P9-BHX-276

JAPANESE EDUCATION SINCE 1945

This volume is a selected study of postwar Japanese education and includes major educational documents that shed new light on this important period and provide a guide to understanding the development of current Japanese educational policy. Some of the documents are taken from records of American occupation forces, while others are original translations from Japanese sources. Taken together, they provide documentary evidence of the development of Japanese education from a devastated system in 1945 to world class status today.

While the collection is not intended to be exhaustive, it provides basic materials that are essential for understanding the development of the postwar Japanese education enterprise. Not only are the documents chosen invaluable for research and teaching, they are suggestive of fruitful topics for further research.

Education/Modern Japan

JAPANESE EDUCATION SINCE 1945

A DOCUMENTARY STUDY

An East Gate Book

M.E. Sharpe
Armonk, New York
London, England

An East Gate Book

Copyright © 1994 by M. E. Sharpe, Inc.

Permission has been received for the following:
For Document 49: From "Early Childhood and School Education" in
Review of National Policies of Education: Japan (excerpts, pp. 57–92).
Paris: Organization for Economic Co-operation and Development, 1971.
Used with permission.

For Document 56: From *Japan's Private Colleges and Universities:
Yesterday, Today and Tomorrow* (Tokyo: The Japan Association of
Private Colleges and Universities, 1987), pp. 54–70. Used with permission.

Library of Congress Cataloging-in-Publication Data

Japanese education since 1945: a documentary study/
Edward R. Beauchamp, James M. Vardaman,
editors.
p. cm.
Chiefly documents previously published in various sources
and translated from Japanese.
"An East Gate Book."
Includes bibliographical references and index.
ISBN 0–87332–561–3
1. Education—Japan—History—20th century. 2. Education—Japan—
History—20th century—Sources. 3. Education and state—Japan—
History—20th century. 4. Educational change—Japan—History—20th
century. I. Beauchamp, Edward R., 1933–.
II. Vardaman, James M., 1947–.
LA1311.82.J39 1993
370'.952'0904—dc20 93–34744
CIP

Printed in the United States of America
The paper used in this publication meets the minimum requirements of
American National Standard for Information Sciences—
Permanence of Paper for Printed Library Materials,
ANSI Z 39.48-1984.

BM (c)   10   9   8   7   6   5   4   3   2   1

Contents

List of Tables and Figures

Tables

Figures

Part I

Japanese Education and the Development of Postwar Education Policy, 1945–1985

Introduction: Japanese Education since 1945

Edward R. Beauchamp

The appointment of an Ad Hoc Reform Council, or Rinkyoshin, on August 21, 1984, was a logical culmination to a lengthy period of concern in Japan over a set of widely perceived educational problems and the future prospects for Japanese education. The charge given to the council by Prime Minister Yasuhiro Nakasone was clear—"to consider basic strategies for necessary reforms . . . so as to secure such education as will be compatible with the social changes and cultural developments of our country." The prime minister went on to remind council members that "if our nation is to build up a society that is full of vitality and creativity as well as relevant to the twenty-first century, it is a matter of great urgency to design necessary reforms . . ."[1] (see Document 61).

With the publication of the Ad Hoc Council's final policy recommendations, several things are clear (see Documents 70–75). The council's recommendations have been the subject of intense interest and comment both within Japan and abroad. The problems that the recommendations are designed to alleviate are not recent ones, but have their roots in earlier phases of Japan's postwar educational development. Finally, this systematic attempt to institute fundamental educational reforms is not a new phenomenon in Japan. Indeed, major attempts to implement basic educational reforms occurred in the 1870s and again following World War II. In the first instance the reform movement was initiated by the new Meiji government, in reaction to a perceived threat, as a means of building a modern state as quickly as possible. In the latter case the reforms were imposed by a powerful occupation force intending to transform Japan from a military dictatorship into a democratic society (see Documents 3, 6, 9, 10, 12, and 22). In both cases the initial sweeping reforms were followed by a more conservative reaction that served to temper the earlier changes.

Japanese Education, 1868–1945

The first of these reforms occurred in the early Meiji period (1868–80) when western education was introduced for the purpose of modernizing the nation. The Japanese approach was a pragmatic one, based on the Imperial Charter Oath of April 6, 1868, which called on the people to eschew old-fashioned ways, insisting that "knowledge shall be sought throughout the world." The major criterion used by the Meiji reformers was simply to borrow the best features of several western educational systems and adapt them to the Japanese situation. As a result, a highly centralized administrative structure with an emphasis on state-run normal schools was borrowed from France; a system of higher education rooted in a handful of elite public universities was the German contribution; the English model of Spartan-like, character-building preparatory schools stressing moral discipline fit nicely into the Japanese context, and from the United States came the model for elementary education, a number of practical pedagogical approaches, and an interest in vocational education.

Another important element in Japan's rush to reform was the double-edged policy of sending promising young students abroad for study while at the same time hiring foreign experts, the so-called *oyatoi gaikokujin* (foreign employees) as teachers and advisers until enough young Japanese could be trained to replace them. Our best estimate of the numbers of these foreign employees in Japan between 1868 and 1923 ranges from 3,000 to 6,000. As Hazel Jones suggests, the latter figure is "too large if applied to foreign employees in government and perhaps too small if private foreign employees are included."[2] In any event, these foreign educators generally served Japan well, for they were instrumental in introducing western educational thought, practice, textbooks, and equipment into the country.[3]

From 1868 to about 1876, the Meiji reformers pursued modernization in a pell-mell fashion. By the latter date, however, they began to recognize that things were moving too rapidly; that certain western ideas (e.g., individualism) were not well suited to the Japanese environment, and they systematically began to slow down the process. By 1880 a widespread attitude had emerged that the reforms of the previous decade had gone too far, and steps needed to be taken to recapture the essence of such traditional values as Confucianism which, in the view of one leading scholar "taught that the meaning of social life lay . . . in cultivating relationships among members of society built on trust, a fundamental sense of one's humaneness, and above all, a commitment to loyal action on behalf of others." This, its advocates insisted, "should be reintegrated as a nutritive value into modern Japanese life."[4] Another student of the subject suggests that from about this time there emerged "a conscious fear of the development of critical attitudes and active attempts to repress them." In fact, Tadashi Fukutake continues, "Basic state schooling was, one might say, schooling for soldiers. Higher education was the education of officers and NCOs. Vocational schools, higher technical schools, and universities, in their graded hierarchy, were the supply system for a status-ranked society. From such an educational process conducted under full pressure from the Imperial state, one could not expect, even from university education, the development of political awareness."[5]

The success of the Meiji educational strategy is affirmed by the former U. S. ambassador to Japan, Edwin O. Reischauer, who concludes that this policy was "closely tailored to national needs as the leaders saw them. It eventually created

a literate mass of soldiers, workers, and housewives, ample middle-level technical skills—an aspect of education that many of today's modernizing countries
have failed adequately to appreciate—and a stream of highly talented young men
emerging from the universities to occupy positions of leadership in government
and society."[6]

Before and during World War II, American policymakers saw Japanese education as a conscious vehicle for carrying out the intent of the 1890 Imperial
Rescript on Education (see Document 1). This document, promulgated by the
Emperor Meiji on October 30, 1890, remained the official statement of the
principles underlying Japanese education until it was scrapped by the Occupation
authorities. The rescript gave both legal form and, perhaps more significantly,
moral force to an educational system that supported the rise of militarism and
ultranationalism during the late 1920s and 1930s.

The Imperial Rescript is a key document from several points of view: On the
one hand, it paraphrases the acceptable and highly moralistic Confucian virtues
to which all loyal Japanese were expected to adhere and sets down the principles
from which much of the militaristic and ultranationalistic emphasis in education
developed. Along the latter lines, it clearly subordinates the individual to the
good of the state and promotes unthinking acceptance of and blind obedience to
instructions from above. An Office of Strategic Services (OSS) document on
Japanese education, prepared during World War II, concludes that "the attitude
that education should be for the purposes of the State rather than for the libera-
tion of the individual has permeated the entire system. Elementary school instruction has been dedicated to the development of unquestioning loyalty. The
Department of Education's exclusive copyright over textbooks, held since 1903,
has made it possible to intensify this process of indoctrination." The minister of
education, in a 1941 speech, called for the "eradication of thoughts based on
individualism and liberalism, and the firm establishment of a national moral
standard with emphasis on service to the state"[7] (see Documents 2 and 7).

William Seabald, a career State Department officer who served as an adviser
to General MacArthur during the Occupation, has written that prewar Japanese
education "had been used by the country's leaders as part of a policy of developing an obedient and subservient population. Schools had been transformed, primarily into agencies of indoctrination in militarism and ultranationalism. For
many years teachers and students had drawn their inspiration from the Imperial
Rescript on Education . . . , with the result that the importance and integrity of
the individual were dwarfed by the growing power of the state."[8]

The Occupation of Japan, 1945–1952

A second major reform period took place immediately following World War II
as a key element in the Allies' determination to transform Japan from an aggres-

sive military dictatorship into a peace-loving democracy.[9] When Japan surrendered to the Allies in August 1945, those Americans charged with planning the eventual occupation of Japan shared an essentially common view of prewar and wartime Japanese education and the role it had played in Japan's military expansion into much of Asia and Oceania[10] (see Documents 10, 22, and 23). Since the Meiji Restoration of 1868, education had been consciously used by Japan's political leaders as an instrument to advance the ends of the state, including economic development, national integration, and military power and conquest.

When the emperor's representatives formally signed the instrument of surrender aboard the USS *Missouri* on September 2, 1945, Japan lay numbed and prostrate before a conquering army. Her education system was in shambles; capitulation found 18 million students idle, four thousand schools destroyed, and only 20 percent of the necessary textbooks available[11] (see Document 7). In addition, large portions of many of those textbooks contained unacceptable nationalist propaganda which had to be removed before they were suitable for pedagogical purposes. Finally, more than one of every three institutions of higher education lay in ruins, thousands of teachers were homeless, hungry, and dispirited, and many of their pupils had been moved to safer areas. In short, a functioning educational system was virtually nonexistent[12] (see Documents 5 and 8).

The primary goals of the Occupation of Japan can be simply stated as the democratization, demilitarization, and decentralization of Japanese society (see Document 6). The Americans recognized that reorienting the educational system was an indispensable element in achieving these objects, especially that of remaking Japan into a functioning democracy. Having surrendered her sovereignty to the Allies, Japan entered a period in which the policymaking function was no longer in her hands. In the words of the Potsdam Proclamation, "There must be eliminated for all time the authority and influence of those who have deceived and misled the people of Japan into embarking on world conquest, for we insist that a new order of peace, security and justice will be impossible until irresponsible militarism is driven from the world" (see Document 4).

As an occupied nation, all Japan could hope was that through persuasion and political skill she could have an influence on the educational policy that the Americans formulated and had the power to force a defeated people to implement. It was during this time that the process of transforming Japan's prewar system proceeded apace. This was a dual process in which the terrible scars of war led the Japanese people to acquire a strong aversion to their military establishment while, simultaneously, the Occupation authorities systematically dismantled the prewar institutions and structures that they saw as causing Japan's slide into the abyss of militarism and nationalism (see Documents 3, 11, 13, 14, 16). The Japanese commitment to nonviolence and peace was evidenced by the widely accepted Article 9 of the 1946 Constitution, which forever renounced war as an instrument of the national policy (see Document 24); the emergence of the so-called "nuclear allergy," which has made discussions of national defense and American nuclear forces in Japan a politically volatile subject; and the increasingly left-of-center political ideology of intellectuals, university students, and the Japan Teachers' Union.[13] The experience of military dictatorship and the horrors of World War II appear to have been indelibly ingrained into the character of the Japanese people.

This new situation, reinforced by surviving remnants of the prewar Japanese willingness to accept and obey instructions from above, enabled American authorities to use the existing instruments of government to implement educational reforms. Indeed, it should be pointed out that the defeated Japanese began to implement significant changes even before the Occupation army was settled into place. For example, on September 15, 1945, the Ministry of Education was "diligently reexamining educational policies in order to establish new policies which meet the demands of the new circumstances," and promising to "humbly reflect upon education and its goals of serving the good of the country and, at the same time, constructing a peaceful nation by the eradication of militarism" (see Document 9). This trend was legitimated and encouraged by the emperor's new Imperial Rescript on Education, promulgated on New Year's Day 1946 (see Document 17).

The Occupation authorities proceeded to censor textbooks, magazines, films, and other media as well as to purge teachers whose pre-Occupation activities were deemed either undemocratic or actively supporting the military's policies.[14] Thus, one of the great ironies of this period was that in encouraging the democratization of Japanese education, the actions of the all-powerful Occupation forces were often not democratic.

What appeared to be wrong with Japanese education, in the eyes of most American policymakers, was that it was not like the American system. American-initiated educational reforms were therefore designed to reform Japanese education along the lines of an American model. This meant that the Occupation authorities would have to transform the prewar orientation of the Japanese people (characterized by an emphasis on filial piety, the perfection of moral powers, group cohesion and harmony, and loyalty and obedience to the emperor and the nation) into one that was congruent with the goals of the United States in Japan.

To assist in carrying out this transformation, the First United States Education Mission, composed of twenty-seven prominent American educators, was invited to spend a month in Japan examining the educational system and recommending reforms of that system (see Documents 15 and 21). True to their American heritage they rejected most of the elements of prewar Japanese education. The mission insisted on the democratization and decentralization of Japan's highly centralized enterprise into a system in which the centralized power of the Ministry of Education would be broken, and local communities would gain control of their own educational destiny. The American reformers also suggested dismantling the highly differentiated multitrack system of prewar days in favor of a nine-year compulsory single track as part of an American-style 6–3–3–4 school ladder, along with steps designed to foster greater individuality, freedom of inquiry, the development of the "whole child," coeducation, greater flexibility in the curriculum, and a radical reform of Japan's written language.[15]

As a number of scholars, both Japanese and American, have pointed out, many of these reforms, such as coeducation, comprehensive schools, and local control, were deeply rooted in the American democratic model but were dysfunctional when transported to the Japanese context (see Document 19). The Japanese educational authorities, however, had little choice but officially to accept the recommendations of the mission's report. Indeed, these recommendations became the basis for a series of important educational laws implemented between 1947 and 1949. The most important of these were the Fundamental Law of Education (see Document 26), and the School Education Law (see Document 25), both promulgated in 1947.[16] The former represented a 180-degree change from the 1890 Imperial Rescript, declaring that "education shall aim at the full development of personality, striving for the rearing of the people sound in mind and body, who shall love truth and justice, esteem individual value, respect labor and have a deep sense of responsibility, and be imbued with the independent spirit, as builders of a peaceful state and society." It also established the important principle that all major educational regulations would be made by parliamentary procedure. The School Education Law, in part, established a new educational structure in which a 6–3–3 school ladder was created, the age at which one could leave school was raised to fifteen years, and coeducation was legitimated. These two basic pieces of legislation are still the legal underpinnings of Japanese education today.

On January 9, 1946, the American authorities officially informed the Japanese that an American Education Mission was on its way to Japan, and "requested" that "the Ministry of Education appoint a committee of highly qualified Japanese educators" whose task would be "to assist the Educational Mission" in studying the problems facing Japanese education (see Document 18). This Japanese committee eventually evolved into the Ministry of Education's prestigious and powerful Central Council on Education.

One of the first contributions of this committee was to shape *A Guide to the New Education,* promulgated by the Ministry of Education on June 30, 1946. It laid down "the task of educators in Japan to take it upon themselves to promote, through reeducation of the people, the construction of a new Japan which is democratic, peace-loving, and civilized" (see Document 22). At about the time this document was published, Minister of Education Morita Tatsuo, whose leftist views had caused his dismissal at Tokyo University in World War I, appealed to educators to fully support the educational reform program.

The only groups in Japan to emerge from World War II with "clean hands" were the opponents of Japan's militarists, i.e., the Communists and Socialists who had often been persecuted and imprisoned until 1945. As a result, the American authorities immediately released them from prison and encouraged their democratic participation in a new and peaceful Japan. Thus, with the emergence of Nikkyoso, or the Japan Teachers' Union (JTU), most of the leadership shared a left-of-center political ideology. This would later evolve into the intractable animosity between the union and the Ministry of Education that endures to this day. In any event, the JTU's first convention, held on June 8, 1947, established the basis for its postwar activities (see Document 27).

Five years later, in June 1952, the JTU promulgated a "Code of Ethics for Teachers" which reinforced its leftist ideology by calling on teachers "to be advocators (*sic*) of the brotherhood of AN, leaders in the reconstruction of life attitudes, and pioneers in respecting human rights, and as such they shall stand as the most courageous defenders of peace against those who advocate war" (see Document 32).

By 1949, however, the major accomplishments of the Occupation were completed. The political and strategic imperatives of the emerging "Cold War" caused American policymakers to reassess their plans for the future of Japan and to ally themselves more closely with conservative Japanese interests.[17] This is perhaps best reflected in a convocation address by the controversial anti-Communist higher education adviser Dr. Walter Ells. At the opening of Niigata University on July 19, 1949, the outspoken Ells called for the dismissal of Communist professors from their positions and the exclusion of students who "deliberately absent themselves in groups from their university classes," or who engage in strikes. His remarks touched off a firestorm of controversy in Japan and, in the view of most intellectuals, tarnished American rhetoric about democracy (see Document 30).

The culmination of the American attempt to decentralize Japanese education along American lines was the Board of Education Law passed on July 15, 1948 (see Document 29). The decentralization issue, pushed very hard by the Occupation authorities, never found roots in Japanese soil. Indeed, even today many American critics of Japanese education are still calling for decentralization as a way of reforming the educational system. And even today, the idea has little support in Japan.

In any event, by 1949 the reforming zeal of the Americans had abated as the environment in Japan underwent an important change. The Korean War's onset in June 1950 resulted in an important impetus to the Japanese economy, and with the end of the Occupation in spring 1952, and the restoration of Japan's sovereignty, American tutors had lost their clout. American reformers had been successful in clearing away the old undemocratic structures and replacing them with ones more to their liking. They had replaced many individuals hostile to democracy with Japanese who seemed committed to democratic values. They had provided Japanese educators with new curricula, textbooks, and methodologies. In short, they had given their best effort and now, as they withdrew to the sidelines, they could only hope that this effort had been good enough.

How did the Japanese view the American efforts? The Ministry of Education, in August 1950, described "the reforms initiated after World War II [as] unprecedented in depth and scope." The official went on to say that "they are unprecedented because there has been a complete revolution in the fundamental concepts that support the education system."[18] Whatever the reality of the American influence from 1945 to 1952, there is widespread agreement that today's Japanese education has played an important, indeed vital, role in Japan's emergence as a world economic power.

The Post-Occupation Period, 1952–1960

April 28, 1952, the day on which the San Francisco Peace Treaty took effect, marked the official end of the American Occupation of Japan. For the first time since Japan's formal surrender on September 2, 1945, sovereignty was returned to the Japanese government. In the six years and eight months separating these two watershed events the social and political systems of the nation had been dramatically transformed into an essentially democratic pattern, albeit not a mirror image of the American model of democracy. Most Japanese preferred the postwar environment to that which had brought them such destruction, but there were many who felt that the Occupation reforms had gone too far and, indeed, had often done considerable violence to cherished Japanese values and traditions.

Given the new political and social systems that existed in 1952, it should not be surprising that the Japanese government undertook a careful reassessment of the recent reforms with an eye to correcting what were widely viewed as excesses. These changes, however, the so-called "reverse course," helped the main features of the American-imposed democratization to take root in Japanese soil. Looking back with the luxury of twenty-twenty hindsight, it appears that the Occupation's emphasis on democracy, individualism, and liberty needed to be balanced with an understanding of what it meant to be a citizen of Japan and all that that implies. The government's reaction may be another illustration of the basic accuracy of Sir George Sansom's dictum that "The power and prestige of a foreign culture seem as if they would overwhelm and transform Japan, but always there is a hard, non-absorbent core of individual character which resists, and in its turn works upon the invading influence." To put it another way, although the changes in Japanese society enabled Japan to accept the general thrust of the reforms forced upon her by American power and prestige, a "hard, non-absorbent core" of "Japanese-ness" converted the reforms into something more harmonious with Japanese traditions and culture.[19] In the long run, this was probably the only way in which the major American reforms could have been institutionalized in the Japanese context.

Education did not escape the government's reassessment, and during the post-1952 period Japanese authorities scrapped a number of American-initiated reforms and modified others to fit more closely traditional Japanese models. For example, the 1948 Board of Education Law (see Document 29), designed to implement the Occupation policy of transferring power from the Ministry of Education to the communities through locally elected boards of education, was abolished. Since 1956 board members have been appointed by the prefectural governors or local mayors with the approval of the appropriate legislative body, thereby making the school board an integrated part of local administration.

The Occupation-imposed abolition of *shushin* (moral education), seen by the Americans as a primary vehicle for inculcating prewar ideas of racial supremacy, the righteousness of Japanese overseas expansion, and the divinity of the emperor, was viewed by many Japanese as having thrown out the baby with the bathwater, leaving public education without a spiritual backbone. In fact in 1949, even before the Occupation ended, Prime Minister Yoshida Shigeru advocated creation of an educational statement on morality to replace the discredited 1890 Imperial Rescript. The Japanese left immediately denounced Yoshida's proposal as an attempt to reinstitute prewar thought-control. The following year, Amano Teiyu, then minister of education, provoked charges of a rebirth of militarism by proposing that national holidays be celebrated by raising the rising sun flag and playing the national anthem. He also echoed Yoshida's call for a new ethical code to replace the discredited Imperial Rescript. By 1958, the Ministry of Education's required course of study included one hour per week for moral education, called *dotoku* in place of the disreputable term *shushin*. By the early 1960s the Ministry of Education's official position was: "Moral education aims to develop a Japanese who will never lose the consistent spirit of respect for his fellow man, who will realize this spirit in home, school and other actual life in the society of which he is a member, who strives for the creation of a culture rich in individuality and for the development of a democratic nation and society, and who is able to make a voluntary contribution to the peaceful international society."[20] This reintroduction of moral education has not led to the evils critics had predicted. After observing several lessons in the mid-1970s, William Cummings, a leading American specialist on Japanese education, concluded, "I quickly overcame my bias against moral education and looked forward to each week's new drama." Rather than finding right-wing patriotic themes in these lessons, Cummings was surprised to see that the lessons "emphasized fundamental matters such as the value of life, the foolishness of fighting, the importance of friendship, the problems of old people."[21]

One of the Occupation's most significant acts was legalizing and even encouraging labor unions as a means of fostering Japanese democracy. One early result was the creation of a powerful Japan Teachers' Union. Organized primarily by a minority of militant Communists and Socialists, the union was quickly recognized by General Headquarters. Perhaps because of the union's close ties with the political opposition and the beginnings of the Cold War in the early 1950s, the conservative Ministry of Education refused to have anything to do with it, claiming that the JTU was devoted to fomenting a Communist revolution and thus its members were unfit to teach Japan's youth (see Documents 33, 35, and 36). A kind of knee-jerk symbiosis has existed between the JTU and the Mombusho [Ministry of Education]; if one side is in favor of virtually anything, one can expect the other to be opposed. Relations between these two major educational forces have not improved significantly in recent years, and prospects for real understanding and cooperation are not yet on the horizon[22] (see Document 38).

This Japanese "counter-reformation" contradicted many of the earlier American reforms, but despite the charges of the radical left these changes did not signal a rejection of democracy and a return to the "bad old days." It should be pointed out, however, that many of the American reforms were not always received well by the business community. Indeed, in the 1950s Nikkeiren, an influential federation of some of Japan's largest industrial firms, issued its first statements on education policy bluntly expressing the industrial circles' unhappiness with the democratically oriented schools, and calling for an educational system more closely reflecting the needs of industry. In practice, this meant more and better vocational courses and a higher degree of professionalization at the university level (see Documents 34, 37, 40, 42, and 43).

Certainly big business favored much of the "reverse course," but more importantly, the phenomenon clearly demonstrated a broadly based Japanese conviction that if they were to have democracy (and there was widespread agreement that they would), they were determined to have a variant that was more or less consistent with their traditions and culture. As one distinguished Japanese scholar explained, "it was easy for liberty to become license," and the "incompatibility of American-style democracy with Japanese traditions was [clear], and the process of developing an amended Japanese version of democratic ideals was pushed forward."[23] The Japanese preference for centralization reasserted itself, but centralization is not necessarily undemocratic; indeed, one can point to France as an example of a democratic society characterized by a highly centralized bureaucracy. In addition, the study of American education amply demonstrates that although local control may result in a greater sensitivity to local needs it can also support racial prejudice, religious bigotry, economic discrimination, textbook censorship, and other undemocratic acts. One can also make the argument, and many Japanese do, that their centralized system ensures that every child—from Okinawa to Hokkaido—enjoys "equality of opportunity" because of substantially equal physical facilities throughout the archipelago, a uniform curriculum administered by a single Ministry of Education, equal access to the same textbooks, teachers of relatively equal competence, and a uniform set of national standards.

There is no doubt that postwar Japan has made enormous strides in providing expanded educational opportunities for her young people. In the thirty-five years between the end of World War II and 1980, the number of students attending school in Japan increased by over 80 percent, from fifteen million to over twenty-seven million. Virtually all youngsters (99.98 percent) complete the nine years of compulsory education, and an impressive 94.2 percent of these graduates go on to a noncompulsory senior secondary school. Perhaps most significantly, the Japanese have persuasively demonstrated that mass education does not have to be purchased with diluted standards. Time and time again international achievement tests have placed the Japanese at or close to the top in a variety of subjects. Furthermore, in 1990, approximately 40 percent of senior high school graduates attended some kind of institution of higher education.

Prior to 1945, Japanese females had very limited access to advanced education, especially an academic program. The secondary education alternatives that were available to them heavily favored domestic education, while university preparatory schools were a male preserve. It has been only recently that educational opportunities for women have improved in Japan. In 1970, for example, "the proportion of Japanese women with an education beyond high school constituted a fraction of the United States distribution, particularly among women between the ages of 35 and 44."[24] Today, although things have changed for the better, much remains to be done. In 1983, 94.5 percent of the female college-age cohort attended the noncompulsory senior high school as opposed to 93.1 percent of the male cohort. In addition, one out of every three female graduates advances to some form of higher education, but the vast majority of these female graduates enroll in junior colleges, and most of those who attend four-year schools major in English literature, home economics, and so forth.

Perhaps a more telling statistic, although somewhat dated, indicative of deeply held attitudes is contained in a 1973 government survey that "found only 14 percent of mothers wanting their daughters to have a university education, in contrast to 49 percent for sons."[25] Still another example of the lingering bias against higher education for women is reflected in a 1983 decision by the administration of the Kyoto Pharmaceutical College that it would give preference to male applicants. It seems that the number of young men successfully passing the entrance examination had been declining for several years and more women than usual were accepted. The university officials felt threatened by what they called the "feminization" of their institution and sought to reverse this trend. They justified their decision on the grounds that Japanese companies overwhelmingly prefer to hire men and that the university sees no point in producing female graduates who will not be hired by the industry. It is clear that although Japanese women have made important educational strides since 1945, they have a long way to go to achieve equality with their brothers.

As governmental authorities turned to "fine tuning" the new system to more faithfully reflect the Japanese cultural environment, they also designed educational policies that reflected the spirit of the nation's new democratic ideology. In addition to honoring its commitment to extend the net of educational opportunity more widely than ever before in Japanese history, the government was simultaneously seeking to improve the quality of the education offered.

Reinforcing these essentially political decisions was the reality of a postwar "baby boom" which began in 1947, after large numbers of military and civilian personnel returned from wartime assignments. The birthrate rose sharply after 1945. For example, the number of births soared from 1,576,000 in 1945 to 2,718,000 in 1947. This resulted in a virtual flood of children reaching elementary school age in 1953, along with the certain knowledge that the same children would enter junior high school in 1959, senior high school in 1962, and the university in 1965 (see Document 37).

This trend required the government to rapidly expand educational facilities systematically, beginning with the elementary grades and continuing through university level as the youngsters wended their way through the system. Providing the necessary facilities would have been difficult enough in normal times, but Japan still suffered from the loss of educational facilities in World War II. In addition, the problem was further exacerbated by the great expansion in education opportunity described earlier and by a significant rise in the percentage of students continuing beyond the elementary and lower secondary levels. According to one researcher, "the new 6–3–3–4 system established in the late 1940s gave people much easier access to higher levels of education than the old system, and an economic revival in the late 1950s followed by a period of high economic growth in the 1960s and the first half of the 1970s, made educational opportunity which had been institutionally offered feasible."[26]

As the government grappled with these problems, it also worked hard to provide the resources and teachers needed to improve the quality of education for steadily increasing numbers of students. In addition, the Mombusho issued four five-year plans, beginning in 1958, to address problems of class size, staffing needs, and other technical issues. Since 1980, an ambitious twelve-year (1980–92) plan has been in operation. Perhaps one of the most effective activities of the Mombusho is the preparation of official revised courses of study, which serve as guides for the various curricula. The first of these was undertaken in the late 1950s in an attempt to evaluate the quality and effectiveness of postwar education. A second revision occurred in 1968, focusing on providing a higher level of study in mathematics and science. These decennial revisions ensure that the curriculum is kept up-to-date and, indeed, provide at least a partial explanation for the success of Japanese students in the International Survey of Educational Achievement (ISEA) Project. This project is the first large-scale, systematic attempt to measure achievement in mathematics, science, social studies, and other subjects across national boundaries.

Whereas the Occupation was an era in which the government's role was generally restricted to implementing reforms laid down by General Headquarters, during the 1950s Japan regained control over her educational future. The government's freedom of action was constrained, however, by the existence of the earlier reforms and a general consensus for a continued democratic system. These new political and social realities resulted in a Japanese educational policy directed at retaining those American-initiated policies that did not violate Japanese traditions and culture while discarding or modifying those that were dysfunctional. This meant a rejection of significant portions of the Occupation changes, including American-style progressive education, and a return to the more traditional subject-centered education congruent with traditional Japanese culture. Similarly, there was a return to earlier forms of centralization, short-circuiting American attempts to shift power to the local communities and allowing the Mombusho to retain its central position in the educational enterprise. Moral education became a matter of public debate and slowly worked its way back into the curriculum although in a much milder form than had existed previously. Finally, the Japan Teachers' Union came into increasingly direct conflict with a conservative government after 1952 and a continuing battle between the JTU and the Mombusho became a familiar occurrence (see Documents 45, 46, and 54).

Not all of this period was characterized by counter-reformation; the post-1952 Japanese government also presided over an impressive expansion of educational opportunity that was fueled by both a baby boom and the scores of new students entering schools as a result of structural changes imposed during the Occupation. Finally, the latter part of the 1950s saw the beginnings of an industry-initiated demand for a greater emphasis on science, technology, and vocational courses in the schools (see Document 34). In brief, the period of the 1950s was characterized by the consolidation of many Occupation reforms, the rejection or modification of others that were dysfunctional within the unique Japanese context, and the laying down of the broad outlines of educational policies that would be pursued during the 1960s and 1970s.

Expansion in the 1960s and 1970s

No less important for Japanese education than the Occupation reforms of the immediate postwar years was the unprecedented period of high economic growth triggered by the restoration of sovereignty and accelerated by the outbreak of the Korean War. This growth continued unabated until the first oil crisis of 1973. Enjoying a steady accretion of her growth rate of over 10 percent yearly (in real terms), Japan experienced rapid changes not only in her economy, but also in the political and social arena. Changes of this magnitude invariably cause changes in a society's educational enterprise, and so it was in Japan's case. It was not so much that the democratizing themes of the Occupation were forgotten, indeed, the more democratic segment of the population would not allow that to happen. But after years of economic hardship there was a wide consensus on the need for economic reconstruction. Educational policy during the 1960s and much of the 1970s was consciously designed to foster economic development (see Documents 39). Indeed, there is little doubt that since the mid-1950s the interests of industry have been extremely influential in shaping educational policy.

Almost immediately after Japan's reassertion of her sovereignty in 1952, the recognition of a serious shortage of scientific and technical manpower emerged as a major educational problem (see Document 43). Major special interest groups, such as Nikkeiren (Japan Federation of Employers), had begun aggressively urging the government to play a major role in overcoming the problem. Industry spokesmen generally agreed on the need for the "functional differentiation of the higher educational structure, and . . . increased specialization in courses and the graduation of more science and engineering specialists"[27] (see Document 47).

In prewar Japan there had been a system of single faculty technical schools providing subprofessional training (roughly comparable to that offered by American community colleges, but of a generally higher quality) to those either unable to pass the university entrance examination or without the necessary economic means to attend a university. Students could enter technical schools directly from the lower middle schools and graduate with certification in a variety of technical fields including drafting, accounting, architecture, engineering, and, in some cases, even as a qualified doctor or dentist. Although such graduates did not enjoy the same level of professional status as a university graduate, "they provided the important battalions that filled the growing needs of Japanese industry."[28]

In postwar Japan, any major firms were nostalgic for the prewar multitrack system that had enabled them to make "use of a status system based on the academic background of their employees. Within companies one found multiple tiers and compartments divided along school-affiliation lines. The school one had been graduated from would determine one's type of job within the organization and the highest position one could hope to reach."[29] In addition, there were complaints from industry about the quality of graduates entering the work force. Viewed from this perspective, the postwar reforms had been a disruptive force within the corporate culture. As the new system's considerable strengths began to be appreciated, however, members of the corporate world "began to use the system to their advantage." They began, for example, "using the rankings into which the new schools were eventually classified," and "a hierarchy among universities took shape in line with the caliber of each university's student body, and companies shifted their internal organization to match the structure of the university hierarchy."[30] This reality was not lost on high school graduates who, quite naturally, saw their futures best served by attending a university in the upper reaches of the new hierarchy. This, in turn, reinforced and expanded the importance of university entrance examinations.[31]

In an extraordinary policy statement issued shortly after assuming office as prime minister in 1960, Hayato Ikeda announced his intent to double Japan's national income in a ten-year period. This, in effect, required an annual growth rate of about 7 percent. In the late 1950s, Japan's share of the world gross national product stood at about 3 percent, but by the time of the first oil crisis of 1973 it had grown to a remarkable 10 percent. Japan had, in fact, achieved an average annual growth rate of about 11 percent between 1961 and 1969, attaining Ikeda's ambitious target in just five years. By 1969 Japan's gross national product was 3.7 times that of its 1960 level (see Documents 39 and 41).

Increases in per capita income kept pace with this dizzying trend, and soon Japan's standard of living reached new levels of prosperity. Per capita income, which had stood at barely $200 in the early 1950s, rocketed to $2,300 per year in 1972.[32] Several important consequences flowed from Japan's newfound economic cornucopia, including increased social mobility, a quickened flow of young people from rural to urban centers, a declining birthrate, and an unprecedented expansion of employment opportunities. An increasing demand for formal education reflected these economic and social developments, and educational officials were hard-pressed to keep up with it.

In 1957, the recently established Economic Planning Agency, the coordinating body for overall governmental economic planning, had issued a long-range plan establishing guidelines for economic development and education's role in achieving it. The Ministry of Education contributed a five-year plan designed to accommodate eight thousand new university places annually for science and technology students and by 1960 was close to achieving its target. Prime Minister Ikeda's scheme to double the national income in a decade, however, required creating an additional 170,000 scientists and engineers. The Ministry of Education planned to meet this need with a seven-year plan that added sixteen thousand places annually, but it was subsequently replaced with a four-year plan adding twenty thousand new places yearly.

Perhaps the single most influential educational document of this period was the so-called "Report on the Long-Range Educational Plan Oriented Toward the Doubling of Income." Prepared by a technical subcommittee of the Economic Planning Agency's Economic Council in 1960, this document stressed the importance of education as an investment in developing human resources. It argued for more and better science and technical education to meet industry's need for skilled workers, and intoned: "Future progress in economics and social welfare depends largely on the effective use of the human resources of the nation."[33] It insisted, in the view of one close observer, on the necessity of "extending upper secondary education to most adolescents, shaping the motivational and cognitive orientations of adolescents toward a complex society through upper secondary education, and training talented human resources to compete economically in the international domain."[34] As we have seen throughout this essay, since the Meiji Restoration of 1868, the Japanese government has been consistent in using education as a vehicle to achieve larger national goals (see Document 42).

In 1962 the government passed legislation creating a system of nineteen technical colleges designed "to train (middle level) technicians with well-rounded general knowledge and a thoroughly specialized knowledge in technology."[35] These institutions, offering a five-year curriculum in a variety of industrial (and sometimes merchant marine) studies, are open to graduates of the lower secondary school. As of May 1983, sixty-two technical colleges had a total enrollment of 47,245 students; 97.2 percent of them were male.[36]

This law, along with subsequent actions of the Ministry of Education, resulted in a highly differentiated system of technical education. At the apex of this system, the universities provided both undergraduate and graduate education for scientists and high-level technical personnel. The elite nature of this arrangement can be seen in the decision to concentrate advanced courses in a handful of important universities. The technical schools described above were designed to train the large numbers of middle-level technicians needed to operate a sophisticated scientific and technical economy. In addition, specialized technical high schools and high quality technical courses in general high schools produced large numbers of lower-level technicians. Finally, a variety of miscellaneous schools was created outside the formal system of education providing technical education. Many of these provide short-term courses in a variety of fields. A sophisticated set of public and private industrial training centers to train skilled workers also was developed. The School Education Law of 1961 allowed, under certain circumstances, work done in them to be credited toward high school graduation. This differentiation clearly served the interests of those industries who as early as 1952 had severely criticized the new educational system.

In the decade between 1960 and 1970 the government succeeded in more than doubling the number of university science and engineering graduates. This, however, tells only part of the story. According to one source, "in 1960, 18.2 percent of the total [university] student enrollment was in the fields of science and engineering; by 1975 this figure was up to 23.2 percent. Even more significant, within the national universities, where the government efforts were most direct, the figure rose from 24 percent to 33 percent in these fields."[37]

Early on, educational planners had identified secondary education as a critical factor in human resource development and, although recognizing the long-term need for overall improvement in general secondary education, they opted to give priority to science and technical education in the short term. The same study that called for training of 170,000 scientists and engineers also insisted on the need for 439,000 technical school graduates in the same period. This goal could not, of course, be met without a substantial increase in the number of technical teachers available, so a number of temporary three-year teacher training institutes, tied to nine major national universities, were created. In the next seven years, eight hundred future teachers were admitted to these schools.[38]

As noted earlier, the postwar period was one of quantitative expansion, but the need for a similar qualitative improvement remained. The level of public funding for education rose from 159,818 million yen in 1950 to 372,006 million yen in 1955, to 1,057,070 million yen in 1963, and to 5,060,245 million yen in 1973. This money went not only toward providing better teachers, but also better facilities (including laboratories and libraries), smaller classes, and in-service training for teachers.[39]

One of the most interesting and successful examples of this in-service training was the creation of a system of Science Education Centers in each prefecture. "In them, with a combination of local initiative and resources and substantial National Government assistance, teachers at all precollege levels received in-service training in the use of the latest materials and methods for science and mathematics teaching."[40]

Increasing differentiation was also a characteristic of higher education following the Occupation period. Government policy assigned the fulfillment of manpower needs to the national sector, while the private sector was encouraged to meet increased social demand for higher education. Thus, public money was invested in the public sector's responsibility to fuel economic development, but not significantly in satisfying increased social demand for higher education that had arisen. From 1960 to 1975, only nine new national universities were established while, in the same period, 165 private institutions were founded! Today, three out of every four Japanese seeking higher education fulfill their ambition in the private sector (see Document 56).

Since 1956, the government has also differentiated *within* national universities; the newly established postwar universities (many upgraded from the old higher schools) operate on an American-style course system, whereas the former seven imperial universities (the most prestigious in Japan) and a handful of others have retained the prewar *chair* system, based on the German model. These prestigious universities have received the bulk of research funds, higher salaries, and better equipment. They also have "attached" research institutes and are charged with both teaching and research functions.

A potent combination of the postwar baby boom, the nation's increasing affluence, and the recognition that the individual's and the nation's future were intimately intertwined with an emerging "information society," led to widespread acceptance of higher education as a prerequisite to maintaining Japan's newly acquired affluence. This reality sent increasing numbers of high school graduates through the narrow gates of the universities. The gatekeepers, however, insisted that those admitted first demonstrate their merit by successfully passing rigorous entrance examinations[41] (see Document 48).

A bizarre but true example of the kind of horror stories associated with entrance examinations is recounted by Ronald Dore. In describing how a preoccupation with these examinations at higher educational levels tends to create a "backwash" into the lower levels of the educational system, he describes its logical conclusion in "a pre-pre-kindergarten which was reported in 1970 to have failed to devise adequate tests for 2-year-olds and decided to test their mothers instead."[42] Although an admittedly extreme case, it would overly surprise few Japanese. Thomas Rohlen characterizes this kind of "obsession with entrance examinations" as "a dark engine powering the entire school system"; if anything, he understates the case.[43]

While most Japanese seem to think entirely too much emphasis is placed on examinations, very little has been done to change this situation. What are the obstacles preventing a change most thoughtful people seem to favor? At least three possible answers, in no particular order of importance, suggest themselves: (1) a deeply ingrained Confucian legacy, (2) powerful vested interests, and (3) too few places for too many applicants.

The Confucian legacy argument stresses the efficacy of memorizing the classics, and a number of scholars have pointed out how deeply this approach seems to be inbred in the Japanese psyche. One distinguished student of Japan, with many years of experience there, has written that Japan's "ferocious race and competition for the best possible places at the best universities, is simply the ancient Chinese system of state examinations to accede to the class of *jugakusha* (literati) in a modern context. Today one may gloss Karl Marx instead of Mencius, or write an essay on spherical trigonometry instead of defining filial piety, but the terms, rules and outcomes of the game have changed very little."[44] Whoever learns the most facts and best develops test-taking skills is most likely to be successful. The criticism by an American teacher in Japan during the 1870s is still valid today. William Elliot Griffis, a Rutgers College graduate serving the Meiji emperor, reproached Japanese teachers who saw it their "chief duty . . . to stuff and cram the minds . . . of pupils" with nothing but information.[45]

The entrance examinations of today are still shaped by this attitude, but it may not be quite as absurd as it sounds. There is a widely held view among many Japanese that the value of entrance examinations is not in the information memorized and regurgitated upon command, but rather in the intense, difficult, and often lonely experience of preparing for those examinations. This, we are told, strengthens one's character and moral fiber and prepares the individual for the arduous challenges lying ahead. Interestingly, Thomas Tohlen lends supports to this view when he suggests that although intelligence is needed to pass the exams, "self-discipline and willpower are equally essential."[46]

A second obstacle to reforming the examination system lies in the powerful vested interests that might suffer financially if significant changes are made. A visit to virtually any book shop in Tokyo or any large urban center will illustrate the profitability of the current examination system to publishers. These book shops are usually crowded with students of all ages who flock to the shelves appropriate to their needs. Shelves are conspicuously marked with signs such as "For Secondary School Entrance Preparation." Other shelves contain such provocative titles as *The Complete Study Guide for Passing "X" University Entrance Examinations,* or *English Vocabulary Most Likely to Appear on the Entrance Examination for "Y" University,* and so forth. Pamphlets containing past examinations and sample examinations are also found in abundance. All of this is, of course, big business for the publishers.

In addition, most students preparing for entrance examinations attend voluntary and often expensive supplementary or cram schools. Many are part of nationwide chains and have made many an entrepreneur affluent. There are also the fat fees charged students for the privilege of taking a university's entrance examination—fees that can make a considerable difference to the financial health of many private institutions. These are not the only enterprises to benefit from the examination system: manufacturers of specially designed student desks and worktables, desk lamps, and other items, would also suffer economically from a weakening of the much-criticized examination system.

Ironically, many of the victims of this system would also be victimized should entrance examinations lose their centrality to the Japanese educational experience. One of the easiest and often lucrative sources of income for Japanese students who have entered university is to tutor students preparing for the examinations.

A third obstacle to examination reform is a simple one: over 90 percent of the relevant age cohort graduate from high school in Japan, and almost two-thirds of them have taken a college preparatory curriculum. In 1980, "there were 590,000 places in higher education available and about 636,000 seniors applying."[47] At first glance, this appears to be a reasonably close fit, but it overlooks another 200,000 applicants, known as *rōnin,* a reference to the masterless samurai of feudal days. These high school graduates from earlier years had failed in earlier attempts to enter their university of choice and rather than admit failure continued their studies in preparation for another try at the examination.

Nagai Michio, a former minister of education and sometime editorial writer for the *Asahi Shimbun,* has concluded that "the overly fast growth in student population caused qualitative deterioration in the levels that expanded with particular rapidity. This was most conspicuous in the sphere of higher education, as evidenced by the financial hardships of private schools, the acceptance of more students than could be officially registered, the admission of students through shady behind-the-scenes procedures and the rigidity of the self-management of national and public universities. Such issues of qualitative deterioration have kept the government occupied since the 1970s."[48] Two important unintended consequences of this rapid expansion have been that it has reinforced both the existing hierarchy of universities and the entrance examination system.

Expanded enrollments for a limited number of university places inevitably meant increased competition for those relatively few places perceived to be of the greatest value. Thus, with more and more applicants striving to attend a handful of famous national universities and an even smaller number of prestigious private universities, the existing hierarchy was not only maintained but strengthened. This trend also reinforced the power of the entrance examination system, and not only for its importance as a sorting device. Every student who takes the university entrance examination, and most take the examination for more than one institution, pays a fee ranging from about sixty-five to one hundred U.S. dollars (based on an exchange rate of 150 yen to a dollar). Thus, the money-starved private sector has come to depend on this income to help meet their operating expenses.

Indeed, one of the most interesting features of Japan's system of higher education (and almost the opposite of the American model) is that her most prestigious universities tend to be state supported and are able to charge significantly lower tuition and fees than do the usually less prestigious but more expensive private institutions. This results in the state-supported national universities, whose graduates make up a disproportionate share of the nation's political and economic leadership, being able to select talented students from all levels of society's economic strata. In the Japanese context the "ability to pay" is replaced by "the ability to pass entrance examinations."

Another important, even spectacular, development in Japanese education was the campus unrest of the 1960s. Although the Occupation authorities had encouraged free speech and academic freedom on university campuses, the environment following Japan's independence in 1952 had changed considerably. The American relationship with Japan was informed by U.S. need for Japanese support in the Cold War and America's perceived need to back a conservative government supportive of its military policy. It should not be surprising that Japan's academic orientation also changed in response to this event.

In this changed academic environment of the post-Occupation years students found the realities of university life disappointing. After working exceptionally hard for many years to pass the examination to a prestigious university, the reality of large classes, rigidly prescribed curricula, disinterested lecturers, seldom-seen professors, and a Byzantine bureaucratic structure clashed with their image of a university. The postwar educational system and its left-of-center teaching force had encouraged students to question both society's materialism and the political assumptions underlying the conservative government's apparent repudiation of the antiwar constitution and its attempts to return Japan to a more authoritarian society.

Student radicals were an important part of the postwar intellectual ferment in Japan, but their numbers proved to be the heart of the great student protest that shook the nation over the ratification of the revised U.S.–Japan Security Treaty in June 1960. The movement continued, using American intervention in Vietnam as an emotional focus culminating in the great Tokyo University protest of 1968. This event marked the high point of the student movement, and student occupation of Todai's facilities not only forced the university's closure for several months but was directly responsible for suspending the 1969 entrance examinations.

The government of Prime Minister Eisaku Sato accepted the challenge in August that year and rammed through the Diet a "Bill for Emergency Measures of University Administration." The significance of this bill, which broke the back of the student movement, was that it gave university presidents and, if necessary, the minister of education extraordinary powers to supersede the authority of the faculty, suspend teaching and research functions, and so forth. Despite spirited opposition from those supporting traditional faculty autonomy, and although it was never applied, the mere existence of this legislation changed the academic environment and the traditional relationship between government and university. The result was that with occasional exceptions, campus unrest subsided and the student movement broke up into increasingly rival factions, each claiming to be more ideologically pure than its opponents. These factions still visited violence upon one another, but their challenge to the state had been successfully met.

Somewhat like the aerodynamics of the gooney bird, the marvel of Japanese higher education is not that it fails to perform as well as critics would like, but that it works at all. Nathan Glazer's generalized characterization of Japanese education seems to be most applicable to higher education. Seemingly puzzled, Glazer has noted: "The basic paradox of Japanese education is that underfunded . . . , devoid of any marked evidence of innovation [and] sharply criticized for its enormous emphasis on examinations, under attack from business for the quality of its college graduates, with limited research facilities, and a modest system of graduate education, torn by conflict between an alienated and radicalized teaching force in the elementary and secondary schools and a firmly conservative Ministry of Education, characterized by a college and university intelligentsia most of whom are opposed to the national government and unsympathetic to the emphasis on economic growth—it manages nevertheless to educate a labor force that serves the needs of Japanese business, industry, and government."[49] Why such a system is "successful" can only be answered by pointing to Japan's unique cultural context. Every nation defines the functions that its schools will serve through a political process, but the specific shapes of these functions is a matter of cultural particularism. Such a system, in other words, can exist only in Japan.

Another aspect of the 1960s was the Ministry of Education's attempt to define the "Ideal Japanese" (see Document 45). This was perceived by the political left as a first step toward reinstituting elements of the prewar system, and the ensuing uproar forced the ministry to back down. This was not unrelated to the JTU's subsequent pledge "to oppose education controlled by the national government" (see Document 38). Finally, the Ministry of Education continued to support the teaching of moral education as part of the curriculum, but continued opposition prevented excesses. For example, in establishing the goal that all Japanese "love your country as a Japanese . . . " it was thought necessary to add "and try to aim to be a man who can contribute to the welfare of his fellow man, as well as to contribute to the development of our country" (see Document 46).

The Third Major Reform Period, 1978 to the Present

The late 1970s and early 1980s served as a "run up" period to Japan's current educational reform movement. In the early 1970s, several important reports calling for various educational reforms stirred widespread discussion among thoughtful Japanese and contributed to the ferment that resulted in the appointment of the Ad Hoc Reform Council, or Rinkyoshin, in 1984 (see Documents 60–64, 68). The first of these early documents, published in 1970, was the Ministry of Education's *Educational Standards in Japan*, which provided a comparative framework within which to evaluate Japan's educational achievements. This was soon followed by a report of one of the ministry's advisory organs, the Central Council for Education, which caused a considerable stir and provoked the Japan Teachers' Union to undertake its own study, which it published in 1975 (see Documents 54 and 55).

The Central Council for Education's report took a swipe at both conservative apologists of the existing system and the radical Japan Teachers' Union when it warned, "Education is rapidly falling behind the times because vested interests protect the status quo, because idealists oppose reforms without paying attention to their actual contents, and because much time is spent wastefully on the discussion of reforms which have no possibility of being implemented."[50] The report advocated "long-range fundamental policies and measures for developing the educational system, basing these proposals on an examination of the educational system's achievements over the past twenty years and on its understanding of the system of education appropriate for the years to come in which rapid technological innovations and national and international changes are anticipated."[51] The then-minister of education, Sakata Michita, was sufficiently impressed by this analysis to refer to it as a plan "for the third major educational reform in Japan's history."[52]

Among its proposals, all of which carried hefty price tags, were: extending free public education to four- and five-year-olds; providing teachers with large salary increases; allowing teachers more time to teach by shifting paperwork to an expanded clerical staff; expanding special education programs; increasing subsidies to private universities; and others along similar lines. One could probably characterize this report as recognizing that educational expansion had run its course, and there was now a need to move toward improving the quality of education. As expected, reactions to specific proposals depended upon whether or not one's ox was being gored.

Still another important document feeding the reform debate was the Organization for Economic Organization and Development (OECD) analysis of Japan's educational policies (see Document 49). Falling back on its traditional practice of actively seeking outside advice, Japan invited the OECD to send a team of education experts to advise it on future directions. The OECD report, which on balance probably had the clearest view of Japan's educational problems, praised education's role in the nation's industrial development, but strongly criticized the conformist nature of the Japanese system, overcentralized control, and an overemphasis on standardization in the name of egalitarianism. It recommended that the time seemed to be ripe "for some practical measures aimed at the development of students' personalities through a more flexible and less pressured scheme of education, with more free time, more curricular freedom, more diversity in extra-curricular activities and more cooperation among pupils" (see Documents 50 and 51). "The time may have come," the OECD examiners continued, "to devote more attention to such matters as *cooperation,* in addition to discipline and competition, and *creativity,* in addition to receptivity and imitation."[53]

Finally, after several years of careful study, the Japan Teachers' Union published its own view of the correct path to educational reform. Arguing that Japanese education "is circumscribed" by the government's "high economic growth policy nationally, and Security Treaty setup with the United States internationally," the JTU report suggests that this has resulted in "environmental destruction, soaring prices, housing problems, [a] traffic mess and energy crisis"[54] (see Documents 54 and 55).

While the reform ferment of the early 1970s was at its height, Japan was hit by the first oil crisis in 1973. As a result of this international economic dislocation, Japan's economy sputtered to a virtual halt and, for a brief period, experienced a negative growth rate. After this sharp decrease in the growth rate, which had averaged 9.1 percent between 1959 and 1973, to a mere 4.0 percent between 1974 and 1980, the government was hard put to provide the resources needed by the education sector and, indeed, has had to find ways to reduce its financial support.

Following the rapid expansion of educational enrollments during the economic boom of the 1960s, the system began to contract after 1973. The birthrate has dropped sharply in recent years and there appears to be no good reason to anticipate a turnaround in the near future. The school-age population has been decreasing since 1979 at the kindergarten level, and since 1981 at the lower elementary level, and this negative wave is gradually making its way through the entire system. Attendance rates among school-age children in the noncompulsory sector have stabilized since the 1970s, suggesting that demand may have peaked. Further, "Japan's birth rate for 1980 equaled the record low level for 1966" and, according to a government spokesman, "the proportion of women of childbearing age will decline during the next four or five years."[55] Also, the percentage of Japan's under-fifteen population decreased from 22.3 percent in 1984 to 21.8 percent in 1985.[56]

Recent reports based on hard data collected and analyzed by the government have concluded that Japan's population of aged people is rapidly growing, and in 1984, the proportion of people age sixty-five or over reached 9.9 percent as compared with 5 percent in 1950. By the year 2000 it is projected that Japan will be the nation with the highest percentage of old people. Government-sponsored research has found this "graying" phenomenon means that by the year 2001 there will be one citizen age sixty-five or over for every three productive citizens (ages fifteen to sixty-four). The current ratio is one to seven.[57]

The educational implications of this trend are not difficult to see. Japan is now paying the price in economic and social consequences for her rapid demographic transition after World War II from a country with high death rates and birthrates to one with low mortality and fertility. The aging phenomenon confronts the society in general, and educational planners and policymakers in particular, with a number of problems. One possible scenario is raising the retirement age, which would enable workers to stay on the job longer but reduce the openings for youths anxious to enter the labor force. Having more older people in jobs may also serve to decrease productivity at a time when higher productivity is needed to meet increased foreign competition. Finally, it appears certain the nation's medical bills will increase substantially. The social implications of all of these scenarios are not easy to predict.

Although Japan's commitment to education as an escalator for success is still very high, cracks are beginning to appear in that commitment. Professor Amano Ikuo of Tokyo University presents a persuasive argument in which he refers to a "crisis of structuration." Amano argues that postwar Japan was successful in creating a society that was both egalitarian and mobile, but since the slowdown of the economy after the oil crisis of 1973 opportunities for mobility have been significantly reduced. He believes that the Occupation's attempt to dismantle the prewar hierarchical system of higher education failed, and that a stable hierarchy of high schools, dominated by a relative few serving as feeder schools to the top universities, has emerged. "The opportunities to the top universities are virtually monopolized by the top high schools," he writes, and graduates of these top schools tend to secure jobs leading to the elite positions in society. In the earlier stage of rapid expansion of secondary and higher education, Amano contends, there existed a healthy competition, but as a result of the kinds of changes described above the number of places in elite universities has decreased, and the desirable jobs available upon graduation are fewer. Although it is still true that a majority of young people continue to play this game, there are increasing numbers who are unwilling to participate.[58]

Big business in Japan has also contributed to this situation as a result of its predilection for recruiting new employees from a select group of universities. (See Document 65 for an important business view of reform.) This causes a downward pressure that distorts pre-university education. One cannot blame children and their parents for following the only real path to economic success in Japanese society. They search with a relentless persistence for whatever experience will give them an "edge" in the great competition for educational certification.

A recent study by Thomas Rohlen tends to support the general thrust of Amano's argument. Rohlen's analysis suggests "a trend toward a greater role for family factors in educational outcomes," pointing out that in the early 1960s the range of applicants to elite national universities was much broader, and there was "little relationship between income and success. Private universities . . . , on the other hand, were filled primarily by students from families in the upper half of the income scale. By the mid-1970s, a significant shift was perceptible with fewer and fewer students from poor families entering the elite universities. A major reason [for this] is the rising significance of privately purchased advantages in the preparation process—namely, *juku* [cram schools] and elite private high schools."[59]

Amano's assertion that most Japanese youths continue to play the competition game is undoubtedly accurate, but for the first time an increasing number of young people are dropping out of that game. In the past, one of the things that distinguished Japanese schools from their American counterparts was their minuscule dropout rate. In 1983, the latest year for which figures are currently available, 111,531 students of public and private senior high schools in Japan dropped out, an increase of 5.2 percent over the preceding year. This figure constitutes only 2.4 percent of all senior high school students and is quite low, especially when compared to the United States, where 23 percent of senior high school students drop out before graduation. What is troubling, however, is that the Japanese figure has increased every year since 1974, when relevant statistics were first collected.[60]

One of the most interesting dimensions of this phenomenon is the so-called "school refusal syndrome," which the Ministry of Education believes is caused by "the rapidity of social change, the proliferation of the nuclear family, loss of community feelings, affluence and urbanization." Another view, however "blames the school system which is theoretically designed so that all children of the same group stay at the same level and work at the same pace." When reality intrudes on this Pollyannaish assumption, however, the result is "great strain on the slower children." These children's complaints of physical ailments that keep them home from school are neither truancy nor delinquency, but "a cry of silence" against the terrible pressures placed upon them by an unyielding system.[61]

Others see the problems emerging in today's Japan as nothing more than what they call "advanced nation disease" *(senshinkoku-byo),* the inevitable, if alarming, results of modern industrial society: "increases in the rates of divorce, juvenile crime, school violence and other social ills associated with countries like the United States."[62] It is undeniable that school violence, although still a minor problem when compared to that in the United States, is seen by most Japanese as simply unimaginable. The actions of this still tiny minority have shocked adult Japan because "their behavior violates the most fundamental code of Confucian-influenced traditional education values—namely, respecting and obeying teachers"[63] (see Document 57).

There is no doubt that the socioeconomic environment of contemporary Japan is very different from that of a decade ago. Young people today are growing up amid an affluence that is in stark contrast to the economic reality of previous generations. Their culture is universal; the music they listen to on their Walkman is the same as that their counterparts in Dusseldorf or Detroit hear. They are sensitive to changing youth culture trends abroad, and it is not uncommon for them to have traveled overseas. They spend much of their time shopping for the latest fashions and playing video games, and increasing numbers drive automobiles. In summary, the consumer orientation of young people in the late 1980s is a far cry from their counterparts of the 1960s. Whereas politically active students a quarter-century ago were committed to idealistic goals and intensely interested in building what they perceived to be a better society, and a majority in the 1970s worked hard to become "salarymen" and share in the nation's economic prosperity, today's youth pursue personal pleasure with a single-minded devotion reminiscent of their older brother's loyalty to his company.

The combination of a rigid and inflexible educational system, along with this new orientation of students, has led not only to an increase in dropouts (as described above) but also to a great increase in school violence. For example, the first half of 1983 saw a 26 percent increase in violent school incidents over 1982 levels. A bewildering increase of violence against teachers occurred and, to the surprise of many, more and more females are becoming violent; the National Police Agency (NPA) reported that in 1984 almost one out of every five youngsters taken into custody by the police was a female.[64]

Both 1983 and 1984, however, saw a slight decline in school violence, according to NPA reports; but violence that did occur has been characterized by authorities as more "vicious" than in the past; indeed the NPA recorded an increase "in such crimes as kidnapping, arson, and assaults by minors."[65] The category showing the greatest increase, however, is that of *ijime*—school "bullying"—and both the vernacular and English-language press have been filled with reports, editorials, and letters to the editor describing it and analyzing its causes. It has become so serious a problem that the Tokyo Metropolitan Police Department has recently created "a special unit for taking into public custody tormentors in school bullying cases." They report that in the period of November 1 through 18, 1985, they received forty calls from victims and "fourteen [of them] were taken up as criminal cases." The complaints included inflicting bodily injuries, blackmailing, being burnt with cigarette butts and a cigarette lighter, forcing victims to drink large quantities of sour milk, poking hot needles under a victim's fingernails, and forcing them to eat insects.[66] Another recent article reports that a significantly large group of children "who are apparently victims of bullying at schools have been admitted to . . . a mental hospital for children in Tokyo." The hospital reports that "many admitted children not only refuse to go to school but also show symptoms of obsessional neurosis . . . out of fear of bullying"[67] (see Documents 58 and 59).

It is important to understand that, as disturbing as such uncivilized behavior may be, bullying is a tragic phenomenon that occurs at schools in all countries and, indeed, is nothing new in Japan.[68] In fact, one cannot be sure that its practice today is of greater magnitude than in the past. The argument can be made that because of changes in society, bullying and school violence are now regularly reported, whereas in the past they went unreported for a variety of reasons. Donald Roden argues, for example, how in the elite prewar higher schools upperclassmen "customarily intimidated" new students, and "any sign of annoyance could lead to more severe forms of harassment." This behavior was not described as bullying, however, but merely as "initiation." More serious was the so-called "welcome storm" *(kangei sutomu)* in which new students "would be attacked in their sleep by a roving band of upperclassmen," while terrified, they "quivered in huddled masses."[69] This is not intended to dismiss the current furor over school bullying; merely to suggest that it is nothing new.

A number of other issues are relevant for the policy process, but lack of space precludes their discussion. There is little doubt, however, that the most important policy issues include the examination system, centralized control over the educational system, the role of the educational system, the role of education in fostering economic development, and the knotty problem of how to reform Japanese education to meet the challenges of the twenty-first century while at the same time taking care that reforms are harmonious with Japanese traditions and values. If the two previous major reforms in early Meiji and following World War II are any guide, we can expect reforms of a rather sweeping nature to be made in the next few years, to be followed shortly by a period of reflection in which modifications of the original reforms are made to bring them into closer conformity with the realities of Japanese life.

One of the major differences between the 1990s and the two earlier reform experiences is that in both the Meiji and the Occupation periods there were foreign models that everyone agreed were worthy of emulation. Whether English, French, German, or American, they were models with which their creators were reasonably satisfied. Today, however, there is no foreign model that stands out as an obvious candidate for adaptation. Virtually all of the countries to which Japan has traditionally looked for educational ideas are themselves engaged in reform efforts to salvage inadequate educational systems. The question facing Japanese reformers is simply whether they can *create* a new model that will not only meet their needs in the twenty-first century but will also serve as a role model with which the former students can instruct their children's teachers (see Documents 69–75).

Notes

This study was originally published, in a slightly different form, in the *History of Education Quarterly* (1988). I wish to thank the editors for encouraging its publication in this format. The research for this paper was commissioned by the National Institute of Education (Contract No. NIE-P-85-3206) as a contribution to the recently completed U.S. Study of Education in Japan Project.

1. Provisional Council for Education Reform, *First Report on Educational Reform* (Tokyo: Goverment of Japan, 1978), pp. 66–67.

2. Hazel J. Jones, *Live Machines: Hired Foreigners in Meiji Japan* (Vancouver: University of British Columbia Press, 1980).

3. Edward R. Beauchamp, *An American Teacher in Early Meiji Japan* (Honolulu: University of Hawaii Press, 1976); Edward R. Beauchamp and Akira Iriye, eds., *Foreign Employees in Nineteenth Century Japan* (Boulder, CO: Westview Press, 1989); Edward R. Beauchamp, ed., *Schoolmaster to an Empire: Richard Henry Brunton in Meiji Japan* (Westport, CT: Greenwood Press, in press); Ardath W. Burks, ed., *The Modernizers: Overseas Students, Foreign Employees, and Meiji Japan* (Boulder, CO: Westview Press, 1985); Foster Rhea Dulles, *Yankees and Samurai: America's Role in the Emergence of Modern Japan* (New York: Harper & Row, 1965); Richard Rubinger, ed., *An American Scientist in Early Meiji Japan: The Autobiographical Notes of Thomas C. Mendenhall* (Honolulu: University of Hawaii Press, 1989); Robert Schwantes, *Japanese and Americans: A Century of Cultural Relations* (New York: Harper & Brothers, 1955).

4. Tetsuo Najita and Irwin Scheiner, eds., *Japanese Thought in the Tokugawa Period, 1600–1868: Methods and Metaphors* (Chicago: University of Chicago Press, 1978), pp. 98–99.

5. Tadashi Fukatake, *The Japanese Social Structure: Its Evolution in the Modern Century,* trans. Ronald P. Dore (Tokyo: University of Tokyo Press, 1982), p. 70.

6. Edwin O. Reischauer, *The Japanese* (Cambridge, MA: Harvard University Press, 1976), p. 169.

7. United States, Department of War, Office of Strategic Services, "Japanese Education" (Washington, DC: National Archives of the United States, n.d.), p. 2.

8. William J. Seabald and Russell Brines, *With MacArthur in Japan: A Personal History of the Occupation* (New York: Macmillan, 1965).

9. Toshio Nishi, *Unconditional Democracy: Education and Politics in Occupied Japan, 1945–1952* (Stanford, CA: Hoover Institution, 1982); Robert E. Ward and Frank Shulman, eds., *The Allied Occupation of Japan, 1945–1952: An Annotated Bibliography of Western Language Materials* (Chicago: American Library Association, 1974).

10. Hugh Borton, "American Presurrender Planning for Postwar Japan," occasional papers of the East Asian Institute, Columbia University (New York: Columbia University,

1967); Hugh Borton, "Preparation for the Occupation of Japan," *Journal of Asian Studies* 25 (February 1966): 203–212; Thomas W. Burkman, ed., *The Education of Japan: Educational and Social Reform* (Norfolk: The MacArthur Memorial, 1982); Marlene J. Mayo, "American Wartime Planning for Japan: The Role of Experts," *Americans as Proconsuls: United States Military Government in Germany and Japan, 1944–1952,* ed. Robert Wolfe (Carbondale: Southern Illinois University Press, 1984), pp. 3–51.

11. Robert King Hall, *Education for a New Japan* (New Haven, CT: Yale University Press, 1949), p. 2.

12. Nishi, *Unconditional Democracy*, pp. 176–180.

13. Benjamin C. Duke, *Japan's Militant Teachers: A History of the Left Wing Teachers' Movement* (Honolulu: University of Hawaii Press, 1973); Donald R. Thurston, *Teachers and Politics in Japan* (Princeton, NJ: Princeton University Press, 1973).

14. Ronald S. Anderson, *Education in Japan: A Century of Modern Development* (Washington, DC: Government Printing Office, 1963). See also Hans H. Baerwald, *The Purge of Japanese Leaders under the Occupation* (Berkeley: University of California Press, 1959).

15. Edward R. Beauchamp, "Education and Social Reform in Japan: The First U.S. Education Mission," in *The Education of Japan,* ed. Burkman, 175–192. Hideo Satow, a Japanese education specialist, has found evidence in the U.S. National Archives that suggests the 6–3–3 system was not imposed on the Japanese, but was instituted on the recommendation of a committee of Japanese educators. See "6–3–3 System Not Imposed by GHQ," *Japan Times,* September 15, 1986, p. 2.

16. Herbert Passin, *Society and Education in Japan* (New York: Teachers College, Columbia University Press, 1965), pp. 293–304.

17. John W. Dower, *Empire and Aftermath: Yoshida Shigeru and the Japanese Experience, 1878–1954* (Cambridge, MA: Harvard University Press, 1979), 369–470; Michael Schaller, *The American Occupation of Japan: The Origins of the Cold War in Asia* (New York: The Free Press, 1985).

18. Ministry of Education, "Progress Report on the Reformation of Japanese Education" (Tokyo: Government of Japan, August 1950).

19. Sir George B. Sansom, *Japan: A Cultural History* (New York: Appleton, Century, Crofts, 1962), p. 15.

20. Ministry of Education, "Outline for Implementing Moral Education" (Tokyo: Government of Japan, March 18, 1958).

21. William K. Cummings, *Education and Equality in Japan* (Princeton, NJ: Princeton University Press, 1980), p. 116.

22. There is evidence to suggest that the power of the Nikkyoso (Japan Teachers' Union) has been declining. For example, "Only 50% of Teachers in JTU, Says Ed. Ministry," *Asahi Evening News,* August 27, 1985, p. 2; "Nikkyoso Teachers Less Than Half of Total for First Time," *Japan Times,* October 1, 1986, p. 3; "Teachers' Union Membership Failing," *Mainichi Daily News,* October 1, 1986, p. 12.

23. Fukatake, *Japanese Social Structure*, p. 70.

24. Samuel Coleman, *Family Planning in Japanese Society: Traditional Birth Control in a Modern Urban Culture* (Princeton, NJ: Princeton University Press, 1983), p. 150.

25. Ibid., p. 151.

26. Shogo Ichikawa, "Japan," in *Educational Policy: An International Survey*, ed. J.R. Hough (New York: Helm-Croom, 1984), p. 105.

27. T.J. Pempel, *Patterns of Japanese Policymaking: Experiences in Higher Education* (Boulder, CO: Westview Press, 1978), p. 163.

28. Passin, *Society and Education in Japan*, p. 97.

29. Ikuo Amano, "Educational Crisis in Japan," in *Educational Policies in Crisis:*

Japanese and American Perspectives, ed. William K. Cummings, Edward R. Beauchamp, et al. (New York: Praeger, 1986), pp. 23–43.

30. Edward R. Beauchamp, "Shiken Jiguoku: The Problem of Entrance Examinations in Japan," *Asian Profile* 6 (December 1978): 543–560; William K. Cummings, *Education and Equality in Japan,* pp. 206–234; Thomas P. Rohlen, *Japan's High Schools* (Berkeley: University of California Press, 1983), pp. 77–110; Nobuo Shimahara, *Adaptation and Education in Japan* (New York: Praeger, 1979), pp. 77–126.

31. Ardath W. Burks, *Japan: A Postindustrial Power* (Boulder, CO: Westview Press, 1981), p. 157.

32. Tetsuya Kobayashi, *Schools, Society, and Progress in Japan* (New York: Pergamon Press, 1976), p. 93.

33. Shimahara, *Adaptation and Education in Japan,* p. 133.

34. Anderson, *Education in Japan,* p. 201.

35. Ministry of Education, *Outline of Education in Japan, 1985* (Tokyo: Government of Japan, 1985), p. 13.

36. Pempel, *Patterns of Japanese Policymaking,* p. 180.

37. Ichikawa, "Japan," p. 115.

38. Ministry of Education, "Education Statistics" (Tokyo: Government of Japan, 1976), p. 73.

39. Anderson, *Education in Japan,* p. 98.

40. Beauchamp, "Shiken Jiguoku," pp. 243–260.

41. Ezra P. Vogel, *Japan's New Middle Class: The Salary Man and His Family in a Tokyo Suburb* (Berkeley: University of California Press, 1965), p. 40.

42. Ronald P. Dore, *The Diploma Disease: Education, Qualification, and Development* (Berkeley: University of California Press, 1976), p. 49.

43. Thomas P. Rohlen, "Japanese Education: If They Can Do It, Should We?" *American Scholar* (Winter 1985–86): 29–43.

44. Fosco Maraini, *Japan: Patterns of Continuity* (Tokyo: Weatherhill, 1971), p. 27.

45. Beauchamp, *An American Teacher in Early Meiji Japan.*

46. Rohlen, "Japanese Education," pp. 19–43.

47. Ministry of Education, *Statistical Abstract of Education, Science and Culture* (Tokyo: Government of Japan, 1981), p. 69.

48. For details, see the Japan Association of Private Colleges and Universities, *Japan's Private Colleges and Universities: Yesterday, Today and Tomorrow* (Tokyo: Japan Association of Private Colleges, 1987), especially pp. 151–172.

49. Nathan Glazer, "Social and Cultural Factors in Japanese Economic Growth," in *Asia's New Giant: How the Japanese Economy Works,* ed. Hugh T. Patrick and Henry Rosovsky (Washington, DC: Brookings Institution, 1976), p. 821.

50. Central Council for Education, "Basic Guidelines for the Reform of Education: On the Basic Guidelines for the Development of an Integrated Educational System Suited to Contemporary Society: Report of the Central Council for Education" (Tokyo: Government of Japan, 1972), p. 2.

51. Ibid.

52. *Mainichi Daily News,* June 12, 1971, p. 8.

53. Organization for Economic Co-operation and Development, *Reviews of National Policies for Education: Japan* (Paris: OECD, 1971).

54. Japan Teachers' Union, *How to Reform Japan's Education* (Tokyo: Japan Teachers' Union, 1975), p. 30.

55. *Japan Times,* February 26, 1981, p. 2.

56. *Mainichi Daily News,* May 5, 1985, p. 12.

57. Mitsuru Uchida, "The Graying of Japan," *Japan Times,* April 19, 1987.

58. Ikuo Amano, "Educational Reform in Historical Perspective," *Japan Echo* 11 (1984): 12.

59. Thomas P. Rohlen, "Order in Japanese Society: Attachment, Authority, and Routine," *The Journal of Japanese Studies,* 15: 1 (Winter 1989).

60. *Japan Times,* April 7, 1985; *Asahi Evening News,* April 5, 1985, p. 4.

61. Margaret Lock, "Plea for Acceptance: School Refusal Syndrome in Japan," *Social Science and Medicine* (Fall 1987).

62. G. Cameron Hurst III, "Japanese Education: Trouble in Paradise?" *Universities Field Staff International Reports, No. 40: Asia* (1984): 10.

63. Hidetoshi Nishimura, "Educational Reform: Commissioning a Master Plan," *Japan Quarterly* 37 (January–March 1985) pp. 18–22.

64. *Mainichi Daily News,* December 30, 1984, p. 12.

65. Ibid.

66. *Japan Times,* November 19, 1985, p. 3.

67. *Mainichi Daily News,* November 13, 1985, p. 13.

68. Yoshio Murakami, "Bullies in the Classroom," *Japan Quarterly* 32 (October–December 1985): 407–411.

69. Donald T. Roden, *Schooldays in Imperial Japan: A Study in the Culture of a Student Elite* (Berkeley: University of California Press, 1980).

Part II

Selected Documents

A. War, Defeat, and Occupation, 1890–1952

1
Imperial Rescript on Education
(Kyoiku Chokugo)

October 30, 1890

Source: General Headquarters, Supreme Commander for Allied Powers, Civil Information and Education Section, Education Division, *Education in the New Japan,* Volume II (Tokyo, 1948), p. 76.

Know Ye, Our Subjects:

Our Imperial Ancestors have founded Our Empire on a basis broad and everlasting, and have deeply and firmly implanted virtue; Our subjects ever united in loyalty and filial piety have from generation to generation illustrated the beauty thereof. This is the glory of the fundamental character of Our Empire, and herein also lies the source of our education. Ye, our subjects, be filial to your parents, affectionate to your brothers and sisters; as husbands and wives be harmonious, as friends true; bear yourselves in modesty and moderation; extend your benevolence to all; pursue learning and cultivate arts; and thereby develop intellectual faculties and perfect moral powers. Furthermore, advance public good and promote common interests; always respect the Constitution and observe the laws; should emergency arise, offer yourselves courageously to the State; and thus guard and maintain the prosperity of Our Imperial Throne coeval with heaven and earth. So shall ye not only be our good and faithful subjects but render illustrious the best traditions of your forefathers.

The way here set forth is indeed the teaching bequeathed by Our Imperial Ancestors, to be observed by their descendants and the subjects, infallible for all ages, and true in all places. It is our wish to lay it to heart in all reverence, in common with you, our subjects, that we may attain to the same virtue.

The thirtieth day of the tenth month of the twenty-third year of Meiji

(Imperial Sign Manual) (Imperial Seal)

2
Japan: The Education System under Military Government (PWC–287a)

November 6, 1944

Source: National Archives of the United States, Modern Military Branch, Record Group 59, General Records of the Department of State. Records of Harley A. Notter, 1939–1945. Records of the Policy and Planning Committees. Box 144.

Originally prepared and reviewed by the Inter-Divisional Area Committee on the Far East. Reviewed and revised by the Committee on Post-War Programs, October 27, 1944.

I. The Problem

What should military government do with the Japanese educational system?

II. Basic Factors

1. General Observations

Careful study of the problem leads to the conclusion that there will not be available to military government the large number of competent and qualified American and other foreign personnel which would be required to carry out such fundamental reforms of the Japanese educational system as might seem desirable and to operate it after such reforms have been inaugurated; that modifications in the educational system imposed on the Japanese by military government can do little more than create conditions favorable to a change in the Japanese mental attitude towards religious, political and social problems; and that therefore military government should await the coming forward in sufficient numbers of cooperative Japanese, themselves proponents of liberal ideas, upon whom can be placed the responsibility for carrying to completion these fundamental educational reforms necessary for the elimination of ultra-nationalism and a militaristic spirit. Consequently, this paper makes certain recommendations which aim at removing some of the reactionary and illiberal influences from the Japanese educational system and which, from a practical point of view, the military government will be able to carry out.

The Japanese educational system, which includes nearly 50,000 schools, 400,000 teachers, and almost 16,000,000 students, combines universal compulsory elementary education with an examination system for educational attainment. The effect of this is to reduce drastically the number of students at the secondary level and even more drastically at the higher level.

The system as it now operates and as it is now controlled supports an authoritarian social and political regime. It does not undertake to develop individual initiative and character but aims to create a general high level of educational attainment so that the supply of well-trained instruments will be available for national service. While equal educational opportunities are given to the rich and poor the effect of the system is in the main to produce obedient members of the state.

The selection of students, as they pass from the lowest to the highest level of the system, channels the best brains of the nation into a small leadership group. The graduates of colleges and universities, being the products of a highly selective system, have a distinct advantage in securing favorable positions in both government and private business. In a relatively poor country such as Japan a highly selective system is probably necessary for obtaining the leadership which is requisite to a modern state.

Individual initiative, however, is discouraged by not permitting the student to do original thinking. He is taught not to question the instructions given him by his teachers. His educational development is usually measured by his proficiency in reproducing the statements and problems of his teachers.

Under present circumstances the military clique that rules the nation manipulates education. The inculcation of an extreme nationalism and a glorification of war, combined with the doctrine of the "divine destiny" of Japan, hold the common people under the control of the state for the service of the state. The body of the population is fixed in the status of followers.

Thus the system is somewhat paradoxical. It succeeds in shaping a closely knit, well-integrated nation whose energies can be easily directed by those who exercise the power of the state. However, the social integration of the nation is incomplete, especially in the highest ranks of the educated group where the largest proportion of non-conformists to the prevailing militaristic norm are found. Some of these non-conformists are the repositories of whatever liberal outlook survives in Japan.

The present operation of the Japanese educational system is obviously out of harmony with democratic conceptions and ideals. Actually, of course, although it provides for universal education and for education advancement on the basis of proved merit, it is devised more to meet the needs of the state than those of the people. Therefore, the many problems which will arise for the occupation authorities can be resolved only as principles are introduced and means adopted which will foster in the minds of the present and future generations of Japanese children and youth the psychological and intellectual basis for a policy of international cooperation by Japan.

2. *Japanese Educational System Centralized*

The Japanese educational system is one of the most centralized, closely knit systems in the world. The ultimate decision of educational policy and administration of schools throughout Japan is concentrated in the Ministry of Education in Tokyo. The Ministry has control over all prefectural and local educational organs, the most important of which is the Division of Educational Affairs of each prefecture.

It is assumed that the military authorities will abolish the purely policy-forming organs of the Ministry of Education. They may find it desirable, however, to continue some or all of the functions of the following bureaus of the Ministry of Education with their administrative machinery—Bureau of General Education (controls the elementary, secondary, normal, and middle schools for the blind and deaf); Bureau of Special School Affairs (supervises higher institutions of learning and special schools); Bureau of Technical Education (supervises industrial, commercial and other technical schools)—and to continue some or all of the functions of the Division of Educational Affairs in each prefecture. Under close supervisory control, they may utilize the non-policy functions of the Bureau of Textbooks and the Bureau of Social Education. The Bureau of Educational Reform should be abolished, the central inspectorate and the "coaching" teachers dismissed.

The supervision of the non-school functions of the Department, such as the control of religions [*sic*] and youth organizations, should be delegated to those civil affairs officers in charge of religion and nationalist organizations.

3. *Textbooks*

Under the present educational system no book may be used in a Japanese school unless it is approved in Tokyo. The Ministry of Education holds exclusive copyright on all indoctrination textbooks. By the careful selection of and control over all textbooks the Ministry of Education with the advice of military officers has a powerful weapon in molding the minds of Japan's students. There was a major revision of elementary texts in 1936 when the militaristic "Showa" morals readers, filled with pictures, stories and illustrations from Japanese history, glorifying Japan's military exploits, were substituted for the more rational "Taisho" morals readers. The "Taisho" readers were written during Japan's peaceful era of the twenties and placed little emphasis on the glorification of Japanese military life. The CAA might consider the substitution of these readers for the recent militant "Showa" readers.

A study of Japanese textbooks might well be undertaken now by the appropriate authorities in order to determine what material is appropriate and what should be discarded. They might in certain instances find available in Japan satisfactory new textbooks which could be used, or they might encourage the Japanese to provide such material. The inspection of textbooks might commence now or be left to the times when the military occupation of Japan is complete.

4. Personnel

It has been previously recommended that the military government retain a considerable number of Japanese personnel within the Ministry of Education to continue administrative functions. In carrying out this recommendation a distinction should be made between the present administrative personnel and those appointed as inspectors and supervisors of thought and teaching methods. Such inspectors, both in the central administration and on the prefectural and local levels, appointed by the authority now in operation, should be dismissed.

In order to carry out the approved administrative functions of the Department of Education it will be necessary to place civil affairs officers in strategic positions within the Ministry. In order to encourage cooperation it would seem advisable for these officers to make themselves no more obtrusive than would be necessary for the performance of their functions. In addition to the civil affairs education officers in Tokyo, occupation authorities should assign a civil affairs officer to each prefectural office, whose duties would be to assist in the enforcement of the education directives from the central authorities. The education program during military occupation will probably function more successfully if these supervisors can be selected from Americans or other established persons who have been teachers and administrators in Japanese schools.

In order to facilitate the carrying out of the functions of civil affairs education officers and the local Japanese school administrations and teachers it may prove desirable to have carefully selected native-born Japanese educated in mission schools or abroad and Americans of Japanese ancestry (*Nisei*) employed to assist the civil affairs officers for administration and in carrying out the educational directives.

5. Schools and Courses

The great majority of the students, some 12,000,000 are to be found in the elementary schools. Here an undue proportion of the student's time is devoted to such indoctrination courses as "morals," Japanese history and group physical training and drill as preparatory to military training. Such basic courses as Japanese language, arithmetic, science, music, and penmanship [calligraphy] are also taught in the elementary schools.

From the elementary school those students who have met certain scholastic requirements enter the middle schools which provide for a five year course. Here the curriculum is expanded to include the natural sciences and foreign languages. Indoctrination courses become more intensive. Military training is required of all the physically fit boys.

Those students who have finished middle school are admitted to higher schools after passing the entrance examination. The courses of study in these higher schools include the arts, sciences, and the usual indoctrination subjects in "morals," history, etc. Students who desire to study for a profession in a university may take basic courses required for entry into a university. Military training is compulsory for all physically fit men students in the higher schools.

Japanese universities, like those of the West, are composed of several colleges, such as Colleges of Medicine, of Law, of Engineering, etc. The course of study is usually three or four years.

Japanese teachers in elementary and middle schools are trained in normal schools established by the prefectures. Each prefecture is required to organize and maintain at least one normal school. An effective if rapid instrument for changing the emphasis in Japanese education from a militaristic to a peaceful philosophy is the normal schools. It would seem advisable for the CAA to place special emphasis on the supervision of these schools.

It would be desirable for appropriate administrative assistants of Japanese ancestry to make periodic visits to the various cities and towns, when the teachers in various schools could be brought together for a brief course in reorientation. The program, which should be designed to cover a period of not more than a day for each occasion, should include addresses to disseminate ideas and information on the United Nations and cognate subjects, and motion pictures on appropriate subjects. The service of Japanese liberals who may be prepared to participate in such programs should be utilized. Competent teachers who have been discharged because of their opposition to militarism should be reinstated.

6. Indoctrination

The indoctrination courses are designed to reduce personal initiative to a minimum, and the students are trained to conform to directives, and, if necessary, to sacrifice themselves readily for the State. The glorification of Japan's military way of life is drilled into the student's mind through such required courses as "morals," ethics and history and military training. Special lectures, radio programs, motion pictures, and phonograph recordings help to remind the students of their duties as "good" Japanese subjects. The indoctrination program is carried on under the direction of the Bureau of Educational Reform and Social Education and the strict guidance of the military.

Indoctrination is also effectively carried on by special convocations, such as those held on national holidays. For example, on the emperor's birthday attendance at school is compulsory and a general assembly is held for several hours in the morning during which the students are subjected to long harangues on the virtues of the sovereign and the superiority of Japan's national characteristics. The emperor's portrait, of which there is one in each school, is the focal point of the program and is treated with awesome respect. Consequently, all such occasions are excellent opportunities for the dissemination of the national cult. To keep the students away from school and a national holiday would be a simple way and an effective way of preventing such indoctrination.

The CAA should bear in mind that modifications of the Japanese educational system during military occupation cannot be far-reaching. It will have neither the time nor the personnel to institute a drastically reformed system of education and to administer it in its completed form. However, the type of initial steps taken to destroy those features which foster militarism in the existing set-up forms the basis for the more permanent re-creation of Japan's education program. The military governments [sic] should initiate such steps where possible and give momentum to a program that will break through and break down Japan's "insularity" and teach her students to know and learn to respect the history and accomplishments of other nations and secure if possible a world outlook.

For example, such measures may include nullification of obnoxious laws, free dissemination of ideas and information from the outside world through the activities of a distributive machinery available in the Bureau of Social Education, and encouragement of the functions of the Bureau of Education Research in studying foreign systems of education and discussion [sic] methods of revising the Japanese system from within.

The fact that the Japanese educational system is so rigidly controlled and so uniform may in some respects make the task of changing it easier. The framework and mechanical channel of control may be used, but the spirit and substance must be to a great extent changed in the course of time.

III. Basic Principles

Measures dealing with the control of the educational system under military occupation should be integrated with the general policy of the United States in building a world in which we can live at peace. In the intellectual field the fundamental proposition is that there should be no areas closed to outside ideas. In applying this policy to this system of education in Japan, the objectives should be (a) to set aside those laws and practices which in recent years have made it a closed ideological area, and (b) to initiate measures or assist indigenous movements which would breakdown Japanese "insularity," develop personal intellectual initiative, and create conditions under which free intellectual intercourse can develop and expand.

IV. Recommendations

The following recommendations are applicable in the main to all Japanese schools, colleges, and universities.

1. To facilitate the maintenance of peace and order, schools should be kept open. Schools closed by Japanese authorities should be reopened. A proclamation should be issued instructing the officials of the Ministry of Education, except the top policy-making officials, to continue their functions and the teachers and students of schools to continue their attendance at school.

2. Where it is practicable administrative and clerical staff in the Ministry of Education and in the Division of Educational Affairs in each prefecture, and teachers in schools, colleges and universities who are willing to cooperate with the occupation authorities should be retained.

3. In conjunction with the abolition of obnoxious laws the Bureau of Educational Reform should be abolished and Japanese inspectors of thought and teaching methods should be dismissed.

4. CAA should use where practicable those Japanese textbooks that are not contrary to the objectives of the United Nations. Textbooks that indoctrinate the student with Japanese militarism and mythology should be revised as rapidly as practicable. As a first step the "Taisho" readers might be substituted for the "Showa" readers.

5. There should be civil affairs education officers placed in strategic positions within the Ministry of Education and the Division of Educational Affairs. The civil affairs officers in prefectures should be selected as is practicable from United Nations nationals who have had teaching and administrative experience in Japanese schools.

6. Americans of Japanese ancestry (*Nisei*) might be assigned to civil affairs officers to assist in enforcing the educational directives and to perform such other work as they may designate. At the appropriate time, carefully selected native-born Japanese educated in mission schools or abroad might also be used if they volunteered for such work.

7. Because of the importance of creating a teaching personnel with a new viewpoint, CAA authorities should give special attention to the supervision and curriculum of the normal schools.

8. The curriculum of the schools should be modified to exclude military training and courses, such as "morals" (*shushin*) and Japanese history, which indoctrinates the student in the way of Japanese militarism. There should be no

effort in the initial stages to revise the curriculum by way of providing instruction with a democratic approach in the suspended or abolished courses and subjects. The phrase "in the initial stages" is defined in the present context as being the period prior to the time when the services of progressive and forward-looking Japanese can be employed to prepare appropriate textbooks and to collaborate in giving instruction in the subjects concerned.

9. The CAA should prohibit such compulsory convocations as those held on national holidays or for the purpose of revering the state. On national holidays they should close the schools and the students should be kept away from the school. Care should be taken to prohibit as a part of the prescribed school curriculum any ceremony connected with the emperor's portrait.

10. The school, radio, motion picture and recording equipment should be used as much as possible by the civil affairs authorities, and perhaps by Japanese liberals, to break down Japan's "insularity" and teach her students to know the history and accomplishments of other nations and secure if possible a world outlook.

3
Positive Policy for Reorientation of the Japanese (SWNCC 162/D)

July 19, 1945

Source: The National Archives of the United States, Record Group 319, Records of the Army Staff, ABC 014 Japan (April 13, 1944), Sec. T-A (excerpts).

The Problem

1. Whether it is desirable to undertake a program of reeducation and reorientation of the Japanese people which, through changes in certain of their ideologies and attitudes of mind, will bring about the development of a peaceful and democratic Japan.

Facts Bearing on the Problem

Failure to prepare a positive and integrated program of reeducation and reorientation is a basic cause of the present chaos in Italy and has already invited severe criticism of our military government in Germany.

Conclusions

6. It is desirable, as part of the function of military government in Japan, to undertake a program of reeducation and reorientation of the Japanese, designed to bring about a Japan which will cease to be a menace to international security.

Discussion

1. Most Japanese, in greater or lesser degree, at present share a common attitude of mind of which the following are salient elements:

a. The persistence of feudal concepts, including class stratification, the glorification of the military, and a habit of subservience to authority.

b. A belief in the "divine mission" of the Japanese in the leadership of the world, closely connected with a cult of emperor-worship fostered in recent years by the military to serve their own purposes.

c. Extreme racial consciousness and an anti-foreign complex, which, however, is often combined with great admiration for foreign achievements and learning.

2. The basic objective of the United States is to insure [*sic*] the emergence of a Japan which will not again disturb the peace of the world and which will eventually assume its proper place as a member of the family of nations.

3. To this end, it is necessary to effect changes in certain ideologies and ways of thinking of the individual Japanese, referred to above, which have in the past motivated the Japanese people as a whole in the pursuit of chauvinistic and militaristic policies.

4. It is not proposed to recast the culture of the Japanese but rather to use it, as far as possible, in establishing new attitudes of mind conforming to the basic principles of democracy and fair dealing.

5. Despite the prevalence in Japan of contrary beliefs, numerous Japanese will be found who, through prior contacts and earlier education, will be disposed to accept and to assist in the development of such democratic principles. It will be the first duty of our military government to seek out such persons and with their assistance to initiate the formation of local democratic groups to further the program herein presented.

6. Similarly, it will be possible to select from the Japanese cultural complex, numerous ideas and beliefs which by appropriate emphasis and development may be used for the furtherance of this program. This will be true of many of the older ethical standards of Japanese home and family life, as distinguished from the chauvinistic and militaristic concepts of Japanese nationalism. Emphasis placed on such ethical standards will go far toward ensuring the support of the

older generation and of the Japanese women, groups which, by reason of their conservatism might otherwise present substantial resistance to any program of reeducation and the inculcation of new ideas. An important additional element will be the ensuring of equal educational opportunities for women.

7. On the national level it will be the purpose of this program to develop the political responsibility of the individual citizen, and thereby to ensure the reorganization of the Japanese political system. It is axiomatic that the only effective political reform must stem from the people themselves. Political reforms imposed solely by the fiat of the military government will either be resisted by the people, or will be ignored by them. The entire program of reeducation is intended, in part, to supply the Japanese themselves the ideas and incentives essential to the spontaneous development of a political reorganization stemming from the people as a whole.

8. To this end, emphasis will be placed on the principles of self-government which have been evolved by the democracies, and upon the dangers to individual freedom and international peace inherent in tyrannical governmental forms, whether oligarchics or dictatorships.

9. The power of the Japanese oligarchy and the ready acceptance of militarism by the population both rest, in part, on the depressed condition of the agricultural and industrial workers of Japan. The ruling classes are powerful by reason of their control over the country's wealth, and the poverty of the rural districts has fostered and intensified the fanaticism of the military groups. Thus, the encouragement of appropriate agrarian and economic reforms should constitute an integral part of the program of reeducation proposed here.

10. Reeducation will only be effective as it goes hand in hand with some gradual improvement in the economic condition of the ordinary Japanese toward whom it is directed, as compared with the conditions existing at the time of defeat or surrender. To this end, again, it is essential that the economic policies of the military government be integrated with the entire program of reeducation, and that whatever relief is furnished and whatever economic improvement is made be identified in the minds of the Japanese as part of such a program.

11. The program of reeducation cannot be restricted to formalized education or to a mere reform of the educational system. It must be aimed at reeducating not only the youth but the whole population, and it must be insinuated [insulated] into the minds of the Japanese through every channel that is available.

12. The Japanese are a literate people. They have been taught that education is desirable and this, coupled with their habit of obedience to authority and uncritical acceptance of the teachings of their leaders, will make them receptive to a process of reeducation which is properly presented. The most effective element will be the supplying of information concerning the world outside of Japan. It is essential, however, that the program and the materials used be con-

formed to the background of the Japanese themselves rather than to purely occidental concepts.

13. All the media should be utilized including books, textbooks, periodicals, motion pictures, radio, lectures, discussion groups, and the school system. It is obvious that extensive advance preparation of materials will be essential to this end.

14. The necessity of prompt determination of United States policies is not dependent on a decision at this time as to the duration of military occupation or control of Japan. Since military control must be maintained long enough to ensure the carrying out of the terms imposed following surrender or total defeat, this will afford adequate time to develop a substantial program of reeducation and reorientation, particularly where advance planning and preparation of materials assures its prompt initiation.

15. The entire program in type and scope should be designed so that it can be carried on by the Japanese themselves following withdrawal of the United States or allied controls, and, to this end, it will be essential from the beginning to encourage participation by local groups or organizations. It must be emphasized that reeducation promptly and adequately made effective will materially speed the development of a responsible and trustworthy government in Japan, and thereby help materially to shorten the period of occupation by our forces.

16. The foregoing program is not predicated on any sympathy for the Japanese people, or on any desire for a "soft peace." It is based solely on the proposition that certain reforms must be instituted in Japanese ideologies if Japan is to emerge as a peaceable nation. There is no intention to permit these considerations to override or impair, in the slightest degree, the demilitarization and just punishment that will be imposed on Japan at the end of the war. The program here proposed should be administered with complete objectivity and detachment to attain the ends desired. Maudlin sympathy and sentimentality should be excluded.

17. The failure to establish in advance policies designed to meet the problems of reorientation in Italy has resulted in the continuance for nearly two years of conditions of internal conflict and instability bordering on chaos. Evidence already exists that, due to lack of advance preparation of a positive and integrated program for Germany, equally disastrous results may ensue in that country. Failure or refusal of the United States to take the lead in providing such a program for Japan will leave the field open to other interested elements, who will not hesitate to enter it. The probable result would be prolonged unrest and civil strife, coupled with the development of a political hegemony inimical to the best interests of the United States and the future peace of the world.

4
The Potsdam Proclamation

July 26, 1945

Source: Department of State Bulletin (July 29, 1945), pp. 137 (excerpts).

1. We—the President of the United States, the President of the National Government of the Republic of China, and the Prime Minister of Great Britain—representing the hundreds of millions of our countrymen, have conferred and agree that Japan shall be given an opportunity to end the war. . . .

4. The time has come for Japan to decide whether she will continue to be controlled by those self-willed militaristic advisors whose unintelligent calculations have brought the Empire of Japan to the threshold of annihilation, or whether she will follow the path of reason.

5. Following are our terms. We shall not deviate from them. There are no alternatives. We shall brook no delay.

6. There must be eliminated for all time the authority and influence of those who have deceived and misled the people of Japan into embarking on world conquest, for we insist that a new order of peace, security and justice will be impossible until irresponsible militarism is driven from the world.

7. Until such a new order is established and until there is convincing proof that Japan's warmaking power is destroyed, points in Japanese territory to be designated by the Allies shall be occupied to secure the achievement of the basic objectives we are here setting forth. . . .

10. We do not intend that the Japanese shall be enslaved as a race or destroyed as a nation, but stern justice shall be meted out to all war criminals, including those who have visited cruelties upon our prisoners. The Japanese Government shall remove all obstacles to the revival and strengthening of democratic tendencies among the Japanese people. Freedom of speech, of religion, and of thought, as well as respect for the fundamental human rights, shall be established. . . .

12. The occupying forces of the Allies shall be withdrawn from Japan as soon as these objectives have been accomplished and there has been established in accordance with the freely expressed will of the Japanese people a peacefully inclined and responsible government.

13. We call upon the government of Japan to proclaim now the unconditional surrender of all Japanese armed forces, and to provide proper and adequate assurances of their good faith in such action. The alternative for Japan is prompt and utter destruction.

5
School Education under the New Situation (I) (*Hatsu Sen* No. 118)

August 28, 1945

[From the Vice-Minister of Education to Prefectural Governors and Presidents of Schools]

Source: General Headquarters, SCAP, CIE, and Education Division. *Education in the New Japan,* vol. 2 (Tokyo, 1948), p. 139.

As regards carrying out school education, a directive has been sent to you by telegram, but as this is a very important problem, you are hereby requested again to carry it out thoroughly paying strict attention to the following items:

1. As regards teaching in schools (including women's schools), you are requested to do your best to return to ordinary conditions. Even the schools whose students were asked to return home shall begin teaching by the middle of September at the latest.

2. However, if needs be, you are allowed to suspend teaching for a time or have the students return home irrespective of the preceding clause.

3. Even those schools which have no prospect of beginning teaching because of war damage are requested to do their best to begin ordinary teaching as soon as possible. As regards equipment of the school buildings and the boarding houses of the teachers and students, it is desirable to keep close connection with the authorities concerned. While it may be a proper measure to entrust the students to other schools, it is also a proper measure to make the students work to increase food production. For the above-mentioned matter, higher schools and colleges are requested to get good results by mutual assistance and cooperation among the schools groups. . . .

6
United States Initial Post-Surrender Policy for Japan

August 29, 1945

Source: National Archives, Record Group 319, Records of the Army Staff, ABC 387, Japan, Joint Civil Affairs Committee 48, "Basic Initial Post-Surrender Directive to Supreme Commander for Allied Powers for the Occupation and Control of Japan" (August 30, 1945), pp. 7, 18–19. (February 15, 1944) Sec. 19 (excerpts).

. . . 3. Basic Objectives of Military Occupation of Japan

A. The ultimate objective of the United Nations with respect to Japan is to foster conditions which will give the greatest possible assurance that Japan will not again become a menace to the peace and security of the world and will permit her eventual admission as a peaceful member of the family of nations. Certain measures considered to be essential for the achievement of this objective . . . include, among others, . . . the abolition of militarism and ultra-nationalism in all their forms; the disarmament and demilitarization of Japan, with continuing control of Japan's capacity to make war; the strengthening of democratic tendencies and processes in governmental, economic and social institutions; and the encouragement and support of liberal political tendencies in Japan. The United States desires that the Japanese government conform as closely as may be to principles of democratic self-government, but it is not the responsibility of the occupational forces to impose on Japan any form of government not supported by the freely expressed will of the people. . . .

10. Education, Arts and Archives

A. As soon as practicable educational institutions will be reopened. As rapidly as possible all teachers who have been exponents of militant nationalism and aggression and those who continue actively to oppose the purposes of the military occupation will be replaced by acceptable and qualified successors. Japanese military and para-military training and drills in all schools will be forbidden. You will assure that curricula acceptable to you are employed in all schools and that they include the concepts indicated in paragraph 3A above.

7
Educational Situation at End of the War

Fall 1945

Source: National Archives, Record Group 718, General Headquarters, Supreme Commander for Allied Powers, "Monthly Summary No. 1" (n.d., probably November 1945), p. 199.

Surrender Day found the Japanese educational system at a standstill; 18,000,000 students idle; 4,000 schools destroyed; 20% of the necessary textbooks available; military officers occupying responsible educational positions; textbooks impregnated with militaristic propaganda; teachers dispersed; the Ministry of Education a tool of the militarists; liberal educators hiding from the Thought Police.

Between the time of Japanese capitulation and the establishment of Allied General Headquarters in Tokyo the Japanese voluntarily undertook many reforms. They conducted a rough school survey, initiated a censorship of existing official textbooks; reorganized the Ministry of Education, reopened the schools, and abrogated the laws, orders and regulations which had been the basis of authority for militaristic and ultranationalistic indoctrination in the schools.

During September and October the Japanese under the guidance of SCAP [Supreme Commander for Allied Powers] personnel, closed the military schools, provided for the transfer of displaced students who had previously been in military academies, war industry or evacuation areas, disposed of school military supplies and weapons, issued directives for the guidance of teachers in using existing textbooks until they could be censored, and dissolved the Youth Corps, which had been a tool of militaristic propaganda.

8
School Education under the New Situation (II) (*Hatsu Koku* No. 184) (From the Chief of the Bureau of Lower Education [Ministry of Education] to all Prefectural Governors)

September 12, 1945

Source: General Headquarters, SCAP, CIE, Education Division. *Education in the New Japan,* vol. 2 (Tokyo, 1948), p. 140 (excerpts).

The Vice-Minister of Education issued notification on . . . the above mentioned subject on August 28, 1945 [see previous document]. On the same subject I hereby notify you that you should bear in mind the points mentioned hereunder concerning the education in elementary schools, youth schools, and secondary schools.

Furthermore, you are requested to take proper measures in order that those girls' schools which have been suspending instruction under special circumstances should do their best to resume it, fixing special lesson hours, and adjusting the time of students attending schools.

A. Concerning Elementary School Education

. . . 2. Although the general principle is to restore peacetime school education as rapidly as possible . . . , it has been decided that the school children evacuated to the country in groups will remain where they are for some time to come. Therefore, it is desired that the education be carried on more intensively than ever in these places. As to the school children remaining in the devastated cities, or in those cities where group evacuation of school children has been carried out, in case it is impossible to restore peacetime school instruction, it is desired that best efforts be made to promote their education. . . .

3. Those school children who, their homes being devastated, have been evacuated in other districts and who have not yet taken the steps necessary for changing schools, and those who, their schools being devastated, remain at home, should be made to apply for admission to elementary schools nearest their residences so that they may study at school.

4. Although the Wartime Education Ordinance is to be abolished, some students will continue their labor service. . . .

5. In view of the present importance of increasing food production, even the lower course of elementary schools in farming villages, mountain villages, etc., should be given agricultural work . . . when they are to be given no lessons.

B. Concerning Youth School Education

1. It is presumed that there must be a great number of students belonging to youth schools which have been set up in factories and workshops and who, due to the sudden changes in the situation, have been dispersed in various areas. It is desirable that such students be immediately made to enter their nearest public youth schools in compliance with the principles of the compulsory school system.

2. Although the Wartime Education Ordinance is to be abolished, the instruction and training to be given in the youth school is to be [continued]. However, the hours assigned to the military training and instruction should be used properly for vocational training and gymnastics, etc. At the same time, efforts should be made to devise original ways of displaying local characteristics in all activities of education.

3. In the girls' youth schools, while feminine virtues are to be fostered, guidance should be especially given in how to conduct daily life more scientifically. Students' attendance at schools should also be encouraged. . . .

5. As food production is an urgent problem under the present circumstances, efforts for it should be continued even after peacetime training and instruction and training are restored. The hours spent for it in collective works should be treated as those of the regular curriculum.

C. Concerning Secondary School Education

1. The hours that remain over, due to the abolition of the military training in schools . . . should be used for work in food production, reconstruction of devastated areas, and the like, making the students actively participate in those kinds of work.

2. Those students who, their homes being devastated, have been evacuated in other districts and who have not taken steps necessary for changing schools, and those who, their schools being devastated, remain at home, should be made to apply for admission in similar secondary schools nearest to their dwellings . . . so as to encourage them to study.

3. The commercial schools which converted into technical schools in the 1944 school year will continue their instruction on the same lines as heretofore until further notice. . . .

D. Concerning School Buildings and Education in Devastated Cities

1. The Elementary Schools and the Secondary Schools in the devastated cities which have been deprived of their buildings by fire should try to accommodate themselves mutually with the general rule of establishing as far as possi-

ble boys' secondary schools in the suburbs and girls' secondary schools and elementary schools near the former areas where the parents and guardians live. In places where such a plan is impracticable, temples, assembly halls, and similar appropriate buildings should be utilized so as to have the facilities necessary for education.

9
Educational Policy for the Construction of a New Japan *(Shin nihon kensetsu no kyoiku hoshin)*

Ministry of Education

September 15, 1945

Source: Kanda Osamu et al., eds., *Shiryo Kyoikuho* (Tokyo: Gakuyo Shobo, 1973), pp. 299–300. Translation by James Vardaman.

In obedience to the purport of the imperial edict concerning the termination of the war, the Ministry of Education is implementing various educational policies to aid in the construction of a new nation which will contribute to the peace and welfare of mankind by reforming the former educational policies based upon the requirements of prosecuting war.

1. Policies for the "New Education"

In obedience to the imperial edict, the Ministry is diligently reexamining educational policies in order to establish new policies which meet the demands of the new circumstances, and it expects to form a concrete program in the near future. We will humbly reflect upon education and its goals of serving the good of the country and, at the same time, constructing a peaceful nation by the eradication of militarism. Emphasis shall be placed on improving the education of the Japanese people, cultivating their ability to think scientifically, strengthening their desire for peace, and raising the general level of knowledge and virtue within our society.

2. Stance of Education

The student brigades organized as part of the war effort are abolished and the wartime system of education has been disassembled in order to return to a normal curriculum of study. Military education in the schools is completely abolished and the research centers directly connected with war activities have begun to redirect their efforts toward research for peace-related purposes.

3. Textbooks

A fundamental revision of textbooks must be carried out in accord with the new educational policies. For the present, the Ministry of Education intends to designate which portions of the textbooks should be corrected or omitted in order to prevent difficulties from the point of view of instruction.

4. Teaching Staff

It is essential that educators understand the new educational policies which have been established in light of the new circumstances and that they dedicate themselves to the actual implementation of these new policies. In this regard, the Ministry of Education is considering a plan for dealing with the reeducation of teachers. It is also considering a similar plan for repatriated soldiers and personnel from the military and industry.

5. Students

The Ministry of Education will provide special education to those who were mobilized for labor or military service, in order to compensate for their academic deficiencies. The Ministry is also examining concrete measures for allowing certain students to transfer to different schools or to change departments. Students and graduates from both the army and naval academies will receive priority to continue on in schools administered by the Department of Education in accordance with their academic achievements and their individual desires.

6. Science Education

The Ministry will promote education that is not aimed solely at utilitarian goals but aimed at creating the ability to think scientifically and obtaining practical knowledge that is generated in the search for scientific truth. The Science Council shall advance its research work in order to assist in the construction of a peaceful nation as well as to contribute to progress.

7. Social Education

Since the construction of a new Japan is grounded in improving the morality of the nation and the people's educational standards, the Ministry plans to promote various types of social education such as adult education, worker education, family education, libraries and museums. The Ministry is also considering concrete plans for enriching the cultural level of the public through art, music, movies, theatre, and publications. We are eager to have art exhibitions held at the earliest opportunity.

8. Youth Groups

The Ministry is determined to encourage the formation of youth groups as there is a need for cooperative organizations to replace the dismantled Student Brigades. In principle, new youth groups will be organized by local youths on a voluntary basis and in a cooperative manner, without central administrative control. These groups shall not be mere replicas of the Greater Japan Youth Brigades which preceded the Student Brigades.

9. Religion

We shall make every effort to encourage recognition of the true worth of religions of Japan and encourage communication between and cooperation among the various religious organizations and denominations while respecting their particular characteristics. Cultivating a religious spirit and a pious faith, worshipping gods and buddhas and fostering a spirit that respects the individual will be a means toward the construction of a moral nation and toward working for world peace, realized through promoting international religious amity.

10. Physical Education

Many students have become mentally and physically strained by the mobilization for factories and by the evacuation during the war period. We should make every effort to help them recover and improve their physical condition by emphasizing hygiene and medical care. It is absolutely essential that we attend to improving conditions of everyday life which also affect education, such as increasing the food supply and reconstructing damaged areas, emphasizing an appropriate balance between labor and study. We will also encourage the holding of athletic events for students in order to revitalize sports. Such an attempt will help young people return to normal life and enhance a spirit of sportsmanship. Furthermore, it will contribute to preparations for opportunities to participate in international athletic competitions in the future and foster international friendship and understanding among the youth of the world.

11. Reform of the Structure of the Ministry of Education

In order to carry out the various policies described above, the Ministry has found it necessary to reform its administrative structure. The Ministry has abolished the

Student Mobilization Bureau and has reestablished the Physical Education Bureau and the Science Education Bureau. Further reforms are under construction.

10
Plan for Educational Control in Japan under Military Occupation

September 26, 1945

Source: National Archives of the United States, Modern Military Branch, Record Group 391, ABC .014 (Japan).

I. The Problem Presented

To utilize the educational system of Japan as an instrument for accomplishing those reforms necessary to bring the basic pattern of Japanese thought, life, and actions into conformity with standards considered essential in a country which is to resume self-direction and a position of dignity in the community of nations.

II. Facts Bearing upon the Problem

A. The Japanese educational system at the beginning of the war provided an ideal instrument for the dissemination of militaristic propaganda. It included 16,000 students, 400,000 teachers, 50,000 schools, and an estimated budget of 600,000,000 Yen. Its importance in the life of Japan is emphasized by the fact that its budget was larger than that of the Army and Navy combined until 1932, that 99.9% adult literacy was claimed, and that 37% of the nation's population was included in the elementary school and pre-school age level. The highly centralized organization with virtually all authority stemming from the Ministry of Education made it possible to introduce a uniform propaganda quickly and efficiently. The adoption of the National School Plan in April 1941 marked the first swing toward war-time militarism with an intensification of ultra-nationalism, vocational training, and physical training.

B. The period of the war brought a complete revision of all textbooks in use in the elementary and secondary schools with the insertion of positive and inflammatory militaristic propaganda in the 1942 and 1943 editions. The 1944 editions indicate a recognition of the inevitability of defeat and explain the trend of the war on the grounds of defeat by supply lines and superior science. On July 11, 1945, a revision in the Ministry occurred with a transfer of powers, some personnel, and records to the Regional Superintendent General. On July 13, 1945, a revision of educational policy was announced by the Ministry designed to prepare the schools for the approaching homeland battle. Virtually all schools had been closed above the elementary level to divert the students to productive war labor. Military officers, who had been distributed among the schools as instructors, were made members of the school staffs on July 17, 1945. Capitulation found education in Japan practically at a standstill, with 18,000,000 former students idle, 4,000 schools destroyed and only 26% of the necessary textbooks available.

C. Between the time of Japanese capitulation and the start of the establishment of General Headquarters in Tokyo, the Japanese educational authorities took five positive steps:

1. Conducted a rough physical school survey which indicated that 4,059 schools had been destroyed by bombing and that approximately 39,053 schools were usable.

2. Initiated a program of censorship of the official textbooks, by marking for elimination all passages and illustrations considered militaristic or ultranationalistic.

3. Collected records, recalled personnel, and transferred powers back to the central authority, the Ministry of Education.

4. Issued Order No. 118 of August 28, 1945, "School Education Under the Changing Circumstances," which reopened all schools.

5. Issued Order No. 20 of August 25, 1945 abrogating all those orders designed to promote militarism and ultranationalism in the schools which came under the jurisdiction of the Ministry of Education, and notified the schools that the Ministry of War and Navy were taking steps to eliminate those phases of military training which came under their jurisdiction.

D. On October 2, 1945 the Supreme Commander for the Allied Powers issued SCAP General Order No. 4, which established the Civil Information and Education section and directed that this special staff section make recommendations, maintain liaison and direct initiation and production of plans and materials dealing with civil education in Japan. . . .

E. On October 22, 1945 the Supreme Commander for the Allied Powers issued SCAP Directive AG 350 (22 Oct 45) CIE to the Imperial Japanese Government directing that the content of all instruction be critically examined, revised, and controlled; that the personnel of all educational institutions be investigated, approved or removed, reinstated, appointed, reoriented, and supervised; and that the instrumentalities of educational processes be critically examined, revised and controlled. . . .

F. Reference is made to JCS 1380/15; SWNCC 175/8; JCB 1512; and SCAP Memo No. 6 of 28 Nov 1945 (all classified).

G. On November 28, 1945 the CI&E Section was instructed to continue staff action necessary to carry through to completion those tasks which had been assigned to it and was authorized and directed to make liberal use of personal contacts and other means in expediting of these tasks.

H. The precise educational tasks assigned CI&E Section included four main categories:

1. *To eliminate* militaristic and ultra-nationalistic propaganda, official sanction of and support of Shinto, and unacceptable teachers.

2. *To introduce* democratic ideas and principles, democratic tendencies in social organizations, information on the Japanese defeat and its implications, and knowledge of the responsibility of the Japanese to maintain their own standard of living without assistance.

3. *To safeguard* religious freedom, and within the limits of security, freedom of opinion, speech, press, and assembly.

4. *To control* the curricula of educational institutions, the eligibility of persons to hold public office or important positions in private organizations, and the opening of schools.

III. Conclusions

A. Five basic projects should be undertaken. These projects should include many sub-projects, some of which will be continuing responsibilities for the duration of the occupation. They are:

1. *Basic Charter for Educational Reform:* This should be a statement to the imperial Japanese Government of the broad policies which are to govern the administration of the Japanese educational system. It should be specific enough to be a guide for future action, but should be general enough so that it does not unnecessarily restrict the actions of those who implement the program.

2. *Basic Plan for Education Reform:* This should be a very detailed statement of the projects which are recommended for the effectuation of the educational policies enunciated in the *Basic Charter for Educational Reform.* It should have the following characteristics:

a. It should be in the form of a continuing inventory of progress made in carrying out the educational policies of the occupation.

b. It should be so arranged that at any time it will indicate the staff studies completed, those in progress, and those in prospect.

c. It should indicate the chronological history of the preparation of each staff study.

d. It should indicate the plans for preparing each prospective or current staff study.

e. It should include each finished study together with recommendations for action to be taken.

f. It should indicate recommended priorities for the completion of each staff study.

g. It should include a monthly summary of progress in the implementation of policies enunciated, based on reports from the Ministry of Education, reports from the occupying Armies, and reports from a sampling of schools by members of the staff of CI&E.

3. *Elimination of Objectionable Elements:* This should include four fundamental programs:

a. The modification of the curriculum to eliminate all elements antagonistic to the policies of the occupation.

b. The censorship of textbooks, teachers' manuals, and other teaching materials, to eliminate all elements antagonistic to the policies of the occupation.

c. The investigation, screening and certification of all teachers and educational officials to eliminate those who are militaristic, ultra-nationalists, and antagonists to the policies of the occupation.

d. The systematic abrogation of all laws, ordinances, regulations, and orders which direct compliance with or are expressive of policies antagonistic to the enunciated policies of the occupation.

4. *Introduction of Desirable Elements:* This should include five fundamental programs:

a. The development of a nucleus of energetic, progressive, informed and liberal Japanese educators, whose ideas have been suppressed by previous Japanese regimes.

b. The invitation to Japan of distinguished foreign educators to advise the Ministry of Education and the staffs of SCAP.

c. The invitation to Japan of foreign teachers in special subject matter fields to teach on contract.

d. The development of appropriate books, teaching manuals, films, recordings, magazines, journals, and other expressions of Japanese scholarship in keeping with the enunciated policies of SCAP.

e. The importation into Japan of books, teaching materials, films, recordings, magazines, journals and other sources of foreign scholarship so that the material contained in these media may be fully available to the Japanese people.

5. *Accessibility to the People of Japan:* This should include two essential programs:

a. The development of all information channels, including radio, films, recordings, lectures, forums, associations, theater, press, books, and magazines, as media for the dissemination of knowledge directly coordinated with the educational system.

b. A study of the simplification of the Japanese written language.

B. In addition to the advisory, liaison, and planning functions of the Education Sub-section provision should be made for the following:

1. *Research:* Routine research by the Research and Analysis Sub-section of CI&E, and educational research involved in planning by the Education Sub-section of CI&E.

2. *Inspection:* Routine inspection to determine compliance with the SCAP directives to be done by the occupying Armies; intensive inspection of a sampling of schools in all prefectures to be done by the Armies on technical information supplied by the Education Sub-section of CI&E; and periodic personal inspections by members of the staff of CI&E to secure information and background for planning.

3. *Punitive Actions:* Routine punitive action to be taken by the occupying Armies at the direction of SCAP, GHQ, and individual punitive actions initiated by the Education Sub-section of CI&E in special cases.

IV. Recommendations

That the accompanying plan for educational control in Japan under military occupation be approved and implemented.

11
Administration of the Educational System of Japan

October 22, 1945

Source: General Headquarters, SCAP, CIE, Education Division, *Education in the New Japan,* vol. 2 (Tokyo), pp. 26–27. (Memorandum AG 350, dated October 22, 1945, to the Imperial Japanese Government, via the Central Liaison Office, from General Headquarters, SCAP.)

1. In order that the newly formed cabinet of the Imperial Japanese Government shall be fully informed of the objectives and policies of the Occupation with regard to Education, it is hereby directed that:

A. The content of all instruction will be critically examined, revised and controlled in accordance with the following policies:

(1) Dissemination of militaristic and ultranationalistic ideology will be prohibited and all military education and drill will be discontinued.

(2) Inculcation of concepts and establishment of practices in harmony with representative government, international peace, the dignity of the individual, and such fundamental human rights as the freedom of assembly, speech, and religion, will be encouraged.

B. The personnel of all educational institutions will be investigated, approved or removed, reinstated, appointed, reoriented, and supervised in accordance with the following practices:

(1) Teachers and education officials will be examined as rapidly as possible and all career military personnel, persons who have been active exponents of militarism and ultranationalism, and those actively antagonistic to the policies of the Occupation will be removed.

(2) Teachers and educational officials who have been dismissed, suspended, or forced to resign for liberal or antimilitaristic opinions or activities, will be declared immediately eligible for and if properly qualified will be given preference in reappointment.

(3) Discrimination against any student, teacher, or educational official on grounds of race, nationality, creed, political opinion, or social position will be prohibited, and immediate steps will be taken to correct inequities which have resulted from such discrimination.

(4) Students, teachers, and educational officials will be encouraged to evaluate critically and intelligently the content of instruction and will be permitted to engage in free and unrestricted discussion of issues involving political, civil and religious liberties.

(5) Students, teachers, educational officials, and [the] public will be informed of the objectives and policies of the Occupation, of the theory and practices of representative government, and of the part played by militaristic leaders, their active collaborators, and those who by passive acquiescence committed the nation to war with the inevitable result of defeat, distress, and the present deplorable state of the Japanese people.

C. The instrumentalities of educational processes will be critically examined, revised and controlled in accordance with the following policies:

(1) Existing curricula, textbooks, teaching manuals, and instructional materials, the use of which is temporarily permitted on an emergency basis, will

be examined as rapidly as possible and those portions designed to promote a militaristic or ultranationalistic ideology will be eliminated.

(2) New curricula, textbooks, teaching manuals, and instructional materials designed to produce an educated, peaceful and responsible citizenry will be prepared and will be substituted for existing materials as rapidly as possible.

(3) A normally operating educational system will be reestablished as rapidly as possible, but where limited facilities exist preference will be given to elementary education and teacher training.

2. The Japanese Ministry of Education will establish and maintain adequate liaison with the appropriate staff section of the Office of the Supreme Commander for the Allied Powers, and upon request will submit reports describing in detail all action taken to comply with the provisions of this directive.

3. All officials and subordinates of the Japanese Government affected by the terms of this directive, and all teachers and school officials, both public and private, will be held personally accountable for compliance with the spirit as well as the letter of the policies enunciated under this directive.

12
Problems Involved in Japanese Educational Reforms

Department of State (Restricted), Interim Research and Intelligence, Research and Analysis Branch

October 26, 1945

Source: Department of State, Division of Library and Reference Services. Declassified May 4, 1950. (097.3 Z109z #3281)

The problems involved in the Allied program of eradicating militarism from Japanese education are especially difficult in the primary and secondary schools, in which the majority of Japanese young people receive their only formal education. Revision of textbooks is hampered by shortages of materials and in consequence, old texts which have been censored under Allied instructions are being used for the time being.[1] A more basic problem, however, is that of the teaching personnel and their attitudes. It has been stated that, even before intensive development of "thought control" and persecution of communists, dating from 1929 "there was hardly a liberal professor left in any high school or college in Japan."[2] Teachers in primary and secondary schools are trained in Japanese normal schools, known as breeding grounds for militant nationalism. There, increasing concentration on technical subjects, moreover, has left little opportunity for studies which might lead to political liberalism among the teachers. Education Minister Maeda Tamon recently announced in a press interview that a program for "changing the ideas of educators" was being planned, based on "the democratic principles peculiar to the Japanese and the ideology of all the Japanese people."[3] The various conferences of school principals being held by the Education Ministry[4] may constitute a first step in this program.

The problem of eradicating militarism from the universities, many of which were important centers of liberal thinking before the war, presents fewer difficulties. Many liberal faculty members survived nationalistic pressures well into the 1930s; some of them, including T[anaka] Kotaro, new chief of the Bureau of School Education, retained their positions even during the war. Education Minister M[aeda] has invited university professors who were ousted because they were liberals to return to their former posts, announcing at the same time that free discussions of the theory of the Emperor as an organ of the state would no longer be considered a violation of national policy.[5]

Important Personnel in the Education Ministry

The attitudes and affiliations of prominent individuals in the field of education have an important bearing on the success of the reform program. In this connection, the present Vice Minister and the new chief of the Bureau of School Education are of interest.

O[mura] Seiichi, who was Vice Minister of Education in the Higashi-Kuni Cabinet, is being retained as Vice Minister under the Education Minister Maeda. Omura is a 47-year-old career government official who served from 1917 to 1938 in various posts under the Home Affairs Ministry, including that of director of the Police Bureau, which he held for five months during 1937. He was Vice Minister of Education, for six months in 1940, then went to North China for a year with the North China Railway Company. In 1943, he was Chairman of the board of the Dai Nippon Scholarship Foundation; subsequently he held various positions in the field of education, including that of Managing Director of the Dai Nippon Education Association, which he left in September 1945 to become Vice Minister of Education under Prince Higashi-Kuni.

Although Maeda, as Education Minister, is in a position to improve Japanese cultural relations with the Americas and Europe, his liberal policies cannot be expected to be markedly effective in Japan without cooperation from his Vice Minister, whose position is very important in the hierarchy of the Ministry. Although little specific information is currently available regarding Omura's political views, it is clear that if he was a convinced liberal he could not have held the prominent positions he did hold during the war, and that he is unlikely to be converted overnight to policies in direct opposition to those which he has carried out in past years. It is perhaps significant that Omura is currently managing the affairs of the Bureau of Social Education.[6]

T[anaka] Kotaro was appointed on October 15 by the Education Minister as head of the Bureau of School Education, which includes departments of elementary school, middle school, college and university education. He was also named to manage the affairs of the Tokyo Music Academy and of the Research and Experiment Station of Education.[7] Tanaka is 55 years old, a Professor of Law at Tokyo Imperial University, and was at one time Dean of the Law Faculty. He is an outstanding Roman Catholic layman who in 1938 vigorously defended academic freedom and political liberalism when a colleague was indicted and imprisoned on the charge of complicity in a Communist movement. As reported by Tokyo radio in January 1945, he is professor, *honoris causa,* at the Catholic University of Chile. Tanaka's wife is the eldest daughter of M[atsumoto] Joji, Minister without portfolio in the present Cabinet.

The appointment of Tanaka reinforces the earlier measure which ended restrictions on religious education in the schools. As a fighter for academic freedom and political liberalism, he may well prove to be of material aid to Education Minister Maeda in eradicating militarism from the Japanese educational system.

Student Strikes and Their Implications

Recent student strikes in Japan present one method by which the replacement of unsatisfactory school principals can be effected under new Education Ministry policies. Students at the Mito Higher School were the first to go on strike, demanding dismissal of Principal Y[asui] Shoichi on the grounds that his education policy was "not in line with the new situation and would harm the true learning power of young fellow students."[8] According to *Asahi,* another basis for the strike was the objection of the students to "high-handed measures."[9] Student representatives took their demands directly to the Education Ministry, which after a few days decided to meet the demands, thus ending the strike.[10] Replacement of Principal Yasui by S[eki] Ttaiyu, formerly a teacher in the first Higher School of Tokyo, was announced shortly thereafter.[11] More recently, students at three agricultural schools have gone on strike against teachers and practices they found objectionable.[12]

These facts indicate that students are utilizing their recently restored freedom of expression to take action against teachers and school policies which they find unjust or oppressive. The Mito Higher School in particular shares the Mito tradition of rebellion against oppression, a tradition which originated with T[okugawa] Mitsukine of Mito.[13] It is to be expected that students will use the announced Education Ministry policy of eradicating militarism from the schools as a slogan for their protests. Its use in this manner, however, does not constitute proof that students now attending Japanese secondary schools are fundamentally antagonistic to the doctrines of militaristic nationalism to which they have long been exposed. (In this connection it is well to remember that higher schools and technical schools will from now on be attended by increasing numbers of demobilized soldiers and students from military schools which are now closed; these students are not likely to be receptive initially to anti-militaristic doctrines.) The real occasions for protest are likely to be measures which appear to the students to be high-handed or unjust; with renewed freedom of expression, students of both sexes can be expected to make further protests as occasion arises. The Education Ministry announcement in connection with the Mito strike, urging the resignation of school principals and teachers "who are not able to discard militaristic principles" and forecasting a large-scale personnel change among school heads[14] indicates that the Ministry is prepared to take advantage of further strikes to replace school heads, just as was done in the case of Mito Higher School.

The current strikes should not be confused with student strikes which took place during the 1930s, tapering off in number after 1929 and disappearing altogether after the invasion of Manchuria in 1931. The student strikes of that period occurred in the universities and were evoked by issues of national importance; sometimes they were held in protest against dismissal of faculty members but more often in opposition to such measures as military training in the universities. Given the genuine encouragement of liberalism in the universities which appears probably under Maeda and Tanaka, university students may again make a positive contribution in the struggle to restore academic freedom in Japan.

Notes

1. *Washington Post,* 23 October (1945).
2. A. Morgan Young, *Imperial Japan, 1926–1938.* As used here, "college" probably means advanced technical schools; it does not include institutions at the university level.
3. Far Eastern Commission, Directorate [hereafter FEC] 11 October (1945).
4. Ibid., 13 October (1945).
5. Ibid., 11 October (1945).
6. Ibid., 17 October (1945).
7. Ibid., 17 October (1945).
8. Ibid., 11 October (1945).
9. *New York Times,* 11 October (1945).
10. FEC, 15 October (1945).
11. Ibid., 17 October (1945).
12. *Washington Post,* 20 October (1945); FEC, 22 October (1945).

13. Mitsukune is known not only for his founding of the Mito historical school, whose research provided fuel for the anti-*bakufu* [anti-government] forces and thus contributed to the restoration of the Emperor's power in 1867, but also for his consistent championship of the subjugated peasant classes under Tokugawa oppression.

14. FEC, 11 October (1945).

13
Memorandum on Investigation, Screening, and Certification of Teachers and Educational Officers

October 30, 1945

Source: General Headquarters, SCAP, CIA, Education Division, *Education in the New Japan* (Tokyo: 1948), vol. 1, pp. 29–30.

General Headquarters, Supreme Commander for the Allied Powers AG 350 (30 Oct 45) CIE

Memorandum for: Imperial Japanese Government

Through: Central Liaison Office, Tokyo

Subject: Investigation, Screening, and Certification of Teachers and Educational Officers

1. In order to eliminate from the educational system of Japan those militaristic and ultranationalistic influences which in the past have contributed to the defeat, war guilt, suffering, privation, and present deplorable state of the Japanese people; and in order to prevent the teachers and educational officials having military experience or affiliation from teaching; it is hereby directed that:

    a. All persons who are known to be militaristic, ultranationalistic, or antagonistic to the objectives and policies of the Occupation and who are at this time actively employed in the educational system of Japan, will be removed immediately and will be barred from occupying any position in the educational system of Japan.

    b. All other persons now actively employed in the educational system of

Japan will be permitted to retain their positions at the discretion of the Ministry of Education until further notice.

c. All persons who are members of or who have been demobilized from the Japanese military forces since the termination of hostilities, and who are not at this time actively employed in the educational system of Japan, will be barred from occupying any position in the educational system of Japan until further notice.

2. In order to determine which of those persons who are now actively employed in or who may in the future become candidates for employment in the educational system of Japan are unacceptable and must be removed, barred, and prohibited from occupying any position in the educational system of Japan, it is hereby directed that:

a. The Japanese Ministry of Education will establish suitable administrative machinery and procedures for the effective investigation, screening, and certification of all present and prospective teachers and educational officials.

b. The Japanese Ministry of Education will submit to this Headquarters as soon as possible a comprehensive report describing all actions taken to comply with the provisions of this directive. The report will contain in addition the following specific information:

(1) A precise statement of how acceptability of the individual is to be determined, together with lists of specific standards which will govern the retention, removal, appointment or reappointment of the individual.

(2) A precise statement of what administrative machinery and procedures are to be established in order to accomplish the investigation, screening and certification of personnel, together with a statement of what provisions are to be made for review of appealed decisions and reconsideration of individuals previously refused certification.

3. All officials and subordinates of the Japanese government affected by the terms of this directive, and all school officials, both public and private, will be held personally accountable for compliance with the spirit as well as the letter of the policies enunciated in this directive.

For the Supreme Commander:

H.W. Allen
Colonel, A.G.D.
Asst. Adjutant General

14
Abolition of State Shinto

December 15, 1945

Source: General Headquarters, SCAP, CIA, Education Division, *Education in the New Japan* (Tokyo, 1948), vol. 1, p. 31 (extract).

(Memorandum to Imperial Japanese Government from GHQ SCAP, abolishing State Shinto, dated 15 December 1945)

1. In order to free the Japanese people from direct or indirect compulsion to believe or profess to believe in a religion or cult officially designated by the state, and

In order to lift from the Japanese people the burden of compulsory financial support of an ideology which has contributed to their war guilt, defeat, suffering, privation, and present deplorable condition, and

In order to prevent a recurrence of the perversion of Shinto theory and beliefs into militaristic and ultranationalistic propaganda designed to delude the Japanese people and lead them into wars of aggression, and

In order to assist the Japanese people in a rededication of their national life to building a new Japan based upon ideals of perpetual peace and democracy,

It is hereby directed that:

a. The sponsorship, support, perpetuation, control, and dissemination of Shinto by the Japanese national, prefectural, and local governments, or by public officials, subordinates, and employees acting in their official capacity, are prohibited and will cease immediately.

b. All financial support from public funds and all official affiliation with Shinto and Shinto shrines are prohibited and will cease immediately.

f. All public educational institutions whose primary function is either the investigation or dissemination of Shinto or the training of a Shinto priesthood will be abolished and their physical properties devoted to other uses. Their present functions, duties, and administrative obligations shall not be assumed by any other governmental or tax-supported agency.

g. Private educational institutions for the investigation and dissemination of Shinto and for the training of [a] priesthood for Shinto will be permitted and will operate with the same privileges and be subject to the same controls and restrictions as any other private educational institution having no affiliation with the government; in no case, however, will they receive support from public funds, and in no case will they propagate or disseminate militarist and ultranationalistic ideology.

h. The dissemination of Shinto doctrines in any form and by any means in any educational institution supported wholly or in part by public funds is prohibited and will cease immediately.

(1) All teachers' manuals and textbooks now in use in any educational institution supported wholly or in part by public funds will be censored, and all Shinto doctrine will be deleted. No teachers' manual or textbook which is published in the future for use in such institutions will contain any Shinto doctrine.

(2) No visits to Shinto shrines and no rites, practices, or ceremonies associated with Shinto will be conducted or sponsored by any educational institution supported wholly or in part by public funds.

i. Circulation by the government of "The Fundamental Principles of the National Structure" *(Kokutai no Hongi)*, "The Way of the Subject" *(Shinmin no Michi)*, and all similar official volumes, commentaries, interpretations, or instructions on Shinto is prohibited.

j. The use in official writings of the terms "Greater East Asian War" *(Dai Toa Senso)*, "The Whole World under One Roof" *(Hakko Ichiu)*, and all other terms whose connotation in Japanese is inextricably connected with State Shinto, militarism, and ultranationalism is prohibited and will cease immediately. . . .

(2a) The purpose of this directive is to separate religion from the state, to prevent misuse of religion for political ends, . . .

(4) All officials, subordinates, and employees of the Japanese national, prefectural and local government, all teachers and education officials . . . will be held personally accountable for compliance with the spirit as well as the letter of all provisions of this directive.

15
Staff Study on Proposed Education Mission (CIE, GHQ, SCAP)

December 27, 1945

Source: Supplied to the editor by Professor Robert King Hall, the study's major author.

I. The Problem Presented

1. To bring to Japan for a period of approximately thirty (30) days a mission composed of distinguished American educators to advise the Education Section of the Civil Information and Education Section and the Japanese Ministry of Education on the rehabilitation of the Japanese System.

II. Facts Bearing on the Problem

1. Japan's educational system is very large and complex. In 1939 it included 16,000,000 students, 400,000 teachers and 50,000 schools. An estimated 39,000 schools survived the war and the total enrollment in 1944 prior to the closing of schools was 18,000,000 students. The school budget ranged from 450,000,000 Yen to 600,000,000 Yen during the ten (10) years prior to the war.

2. Japan's educational system offers an effective instrument for changing the pattern of Japanese life, thought and action. Approximately 37% of the total population of the nation is in the elementary school or pre-school age group. The children comprising this 37% are still in the formative stage of development and presumably may be reclaimed by reeducation.

3. Japan's educational system offers an efficient instrument for this change. The cost of elementary education, which enrolls nearly 16,000,000 of the 18,000,000 students, is approximately 27 Yen per student annually as compared with 763 Yen for university education. The Japanese Ministry of Education exercises a very rigid control over the content and method of teaching in all schools below the university level. Effective supervision and control of Japanese education with a minimum of personnel from the Allied Powers is possible through manipulation of the Ministry.

4. Basic policy with regard to post-war Japan has been enunciated by "Administration of the Educational System of Japan" [see Document 11]. It deals with the content of instruction, personnel, and instrumentalities of educational processes.

5. The Japanese Ministry of Education has demonstrated both cooperation and industry in undertaking voluntary reforms. On 20 September 1945 an order was issued directing that various sections of textbooks be deleted. Order No. 20 of 15 October 1945 abolished many abuses with the abrogation of most of the war-time educational legislation. Order No. 118 of 28 August 1945 re-established schools suspended during the war. Order No. 83 of 25 September 1945 directed the reform and re-establishment of youth organizations along non-militaristic lines. Order No. 184 of 12 September 1945 directed a revision of lower education. Order No. 120 of 5 September 1945 provides for the absorption of students from military schools. On 14 October 1945 the Ministry of Education was partially re-organized.

6. Studies are now underway for the revision of textbooks, the screening of teachers, the re-orientation of teachers, and the further re-organization of the Ministry of Education.

7. The Japanese educational authorities are technically not qualified to complete in a satisfactory manner the reforms which are directed in AG 350 (22 Oct 45) CIE without technical advice and assistance from foreign sources.

8. The Education Staff of Civil Information and Education Section requires certain technical advice and assistance unavailable from military sources, for the efficient accomplishment of its mission. . . .

9. Qualified technical advice is available from civilian educators now in the United States. A very careful survey of such educators has been made, based on the technical needs indicated in AG 350 (22 Oct 45) CIE and upon requests for assistance voiced by Japanese educators in interviews, letters, and editorials. A list of qualified educators appropriate to the needs of such a mission has been prepared. The selection of the membership of this list was based on Embree's study of The Order of Eminence Foundation; upon the geographical distribution of the population, American educational institutions, and concentration of talent; and upon the international reputation of the individual scholars.

10. Such technical advice must be given in the immediate future if the results are to be felt in the revision of the textbooks and in the conduct of schools during the next academic year, which begins on or about 1 April 1946.

III. Action Recommended

1. That an Educational Mission of distinguished educators be invited to Japan to study the Japanese educational system and to advise the Education Section and the Japanese Ministry of Education on technical matters.

2. That this Mission be requested to make studies of the following problems and submit reports and recommendations to the Supreme Commander of the Allied Powers upon completion of the mission.

a. *Education for Democracy in Japan*: A study leading to recommendations as to the content of courses, curricula, textbooks, teachers' manuals, and visual and auditory aids.

b. *Psychology in the Re-education of Japan*: A study leading to recommendations as to the educational methodology, language revision, timing and priority of educational reforms, the development of student initiative and critical analysis, and reorientation of teachers.

c. *Administrative Reorganization of the Educational System of Japan*: A study leading to recommendations as to the immediate and long range administrative reforms, the reorganization of the Ministry of Education, and the problems of decentralization.

d. *Higher Education in the Rehabilitation of Japan*: A study leading to recommendations in regard to the use of libraries, archives, scientific laboratories, museums in higher education; to student and faculty freedom; to re-orientation of the social sciences; and to more active participation in the life of the community and of Japan.

3. That this mission be requested to recommend technical experts in subject-matter fields to assist the Japanese Ministry of Education and autonomous educational institutions.

4. That the United States Office of Education be requested to make recommendations for substitutions in the suggested membership of the Mission where suggested personnel are unavailable or where the United States Office of Education believes substitutions are desirable.

5. That the membership of the Mission be selected from those persons indicated in Appendix A (deleted) of this Staff Study.

6. That this Mission be requested at the earliest possible date, preferably by 1 February 1946, for a period of approximately thirty (30) days' study.

Ken R. Dyke
Brig. General, AUS

16
Suspension of Courses in Morals *(Shushin)*, Japanese History, and Geography

December 31, 1945

Source: General Headquarters, SCAP, CIE, Education Division, Education in the New Japan (Tokyo, May 1948), vol. 2, pp. 36–37.

(Memorandum to Imperial Japanese Government, via Tokyo Central Liaison Office from GHQ, SCAP, dated December 31, 1945)

1. In accordance with the basic directive (December 15, 1945) proclaiming the abolition of government sponsorship and support of State Shinto and Doctrine; and inasmuch as the Japanese Government has used education to inculcate militaristic and ultranationalistic ideologies which have been inextricably interwoven in certain textbooks imposed upon students; it is hereby directed that:

a. All courses in Morals *(Shushin)*, Japanese History and Geography in all educational institutions, including government, public and private schools, for which textbooks and teachers' manuals have been published or sanctioned by the Ministry of Education shall be suspended immediately and will not be resumed until permission has been given by this headquarters.

b. The Ministry of Education shall suspend immediately all ordinances *(horei)*, regulations, or instructions directing the manner in which the specific subjects of Morals *(Shushin)*, Japanese History and Geography shall be taught.

c. The Ministry of Education shall collect all textbooks and teachers' manuals used in every course and education institution affected by 1.a. for disposal. . . .

d. The Ministry of Education shall prepare and submit to this Headquarters a plan for the introduction of substitute programs to take the place of courses affected by this memorandum. . . . These substitute programs will continue in force until such time as this Headquarters authorizes the resumption of the courses suspended herein.

2. The Ministry of Education shall prepare and submit to this Headquarters a plan for revising textbooks to be used in Morals *(Shushin)*, Japanese History, and Geography. . . .

3. All officials, subordinates, and employees of the Japanese Government affected by the terms of this directive, and school officials and teachers, both public and private, will be held personally accountable for compliance with the spirit as well as the letter of the terms of this directive.

17
Imperial Rescript on Reconstruction

January 1, 1946

Source: General Headquarters, SCAP, CIE, Education Division, *Education in the New Japan*, vol. 2 (Tokyo, 1948), pp. 77–78.

In greeting the New Year, we recall to our mind that Emperor Meiji proclaimed, as the basis of our national policy, the five clauses of the Charter Oath at the beginning of the Meiji Era (1868–1912). The Charter Oath signified:

1. Deliberative assemblies shall be established and all measures of government decided in accordance with public opinion;

2. All classes, high and low, shall unite in vigorously carrying on the affairs of State;

3. All common people, no less than the civil and military officials, shall be allowed to fulfill their just desires, so that there may not be any discontent among them;

4. All the abused usages of the old shall be broken through, and equity and justice to be found in the workings of nature shall serve as the basis of action;

5. Wisdom and knowledge shall be sought throughout the world for the purpose of promoting the welfare of the Empire.

The proclamation is evident in significance and high in its ideals. We wish to make this oath anew and to restore the country to stand on its own feet again. We have to reaffirm the principles embodied in the Charter, and proceed unflinchingly towards elimination of misguided practices of the past, and keeping in close touch with the desires of the people. We will construct a new Japan through being thoroughly pacific, the officials and people alike, attaining rich culture, and advancing the standard of living of the people.

The devastation of war, inflicted upon our cities, the miseries of the destitute, the stagnation of trade, the shortage of food, and the great and growing number of unemployed are indeed heart-rending. But if the nation is firmly united in its resolve to face the present ordeal and to seek civilization consistently in peace, a bright future will undoubtedly be ours, not only for our country, but for all humanity.

Love of family and love of country are especially strong in this country. With more of this devotion we should now work towards love of mankind.

We feel deeply concerned to note that because of the protracted war ending in our defeat, our people are liable to grow restless and fall into the Slough of Despond. Radical tendencies in excess are rapidly spreading and the sense of morality tends to lose its hold on the people, with the result that there are signs of confusion of thought.

We stand by the people and wish always to share with them their moments of joys and sorrows. The ties between us and our people have always stood upon mutual trust and affection. They do not depend upon mere legends and myths. They are not predicated on the false conception that the Emperor is divine, and that the Japanese people are superior to other races and destined to rule the world.

Our government should make every effort to alleviate the trials and tribulations of the people. At the same time, we trust that the people will rise to the occasion, and will strive courageously for the solution of their outstanding difficulties and for the development of industry and culture. Acting upon a consciousness of solidarity and of mutual aid and broad tolerance of their civic life, they will prove themselves worthy of their best tradition. By their supreme endeavors in that direction, they will be able to render their substantial contribution to the welfare and advancement of mankind.

The resolution for the year should be made at the beginning of the year. We expect our people to join us in working to accomplish this great undertaking with an indomitable spirit.

18
Committee of Japanese Educators

January 9, 1946

Source: Provided by the late Professor Ronald S. Anderson, a colleague of the senior editor at the University of Hawaii, and a participant in the Occupation of Japan.

1. This Headquarters has requested that an Educational Mission, consisting of approximately twenty (20) distinguished American educators, be sent to Japan, to arrive in the month of February.

2. The Educational Mission will study the Japanese educational system for approximately thirty (30) days and will advise the Supreme Commander for the Allied Powers and the Japanese Ministry of Education on technical matters.

3. The Educational Mission will make studies of the following problems and submit reports and recommendations to the Supreme Commander for the Allied Powers upon completion of the mission.

a. *Education for Democracy in Japan:* A study leading to recommendations as to the content of courses, curricula, textbooks, teachers' manuals, and visual, and auditory aids.

b. *Psychology in the Reeducation of Japan:* A study leading to recommendations as to the educational methodology, language revision, timing and priority of educational reforms, the development of student initiative and critical analysis, and reorientation of teachers.

c. *Administrative Reorganization of the Educational System of Japan:* A study leading to recommendations as to the immediate and long-range administrative reforms, the reorganization of the Ministry of Education, and the problems of decentralization.

d. *Higher Education in the Rehabilitation of Japan:* A study leading to recommendations in regard to the use of libraries, archives, scientific laboratories, and museums in higher education; to student and faculty freedom; to reorientation of the social sciences; and to more active participation in the life of the community and of Japan.

4. The Educational Mission will be requested also to recommend technical experts in subject-matter fields to assist the Japanese Ministry of Education and autonomous educational institutions.

5. In order to facilitate the work of the Educational Mission and in order that the Japanese educational system derive the maximum benefit from its studies and findings, it is suggested:

a. That the Ministry of Education appoint a committee of highly qualified Japanese educators to work with the Educational Mission;

b. That the committee consist of not less than eighteen (18) nor more than twenty-five (25) members;

c. That the members of the committee be selected with particular reference to their qualifications to assist the Educational Mission in the study of the problems set forth in paragraph 3 above;

d. That the membership of the committee be representative of (1) various fields of teaching and educational administration; (2) various levels and types of educational institutions;

e. That the names of the educators proposed for membership in the committee, together with the proposed assignments for the study of the problems set forth in paragraph 3 above, be submitted to the Education Division, Civil Information and Education Staff Section, not later than 20 January 1946;

f. That the names so proposed be accompanied by all available information as to age, educational background, past and present positions, publications (if any), membership in professional organizations, honorary degrees or other honors received, and any other pertinent facts which will be of interest and value to the Educational Mission;

g. That the committee be appointed and assembled in sufficient time to permit its briefing by this Headquarters and by the Ministry of Education as to the purposes of the Educational Mission and the type of cooperation desired from the committee;

h. That the committee, with such later additions from business and professional fields as may be found desirable, be a continuing committee to advise the Ministry of Education on the reform of Japanese education;

i. That the committee, after the departure of the Educational Mission, continue to study the problems set forth in paragraph 3 above and submit periodic reports on its findings and recommendations to the Ministry of Education and to the Education Division, Civil Information and Education Staff Section.

19
Reorientation of the Japanese

February 15, 1946

Source: National Archives, Record Group 218, Records of the United States Joint Chiefs of Staff, CCAC 014 Japan (9–20–44) SCC. 4 (excerpts).

(Joint Civil Affairs Committee memo to the State-War-Navy Coordinating Committee)

Appendix A: Facts Bearing on the Problem

. . . 2. "The United States Initial Post-Surrender Policy for Japan . . . " made public by the President [Harry S. Truman] on 22 September 1945 states:

"The ultimate objectives of the United States in regard to Japan, to which policies in the initial period must conform, are:

"(a) To insure that Japan will not again become a menace to the United States or to the peace and security of the world.

"(b) To bring about the eventual establishment of a peaceful and responsible government which will respect the rights of other states and will support the objectives of the United States as reflected in the ideals and principles of the Charter of the United Nations."

3. Among the principle means for the achievement of these objectives this statement indicates the following:

"The Japanese people shall be encouraged to develop a desire for individual liberties and respect for fundamental human rights, particularly the freedoms of religion, assembly, speech, and the press. They shall also be encouraged to form democratic and representative organizations."

"The Japanese people shall be afforded opportunity and encouraged to become familiar with the history, institutions, culture, and accomplishments of the United States and other United Nations. . . ."

6. By directive of the Supreme Commander for the Allied Powers [General Douglas MacArthur] issued on 22 September 1945 a special staff division of Supreme Headquarters was established, designated as the Civil Information and Education section, charged with advising the Supreme Commander on policies "relating to public information, education, religion and other sociological problems of Japan and Korea." The section is further charged with "expediting the

establishment of freedom of religious worship, freedom of opinion, speech, press and assembly by the dissemination of democratic ideals and principles through all media of public information. It has the responsibility of making clear to all levels of the Japanese public the true facts of their defeat, their war guilt, the responsibility of the militarists for present and future Japanese suffering and privation and the reason for and objectives of the military occupation of the Allied powers. It is also responsible for keeping the Supreme Commander factually informed of public reactions to the occupation and rehabilitation program in order to ensure a dependable basis for program formulation and modification of policies and plans."

Appendix B. Discussion

1. Most Japanese, in greater or lesser degree, at present share a common attitude of mind of which the following are salient elements:

a. The persistence of feudal concepts, including class stratification, the glorification of the military, and a habit of subservience to authority.

b. A belief in the superior qualifications of the Japanese for world leadership, closely connected with the cult of emperor-worship fostered in recent years by the military to serve their own purposes.

c. Extreme racial consciousness, and an anti-foreign complex, which, however, is often combined with great admiration for foreign achievements and learning.

2. It is probable that the attainment of the ultimate objectives of the Allied powers in regard to Japan cannot be assured in the absence of changes in these ideologies and ways of thinking, which have in the past motivated the Japanese people as a whole in the pursuit of chauvinistic and militaristic policies.

3. It will not be necessary to recast all Japanese cultural concepts, rather, it is proposed to develop these particular Japanese concepts which will create new attitudes of mind conforming to the basic principles of democracy and fair dealing.

4. It is recognized that the character of our occupation of Japan and the commitment to act through the Japanese Government requires that the approach to the Japanese be made through their own leaders. It is also recognized that the Japanese may offer resistance to new ideas and points of view advanced directly by the occupation authorities, whereas the same ideas put forward by leaders of their own and in whom they have confidence, may very well be favorably received and acted upon. There are numerous Japanese who, through prior contacts and earlier education, will be disposed to accept and assist in the development of our ultimate objectives and along lines which will further the interests of the

United States. For this reason a fundamental responsibility of the Allied authorities in Japan should be to seek out such persons, ensure that they are placed in positions that will enable them to accomplish these aims, and afford them counsel, guidance and support.

5. If it is to be successful the process of reorientation cannot be restricted to formalized education or to a mere reform of the educational system. It must be extended to a reeducation not only of the youth but of the population as a whole, and must be developed in such manner as to reach into the minds of the Japanese through every available channel. The influence of the Japanese leaders in every field should be utilized as well as all appropriate media, including books, textbooks, periodicals, motion pictures, radio, lectures, discussion groups and the schools. The methods of approach and character of materials used must be carefully considered, must be persuasive rather than didactic, and must be designed to ensure the maximum response and acceptance by the Japanese. . . .

7. The Japanese are a literate people. They realize that an education is desirable and this fact coupled with their habit of obedience to authority and uncritical acceptance of the teachings of their leaders, makes them receptive to a process of ideological reorientation which is properly presented. One of the most effective means of achieving this objective will be to furnish information concerning the world outside Japan.

8. It will be the policy of the United States not to repress ideas and information from other sources, but to ensure an adequate presentation through Japanese media and channels and an adequate understanding by the Japanese of the aims and ideals of the United States. Other aims and ideals will undoubtedly be promoted, and it is essential, in order to give the Japanese a true picture and enable them to make up their minds intelligently as to their future in relation to the United States and the world at large, that we present our case effectively and comprehensively. . . .

10. The entire program in type and scope should be designed so that it can be carried on by the Japanese themselves following withdrawal of controls, and, to this end, it will be essential from the beginning to encourage participation by local groups and organizations. It must be emphasized that reeducation promptly and adequately made effective will materially speed the development of a responsible and trustworthy government in Japan, thereby materially shortening the period of occupation and reducing the commitments of the United States.

11. In the main, reorientation will be accomplished through the channels of information, education and religion. Unlike other aspects of the occupation, information, education and religion will present long-range problems extending in some instances over several decades. At the same time the groundwork for these aspects of the reorientation program must be laid at once, lest there crystallize in the Japanese mind attitudes and concepts the possession of which would defeat the purposes of occupation. Reorientation and reeducation are primarily civilian

tasks and will require large numbers of civilian experts for their performance. Their early recruitment by some agency of the U.S. Government would appear to be essential to the success of any program.

20
Bases for Educational Reconstruction

March 8, 1946

Source: General Headquarters, SCAP, CIE, Education Division, *Education in the New Japan*, vol. 2 (Tokyo, 1948) pp. 248–265 (excerpts).

(Address by Japanese Minister of Education, Abe Yoshishige, at first meeting of the U.S. Education Mission to Japan)

. . . While war is the most deplorable and abominable happening for the human race, we cannot overlook the fact that through war peoples are brought into closer contact with each other. Actually, as the result of our defeat, an unprecented number of your countrymen have come to our land. We see them everywhere, and we come into daily contact with their ways of thinking and acting. Moreover, we are to be under the control of your countrymen in everything, in our politics, economy, culture, and education. Although we cannot call it an honor for us, it is yet undeniable that it serves to make our contact with your people more frequent and more profound than ever. In fact, our daily life materially and spiritually has come to be unthinkable without taking into account the influence which your country and your people are exercising upon it. . . .

. . . We believe that your country is not going to violate truth and justice on the strength of being a victor. And we pray that the pressure brought upon us by this victory—for we cannot help feeling it as a pressure—will help to make truth and justice permeate all our country, and serve as a chance for us to eliminate quickly and vigorously all the injustices and defects existing in our society and all the weaknesses and evils underlying our national character and customs. . . . As you may guess it is a severe trial and a hard task to be a defeated country and a defeated people, but if I may say so, it must also be a very difficult thing to be a good victor. While we hope that we are not going to be mean and servile as a defeated nation, we believe that you are not going to be needlessly proud and arrogant as a victorious nation. . . .

After this miserable defeat of ours, our people have suddenly turned their eyes on education and become keenly aware of the fact that the present condition of our country is due to errors and defects in education, and also to the low cultural standard of the Japanese, as individuals, so that for the first time our people are realizing the importance of education. But still they do not realize fully enough how permanent and difficult a job education is and are not thoughtful enough in translating their ideas into concrete actions and institutions, for some of them seem to think that, in order to promote education, one simply has to increase the number of schools.

Up to the present in our country there were, of course, imperfections, short-comings, and mistakes in our education itself. But what is more important, we did not fully realize what position education is to occupy . . . the educators were not allowed to do their work according to their conscience and convictions. This led to the evil custom of letting the educators be used as easy tools in the hands of those in political power at the time. That is to say, education, which naturally is to govern politics, was made its slave.

. . . We believe that it is first of all in our education and our educators that the American demand for democratization should be fulfilled in the most essential and exact sense of the word. . . . In a mad reaction against the wartime hardships and restraints placed upon freedom, the people are now rushing from one extreme to another, and are facing the danger of falling into either a state of vacuum or anarchy. This is an unavoidable phenomenon after a war. . . . But the cause for this too lies after all in the lack of education based on the right view of life, and in the lack of a clear consciousness of personality and respect for individuality. This fact undeniably reveals the fundamental weakness underlying our education. . . .

Since our surrender, we have been making efforts day and night in order to rebuild Japanese education in that direction. Under the postwar condition of exhaustion and terrible devastation, there is an enormous amount of obstacles to be surmounted and of difficult problems to be solved. Measures to be taken with respect to war-damaged schools, correction or reconversion of abnormal phenomena due to wartime distortions . . . there are endless tasks of a more permanent nature such as social education which has been the poorest in our country. . . .

It is my conviction that democracy is to be the basis of . . . education since education is the foundation. . . . I hold this conviction not simply because this was the principle forced upon us by America, but because this derives from a fundamental principle of the universe and is based upon the essential nature of human beings. A right democracy should naturally be founded upon the right sense of the relationship between the individual and society. . . .

The nature of all profound and lively manifestations of spiritual culture in mankind is both universal and individual at the same time, this being also true with education. . . . The most original culture always arises in a place where the stimuli from foreign cultures are the most active. Consequently, an ultra-nationalistic culture or education cannot foster a healthy national character in the true sense. . . . I am setting my hopes of an original flowering of Japanese culture on the future of Japanese education which is now making a fundamental change of direction. . . . As a result of her defeat, Japan is now placed in the most absolute state of isolation ever experienced since the beginning of the Meiji Era. This is one of the inevitable punishments we are receiving for our faults, but things may gradually get better in the future . . . [and] I would like to ask you to help us in bringing this about as soon as possible . . . for then only will it be possible for Japanese education to receive constant stimulation and enlightenment from the world. . . .

. . . Just as democracy is meant to combine respect of individuality with the idea of equality of human beings, so should culture and education in a nation also respect both the national and the international. National superstitions should, of course, be rejected, especially the case of a false history construed by ultra-nationalistic policies and that of an irrational interpretation of mythology. But the characteristics of a tradition that is still alive among the people should be respected. Thus I would like to ask America not to deal with us simply from an American point of view. You must know that it was a great failure for Japan to have treated Korea and China in such a manner. America, as a victorious country, is in a position to do anything it pleases with Japan. I hope that I am not too bold in expressing the wish that America may not avail herself of this position to impose upon us simply what is characteristic of America or of Europe. For that matter, if I may say so, this is a mistake which a victorious people is always apt to make either consciously or unconsciously. And if this is also the case this time, I fear that we shall never be able to have a true Japanese education which is firmly rooted in our soil and which can work on the innermost soul of the Japanese people. If so, it will also be impossible to have a true development of Japanese culture. On the other hand there are some young idealists among the Americans coming to our country who tend to see Japan as a kind of a laboratory in a rash attempt to experiment on some abstract ideals of their own, ideals which have not yet been realized even in their own country. While the Japanese people should open-mindedly accept all the advice that America gives to them and should effect a radical reform in education, you will agree that in accepting such advice, the Japanese people should do it on the basis of their own consciences and critical judgment.

. . . It is a natural fact that everything that is universal and human in concept takes in its concrete realization a special form according to the racial characteristics, history and tradition of each country. Therefore, when you come to know during your stay here the characteristics and weaknesses of our people, you will realize that democratic education cannot be carried out in our country in exactly the same way as it is in yours.

I want to ask you here not to take the present condition of Japan for the direct picture of the original, permanent Japan. Far from being proud, we are really ashamed of the conditions prevailing among us. This is, however, due to the impoverishment and exhaustion caused by a long and impracticable war. . . . The reason why the Japanese culture in the past failed to show an international character lies partly in the character of the Japanese people, but it is also due to the fact that they were not given enough opportunity in international contracts. We are, however, still holding the ambition of having Japanese culture take part in future world civilization, and we believe that this is possible if we are going to receive Western culture more critically, deeply and fundamentally than we have done since the beginning of the Meiji Era.

I would like also to mention . . . that, in spite of the mistakes we committed in the past, there were in our educational circles still some conscientious elements that were preserved even during the war, and that these elements were not very strong, it was still owing to them that a part of our educational world was able to keep healthy as compared to other totalitarian nations. And we can expect that these elements will play a great role in the reconstruction of Japanese education in the days to come.

. . . We are determined to open our eyes widely, to reflect sincerely upon our shortcomings, to listen to your advice, and to carry out boldly any reforms that may prove to be necessary. We believe that weaknesses of ours, which are invisible to our eyes, will be easily detected by the fresh and unbiased senses of our newly arrived guests. Relying upon your wisdom and experience, we shall try to study in a cold and objective manner our own educational institutions, their substance, and the practical ways of operating them so as to help pave the way for a substantial reform in education.

21
Report of the [First] U.S. Education Mission: Digest

March 1946

Source: Report of the United States Education Mission to Japan, Submitted to the Supreme Commander for the Allied Powers (Tokyo: GHQ, SCAP, March 30, 1948), pp. 42–46.

The Aims and Content of Japanese Education

A highly centralized educational system, even if it is not caught in the net of ultra-nationalism and militarism, is endangered by the evils that accompany an entrenched bureaucracy. Decentralization is necessary in order that teachers may be freed to develop more professionally under guidance, without regimentation. They, in turn, may then do their part in the development of free Japanese citizens.

To this end, knowledge must be acquired that is broader than available in a single prescribed textbook or manual, and deeper than can be tested by stereotyped examinations. A curriculum consists not merely of an accepted body of knowledge, but of the pupils' physical and mental activities. It should therefore be set up through cooperative action involving teachers, calling on their experience and releasing their creative talents.

Morals which in Japanese education occupy a separate place, and have tended to promote submissiveness, should be differently construed and should interpenetrate all phases of a free people's life. Manners that encourage equality, the give-and-take of democratic government, and the ideal of good workmanship in daily life—all these are morals in the wider sense. They should be developed and practiced in the varied programs and activities of the democratic school.

Books in the fields of geography and history will have to be rewritten to recognize mythology for what it is, and to embody a more objective viewpoint in textbooks and reference materials. On the lower levels more use should be made of the community and local resources; at higher levels competent scholarship should be encouraged in various ways.

The program in health education and physical education is basic to the educational program as a whole. Medical examinations, instruction in nutrition and public health, the extension of the physical education and recreation program at the university level, and the replacement of equipment as rapidly as possible are recommended.

At all levels vocational education should be emphasized. A variety of vocation experiences is needed under well trained staff members, with an emphasis on technology and its supporting arts and sciences. The contributions of artisans and workers should find a place in the social studies program, and opportunities for originality and creativity should be provided.

Language Reform

The problem of the written language is fundamental to all modifications in educational practice. While any change in the form of language must come from within the nation, the stimulus for such change may come from any source. Encouragement may be given to those who recognize the value of language reform, not only to the educational program but also to the development of the Japanese people throughout future generations.

It is recommended that some form of Romaji [western alphabetization of Japanese words] be brought into common use. It is proposed that a language commission made up of Japanese scholars, educational leaders and statesmen be formed promptly in order that a comprehensive program may be announced within a reasonable period. In addition to deciding the form of Romaji to be chosen, this commission would have the following functions: (1) to assume the responsibility for coordinating the program of language reform during the transitional stages; (2) to formulate a plan for introducing Romaji into the schools and into the life of the community and nation through newspapers, periodicals, books, and other writings, and (3) to study the means of bringing about a more democratic form of the spoken language. The commission might, in time, grow into a national language institute.

The need for a single and efficient medium of written communication is well recognized, and the time for taking this momentous step is perhaps more favorable now than it will be for many years to come. Language should be a highway and not a barrier. Within Japan itself, and across national borders, this highway should be open for the transmission of knowledge and ideas in the interest of a better world understanding.

Administration of Education at the Primary and Secondary Levels

The principle is accepted that, for the purpose of democratic education, control of the schools should be widely dispersed rather than highly centralized as at present. The observance of ceremonies in the reading of the Imperial Rescript and obeisances to the Imperial Portrait in the schools are regarded as undesirable. The Ministry of Education, under the proposals of the Mission, would have important duties to perform in providing technical aid and professional counsel to the schools, but its direct control over local schools would be greatly curtailed.

In order to provide for greater participation by the people at both the local and prefectural levels, and to remove the schools from the administrative control by representatives of the Ministry of Home Affairs at the local level, it is proposed to create educational agencies elected by popular vote, at both local and prefectural level. Such agencies would be granted considerable power in the approval of schools, the licensing of teachers, the selection of textbooks—power now centralized in the Ministry of Education.

There is proposed an upward revision of compulsory education in schools to be tax-supported, co-educational and tuition-free, such education to cover nine years of schooling, or until the boy or girl reaches the age of sixteen. It is further proposed that the first six years be spent in primary school as at present, and the next three years in a "lower secondary school" to be developed through merging and modifying the many kinds of schools which those completing primary school may now enter. The schools should provide general education for all, including vocational and educational guidance, and should be flexible enough to meet the individual differences in the abilities of the pupils. It is proposed further that a three year "upper secondary school" be established, free of tuition costs, in time to be co-educational, and providing varied opportunities for all who wish to continue their education.

Together the lower and upper secondary schools would continue the varied functions of other tax-supported schools now at this level: higher elementary schools, girls' high schools, preparatory courses, vocational schools, and youth schools. Graduation from the upper secondary school would be made a condition of entrance to institutions of higher learning.

Private schools under the proposal would retain full freedom, except that they would be expected to conform to the minimum standards necessary to assure ready transfer by the pupil from one school to another, whether public or private.

Teaching and Education of Teachers

In order that the newer aims of education may be achieved, teaching methods emphasizing memorization, conformity and a vertical system of duties and loyalties should be modified to encourage independent thinking, the development of personality, and the rights and responsibilities of democratic citizenship. The teaching of morals, for example, should be less by precept than by instruction deriving from experiences in concrete situations in school and community.

A program for the reeducation of teachers should be set up to further the adoption of democratic methods in the transitional period. Suggestions are made for a program which will gradually merge into one of in-service education.

Normal schools should be modified so as to provide the kinds of teachers needed. They should admit students only after completion of a course in the upper secondary school equivalent in standards to that of the present middle school, thus eliminating the normal preparatory courses. The reorganized normal schools, all more nearly at the level of the higher normal schools, should become four year institutions; they would continue general education and provide adequate professional training for teachers in elementary and secondary schools.

Other institutions for preparing teachers for certification, whether private or tax-supported, should satisfy teacher-training standards equivalent to those of the reorganized normal schools.

School administrators and supervisors should have a professional education equivalent to that for teachers and should have, in addition, such special preparation as will fit them for their assigned duties.

Universities and other higher institutions should develop facilities for advanced study on the part of teachers and administrators; they should promote research and exert educational leadership.

Adult Education

During this period of crisis for the Japanese people, adult education is of paramount importance, for a democratic state places much responsibility on each citizen.

The schools are but one agency for adult education, but through parent-teacher activities, evening and extension classes for adults, and the opening of buildings to a variety of community activities, adult education may be fostered.

Another important institution for adult education is the public library. It is recommended that central public libraries, with branches, be established in the larger cities, and that appropriate arrangements be made for library services in all prefectures. The appointment of a director of public library service in the Ministry of Education would facilitate this program. Museums of science, art, and industry may serve educational purposes paralleling those of the library.

In addition, organizations of all kinds, including community and professional societies, labor unions, and political groups, should be helped to use effectively the techniques of forum and discussion.

In the furtherance of these ends, the present adult education services of the Ministry of Education should be vitalized and democratized.

Higher Education

For a period of years following the first world war currents of liberal thought were fostered largely by men and women educated in the colleges and universities of Japan. Higher education now has the opportunity of again setting a standard of free thought, bold inquiry, and hopeful action for the people. To fulfill these purposes, higher education should become an opportunity for the many, not a privilege for the few. In order to increase the opportunities for liberal education at higher levels, it would be desirable to liberalize to a considerable extent the curricula of the preparatory schools (Koto Gakko) leading to the universities and those of the more specialized colleges (Semmon Gakko), so that a general college training would become more widely available. This would lead, on the one hand, to university study, and, on the other, to specialized training at the semi-professional level such as is provided by the Semmon Gakko, but rounded out with training of broader cultural and social significance.

In addition to providing more colleges, it is proposed that more universities be established according to a considered plan. Some governmental agency should be responsible for supervising the establishment of higher institutions and the maintenance of the requirements first set down. Except for examining the qualifications of a proposed institution of higher education before it is permitted to open its doors, and assuring that these initial requirements are met, the governmental agency should have practically no control over institutions of higher education. The institutions should be entirely free in all respects to pursue their objectives in the manner which they themselves deem best.

Establishment of economic and academic freedom for faculties in institutions of higher education is of primary importance. To this end it is recommended that the present civil service plan be discontinued.

For the student, the freedom which should be guaranteed is the freedom of access, on the basis of merit, to all levels of higher studies. Financial help should be given, in order that further education may be positively assured for talented men and women unable to study on their own resources. Freedom of access to higher institutions should be provided immediately for all women now prepared for advanced study; steps should also be taken to improve the earlier training of women.

The extension of libraries, of research facilities, and institutes is recommended; such agencies can make invaluable contributions to the public welfare during the period of reconstruction and beyond. Attention needs to be given to the improvement of professional education in fields such as medicine, school administration, journalism, labor relations, and public administration. A special commission is recommended for the study of the whole question of medicine and public health.

22
A Guide for the "New Education"
(Shin Kyoiku Hoshin)

June 30, 1946

Source: Kanda Osamu et al., eds., *Shiryo Kyoikuho* (Tokyo: Gakuyo Shobo, 1973), pp. 309–314. Translated by James Vardaman (abridged).

Foreword

This volume is designed to serve as a guide for educators in determining the objectives of education, where emphasis ought to be laid, and how to implement these aims, . . . Part I discusses the theoretical aspects of the new education and Part II discusses the practical applications thereof.

It is the task of educators in Japan to take it upon themselves to promote, through a reeducation of the people, the construction of a new Japan which is democratic, peace-loving and civilized. The practice of the MacArthur GHQ, especially the four directives on education, also hew to this line and they are extremely valuable in determining what the new education should become. . . . The contents of this volume have been written with those directives clearly in mind.

It is not the intention of the Ministry of Education to force the contents herein compiled upon the educator in any way. Accordingly it is necessary neither for educators to commit this material to memory nor for them to use the materials for a textbook with students. Rather it is hoped that educators will use it as a guide in thinking freely and critically, and that they themselves will determine the goals of the new education and devise the methods for themselves. Above all it is to be desired that these volumes will serve as material for joint study and open discussion in the development of the most appropriate educational policy. It is precisely this independent, cooperative attitude of educators which will form the cornerstone of democratic education. . . .

The initial draft of this volume was prepared through the tireless efforts of several authorities outside of the Ministry of Education. As a result of consultations with GHQ, the Ministry, in an attempt to make both the content and the language of expression as easily understood as possible, has taken the responsibility for rewriting the draft. In particular, the Ministry is mindful of limiting the use of characters *(kanji)* and has observed this limitation in preparing these volumes as well, using only the 1,134 characters in common use *(joyo kanji)* established by the Kokugo Shingikai in 1942. Due to the conditions under which this material was revised, we wish to express our deep gratitude to those who wrote the early drafts and ask for their understanding concerning the major revisions present in the final version.

In order to complete the publication and distribution of this material as rapidly as possible, we have divided the material into several volumes and have published the directives as a supplementary volume. We trust that the reader will arrange the volumes accordingly.

May 1946
Ministry of Education

Chapter 6 Conclusion

The Role of Educators in the Construction of a Peaceful and Civilized Nation

1. What Are the True Desires of Humanity?

We have discussed a wide variety of topics and we must now state our conclusions. Probably every teacher today is asking what kind of country

Japan should try to become and what kind of person education should attempt to cultivate. Our answer is this: Let us build a new Japan that is peace-loving and civilized and let us cultivate the kind of person who loves peace and seeks culture.

(a) *The Desire for Peace.* This does not mean to love peace out of necessity, simply because we lost the war and had our armaments taken from us, but rather to satisfy the human being's true desire for peace. The desire for peace is found deep in hearts. Once war commenced our people endured on behalf of the motherland, even at the cost of giving up their husbands, losing their children, and having their homes burned to the ground. But deep in everyone's heart was the thought that if war could possibly be avoided, such cruel events would not have to occur. Even those who urged the people on to war maintained that we were fighting not to have war, but in order to attain peace, to remove the injustices and inequalities that disturb peace, and that war was simply unavoidable. Such calls for struggle would appear to spring from a distrust of other nations and appear to disguise similar designs; however, once we realize that such pretexts must be created in order to fight a war, we can see that the true desire of humanity is to enjoy peace. Militarism and ultranationalism run counter to the true desires of all humanity.

(b) *The Desire for Culture.* The development of culture is another true desire of humanity. The reason one loves peace is because peace allows the development of culture. As we have already noted [in an earlier chapter], human beings are not like domestic animals who live a life of comfort, eating and sleeping their lives away. It is a specific characteristic of humanity that it makes an effort to make life reasonable, honest and well-intentioned, beautiful and pleasurable, and humbly devout. In other words, our true desire is to seek noble qualities like truth, goodness, beauty, and spirit, to realize them in everyday life through the development of cultural elements such as technology, economics, politics, scholarship, ethics, art, and religion.

2. What Type of Country Shall Japan Become?

The people's requirements are to love peace and seek civilization and it is therefore the work of the nation to provide the necessary conditions and to encourage the accomplishment thereof. . . .

3. What Kind of Person Should Education Now Cultivate?

(a) *A Person Who Holds Culture as an Ideal?* On one occasion an exchange student from China was observing Japanese children at play. "Children in Japan enthusiastically play at soldiers and war, and their parents and teachers do nothing to stop them. Why?" According to this student, in his country playing war was considered to be even worse than playing robbers. Someone replied that the Japanese think that there is nothing wrong with playing war; children grow up dreaming about becoming soldiers and performing great feats. The Chinese student replied that this way of thinking is the basis of militarism. Once this was pointed out to us we could see that what we had previously considered to be commendable and what we had been unconscious of actually had the effect of leading our people to war. The reading material, songs, and even games of our children were filled with war. The education of a peaceful nation should rid itself of such elements and direct its youth in an entirely different direction. The education of a nation which honors civilization should not allow its children to embrace ideas such as becoming a soldier or to "make Japan a greater nation," but rather should encourage them to idealize the pursuit of learning, morality, and art and to desire to make a contribution to the world at large. The new ideals of children should be to become like the scientist Madame Curie, the doctor Hideo Noguchi, the developer of the weaving loom Sakichi Toyota, the master of electricity Thomas Edison, and the discoverer of immunization Edward Jenner.

(b) *Cultivating the Seedlings of Culture in Everyday Life.* This does not mean that from the very beginning children should set out to become such a genius, but it means that the task of education is to nurture the seedlings of cultural endeavor in study and play, at home and in school. When young people reveal their true character, they eagerly seek truth, beauty, and goodness, in and of themselves. For example, in arithmetic, children become interested in solving problems, and in studying arithmetic they gain satisfaction from performing calculations accurately and quickly, not from getting good grades or from being praised by parents or teachers. In drawing, they become engrossed in the beauty of the colors and shapes; they do not draw against their will in pursuit of some other goal. Whether they are piling up wooden blocks or knocking them down or putting toys together or taking them apart, they play completely absorbed in what they are doing. These young people, when they exhibit their true natures, make use of their sense of justice and the desire to learn. They reject the injustices in their own behavior and that of other people as they search for justice in the world and in life. Within this attitude of children and young people is contained the capacity to create a culture of science, art, and morality. Education promotes this growth, without restricting it and without distorting it. The education of a peaceful nation need not be extraordinary, but it should respect the true nature of youth, cultivate a mind that seeks culture, and promote the strength to create culture. This is true progress along the road of true education.

During the war education was used as a device of war and became narrow and distorted. Even though one wanted to let students have a variety of learning experiences, one had to abstain from doing it if it was not directly related to the war effort. The goals, content and methods of education were determined not by what people wanted but by what war demanded. Now it is time to make headway along the main road of education, in the direction of true human desire and toward a broad, abundant civilization.

4. *Wherein Lies the Joy and Aspiration of the Educator?*

We have discussed what ought to be abandoned and what ought to be further developed in order to construct the new Japan. Educators must first attain a sufficient understanding of this and then help young people become aware of it and put it into practice.

(a) The Improvement of Material Livelihood. One cannot help but feel sympathy for the steadily worsening plight of educators, whose hardships were already numerous and whose rewards were already few enough. In addition, school facilities were damaged in the war, teaching equipment and writing materials are inadequate, and the number of textbooks is insufficient, so even though new policies and high ideals are set forth, their realization will be very difficult to carry out. In this respect the authorities are making every effort and it is hoped that educators themselves will actively advance educational associations and teachers' unions and help both themselves and others in addressing the various problems.

(b) The Joy of Progressing Along the True Road of Education. However hard the material difficulties are, it should not be forgotten that the real strength for overcoming these difficulties lies within the spirit. Improving the physical circumstances requires thorough planning, tremendous patience, and cooperation with all those concerned, and the spiritual hopes and joys are extremely important in compensating for material hardships. Educators are quite fortunate in this respect. As noted earlier, under the militaristic, ultranationalistic regime education became an instrument of warfare and authorities supervised education "for the sake of the nation." Accordingly educators were unable to move along in what they believed to be the true direction of education with a free will, but had to follow orders from above, submit to outside pressures, and restrain themselves in many ways. Now that the nation has become a nation of peace and culture, education has returned to the true path, so educators need not be restrained by anyone and may freely devote their energies to performing their duties. This must be a great joy for educators today.

(c) Hope for the Future. When we look to the future, educators can entertain brilliant hopes. "The future lies in youth." The only way to realize ambitions for the nation, and the world of the future is through the education of today's youth. . . . It is the duty of educators to look into the future of our nation, in the light of world history, and to realize that future through today's youth. Here the educator must be a farsighted leader.

During the Meiji Restoration, precisely at the time when the Imperial forces were battling the shogunal forces in the woods at Ueno, that pioneer Fukuzawa Yukichi was calmly telling his youthful followers about the future path of Japan. Fukuzawa knew the trends of international affairs and perceived the future of the homeland, and he embraced great hope and joy. Today's educators must take a similar attitude.

Let us look at the life of [Johann] Pestalozzi, the man celebrated as the saint of educators and revered as a paragon of educational virtues. The tempest of the French Revolution raged through his own homeland, Switzerland, and destitute orphans who had lost parents, lost their homes, and had no one to turn to were wandering the streets. Pestalozzi, who had sustained a deep interest in the revolutionary movement from his youth, eventually devoted his entire life to the education of those unfortunate children. He avowed that to educate a beggar as a human being he himself had to become a beggar. This is not to suggest that Japanese educators today should live the life of a beggar, but that the spirit of Pestalozzi, which turns its face upward to higher ideals in even the hardest of times and comforts itself in the preciousness of its tasks, is an eternal source of strength and light for educators. The young sprouts which educators cultivate and nurture in the hearts of young people today will in five, ten, or thirty years extend themselves gloriously, and all vestiges of militarism and ultranationalism will vanish without a trace. True strength, which includes human nature, character, and individuality will act with the accuracy of science, the breadth of philosophy, and the depth of religion. In it the principles of democracy will be practiced, a peace-loving nation enamored of culture will be constructed, and the people of the world will enjoy eternal peace and happiness. That this remote ideal not end up as a dream, but rather through daily educational activity move one step at a time toward reality, is the hope and the joy of the educator.

23
The Constitution of Japan

(Passed by the Diet on October 7, 1946, the Constitution was promulgated November 3, 1946, and went into effect May 3, 1947.)

Source: Japan, Ministry of Education, *Educational Laws and Regulations in Japan*, Ser. 1, The Constitution, the Fundamental Law of Education, 1953 (abridged).

We the Japanese people, acting through our duly elected representatives in the National Diet, determined that we shall secure for ourselves and our posterity the fruits of peaceful cooperation with all nations and the blessings of liberty throughout this land, and resolved that never again shall we be visited with the horrors of war through the action of government, do proclaim that sovereign power resides with the people and do firmly establish this Constitution. . . .

We, the Japanese people, desire peace for all time and are deeply conscious of the high ideals controlling human relationships, and we have determined to preserve our security and existence, trusting in the justice and faith of the peace-loving people of the world. We desire to occupy an honored place in an international society striving for the preservation of peace, and the banishment of tyranny and slavery, oppression and tolerance for all time from the earth. We recognize that all peoples of the world have the right to live in peace, free from fear and want.

We believe that no nation is responsible to itself alone, but that laws of political morality are universal; and that obedience to such laws is incumbent upon all nations who would sustain their own sovereignty and justify their sovereign relationship with other nations.

We, the Japanese people, pledge our national honor to accomplish these high ideals and purposes with all our resources. . . .

Article 9. Aspiring sincerely to an international peace [we] renounce war as a sovereign right of the nation and the threat or use of force as a means of settling international disputes.

In order to accomplish the aim of the preceding paragraph, land, sea, and air forces, as well as other war potential, will never be maintained. The right of belligerency of the state will not be recognized. . . .

Article 11. The people shall not be prevented from enjoying any of the fundamental human rights. These fundamental human rights guaranteed to the people by the Constitution shall be conferred upon the people of this, and future generations as eternal and inviolate rights. . . .

Article 14. All of the people are equal under the law and there shall be no discrimination in political, economic or social relations because of race, creed, sex, social status or family origin.

Article 19. Freedom of thought and conscience shall not be violated. . . .

Article 20. Freedom of religion is guaranteed to all. No religious organization shall receive any privileges from the State, nor exercise any political authority.

No person shall be compelled to take part in any religious act, celebration, rite or practice.

The State and its organs shall refrain from religious education or any other religious activity.

Article 21. Freedom of assembly and association as well as speech, press and all other forms of expression are guaranteed.

No censorship shall be maintained, nor shall the secrecy of any means of communication be violated. . . .

Article 23. Academic freedom is guaranteed. . . .

Article 25. All people shall have the right to maintain the minimum standards of wholesome and cultured living. . . .

Article 26. All people shall have the right to receive an equal education correspondent to their abilities, as provided by law.

All people shall be obligated to have all boys and girls under their protection receive ordinary education as provided by law. Such compulsory education shall be free.

Article 27. . . . Children shall not be exploited. . . .

Article 89. No public money or other property shall be expended or appropriated for the use, benefit or maintenance of any religious institution or association, or for any charitable, educational or benevolent enterprise not under the control of public authority. . . .

24
Revision of the Japanese Educational System

March 27, 1947

Source: U.S. Department of State revision of the Japanese Educational System, Directive, Serial No. 74.

A. Guiding Principles and Objectives

1. Education should be looked upon as the pursuit of truth, as a preparation for life in a democratic nation, and as a training for the social and political responsibilities which freedom entails. Emphasis should be placed on the dignity and worth of the individual, on independent thought and initiative, and on developing a spirit of inquiry. The independent character of international life should be stressed. The spirit of justice, fair play and respect for the rights of others, particularly minorities, and the necessity for friendship based upon mutual respect for people of all races and religions, should be emphasized. Special emphasis should also be placed on the teaching of the sanctity of the pledged word in all human relations, whether between individuals or nations. Measures should be taken as rapidly as possible to achieve equality of educational opportunity for all

regardless of sex or social position. The revision of the Japanese educational system should, in large measure, be undertaken by the Japanese themselves and steps should be taken to carry out such revision in accordance with the principles and objectives set forth in this paper.

B. Training, Recruitment, and Conditions of Service of Teachers

2. Those teachers and other educational officials whose record shows them to have been pronounced exponents of ultranationalistic, militaristic or totalitarian ideas, should be forbidden to teach or engage in other employment connected with education.

3. Short refresher courses and vacation schools for teachers should be opened, so far as possible, in order to train them in democratic ideas.

4. The development of modern techniques of teaching should be encouraged and opportunities should be provided for teachers to become acquainted with these techniques. In this connection, regard should be had to the value of affording teachers opportunity of transferring from one institution to another.

5. As a corrective to the regimented and limiting nature of normal school training in the past, and to provide teachers with aims and techniques in harmony with the objectives of the Occupation, special emphasis should be placed upon the reorganization of normal schools and the establishment of teacher training institutions staffed with the most competent instructors available for inculcating democratic principles. Endeavors should be made to increase the proportion of teachers who have had a university training.

6. The teaching profession should be recognized as of vital importance to the future welfare and democratic development of the nation, and its economic status should be improved to a degree commensurate with this importance. Consideration should be given to the establishment of salary scales affording all teachers a reasonable standard of living according to their abilities, qualifications, and responsibilities without the necessity of supplementing their income from outside sources. A basic living wage should be guaranteed for all teachers, with increases according to their qualifications.

C. Textbooks, Curricula and Teaching Methods

7. Teaching of ultranationalism, state Shintoism, veneration of the Emperor, exaltation of the state over the individual, and race superiority should be eliminated from the educational system.

8. Textbooks and other reading material that contains such ideas as those outlined above should be withdrawn from use in schools. New textbooks should be issued which give an understanding of progressive ideas. Foreign books should be made available, especially in central libraries, and for teachers. These

objectives should be given due weight when allocations of paper supplies and imports of foreign publications are made.

9. Courses in social sciences, civics, constitutional law and government, current events, world affairs, and international cooperation should be made an integral part of the educational system at the appropriate levels of teaching.

10. Teaching of military subjects should be totally forbidden in all educational institutions. The wearing by students of military-style uniforms should be forbidden. Classical sports such as *kendo,* which encourage the martial spirit, should be totally abandoned. Physical training should no longer be associated with the *Seishin Kyoiku* [spiritual education]. Greater emphasis should be placed on games and other recreational activities than on pure calisthenics and drill. If former servicemen are employed as drill instructors, or in connection with physical training or sports, they should be carefully screened.

11. Imperial rescripts should not be used as a basis of instruction, study, or ceremonies in schools.

12. Independent thinking on the part of teachers and students should be encouraged.

13. Uniform minimum standards should be prescribed for the different levels of instruction in all the schools of Japan, whether public or private.

D. Adult Education

14. Adult education should be promoted rapidly by the use of all suitable facilities such as evening classes, university extension courses, the radio, the cinema, and libraries.

E. Vocational Education

15. Japanese youth should be provided with opportunities for varied vocational training and guidance and appropriate organizations for this purpose.

F. Educational Administration and Finance

16. The Japanese Government should seek advice from representatives of all walks of life either through a non-official advisory council or otherwise.

17. The Japanese Government should exercise such control over the educational system as will ensure the achievement of the objectives of the Occupation, particularly the reforms called for by this policy decision. Subject to the foregoing, and to maintenance of standards prescribed by the government, the responsibility for the local administration of educational establishments should in due time be decentralized. Japanese parents and citizens should be encouraged to feel a sense of individual responsibility for the achievements of the objectives set out

in Paragraph 1. Where practicable they should be associated with the control, development, and work of the schools and other educational institutions.

18. The plans enumerated in this paper should be closely correlated with the reforms in the social, economic, and political life of the nation. In the implementation of the educational policies outlined above, funds should be allocated for all essential educational reforms commensurate with the needs and resources of the nations.

19. In order that educational standards in poor districts should not be lowered by the inability of some local bodies to provide sufficient finance from local revenue, finance for education should come for the most part from the national government, which should be responsible for the maintenance of an adequate level of education throughout Japan. Local and private bodies should be encouraged to supplement these funds provided by the national government.

G. General

20. Free and compulsory education should be provided for all Japanese children for a minimum period of six years and should be extended to higher age groups as rapidly as possible.

21. More opportunities should be provided for higher education.

22. Equal opportunity for both sexes should be provided at all levels of education—primary, secondary and tertiary.

23. Encouragement should be given to the formation and reorientation of educational associations and parent-teacher associations; and to assist in making the Japanese people aware of the significant changes in the direction of education in a democratic Japan, such groups should be encouraged to consider practical problems of education.

24. Discrimination against the graduates of private schools in civil service appointments should be eliminated, provided the schools in question conform to educational standards laid down for the public school system.

25. Educational institutions of foreign foundation in Japan have played a useful part in the past in widening and deepening the scope of Japanese education and should be given equal rights to those of Japanese institutions in the future.

25

School Education Law (Law No. 26)
(Gakko Kyoiku Ho)

March 29, 1947

Source: General Headquarters, SCAP, CIE, Education Division, *Education in the New Japan*, vol. 2 (Tokyo, 1948), pp. 112–130 (abridged).

Chapter I. General Regulations

Article 1. The schools provided for in this law shall be primary schools, secondary schools, high schools, universities, higher professional schools, schools for the blind, schools for the deaf, schools for the handicapped and kindergarten.

Article 2. The State, prefectural and local public entities and school juridical persons . . . alone can establish schools.

Article 3. The "Government schools" in this law means the schools established by the State; the "public schools" are schools established by prefectural and local public entities, and the "private schools" are schools established by school juridical persons. . . .

Article 4. The establishment and abolition of schools . . . , the teaching at night or other special time or period . . . , and educating by correspondence . . . , the faculties of universities, the postgraduate school, and the postgraduate courses of the postgraduate school, as well as the faculties of universities . . . , changes of their founders and other items to be decided by Cabinet Order, except for government schools and those schools established by agencies responsible for establishing schools in compliance with this Law, shall be subject to the approval of competent authorities.

Article 5. The founders of schools shall manage the schools which they establish and defray the expenses of the schools, except for the cases specifically stipulated by laws and ordinances.

Article 6. Schools may collect tuition fees. No tuition fees shall be collected for compulsory education, however, in government public and primary schools and secondary schools, or schools for the blind, schools for the deaf and schools for the handicapped, which are equivalent to the above. . . .

Article 9. Persons in the following categories shall not be principals or teachers:

(1) Incompetent and quasi-incompetent;

(2) Those condemned to imprisonment with or without hard labor;

(3) Those who have been sentenced to the cancellation of their certificate and of which a period of two years has not expired since the date of the disposition;

(4) Those persons who, on or after the date of the enforcement of the Constitution of Japan, have organized or belonged to a political party or association which advocates the overthrow by force of the Constitution of Japan or the Government formed thereunder.

Article 10. Private schools shall appoint their principals and the appointment shall be reported to the competent authorities.

Article 11. Principals and teachers of schools may punish their students, pupils and children, when necessary in the light of education, in compliance with the regulations issued by competent authorities. They shall not, however, inflict corporal punishment.

Article 12. Schools shall, as otherwise prescribed by law, conduct health examinations in order to increase the health of students, pupils and children as well as teachers, and take necessary measures to preserve health.

Article 13. The competent authorities may order the closing of schools in any of the following cases:

(1) In cases where they have intentionally violated the provisions of laws and ordinances;

(2) In cases where they have acted against the instruction issued by competent authorities in compliance with the provisions of laws and ordinances;

(3) In cases where they have not conducted teaching for more than six months.

Article 14. In cases where schools acted against the provisions of laws and ordinances or the regulations established by competent authorities as to equipment, teaching and other items, the competent authorities may order changes of the item. . . .

Article 16. Those persons who employ children shall not prevent the said children from receiving compulsory education because of that employment.

Chapter II. Primary School

Article 17. The primary school shall aim at giving children elementary general education according to the development of their minds and bodies.

Article 18. In primary school education efforts shall be made to attain the principles mentioned in each of the following items in order to effect the aim stated in the foregoing Article:

(1) To cultivate a right understanding and the spirit of cooperation and independence in connection with relationship[s] between human beings on the basis of the children's experience in social life both in and outside the schools;

(2) To develop a proper understanding of the actual conditions and traditions both of children's native communities and of the country and, further, to cultivate the spirit of international cooperation;

(3) To cultivate a basic understanding and skills relating to food, clothing, housing, industries, etc. needed in everyday life;

(4) To cultivate the ability to understand and correctly use words and expressions of the Japanese language needed in everyday life;

(5) To cultivate the ability to understand and correctly manage mathematical relations needed in everyday life;

(6) To cultivate the ability to observe and understand natural phenomena of everyday life in a scientific manner;

(7) To cultivate habits needed for a sound, safe and happy life, and to effect the harmonious development of minds and bodies;

(8) To cultivate a basic understanding and skills in music, fine arts, literature, etc. which make life bright and rich.

Article 19. The course of the primary school shall cover six years. . . .

Article 21. At elementary school, the textbooks to be used shall be those authorized by the Minister of Education, Science and Culture, or textbooks, copyrighted by the said Ministry. [This amendment from "NIER Teaching Materials," Occasional Paper 02/84 (Tokyo: National Institute for Educational Research, 1984).]

Article 22. The protectors (i.e., those persons who exercise parental authority over the children, or where there are no such persons, the guardians; hereinafter the same) shall be obliged to send their children to the primary school, or the primary school section of the school for the blind, the school for the deaf or the school for the handicapped, for the period from the beginning of that school year which is the first to begin on or after the day following the children's attaining a sixth birthday to the end of the school year in which the children attain full twelve years of age. . . .

Article 23. As for the protectors of those children who are to be sent to school according to the provisions of the foregoing Article . . . but who are acknowledged as being difficult . . . because of their invalidity, imperfect growth or other unavoidable obstacles, the board of education in a city, town, or village may allow them to postpone the fulfillment of their obligation . . . or exempt them from their obligation according to the regulations stipulated by the competent authorities. . . .

Article 25. The city, town or village shall give necessary help to the protectors of school age children whose financial situations are recognized [as] making it difficult to attend school.

Article 26. The board of education of a city, town or village may suspend those children from school whose character and conduct are so bad that they may obstruct the education of other children.

Article 27. Those children who have not attained the age for entering the primary school shall not enter the school. . . .

Article 29. Each city, town or village shall establish primary schools sufficient for admitting the school age children living within its own boundary. . . .

Article 32. In cases where the prefectural board of education recognizes that some towns or villages are unable to afford primary school education, the prefectures concerned shall give necessary aid to the towns or villages. . . .

Chapter III. Secondary School

Article 35. The secondary school shall aim at giving the pupils secondary general education according to the development of their minds and bodies on the basis of the education given at the primary school.

Article 36. In secondary school education efforts shall be made to attain the principles mentioned in each of the following items in order to realize the aim stated in the foregoing Article:

(1) To cultivate the qualities necessary as the members of a society and State, securing the objectives of the primary school education more thoroughly;

(2) To cultivate the fundamental knowledge and skill of the vocations required in the society, the attitude to respect labor and the ability to select their future course according to their individuality;

(3) To promote their social activities in and out of school, to guide the sentiment rightly, and to cultivate their judgment.

Article 37. The course of the secondary school shall cover three years. . . .

Article 39. Guardians shall be obliged to send their children to the secondary school, or the secondary school section of the school for the blind, the school for the deaf, or the school for the handicapped from the beginning of that school year which begins on, or after the day following their finishing the course of the primary school . . . to the end of that school year in which they attain full fifteen years of age. . . .

Chapter IV. High School

Article 41. The high school shall aim at giving the students higher general education and technical education according to the development of their minds and bodies on the basis of the education given at the secondary school.

Article 42. In high school education efforts shall be made to attain the principles in each of the following items in order to realize the aim stated in the foregoing Article:

(1) To cultivate the qualities necessary as able members of the society and the state, developing the results of secondary school education;

(2) To make them [students] decide on the future according to their individuality on the basis of their awareness of their mission in the society, to cultivate the higher general culture and to make them skilled in technical arts;

(3) To cultivate broad and deep understanding and sound judgment regarding society and to help establish their individuality. . . .

Article 44. The high school may have part-time courses in addition to the full-time course.

. . . (2) The high school may choose to have part-time courses only.

Article 45. The high school may have correspondence courses, in addition to the full-time course and the part-time course.

. . . (2) The high school may choose to have the correspondence course only.

Article 46. The course of the high school shall cover three years for the full-time course, and shall cover four years for the part-time courses and the correspondence course.

Article 47. Those who can enter high school shall have graduated from the secondary school or the equivalent school or have attained equal scholastic levels, according to the provisions laid down by competent authorities.

Article 48. The high school may offer graduate and special courses.

Chapter V. University

Article 52. The university, as a center of learning, shall aim at teaching and studying higher learning and technical arts, as well as giving broad general culture and developing intellectual, moral and practical abilities.

Article 53. It is normal for a university to have faculties therein. Provided that, in the case where it is useful and adequate for achieving the educational object of said university, it may have systems to be the basis for education other than the faculties.

Article 54. The university faculty may teach in the evening.

. . . (2) The university may conduct correspondence courses.

Article 55. The course of the university shall cover four years . . . or more.

. . . (2) As to a regular course of medicine or dentistry in the faculty of medicine or dentistry, the course shall, notwithstanding the provisions of the main clause of the preceding paragraph, be not less than six years; and in the event of dividing said course into the professional course and the pre- professional course, these courses shall, respectively, be four years and two years.

. . . (5) Those who may go on to the professional course . . . shall be persons who have completed not less than [the] two years' course . . . , or persons of equal or better scholastic attainment according to the provisions laid down by competent authorities.

Article 56. To enter the university, students shall have graduated from the high school or completed the twelve-year schooling of regular courses (including those who have completed the schooling equivalent to this, in other courses), or those whose scholastic attainments are recognized as equal to this under provisions laid down by competent authorities. . . .

Article 57. The university may have graduate courses and special courses.

. . . (2) The graduate course of the university shall aim at providing instruction on special matters to a more advanced degree and guiding the study of those who have graduated from the university or those whose scholastic attainments are equal to them under the provisions laid down by competent authorities. The course shall cover more than one year.

Article 58. The university shall have a president, professors, assistant professors, assistants and business clerks. . . .

(3) The president shall govern all the affairs of the university and supervise all staff. . . .

(5) The professors shall instruct the students, guiding them in their study or pursuing their own study.

(6) Assistant professors shall assist the professors in their duties.

Article 61. The university may have research institutes or other research facilities attached to it.

Article 62. The university may have a post-graduate school. . . .

Article 64. Public or private universities shall be under the jurisdiction of the Minister of Education.

Article 65. The post-graduate school shall aim at teaching and studying the theory and practice of learning, mastering the secrets of it and, thus, contributing to the development of culture. . . .

Article 67. Those who can enter post-graduate school shall be the graduates from the universities of Article 52, or those persons who are recognized to have equivalent or more scholastic ability than said graduates, as prescribed by the competent authorities. . . .

Chapter VI. Education for the Handicapped

Article 71. The school for the blind, the school for the deaf and the school for the handicapped shall educate, respectively, the blind (including the intensively weak-sighted, hereinafter the same), the deaf (including the intensively hard-of-hearing, hereinafter the same), and the mentally and physically handicapped, the mentally weak, the physically handicapped, or sickly weak (including the physically weak, hereinafter the same), on the same levels as the kindergarten, the primary school, the secondary school, or the high school, and at the same time giving knowledge and skill to supplement their infirmities. . . .

Article 73.2. The school for the blind, the school for the deaf and the school for the handicapped shall have boarding houses. In special circumstances they need not have them. . . .

Article 75. The primary school, the secondary school and the high school may provide special classes for the children and pupils who come under any of the following items:

(1) Those mentally weak;
(2) Those physically handicapped;
(3) Those physically weak;
(4) Those weak-sighted;
(5) Those hard-of-hearing;
(6) Those others defective in mind or body who can be appropriately educated in a special school.

. . . The schools mentioned in the preceding paragraph may give education to those children and pupils who are under medical care by providing special classes or by dispatching teachers.

Chapter VII. Kindergarten

Article 77. The kindergarten's aim shall be bringing up young children and developing their minds and bodies, and providing a suitable environment for them.

Article 78. In order to realize the aim in the foregoing Article, the kindergarten shall endeavor to attain the objective in each of the following items:

(1) To cultivate everyday habits necessary for a sound, safe and happy life and to effect a harmonious development of bodily functions;
(2) To make children experience group life and to cultivate a willingness to take part in it, as well as to foster the spirit of co-operation and independence;
(3) To foster an understanding of the correct attitude toward social life and events;

(4) To guide the correct usage of language and foster an interest in fairy-tales and picture books;

(5) To cultivate an interest in expressing themselves through music, dances, pictures and other means.

... *Article 80.* Those who can enter the kindergarten shall be children from the age of full three years up to the age [six] at which they are sent to primary school.

Chapter VII, section II

Special Course School
(Senshu Gakko)

... *Article 82.2.* Educational institutions other than those mentioned in Article 1 which affect the systematic education (excluding those covered by special provisions in another law and those exclusively for foreigners residing in Japan) must meet the following criteria, and exist to develop the abilities needed for work or practical life, or to elevate cultures:

(1) That the course is one year or more;

(2) That the number of hours of lessons is not less than the number of hours prescribed by the Minister of Education;

(3) That there are regularly at least 40 students;

Article 82.3. The special course school shall offer a higher course, special course and general course.

(2) The education of the preceding Article shall be effected, in the higher course of such special course schools, according to the development of their minds and bodies, on the basis of the education in the middle school, to graduates of the middle school of equivalent school, or to those whose scholastic attainment is equal to or surpasses that level, as prescribed by the Minister of Education.

(3) The special course of the special course school, shall effect the education of the preceding Article, based on the education in high school, to graduates of high school or equivalent school, or those with similar scholastic attainments, as prescribed by the Minister of Education.

(4) In the general course of the special course school, the education of the preceding Article other than the higher course or the special course shall be effected.

Chapter VIII. Miscellaneous Regulations

Article 83. Those institutions other than those mentioned in Article 1 which give education similar to school education (excluding those specially provided for in other laws for effecting said education, and those effecting the education of a special course school under the provisions of Article 82.2), shall be classified as miscellaneous schools.

26
The Fundamental Law of Education
(Law No. 25) *(Kyoiku Kihon Ho)*

March 31, 1947

Source: General Headquarters, SCAP, CIE, Educational Division, *Education in the New Japan*, vol. 2 (Tokyo, 1948), pp. 109–111..

Having established the Constitution of Japan, we have shown our resolution to contribute to the peace of the world and welfare of humanity by building a democratic and cultural state. The realization of this idea shall depend fundamentally on the power of education.

We shall esteem individual dignity and endeavor to bring up the people who love truth and peace, while education aimed at the creation of culture, general and rich in individuality, shall be spread far and wide.

We hereby enact this Law, in accordance with the spirit of the Constitution of Japan, with a view to clarifying the aim of education and establishing the foundation of education for new Japan.

Article 1. Aim of Education

Education shall aim at the full development of personality, striving for the rearing of the people, sound in mind and body, who shall love truth and justice, esteem individual value, respect labor and have a deep sense of responsibility, and be imbued with the independent spirit, as builders of a peaceful state and society.

Article 2. Educational Principle

The aim of education shall be realized on all occasions and in all places. In order to achieve the aim, we shall endeavor to contribute to the creation and development of culture by mutual esteem and cooperation, respecting academic freedom, having a regard to actual life and cultivating a spontaneous spirit.

Article 3. Equal Opportunity in Education

The people shall all be given equal opportunities of receiving education according to their ability, and they shall not be subject to educational discrimination on account of race, creed, sex, social status, economic position, or family origin.

The state and local public corporations shall take measures to give financial assistance to those who have, in spite of their ability, difficulty in receiving education for economic reasons.

Article 4. Compulsory Education

The people shall be obligated to have boys and girls under their protection receive nine years' general education.

No tuition fee shall be charged for general education in schools established by the state and local bodies.

Article 5. Coeducation

Men and women shall esteem and cooperate with each other. Coeducation, therefore, shall be recognized in education.

Article 6. School Education

The schools prescribed by law shall be of public nature and, besides the state and local public bodies, only the juridical persons prescribed by law shall be entitled to establish such schools.

Teachers of the schools prescribed by law shall be servants of the whole community. They shall be conscious of their mission and endeavor to discharge their duties. For this purpose, the status of teachers shall be respected and their fair and appropriate treatment shall be secured.

Article 7. Social Education

The state and local bodies shall encourage home education and education carried out in places of work or elsewhere in society.

The state and local public bodies shall endeavor to attain the aim of education by the establishment of such institutions as libraries, museums, citizens' public halls, et cetera, by the utilization of school institutions, and by other appropriate methods.

Article 8. Political Education

The political knowledge necessary for intelligent citizenship shall be valued in education.

The schools prescribed by law shall refrain from political education or other political activities for or against any political party.

Article 9. Religious Education

The attitude of religious tolerance and the position of religion in the social life shall be valued in education.

The schools established by the state and local public bodies shall refrain from religious education or the activities for a specified religion.

Article 10. School Administration

Education shall not be subject to improper control, but shall be directly responsible to the whole people.

School administration shall, on the basis of this realization, aim at the adjustment and establishment of the various conditions required for the pursuit of the aim of education.

Article 11. Additional Rule

In case of necessity appropriate laws shall be enacted to carry the foregoing stipulations into effect.

Supplementary Provision:

This present law shall come into force as from the date of its promulgation.

27
Japan Teachers' Union: Main Principles, Bylaws, Proclamations, Resolutions, Summary of Activities, Public Statements *(Nihon Kyoshokuin Kumiai Soritsukai)*

Japan Teachers' Union

First Convention, June 8, 1947

Source: Document provided by the late Professor Ronald S. Anderson of the University of Hawaii, who was a participant in the Occupation of Japan.

In order to carry out our serious responsibilities, we [wish to] establish our position economically, socially and politically.

We strive for the democratization of education and the acquisition of freedom of research.

Bylaws

Chapter 1. General Provisions

Article *1*. This union shall be called Nihon Kyoshokuin Kumiai (Nikkyoso) [Japan Teachers' Union].

Article 2. This union shall be an association constituted of teachers' unions of the municipal, prefectural, and district levels.

Article 3. This union shall be a juridical person.

Article 4. This union shall establish its headquarters within the Kyoiku Kaikan at 2–9 Hitotsubashi, Kanda, Chiyoda-ku, Tokyo.

Article 5. This union shall aim at raising the economic, social and political position of the union members, and endeavor to construct a cultural nation through the democratization of education and research.

Article 6. This union, to achieve the above-mentioned purposes, shall address the following concerns:

1. Matters concerned with maintenance and improvements of teachers' payment and working conditions.
2. Matters concerned with democratization of academic research.
3. Matters concerned with enhancing democratic education.

4. Matters concerned with the cultural enrichment of teachers.
5. Matters concerned with liaison and cooperation with other organizations.
6. Other matters required to achieve the purposes of this union.

Proclamation

We have now organized the Japan Teachers' Union with the expectations and support of 500,000 teachers from all over Japan.

The Japan Teachers' Union shall concentrate the hopes, determination and strength of these teachers in one organization and it shall shoulder the responsibility of constructing a new democratic order and creating a new Japanese society.

We believe that democratization of education is the basis of the democratization of the nation, and that education holds the key to the future of our nation.

However, the present situation of education in our nation is extremely deficient both in terms of democratization and educational facilities, and the future does not seem bright.

These difficulties must be overcome as soon as possible through our conscious efforts. We solemnly swear that with the strength of the 500,000 teachers here united, we shall endeavor not only to improve the conditions of teachers and raise their social and political position, but also with the cooperation of laborers and farmers all over Japan and the world, we shall struggle to eliminate all of the evils still existing in our nation, and push forward to construct a nation that is democratic as well as well-educated.

June 8, 1947
Japan Teachers' Union

Resolutions

We call for the following measures to aid in the reconstruction of education:

1. The complete reconstruction of major expenditures from the national treasury, democratization of educational administration, democratization of school education, implementation of compulsory education in regular secondary schools, granting permission to borrow money for the construction of school buildings.
2. The immediate implementation of compulsory education for the physically handicapped and mentally retarded.
3. The assurance of democratization of academic research.
4. An increase in expenditures for research.
5. The reconstruction of war-damaged and earthquake-damaged schools.
6. The promotion of legislative measures concerning education.

7. Democratization of Education Reform Council.
8. Democratization of the Teachers' Screening Committee.
9. Democratic reorganization of educational societies.
10. Universal provision of school textbooks at moderate prices and the democratization of editorial policies.
11. Major increases in national government support to private schools.
12. Improvement of the quality of teachers and the promotion of educational vigor.

We call for the following measures concerning the improvement of living conditions:

1. Establishment of a minimum wage system.
2. Abolition of discrimination against youth and women.
3. Medical compensation for tubercular teachers.
4. Promoting the Mutual Benefit Association.
5. Establishment of teachers' dwellings.
6. Price stabilization.
7. Addressing the problem of treatment of underpaid employees.

We call for the following measures concerning collective [bargaining] agreements:

1. Continuation of collective bargaining.
2. Conclusion of collective [bargaining] agreements in local areas.

We call for the following measures concerning union management:

1. Presentation of a united front through participation in Liaison Council of All Trade Unions of Japan, and the World Federation of Trade Unions.
2. Establishment of the right to organize and the right to strike.
3. Educational and enrichment activities for union members.
4. Establishment of a research organ for the union.
5. Publication of a union bulletin.

We call for the following measures concerning youth and children:

1. Expansion of the educational system.
2. Expansion of institutions for infants and bolstering of nursery school teachers.
3. Education of delinquent students.
4. Relief for Japanese citizens abroad, the children and families of those who suffered during the war, and repatriates.

5. Generalization of school lunch programs at public expense.
6. Taking good care of youth.
7. Securing an adequate supplement of clothes and school materials for students.

Summary of Activities

1. Reconstruct education and establish a new Japan.
2. Implement completely the 6–3–3 educational system with national government support.
3. Ensure the freedom and democratization of research activities.
4. Establish the living wage system.
5. Stabilize prices and the cost of living.
6. Carry out collective [bargaining] agreements.
7. Promote nursery facilities.
8. Liberate women and young people.
9. Promote the national unification of teachers and prepare for participation in the World Federation of Trade Unions.
10. Expel war criminals from the educational world and overthrow Fascism.
11. Join with labor and farming organizations and unify workers.

Public Statement

There is currently a great amount of anxiety concerning social welfare and the lack of thoroughgoing educational policy in Japan. The actual conditions of the new educational system are gradually becoming apparent. It is this common concern which has led 500,000 [teachers] to organize together.

This union shall do its utmost to rationalize the treatment of teachers, raise their social and political position, and push forward in solving the present crisis in education.

We sincerely hope that all people, especially the laborers and farmers of Japan and the world, will offer us their understanding and hearty support.

June 8, 1947
Japan Teachers' Union

28
Appeal to Educators

(From a radio address by Minister of Education
Morita Tatsuo)

June 20, 1947

Source: General Headquarters, SCAP, CIE, Education Division, *Education in the New Japan*, vol. 2 (Tokyo, 1948), appendix, pp. 269–272 (excerpts).

If our country is to be a really democratic nation with respect for fundamental human rights living up to the terms of the new Constitution, the humanistic and democratic spirit underlying this Constitution must permeate into the minds of the people. In other words, Japan needs a brilliant political revolution and cultural uplift. It needs renaissance and reformation. To bring about renaissance aimed at the establishment of a new culture and a new national spirit is our glorious task as educators. . . . And so the task must be discharged . . . by the younger generation. In this way, the perfection of Japan's renaissance lies in the growth of younger generations, and in view of this our responsibilities as educators of youth are indeed heavy.

. . . Japan was once a militaristic and rising capitalistic nation . . . while hereafter she will have to pave her way as a peace-loving and cultural nation. This is a fundamental change in our national ideals. According to an expression of many ancient wise men, this cultural nation will be one where wisdom prevails over economy and armed strength, virtues are clarified, people renewed and utmost good remains. . . . Such a nation was the ultimate ideal . . . cherished by many idealistic political men and theorists of state. But I am sorry to say this has remained a mere utopian world remote from the real state of affairs. But this cultural country, which was only a world in dreamy ideals, is now the actual political objective of our country as the result of the surrender. . . .

Though this is now an ideal objective of our country we do not think this ideal will soon be set up in our country, where postwar miseries and privations prevail. The collapse of militarism and the crisis of our capitalistic social order does not mean the elevation of our culture and the supremacy of our civilization. . . .

Our country has established a foundation along the[se] lines by revising our educational principles and system. . . . The entire nation of Japan is duty-bound to establish a cultural nation, because it would be to build a castle in the air, trying to establish a cultural nation on a foundation lacking in democratic, peaceful and socialistic atmosphere. We educators must first lay a foundation on which to sow the seeds and bring up the new plant of a civilized cultural nation. The duties along the path are very grave for educators. . . .

29
The Board of Education Law (Law No. 170)
(Kyoiku Iinkai Ho)

July 15, 1948

Source: General Headquarters, SCAP, CIE, Educational Division, *Post-War Developments in Japanese Education*, vol. 2 (Tokyo, April 1952), pp. 231–251 (abridged).

Chapter 1. General Provisions

Article 1. This law aims at attaining the primary objectives of education by establishing the Board of Education to administer education based upon their equitable popular will and befitting actual local conditions, realizing that education should not submit to undue control and should be responsible directly to the entire people. . . .

Article 5. The expenses necessary for [conducting] the business of the Boards of Education shall be borne by the local public body concerned.

Article 6. The expenses necessary to conduct business of the Boards of Education as well as those under their control may be subsidized by a national treasury.

Chapter II. Organization of the Board of Education

Article 7. Prefectural Boards of Education shall consist of seven members, and local Boards of Education shall consist of five members.

Article 8. The term of office of the elective members of the board shall be four years.

Article 31. The local public bodies shall pay remuneration to the members of the boards concerned, but shall pay no salary.

Article 41 (Section 2). The superintendent of education shall be appointed by the Board of Education from among those who have certificates for educational personnel as prescribed by the Educational Personnel certification law. . . .

Article 41 (Section 3). The term of the office of superintendent of education shall be four years. They may, however, be reappointed.

Chapter III. Powers and Duties of Boards of Education

Article 48. Prefectural Boards of Education shall have control over all schools and other educational institutions established by the prefectures concerned, and local Boards of Education shall have control over all schools established by the local public bodies concerned.

Article 49. The Board of Education shall take charge of the following matters: (1) Matters concerning establishment, control and abolishment of schools and other educational institutions; . . . (3) Matters concerning the curriculum contents to be taught and their treatment; (4) Matters concerning selection of textbooks; . . . (12) Matters concerning social education; (13) Matters concerning study and self-improvement of principals, teachers and professional educational personnel; . . . (20) Other matters concerning educational affairs of the community under its jurisdiction.

Article 50. Of the affairs placed under the powers of the Board of Education, the following matters shall be taken charge of by the prefectural Board of Education exclusively: (1) Matters concerning the certificates of principals and teachers of national and public schools, superintendents of education and teacher consultants . . . ; (2) Approving textbooks for all schools within the prefecture concerned in accordance with the standards established by the Minister of Education; (3) Giving technical and professional advice to the local Board of Education. . . .

30
Dr. Walter Ells's Convocation Address at the Opening of Niigata University

July 19, 1949

Source: Provided by the late Professor Ronald S. Anderson, University of Hawaii, a participant in the Occupation of Japan.

Function of the University

What is the purpose of a university? According to the School Education Law, passed by the Diet two years ago [March 29, 1947], "the university as a center of learning, shall aim at teaching and studying higher learning and technical arts as well as giving broad general culture and developing intellectual, moral and practical abilities." This is an excellent statement. Notice that it speaks of *teaching* and *studying*. It is the professors who are chiefly responsible for the *teaching* and the students for the *studying*. Let us consider briefly, then, something of the privileges and the responsibilities, first of professors, and second of students.

The Professors

Freedom of teaching and freedom of research are the most widely held and jealously guarded functions of a university. In our country, the American Association of University Professors has some 15,000 members. With the cooperation of various organizations of colleges and universities, during the past 25 years it has published carefully prepared and widely influential statements of principles to assure academic freedom—freedom of teaching and freedom of research in universities. One sentence from one of its statements reads as follows: "No teacher may claim as his right the privilege of discussing in his classroom controversial topics outside of his own field of study." This means that a mathematics teacher, for example, has complete academic freedom to study or teach his own field of mathematics, but does not have freedom to teach such a subject as communism.

In the past few years the question has come up in the United States, as it has recently in Japan and in other countries, whether in a democracy a member of the Communist Party should be discharged from his position as a university professor because he is a Communist. It has been claimed that academic freedom means that a professor is free to believe in communism, to be a Communist, and to teach Communist doctrines and practices in the universities. Communism is a dangerous and destructive doctrine since it advocates the overthrow of established democratic governments by force. Must those who may believe in this dangerous doctrine be allowed in the name of academic freedom to teach such doctrines to the youth of the country? This is a problem of basic importance demanding the best educational thought for a correct answer.

In the United States we have an important organization known as the Educational Policies Commission, composed of the leading educators of the country. It may be thought of as similar in many respects to your JERC (Japanese Educational Reform Council). Its carefully considered statements have been given thoughtful consideration by the educators of the country. This commission, with such men as President [James Bryant] Conant of Harvard University and President [Dwight David] Eisenhower of Columbia University as members, only a few weeks ago issued a document which advocates and defends the discharge of proved Communists from the schools of America. The report has been approved by the United States Commissioner of Education and by President [Harry S.] Truman.

Do the recommendations of this document violate the long and jealously guarded academic freedom of the universities? By no means. Their basic reason for advising exclusion of Communist professors is that they are *not free*. Their thoughts, their beliefs, their teachings are controlled from outside. Communists are told from headquarters *what to think* and *what to teach*. In the very name of academic freedom, therefore, the most important right and duty of a university, we dare not have known Communists as university professors because they [the universities] are then no longer really *free* to teach and carry on research. The argument of the American Commission is simple, logical and convincing. In brief it is as follows: Freedom of thought is basic to the whole spirit of American education. Communist Party members are not free to think. They have surrendered that freedom when they joined the party. Therefore, they cannot be allowed to be university professors in a democracy.

I hope that this question will not come up to disturb the peace and freedom of Niigata University. But if it should, it is clear that the university administration and the Ministry of Education which, according to present Japanese Law, has ultimate authority for university policies and personnel, will not hesitate to take a positive and vigorous stand against Communist professors on its staff. The university not only has the right, it has the duty to preserve *true* academic freedom, to refuse to allow members of the Communist Party on its faculty.

The Students

So much for the professors who, we have seen by the law, are chiefly responsible for teaching. What of the students, who would be chiefly responsible for *studying?* Let us consider briefly the rights, privileges and duties of students in Niigata University and other national universities. Not all students want a university education or can profit by university study. Not all can afford it. In the past less than one percent of the children of the country have ever reached the university.

You young men and young women (I wish there were more young women, but I trust that will come in the near future) who are here today, therefore, represent a highly selected group. You have therefore special obligations to the government which is paying a greater part of the cost of your university education. Many of you are here as the result of sacrifices made by your parents who are eager to have you secure a better education than they have. . . .

I trust, therefore, that you will not waste your time—any of your time—in the university. You will have greater freedom than in the secondary school. But that freedom involves responsibility to use your time wisely. The new university credit plan expects two hours of your outside study in the library or laboratory or field for every hour that you are in classroom or lecture. Your professors should suggest the most helpful reading, study, problems for solution, outside activities related to classwork, but the responsibility is chiefly yours to carry out these suggestions. You cannot afford to waste any of that time, in the classroom or outside of the classroom. You have no right to waste it.

Like your professors you should have freedom to study—freedom to seek the truth. I regret that in many schools in Japan today there has been an unfortunate tendency for some students to go on strikes. Such students are wasting their time. They are wasting their money. They are wasting the money of their parents. They are wasting the money of a generous government which has provided educational opportunities for them.

But even worse, many of these students are actually wasting their freedom of study. For they have been striking for the most part because of interference and instructions from an outside group. In many cases they have gone on strike, not because of any real grievance on their own campus, or knowledge of possible causes, but because they have been instructed to do so by an outside group, the executive committee of Zengakuren [acronym for the National Federation of Student Self-Governing Associations] in Tokyo, commonly known to be a Communist-controlled group, not interested in real student welfare nor in the development of democracy in Japan. Students as well as professors cannot afford to sacrifice their freedom of study and freedom of action to any Communist group.

A strike is a weapon used by labor unions. It is an effort to make the employer come to terms by hurting the business of the employer. The laborer is hired by the employer. But students are not laborers. They are not hired by their professors. They are not hurting their professors when they go on strike. They are hurting themselves. They are hurting the good name of their university. Thus a strike is a completely illogical weapon for a student to use. He is paying hard-earned money for an opportunity to study. Then by striking he is refusing to use that opportunity. Could anything be more foolish, less logical? It is a pity that promising young students, perhaps not always fully matured, become victims of such movements. They are losing their freedom of thought, not gaining it. University students, of all people, should not be puppets but independent thinkers.

To be a student in a university is not only a right, but also a privilege and an opportunity. It imposes distinct obligation to prepare yourself for greater service to the country—in government, in commerce, in agriculture, in the home, as a citizen in the community. The number of positions open in universities in Japan is far less than the number of students prepared and qualified to enter them. For example, in the government higher educational institutions of the country, for the last year the Ministry of Education has furnished me information, the number of entrants was less than one-third the number of applicants. For the institutions now making up the new Niigata University there were over 3,300 applicants two years ago, but only about 1,100 were admitted. In the Niigata Koto Gakko [high school] only one student of six applying was admitted.

In my judgment, students who deliberately absent themselves in groups from their university classes (in other words go on strike) are unfair to the university, are unfair to their parents, are unfair to their government, and are unfair to the people of the country. The people of the country, in a time of terrific economic stress, through their taxes, are paying most of the costs for a university education for students who by striking deliberately and in organized groups spurn that education. By striking they not only fail to take advantage of these educational opportunities themselves but at the same time keep hundreds of their fellows from enjoying them. I feel sure that the only fair thing is for such students, after fair warning, to be discharged from the university in order to give their places to others who are eager for the educational opportunities which they spurn. A striking student has forfeited his right to education at public expense. . . .

A Successful University

You will not have a successful university if students and professors are fighting one another. You will not have a successful university if students are constantly striking or threatening to strike, particularly under instructions from outside Communist groups. You will not have a successful university if Communists are allowed to control any part of it and constantly stir up resentment, hatred and misunderstanding.

You *will* have a successful university if students, administration, and professors work together for the common interest—if they respect the true principles of academic freedom—if they constantly try to understand each other—and if they recognize that membership in the university family is an opportunity and an obligation to the future of democracy in Japan. I hope and trust that Niigata University will be such a successful university.

31
White Paper on Education Prepared by the Japan Teachers' Union

May 1, 1950

Source: National Archives of the United States, Record Group No. 331, SCAP, CIE, Occupied Countries, NEW 5386 (abridged).

Preface

We have resolved the evils of nationalism and militarism at a very high cost—surrender. We sacrificed millions of precious lives, historical inheritances that cannot be replaced, 40 percent of our national land and 70 percent of production facilities for that little piece of knowledge.

When we evaluate those precious things lost in the war, we cannot help renewing our hatred against the past nationalism. Those days were really the dark age of Japan's education, too. No individual dignity was respected. Japan's education was literally controlled by a force of faith that allowed no criticism. All educators were threatened or persuaded to devote themselves to the spreading of the faith. Japan's education paved the road to the reckless war and eventually to the ruin of the country. We cannot recall these experiences without shuddering and making a new resolution not to have another such era.

But the surrender brought about democracy with it. We became aware of the importance of human rights and dignity. We are now learning how to respect fundamental human rights and how to protect them. The new age is with us now, but it is our effort that makes it fruitful. To the new age we must give all the efforts of our organizations. The new age has just begun, where fundamental human rights, freedom, healthy and cultural life and equal chances for education are guaranteed by the Constitution, but, at the present stage, they are in name only. Democracy exists with us as a principle that regulates our life but has not yet materialized in our life.

The one-sided economic policy of the Japanese Government brought about a wide gulf between the rich and poor which inevitably resulted in the struggle between the two parties. We now understand, from the experience of the intense labor movement, what the basic cause of the struggle is. The renaissance is with us, but the old-line bourgeoisie has no power to bring about peace, freedom and democracy in the true sense of the words. The old idea is absolutely useless to us who are anxious for the reconstruction of this devastated land. We expect much of revolutionary ideas on a different basis. We want a new world where nobody exploits others, everybody cooperates with each other, and the working people can live happily. For the realization of such a happy world, we expect very much of education, since education is the only motive power that enables a peaceful revolution.

Once, an ignorant minister of our country provoked us by declaring: "The world is too busy to pay any attention to education." Education is badly needed in this country where such ignorance is allowed to exist. But our anger is now being organized into a motive power for the reconstruction of education.

It must be admitted that there are some teachers among us who cannot outgrow feudalistic ideas. But they are very few and can easily be [re-]oriented. Sentimental preachings on educational love and novel but short-lived educational techniques provide no solution of basic problems of education, no matter how beautiful and ingenious they may appear.

Motivated by zeal for educational reconstruction and in protest against the faulty politics administered by the Government, we have made this "White Paper on Education" in odd moments from our daily struggle. There are many things which are obstructing educational reconstruction but the worst thing of all is that education is given consideration apart from politics. Especially, the reactionary politicians attempt to purposely ignore the political elements which are hampering reconstruction of education, and seek temporary solutions. If politics are not connected with education, there is no need of the Minister of Education or of Boards of Education. Politics should play an active part in the reconstruction of education. We are trying to show the reason in this book.

As we stated above, this is not a perfect report, since it was prepared in odd hours. But we believe that we have shown the whereabouts of problems. We present this for your criticism.

In Book I, we take up the living and scholastic attainments of children. Children are "our greatest hopes" and the true foundations of education with regard to children's living. We surveyed their interest in play, reading and motion pictures, but we placed emphasis on the housing situation and the parents' economic conditions. For we thought that new education should start with a survey of the living environment of children rather than with competition of new teaching techniques. The most important thing this survey suggests is that chances for education are not equalized at all and that the cause of inequality lies in differences in the economic ability of parents. What we want to place special emphasis on is the fact that the current deflationary panic is exerting serious effects on the living of laborers, farmers and small tradesmen to the point where their children's lives are twisted and distorted. Deterioration in scholastic attainments is, as was reported in some commercial papers, now an unquestionable fact, casting a dark shadow over us. Troubles of the distressed people are shifted to their children. Juvenile delinquency and deterioration in scholarship ability cannot be solved with simple preachings of love. These are serious social problems.

In Book II, we present actualities of the implementation of the most imperfect new education system. The survey covers kindergartens, special schools, elementary schools, lower and upper secondary schools and universities, all of which show signs of the collapse of education resulting from meager educational appropriations.

Problems of lower secondary schools are so serious that they will eventually develop into serious social problems, along with deterioration in scholastic ability of lower secondary children. This section is about the schooling circumstances of students which are by no means favorable for them.

In Book III, we record actual conditions of teachers who are struggling under such circumstances. The data in this section are based on a long-range survey of a national scale. The hard living of teachers is widely known but statistics present the stern actualities which are far worse than is generally believed. These facts, while casting a shadow on Japan's education, drive us to the struggle for the improvement of teachers' livelihood. In Book III, qualities of teachers are also discussed, which, coupled with the sharp decline in the application for enrollment at teacher training schools, are major problems.

Book IV contains laws and regulations which provide bases for unfavorable educational circumstances. These laws and regulations, instead of providing political conditions favorable for educational reconstruction, are working as a brake to democratization of education. In this Book, we refer to the suppression of students' political activities. This was not a pleasant job because it reminded us of those dark days a few years ago.

In the last book, Book V, we examine educational appropriations as part of national and local finance. [Book V is not included here.]

We have described the outline of the "White Paper." But what we want to reiterate is that the new age has just started its Page One. Our workshops are left devastated and children are still suffering under pitiable circumstances. Our fighting spirit should be directed to the overcoming of these bad conditions. Political solution of these problems is most urgent.

Book I: Life of Children and Their Scholastic Achievements
(Brief)

Chapter 1: Life of Children

A study was made of all the children in the highest grade at 55 schools in Tokyo, including 706 children of lower secondary schools and 1,406 of elementary schools.

Education of Children and the Home

Of the 2,112 children studied, we find 210 elementary school children and 140 lower secondary school children with one or no parents, that is, 14.9% of the total respectively. According to a survey of the Women and Children's Bureau, Ministry of Welfare, an increase of about 565,000 widows occurred as a result of the war. With no statistics of pre-war conditions at hand we have no way of making a comparative study, but it is clear that children with one or no parents have been on the increase. A fairly detailed study was made of these children in connection with their family income.

Especially the children who have no father are in the worst conditions. A family income of less than 7,000 yen a month is true for 53—that is 33.5% of them—in the case of elementary schools, and 32—that is, 33.7%—in the case of lower secondary schools.

No decent home discipline can be expected of a family in such a wretched state, it is concluded.

Living Conditions

According to the *Ji ji* [a Tokyo newspaper] of 17 October, 55.7% of elementary school children live in owned houses, 26% in rented houses, 6.5% in rented rooms and 6.5% in official residences, government or otherwise, in the old city area of Tokyo, while 54.5% of lower secondary school children live in owned houses, 25.9% in rented houses, 7% in rented rooms and 8.2% in official residences.

That more than half of them live in their own houses gives us a rather rosy picture of the situation, but when we come to realize that most of those houses are nothing but shacks, things are not so bright as they appear.

The worst situation occurs in the case of the children who live in rented rooms. It fosters the habit of loafing around outside their homes. It is clearly shown in the increased number of run-away cases of children in these days.

In addition to the items mentioned above, "home study," "helping with the work at home," "play-ground," "movies and reading," "pocket-money and school expenses," "non-attendance and side jobs" and "conclusion: desirable home and school" are discussed in this chapter. However, these are merely studies and no reference is made to the policies which should be adopted to remedy the situation.

Chapter 2: Scholastic Achievements of Children

Here it was found that the scholastic achievements are vitally connected with the economic conditions of the family, educational environment (qualifications and experience of teacher and sex of teacher), facilities at school and cultural environment (urban and rural). It is concluded that economic conditions are the most important factor in determining the degree of scholastic achievement.

Book II: Condition of the New School System
(Brief)

Chapter 1: Actual Condition of Schools, Organization of Classes, School Buildings, Facilities, and Materials

Schools

The schools in Japan range in size all the way from those that have less than 10 students to those with more than 4,000. The average number of students is 373 for lower secondary schools, and 436 for elementary schools. Besides, there are 1,534 branch lower secondary schools, and 4,227 branch elementary schools. In fact there are too many small schools due to inconvenient geographical conditions.

Classes

Article 18 of the School Education Provisions Enforcement Regulations prescribes that the number of students per class shall be "less than 50." The average size of the class in Japan is 48.0 students per class for lower secondary schools, and 44.3 for elementary schools.

Attention should be called, however, to the fact that there are many single-class schools, classes in which the students of the second year and up are put together, and over-sized classes with more than 50 students. These evil conditions bear heavily upon the health of teachers, resulting in their frequent absence and an indifferent attitude in training children. This in turn brings about a lack of application to studies on the part of students.

School Buildings, Facilities, and Materials

Even the minimum standards on these points are not secured.

According to the statistics published by the Ministry of Education last year, 7,338 elementary and lower secondary schools, that is, 22.8% of all, had only 0.7 *tsubo* [a unit of measure equal to 3.952 square yards] school building space per student. In order to do away with such a condition, 521,164 *tsubo* is required for school building space.

One hundred forty-seven thousand more classrooms are required to meet the provision on the size of the class prescribed in the Regulations.

Chapter 2: *Actual Condition of the Distribution and Organization of Teachers*

Distribution of Teachers

At present the number of teachers per class is 1.21 for elementary schools and 1.59 for lower secondary schools. These figures include nurse-teachers and long-term absentees such as suspended teachers, tubercular teachers and those in child-bed. So the actual figures are still lower.

According to the notification of the Ministry of Education of May 28, 1949, the number of teachers per class necessary for lower secondary schools is set at 1.83. In toto, 68,700 more elementary school teachers and 43,400 more lower secondary school teachers, that is, 112,100 in all, are needed at present. If principals and nurse-teachers who do not engage themselves in actual teaching are deducted, the number will be still greater.

The result is the overburdening of teachers. The average teaching hours per teacher per day are: 3.9 in elementary schools and 3.4 in lower secondary schools. Besides, they put time in preparing lessons, filing, guiding students in life and studies in and outside school, their own studies, health guidance and clerical work if nurse-teachers and clerks are not adequately installed. This means that they work 10 hours a day. In addition, they go on official trips, teach class for absentees and attend workshops. These evil conditions reflect upon students, lowering their scholastic accomplishments and resulting in the deterioration of their morals.

Organization of Teachers

The organization of teachers should be considered in terms of their academic careers and experience.

In elementary schools the teachers who have not even finished the old system middle school are overwhelmingly great in number; that is, 51.7% of all teachers and 68.2% of women teachers fall into this category. Practically all of them have a teaching experience of less than 10 years; 52.9% of them have taught for less than 3 years.

In lower secondary schools 12.4% of all the teachers are those who have not finished the old system middle school.

In elementary schools, among the teachers who have not finished the old system middle school, 24.8% of them possess the teacher's certificate, while in lower secondary schools 20.6% of them have it. In other words, putting the elementary schools and the lower secondary schools together, we find 73,827 teachers of the sort mentioned above are unqualified.

Book III: Actual Condition of the Life of Teachers

According to the study by the Teachers' Union of 483 families of teachers with 5 members, it was found that they have a deficit of 800 yen per month.

We hear very often that teachers are not economically favored, but that they are blessed with time. This is not true. According to the study by the Teachers' Union of 1,100 teachers of elementary and lower secondary schools, the greatest number of men teachers works for 9 hours a day and [the greatest number] of women teachers for 8 hours a day. These are merely regular hours they put in for class work, guidance, care of school lunch, clerical work, etc. But in addition they are burdened with their work for the young men's or women's organizations, public citizens' halls, preparation for lessons, athletic meetings, report meetings, etc.

Next to spinning, teaching is the occupation in which the greatest number of women workers are found.

Of 2,315 childbirths by teachers in 1948, 11.8% were miscarriages, premature births and stillbirths, while the rate for ordinary housewives since the end of the war was 1.2%.

Book IV: Laws and Regulations on Education and the Question of Ban on Political Activities

The Fundamental Rights of Laborers Lost

1. The Ashida Cabinet enacted the National Public Service Law on October 21, 1947. A clear line drawn between government employees including teachers and ordinary workers restricted the labor movement and political activities of the former.

2. Soon after this, Cabinet Order No. 201, the so-called Potsdam Declaration Cabinet Order, was promulgated. Worse than the National Public Service Law in suppressing the Labor movement of government employees, it denied all the fundamental aspects of labor unions.

3. The Yoshida Cabinet enforced the Revised National Public Service Law on December 3; restricted extensively or forbade the group right, collective bargaining, freedom of political activities of national public employees; deprived teachers completely of the application of the three labor laws; put the management of labor relations under the jurisdiction of the National Personnel Authority, turning the teachers' union, a labor union, into a mere personnel union.

4. The National Personnel Authority issued all kinds of restrictive regulations one after another resulting in a complete loss of the fundamental rights of laborers.

5. The Yoshida Cabinet plans to establish a local public service law.

6. That the basic policy of the government is to suppress labor activities is an obvious fact.

1. Board of Education Law

The Board of Education Law aims at the local decentralization of educational authority as against the centralized, nationalistic school administration of Japan.

The greatest weakness of the Board of Education Law is that it is not vested with any financial power.

The next is the question of establishing Boards of Education. The existing law provides that Boards of Education be established in Tokyo-to, Hokkaido, prefectures, cities, towns and villages. The regional width of educational administration is something which should be determined by itself apart from the existing political demarcation. We have come to the conclusion that Boards of Education should be established in Tokyo-to, Hokkaido, prefectures and the five big cities.

2. Private School Law

The Private School Law was promulgated on December 15, 1949 and put into effect on March 15, 1950.

What we demand of the Private School Law is as follows:

1. Set private schools free from bureaucratic control.
2. Democratize the management of private schools to enhance their public significance.
3. In correlation to Article 89 of the Constitution, legalize government aid to private schools by local public bodies.
4. Establish a tax exemption policy for private schools. These points have not been satisfactorily realized.

3. University Management Bill

Starting from December 3 last year, the University Management Law Drafting Conference went into discussion on this matter.

The important points of the draft are as follows:

a. The view of the Japan Teachers' Union that the two members of the National University Council representing the Japan Teachers' Union be openly elected all over Japan was denied, and it was decided that they be appointed by the Minister of Education.

b. The idea of the Japan Teachers' Union that the National University Council should be placed under the direct control of the Cabinet was denied, and it was [put under control by] the Minister of Education.

4. Law Concerning Educational Finance

By the standard educational expense bill drafted by the Minister of Education, the School Finance Law and the School Standards Law are to be revised and the School Facilities Standards Law is expected to be enacted.

5. Law Concerning the Status of Teachers and Other Matters

a. *Teacher Certification Law.* The Teacher Certification Law was put into effect on September 1 last year [1949], but the greatest weakness of this law is its impracticability in connection with the matter of teachers in service who have qualified under previous certification standards.

On the basis of the assumed minimum expense for each teacher, 100 million yen is estimated to be necessary to effect workshops for certification in order to comply with the request of all the teachers. Everywhere workshops are confronted with difficulties.

b. *Law for the Special Regulations Governing Educational Public Service.* The law for the special regulations governing educational public service is the law which concerns itself with the status of teachers. As a whole, the law is weak in its protective aspect for teachers.

32
A Code of Ethics for Teachers
(Kyoshi no Ronri Koryo)

Japan Teachers' Union

June 1952

Source: Center for Japanese Social and Political Studies, *Journal of Political and Social Ideas in Japan,* 1:3 (1963), pp. 129–131.

Article 1. Teachers Shall Work with the Youth of the Country in Fulfilling the Tasks of Society

Upon our shoulders have been laid the historical tasks of promoting peace, ensuring the independence of the country, and realizing a society free from exploitation, poverty and unemployment. Believing in democracy, we are unswerving in our desire to fulfill these tasks.

The youth of the country must be raised and educated to become capable workers who will give themselves, each according to his own abilities, to the accomplishment of these tasks. There is no other road by which the youth of Japan can attain freedom and happiness.

Teachers shall live and work with the youth and shall be the organizers of and counselors in a schooling designed to meet this necessity. Each teacher shall make an intensive critical examination of himself and shall study and make efforts to prepare himself for his new role in education.

Article 2. Teachers Shall Fight for Equal Opportunity in Education

Equal opportunity in education and respect for the dignity of the individual as guaranteed by the Constitution are today still dead letters. The youth of today are severely restricted in their educational opportunities because of the social and economic limitations placed upon the individual. It may be said in particular that no serious consideration has been given to educating either the multitudes of working young people or mentally and physically handicapped children. Children are not being guaranteed equality of conditions for life and growth either within or without the schools. We have reached a point where eighteenth century individualism no longer opens the way to the development of the individual. Today social procedures must be followed in order to create equal opportunities in education.

Teachers shall of themselves be keenly aware of this necessity and shall in all quarters fight for equality in education.

Article 3. Teachers Shall Protect Peace

Peace is the ideal of mankind; war destroys all the hopes of mankind. Without peace the historical tasks facing Japanese society cannot be accomplished. The desire of the people for peace becomes strongest when individual rights are respected and when people are able to hold hopes for an improvement in social conditions and have a strong faith in progress. Discontent and loss of hope on the part of the people may serve to impel a country down the road to war.

Teachers shall be advocators of the brotherhood of man, leaders in the reconstruction of life attitudes, and pioneers in respecting human rights, and as such they shall stand as the most courageous defenders of peace against those who advocate war.

Article 4. Teachers Shall Act on Behalf of Scientific Truth

Progress takes place within a society when the members of that society, acting on behalf of scientific truth, seek a rational approach to historical tasks. Actions which ignore the fruits of science serve to suppress that in man which makes him seek progress. Teachers shall respect the progressive-seeking element in man, shall carry out scientific explorations on nature and society, and shall create a rational environment conducive to the growth and development of young people.

To these ends teachers shall share their experiences and shall work closely with scholars and specialists in all fields.

Article 5. Teachers Shall Allow No Infringements on Freedom in Education

Our freedom of research in education as well as action is often suppressed by improper forces. Academic freedom as well as freedom of speech, thought and assembly, although guaranteed in the Constitution, are nevertheless actually being restricted severely. Infringements on freedom in education serve to obstruct healthy learning by young people, to hinder intellectual activity, and furthermore to endanger the proper development of the nation. Teachers being deeply aware of this shall fight against all improper pressures in education.

Article 6. Teachers Shall Seek after Proper Government

Successive governments, under the pretext of making education politically neutral, have long deprived the teachers of Japan of their freedoms and have forced them to serve in whatever way the government has desired. After the war, having been given the freedom to participate in political activities, teachers banded together and fought for proper government, but now such political freedom is being taken from them. Government is not something to serve the interests of any one group; it belongs to all the people. It is the means for us to attain our desires in a peaceful manner.

Teachers, together with all working men, shall participate in political activities and shall pool their resources in seeking proper government.

Article 7. Teachers Shall Fight Side by Side with Parents against Corruption in Society and Shall Create a New Culture

In our towns and villages our young people are surrounded day and night by corruption of all kinds which is exerting a degenerative influence on their wholesome minds. Unwholesome amusements are suggested in movies, plays and even in the tales told by the neighborhood children's storytellers; degenerative tendencies are to be found in newspapers, radio programs, and in books and magazines; the type of atmosphere surrounding bicycle and race tracks and urban amusement districts tends to weaken the soul of the nation. All these exert a particularly strong and poisonous influence on the youth of the country.

Teachers shall combine their efforts with parents in protecting youth from the corrupting influences of society, shall live and work with youth in a proper manner, and shall create a new culture of the working man.

Article 8. Teachers Are Laborers

Teachers are laborers whose workshops are in the schools. Teachers, in the knowledge that labor is the foundation of everything in society, shall be proud of the fact that they themselves are laborers. At the present stage of history, the realization of a new society of mankind which respects fundamental human rights, not only in a word but in deed as well, and which utilizes resources, technology, and science for the welfare of all men is possible only through the power of the working masses whose nucleus is the laboring class. Teachers shall be aware of their positions as laborers, shall live forcefully believing in the historical progress of man, and shall consider all stagnation and reaction as enemies.

Article 9. Teachers Shall Defend Their Rights to Maintain a Minimum Standard of Living

Having been forced thus far to live in noble poverty under the proud name of educator, teachers have been ashamed to voice their demands for even the minimal material benefits necessary for their existence. To demand just recompense for their own labors would have been unthinkable to teachers of the past. Because of this situation, teachers have lost all desire and zeal for imparting to their students a proper education, and their lives have come to be ruled by exhaustion, indolence and opportunism.

Teachers shall consider it their right and duty to protect their own right to maintain a minimum standard of living and to fight for optimum conditions under which to live and labor.

Article 10. Teachers Shall Unite

The obligation which history has given to the teacher can only be fulfilled if teachers unite. The strength of the teacher is exhibited through organization and unity; organization and unity giving constant courage and strength to the activities of the teacher. Moreover, there is no other way today in which the teacher can establish himself as an individual except through unity of action. The teachers of Japan, through the labor movement, shall unite with the teachers of the world and shall join hands with all laborers.

Unity is the highest ethic of the teacher.

B. Consolidation and Reversal of Course, 1953–1960

33
Maintaining the Neutrality of Education
(Kyoiku no Churitsu no Iji ni tsuite [Tsutatsu])

Ministry of Education

July 8, 1953

Source: Ministry of Education Circular (Tokyo, 1953). Translated by James Vardaman.

As a fundamental of the educational system, neutrality in education must be rigorously maintained.

However, as can be seen in the recent case of the "Elementary School Pupil Diaries" and the "Junior High School Student Diaries," regrettably it too often happens that certain political parties seek to impose their political views upon the consciousness of students. You are hereby notified to take special care concerning the following points throughout the educational organization under your administration.

Furthermore, you are requested to advise the various school boards and school principals under your supervision.

1. Pay special attention that education is not used or distorted, to even the slightest degree, by any vested interest or particular political position.

2. As is apparent in the above-mentioned "Elementary School Pupil Diaries" and "Junior High School Student Diaries" carried out by the Yamaguchi Prefecture Teachers' Union editors, a diversity of educational materials can sometimes be selected and distorted to reflect certain positions. Because some materials are unsuitable as educational materials, related persons should pay special attention to the selection and omission of such materials.

3. Each responsible person should exercise appropriate supervision to ensure that staff members are earnestly carrying out their official duties. Whenever there is any infraction, however minor, the responsible person should take strict

measures to correct it. By these means we hope to totally eliminate unsuitable educational employees.

34
Law for the Promotion of Science Education
(Rika Kyoiku Shinko Ho)

August 8, 1953

Source: "Teaching Materials System in Japan" (Tokyo: National Institute for Educational Research, February 1984), p. 4.

Article 1. [Objective]: In view of the fact that science education is most important as the basis for establishing a cultural state, this law, in conformity with the spirit of the Fundamental Law of Education and the School Education Law, has as its objective the promotion of science education, assisting the citizens to acquire scientific knowledge, skills and attitudes and to cultivate their ingenuity and creativity with a view to enabling them to carry on their everyday life in a more rational manner and to contribute to the progress of our nation.

35
Report Concerning the Preservation of Political Neutrality of Teaching Staff *(Kyoin no Seijiteki Churitsusei Iji ni Kansuru Toshin)*

Central Council of Education

January 18, 1954

Source: Ministry of Education, Central Council for Education, Tokyo, 1954. Translated by James Vardaman.

The Council, recognizing the need to maintain the political neutrality of teachers, especially those in high schools and below, established a special committee for studying the subject. The entire Council met to deliberate the conclusions reached by the special committee and we herein report the results of the Council's discussions.

1

Teachers, like other ordinary public service personnel, hold the status of public servant, and according to the National Civil Service Law and Local Civil Service Law they are restricted in terms of political activity. Moreover, the Fundamental Law of Education proscribes all educational employees from participation in certain political activities. These laws emphasize the neutrality of education and attempt to maintain neutrality by restricting teachers from specific types of political activity. As we need hardly mention, children of high school age and younger, because they are immature spiritually and physically, are restricted in economic capability and legal capacity. Thus, even in terms of political consciousness, they have still not developed sufficiently to be able to make accurate decisions and therefore can easily be influenced in one direction or another by their education. At the same time, one cannot for whatever reason permit a teacher, who occupies a position of leadership and inspiration vis-à-vis these students, to advocate the special political philosophy which he or she believes in or to attack an opposing view. The various problems concerning the political neutrality of teachers must be addressed from this fundamental principle.

Since from the outset freedom of expression has been guaranteed for all citizens by the Constitution, restrictions concerning political neutrality, which teachers should observe, ought to be imposed only where they are deemed necessary for reasons of public welfare. Such activities ought to be restricted only so that they do not directly affect students and pupils, and the limitations established by current regulations generally fix the limits at this point.

However, teachers' union activities of late, although they may be said to be only indirect political activities, leave little room for distinguishing them from activities of political groups. And their influence upon pupils of high school and below, who are not yet capable of independent judgment, cannot be easily dismissed.

2

In an effort to determine the true situation of teachers' political activities at present, this Council has enlisted the assistance of the Justice Ministry and the police. In cases where investigations involved facts that have not been made public, we believed that we should avoid them, and we have therefore depended entirely on data which are universally recognized.

One of these materials is the fundamental policy for activities and "struggle goals" voted upon at the national convention of the Japan Teachers' Union. . . . But most of the activities are political in nature, and, setting aside for the moment the question of whether they support any particular political party, it cannot be denied that they are inclined in a definite direction. The 1953 basic policy contains the phrase "protect the children from Fascist educational policies based on rearmament." In the original, this read "in order to protect children from Fascist educational policies on the axis of the revival of the emperor system," but this was revised as a result of deliberations. Regardless, this cannot be considered neutrality in regard to government policy for education.

The second document studied is the second general meeting report, "Japan's Education," published by the Educational Research Conference, a cultural activity of the Japan Teachers' Union. The overall tenor of the Educational Research Conference is made clear in the report following, and it is anticipated that teachers who are union members will carry out education with particular political intentions and aims. . . . According to the preface to "Japan's Education," written by Oka Saburo, then chairman of the Japan Teachers' Union, in order to "confront the educational policies of the reactionary camp which is enthusiastically building militarism within education" it is hoped that the results of the research activities condensed in this report will be put to practical use. This conclusion is excessively political and unilateral.

Moreover, the section describing the report's contents includes the following passage: "The Educational Research Conference has determined the contents of this report aiming at the establishment of educational conditions for peace and independence, our fundamental historical task as teachers. The Conference investigated the conditions, resulting from the one-sided peace treaty which came into existence from the combination of the [Japan–United States] Security Pact and government accords, which we Japanese currently face not only in terms of politics and economics but in the distortion of education. For the true well-being of the citizens and children of Japan, this volume pursues how we must change education." Due to the fact that there are political parties that favor or oppose the peace and/or security treaties, this cannot but be seen as support for the policies of certain political parties.

One could conclude that as a result of the two treaties education has been distorted. On the other hand, however, this is also a biased political view, or at least a potentially political one, and it is extremely inappropriate to invoke it within education. In some current social studies textbooks, these two treaties are raised as items for study and debate, and it is hardly necessary to explain what type of influence the union-member teachers would have on the political consciousness of pupils if those teachers followed the guidance of the union's research conference.

3

Of the various problems involving political neutrality of teachers, the most important are: (1) That the actions of the Japan Teachers' Union, which embraces a large majority of elementary, junior high, and senior high school teachers, are overly political and, moreover, exceedingly biased; (2) That the union's resolutions and its course of action are binding upon 500,000 teachers who are its members; and (3) That 18,000,000 physically and mentally immature pupils receive instruction from those teachers.

The Japan Teachers' Union is an employees' association freely formed according to the Local Public Employees Law, and the formation of the organization itself is completely free. However, when one observes the actual activities, as previously described, the union-member teachers bring the political goals of the union into the schools. When one considers that this directly affects education, one cannot help but be apprehensive. Of course, we do not believe that at present all of education is as described, but to let matters take their own course would eventually be likely to yield an uncorrectable situation.

Therefore appropriate measures should be conceived to eliminate opportunities for employee organizations formed by teachers and/or federations of such organizations to exert biased political influence upon the pure political consciousness of young people.

4

Further, in addition to this, we believe the following are needed to establish political neutrality within education:

(1) It is necessary to establish even closer communication between the Ministry of Education and boards of education by various means including consultative conferences.

(2) As mentioned in the Council's first report ["Report Concerning Compulsory Education," July 25, 1953], teachers should not be allowed to become candidates for election to boards of education until one term of office has lapsed following their retirement.

(3) When teachers intend to make use of books other than textbooks—for example, summer vacation diaries—the principal of the school should notify the board of education. Further, jurisdiction of the Ministry of Education and boards of education concerning this matter should be stipulated.

36
Law No. 157: Concerning Temporary Measures for Ensuring Political Neutrality in Compulsory Education *(Gimu Kyoiku Sho-gakko ni okeru Kyoiku no Seijiteki Churitsu no Kakuho ni kansuru Rinji Setchi Ho)*

June 3, 1954

Source: Kanda Osamu et al., ed., *Shiryo Kyoikuho* (Tokyo: Gakuyo Shobo, 1973), pp. 468–69. Translated by James Vardaman.

Article 1 (Purpose of the Law)

Based on the spirit of the Fundamental Law of Education (Law No. 25, 1947), this law protects education in the various schools within compulsory education from undue influence and control by factional powers. This law aims at ensuring political neutrality in compulsory education, as well as supporting independence of the teaching staff of these schools.

Article 2 (Definition)

In this law, "compulsory education schools" means elementary schools, middle schools, and elementary school departments of schools for the blind, the deaf, and/or the handicapped that are established under the School Education Law (Law No. 26, 1947).

In this law, "teaching staff" means principals (in the case of elementary or middle school departments of schools for the deaf, blind, and/or the handicapped, it means the principal of the school to which that school is affiliated), teachers, assistant teachers, and instructors.

Article 3 (Prohibition of Instigation and Agitation by Means of Education in Support of a Particular Political Organization)

No one shall instigate or encourage the teaching staff of a compulsory school to make their pupils support a particular party or to educate them against a particular party, using the organization and activity of groups whose members are mainly the staff of schools regulated by the School Education Law (including organizations which mainly consist of such members) to promote or work against a particular political party or other political group (hereafter called "particular political organization") by means of education.

Article 4 (Penal Regulations)

Persons who violate the regulation of the last article are subject to imprisonment not to exceed one year or a fine not to exceed 30,000 yen.

Article 5 (Prosecution)

The following shall be responsible for the charges against these regulations:

1. In the national compulsory schools, the president of the national university (or its faculty) to which the school is attached.

2. In the public compulsory schools, the board of education of the local public body to which the school is attached (if the local public body is in a special district this would be the metropolitan board of education, or, in the event that there is no board of education, the executive organ in charge of the school concerned).

3. In private educational institutions of compulsory education, the governor of the respective prefecture.

Government procedure shall regulate the procedure of the above claims.

Addendum

This law shall be enforced ten days following the promulgation and will be effective until further notice.

37
Opinion on Technical Education to Meet the Needs of the New Era *(Shinjidai no Yosei ni Taio Suru Gijutsu Kyoiku ni kansuru Iken)*

Federation of Economic Organizations

November 9, 1956

Source: Federation of Economic Organizations, Education Section *(Nikkeiren)* (Tokyo, 1956). Translated by James Vardaman.

Recent progress in scientific technology in the advanced countries has been truly remarkable. In various countries, in order to deal with what could be called a second industrial revolution brought on by the sudden rise of atomic energy industries, electronic manufacturing and the diffusion of automation, serious effort is being concentrated on the systematic training of engineers and others with technical skills. For example, the USSR is training sixty thousand specialist engineers and seventy thousand middle level engineers every year. In the sixth five-year plan this is to be stepped up to produce another nine hundred thousand within five years. In Great Britain, the number of students in technical fields in universities exceeds by two times the number prior to World War II. This spring a plan was adopted that would in five years increase by fifty percent the number of senior technicians and double the number of junior technicians and skilled workers; and 100 million pounds (100 billion yen) have been appropriated to meet necessary expenses. In America, President Eisenhower has established a committee charged with establishing a positive plan for the training of scientists and technicians to counter those of the Soviets. However, in our country, though the postwar period has seen a reformation of the school system, virtually no attention has been paid to the importance of technical education. In universities the emphasis on law and humanities over and above science and engineering remains unabated. Even in compulsory education no significance at all is attached to scientific education or vocational education. If we do not establish a plan for the education of engineers to cope with the development of planned economic growth and strive to ensure the advancement of industrial technology, the scientific technology of our nation will gradually slip below the level of the rest of the world, and the inevitable outcome will be our losing out in competition with other nations. Our legacy to the next generation will be most regrettable.

We believe that the promotion of technical education is a pressing matter that will allow not a single day's delay. Therefore, to reform industrial technological education to meet the demands of the new era and to systematically cultivate scientists, technicians and engineers, we urge the government to take the following measures.

I. Systematic Training of Engineers and Technicians to Cope with Future Economic Development

It is of vital importance to estimate the number of engineers and technicians needed to meet the demands of expanding the domestic economy over the next five to ten years, the development of Southeast Asia, and the advance of technology. Furthermore, it is essential to establish annual guidelines and immediately implement plans for increasing funding to establish required specialty colleges (Semmon Daigaku), the constriction of the number of students in the humanities and the expansion of the number of students in science and engineering, the enrichment of technical high schools, the reform of technical education of working youth, and the promotion of science and vocational education in the elementary and junior high schools.

II. Promotion of Science Education and Vocational Education in Compulsory Education

Currently approximately half of junior high school graduates immediately take up occupations, and of these almost half work in industries as general technician factory workers. The foundation for the promotion of a nation's scientific technology is the thoroughness of scientific and vocational education in these early years. Therefore, efforts must be made to actively promote and expand these forms of education in elementary and junior high schools. In order to achieve this, reforms should be carried out concerning scientific and vocational education within teacher training and efforts should be made to raise the ordinary citizen's awareness of science education.

III. Promotion of Technical Education of Working Youth

1. In order to raise the general technological level of our nation's industry and increase productivity, it is necessary to train multi-skilled and specific-skilled workers to meet the needs of various industries. The training system for engineers under the current labor standards law is established as supervisory administration. Because uniform restrictions are in effect, the system is training too few engineers; currently in the basic heavy chemical industry there is a shortage of twenty thousand engineers. Henceforth, in order to train basic workers in sufficient numbers and with the level of training the industry needs, it is urgent that a special law be enacted that would actively foster this system. Large enterprises could, on the basis of this new law, organize the training facilities for multi-skilled workers and specific-skilled workers independently. But small- and medium-size enterprises which cannot set up training facilities within their firms could encourage cooperative training methods. The national government should devise means of financial support, and the national government or regional self-governing bodies should establish prominent facilities for training technical workers and support the training within these various enterprises. As to the train- ing of supervisory personnel, it is desirable that the national government establish a supervisory center. It would also be appropriate if a government institution could carry out the technical examinations for classifying trainees. To meet the desire of trainees to improve themselves, it is also desirable that, where necessary, training be tied to the part-time high school system and correspondence education so that trainees could attain high school equivalency certification.

2. The present circumstances of part-time high schools in which young labor-ers work during the daytime and attend high school at night, with the exception of special cases by region and type of industries, are hardly desirable either from the standpoint of efficiency in the workplace or from the [standpoint of] health of the worker. Therefore, the part-time schooling of youth with daytime occupa-tions should emphasize the vocational course rather than the regular course. Also, current correspondence education only offers the regular course; the voca-tional course should not only be added but made widely available. If both part-time and correspondence education offered these two options it would alleviate the burden of attending school part-time.

IV. Enrichment of Technical High Schools for the Training of First-Grade Engineers and Supervisors

1. In addition to training qualified skilled laborers to become first-grade engi-neers who assist middle-grade engineers and front-line site supervisors, industry for the most part employs graduates of technical high schools and trains them at the working place. However, in the high schools as in the colleges, the balance between the regular course and the vocational course has been lost. Even includ-ing part-time schools, the graduates of industrial high schools number no more than fifty thousand annually. This is insufficient for the future requirements of industry; therefore, the regular course high schools should be reduced as much as possible and technical high schools should be expanded.

2. Concerning the educational content of technical high schools, due consid-eration should be paid to the special characteristics of the local industries. Not only should necessary skills and knowledge be taught, but priority should be given to cultivating the character for becoming an industrialist and for achieving personal discipline. Since World War II, students of technical high schools have been seriously lacking in technical skills and fundamental knowledge. This is mainly attributable to the fact that the schools are limited to three years and that the quality of teaching staff has declined. Therefore, in order to attain an effec-tive beginning technical education, it is necessary to clear the way for coherent education which ties high schools and junior high schools in a six-year system. In order to raise the quality of teaching staff, reeducation and personnel ex-changes should be emphasized, [and] a consistent education in which courses of study and practical training are closely interrelated be imparted.

3. Training facilities of technical high schools are quite inferior to those of the workplace. Therefore, it is necessary to reconsider the Vocational Education Promotion Law and enrich the quality and quantity of education. Under present conditions, it is generally difficult for students to have off-campus training, but industry is willing to cooperate in on-the-job internships and the dispatching of instructors.

V. Reform of Education in Science and Engineering Universities for the Education of Engineers

1. Industry strongly feels the need for the kind of middle-grade engineers that pre-war industrial specialty schools supplied. In the long run, the present two-year junior colleges are unable to fill this need. Accordingly, two-year junior college should be tied with high schools to establish five-year specialty technical colleges, and these should be progressively enlarged. The inefficient overlapping of high school and college education should be corrected, and practical training and specialty courses should be enriched to fill the needs of industry.

2. In four-year universities, there is an imbalance favoring law and humanities compared with science and technology. In terms of student enrollment, the ratio is 75 to 25, even less than the pre-war 65 to 35. The number of science and technology students in colleges and junior colleges together—the future scientists and engineers—total only eighty thousand (twenty thousand in each year of university). Moreover, national expenditures for science and technology are extremely limited. Based on its long-range national policies, the government ought to reduce law and humanities and convert to science and technology (including special technical colleges), increasing national expenditures and subsidies for science and technology universities.

3. The number of class hours given to specialty courses during the four years of technology-related universities is thirty to forty percent less than that of pre-war three-year colleges. Therefore it is necessary to promote enrichment specialty courses within the framework of the current four-year system and to formalize and organize as regular course work students' off-campus practical training. It is necessary to greatly enrich fundamental courses and specialty courses, but in reality it is difficult to attain both completely. Rather, each university should take into consideration the special features of its location and its faculty, place emphasis on one or the other, and work for the realization of its various distinctive characteristics.

Needless to say, the purpose of school education lies not merely in imparting knowledge but in creating human character; therefore, in technology-related colleges it is extremely important to press home the logic of engineering. Accompanying the innovations in machine technology is the phenomenal advance of maintenance technology; therefore from now on courses on maintenance technology cannot be neglected in engineers' education.

4. To help advance scientific technology and elevate industrial technology, in addition to strengthening science and technology-related university graduate schools and striving for the cultivation of specialty science engineers and high-grade engineers, the system of assigning students to industries should be recognized as part of the master's degree program.

5. It is desirable to improve the quality of the teaching staff of science and

technology-related universities by means of study abroad and within the country. It is also desirable for universities to make arrangements for the reeducation of industrial engineers that will accompany the advance of industrial technology.

6. Science and technology-related universities should ceaselessly maintain close relations with industry, accurately grasp the requirements of industry, and give careful thought to means for answering those needs. For its part, industry should cooperate as much as possible by dispatching instructors, assisting professors in on-site visits, and promoting overall technical education and research.

38
The Emergency Declaration of the Japan Teachers' Union

December 22, 1957

Source: Nihon Kyōshokuin Kumiai, *Nikkyōso Nijunen Shi* (The Twenty Years' History of the Japan Teachers' Union) (Tokyo: Rōdō Junpō Sha, 1967), pp. 347–348. Translated by Denji Suzuki.

Through the tragic war we were able to realize fully that it was the educational control by the authorities that made men uniform and drove the people on to great suffering. However, now, ten years after the end of the war, Japanese education is confronting a crisis again.

The enactment of a new system of appointing local boards of education neglected public opinion and meant the complete control of education by the government and the control of education by the party. During the past year, the Ministry of Education has tried to restrain the teachers' freedom of activities by consolidating the former school inspection system, by enforcing the use of State textbooks at schools, and by making unilateral regulations of school administration. We are concerned about this situation.

Furthermore, with untiring ambition the government and the Liberal Democratic Party are planning to revive the subject of authoritarian ethics under the cloak of moral education, and are trying to enforce the Teachers' Efficiency Rating System under the pretense of promoting scientific personnel management.

There is no doubt that the Teachers' Efficiency Rating System is the means of giving the finishing touch to a series of reactionary policies in education, the prompt realization of which has been urgently desired. Its aim is to control the teachers by power and to crush their freedom. It also aims to deprive the teachers of educational autonomy, to restrain their free and creative educational activities, and to prohibit the activities of the teachers' union in a deceptive way.

The interference in education by the Liberal Democratic Party, as we have seen in Ehime Prefecture, is now done openly, and its method is even violent. For example, the declaration on December 10, 1957 by the Conference of Metropolitan and Prefectural Presidents on the Boards of Education throughout Japan vividly illustrates that the boards of education have become instruments of the Liberal Democratic Party. Thus, the spirit of the Fundamental Law of Education, by which educators should take direct responsibility for the whole nation without unjust control by a party, is thoroughly destroyed. We have come to the conclusion that such a tendency by the government, the Liberal Democratic Party, and the boards of education which are no longer autonomous, may cause a serious crisis in the future education of the nation.

Education belongs to the whole nation. It is closely related to the growth of each individual child. Also, the future of Japan depends on it. We who have direct responsibility for education, expect that the whole nation will give its positive opinion about education. At the same time, we swear that we will never neglect to keep an eye on this, and to resist strongly the reversed trend of educational administration.

Despite our strong warning, the Teachers' Efficiency Rating System has turned out to be a definite problem throughout the country. Because of our conscience, we teachers cannot but resent the violent acts which drive education into confusion and lead Japan into misery again.

Therefore, we five-hundred thousand teachers throughout Japan confirm that we are now in an emergency situation, and declare that we will persistently fight against the Teachers' Efficiency Rating System with renewed resolution, firm unity, and systematic activity in order to destroy the control of education by the powers.

The Japan Teachers' Union
December 22, 1957

C. Economic Expansion and Student Unrest, 1960–1973

39
The Advance of Manpower Capability and Promotion of Scientific Technology
(Kokumin Shotoko Baizo Keikake)

Economic Advisory Committee

July 1960

Source: Abstracted from "Government Public Sector Report," Chapter 3 of part 2 of the four-part *National Income Doubling Plan* (Tokyo, 1961). Translated by James Vardaman. (Abstract.)

1. Economic Growth and Manpower

Labor has never restrained our nation's economic growth. This has been due to an abundance of inexpensive labor. However, long-term forecasts reveal a slow-down in the increase in the number of workers, and as science and technology advance and the industrial structure changes there will be demand for an improvement in the quality of labor.

The main characteristic of the contemporary economy in this particular situation is that of technological innovation supported by continuous high-level economic growth and rapid advances in science and technology. It is essential to promote manpower development as part of economic policy in order to fully comprehend and utilize science and technology, and to sustain further development of our economic life in order to meet the needs of society and industry.

Manpower development can be attained by raising the educational standards of the nation and thereby instilling broad knowledge, the ability to make accurate judgments, and a proper sense of values. This means that it is necessary to create those primary conditions which build a modern society and thereby support high economic growth. Naturally, we should raise educational standards gradually over the long term, for such changes cannot be made overnight. Our nation's long-term task at this point is to complete secondary education. Yet the most important goals of this plan are to secure sufficient numbers of scientific technicians and skilled labor and to improve their abilities. Although technological advancement in the past has been achieved primarily by importing technical know-how from overseas, in the future it will be increasingly necessary to develop technology domestically, not merely assimilate technology from abroad. Therefore, measures must be taken immediately to train more technicians, so that their lack will not impede economic growth.

From the preceding considerations, we must strive to spread and improve secondary education, enrich scientific and technological education, and enhance vocational training.

Human resource development and deployment will become increasingly significant in the future. Due to the fact that human resources involve not only education and training, but also the economy, technology and social life, we will examine this issue in relation to economic growth and devise concrete solutions.

2. Technological Advance

Technology must be used to enhance the economic strength of the nation and to improve the standard of living of its citizens. In order to accomplish this plan, it is essential that standards of science and technology make remarkable progress, especially in establishing a domestic foundation from which to develop new technology. To do this it is necessary to reform the technology imbalance that has heretofore existed in industry and to take prompt steps to raise the standards of research at each stage, from basic research to application and development. It is also necessary to foster a closer organic connection between education, research, and production.

The fundamental issues in the advancement of science and technology are training capable persons, promoting research and development, and improving measures for industrialization centered on scientific and technical education. Cultivating capable people will be increasingly important in the future, due to the increasing need for researchers in new technological development and to the need for new types of experts in instrumentation and production control, and facility maintenance in the spread of automation. There is also rising demand for technicians in management and sales, while general managers and other staff members agree that they should acquire technical knowledge. Accordingly, in considering the greater demand for technicians there is immediate need for a concrete plan for increasing the fixed number of students in college departments of science and engineering. Otherwise there will be a shortfall of approximately 170,000 graduates within the period of this plan for national income-doubling. In addition to increasing the total number of students in the above-mentioned faculties, we must reexamine faculty and department structures in existing universities, and expand facilities in colleges of science and engineering and promote their efficient use in response to economic growth. It is also necessary to establish engineering schools in appropriate areas in accord with industry location policies and educational facilities distribution. These new technology universities should pay less attention to present educational methodology and should introduce new, more efficient methods of instruction.

In addition, in order to improve the quality of scientific technology, it is necessary to raise the standards of facilities, improve obsolete facilities and equipment, promote mutual use of both private and university facilities, encourage on-the-job training for students in private enterprise, and increase private industry support of university facilities. Due to the increased number of students in faculties of science and engineering, more teachers will be necessary, and therefore it is important for graduate schools of universities to train more teachers and actively participate in exchanges of personnel with industry.

Because of its technological backwardness, Japan has depended upon overseas technological know-how. However, in order to realize high economic growth in the years to come, it is desirable not only to import technology but also to promote creative research and development at home. In correlation with the national income, total research investment is estimated to be approximately 300 billion yen in the target year. This is approximately four times larger than the expenditures in 1958. The proportion of the national income devoted to research will increase from the 0.9% of 1958 to 1.3% in the target year. However, in considering the demands for raising the standards of technology in our country, it is desirable that the share of the national income used for research be raised to 2% (four hundred billion yen), similar to the percentage devoted to research in advanced countries.

In addition to expanding research investment, we must also coordinate its organization. It is necessary to improve research circumstances where superior researchers may demonstrate their abilities to the fullest, to enforce the function of the graduate school for cultivating researchers, and to establish a cooperative atmosphere as the scale of research enlarges, deepening the research done at each level and coordinating the various levels. It is also necessary to promote the exchange of information domestically and internationally.

We must further encourage coordination to assure that research consistently be done as an element of business activity, from the level of basic research to development research. Private enterprise should play an active role, especially in experiments in industrial application. In basic research, research related to national government projects, and research which cannot feasibly be handled by the private sector, university and national research institutions should in the future play a greater role in providing research information and technical assistance to small- and medium-size businesses with limited capacity for research development.

Further facilitating industrialization requires vigorous technological exchange, the establishment of cooperative efforts, and the concentrated application of capital. In order to increase the desire of enterprise to industrialize, it is hoped that the government will reform the patent system and reform the tax system with respect to experimental research. It is also necessary to assist the development of research in small- and medium-size businesses. Moreover, as technology and mass production increase, it will be necessary to institute reasonable standards.

3. Establishment of Education and Vocational Training

As the labor structure modernizes, more engineers and skilled laborers will become necessary. Under the present system of enrollment, there will be a shortage of 440,000 engineers with technical high school diplomas in the target year. Therefore it is necessary to greatly increase the fixed number of students in technical high schools. It is estimated approximately 1.6 million school-trained engineers and approximately 1.8 million retrained engineers will be needed.

In order to cultivate these high school–educated engineers, it is necessary to establish more industrial high schools, based upon industrial and population distributions. Courses should emphasize basic scientific knowledge and basic specialty knowledge, students' ability to apply knowledge should be cultivated, and the quality of facilities should be improved. Measures should also be implemented immediately to train and reeducate the teachers who will be needed in this expansion.

The significance and urgency of vocational training, alongside school education, has increased. It remains to set this forth in actual practice, as the nation still lacks understanding of this necessity. As industrialization advances to higher levels, we must institute retraining so that present workers may acquire the needed special skills and knowledge, and we must expand and improve apprenticeship systems for those who will enter the work force. This is also necessary for the smooth transfer of workers from sectors where productivity is low. Therefore it is necessary to examine laws to expand facilities of public vocational training institutions and measures for providing income during vocational retraining. Regarding technical training, we must strengthen vocational training in large enterprises and assist it in smaller firms where it is more difficult. It is desirable that technical proficiency examinations be disseminated in order to raise the public's estimation of those who have such skills.

Cooperation between industry and education regarding educational training will become more significant. The cooperation of technical experts and skilled workers in the private sector will be necessary to obtain a sufficient number of teachers and instructors and it will be important to coordinate school education with vocational training.

On the other hand, in the employment of youth it is vital to expand and strengthen vocational guidance so that young people may choose a profession that is appropriate and in which they may demonstrate their abilities to the fullest.

In addition to cultivating technical experts and skilled labor, a highly developed economy requires a policy that attempts to improve the aptitude of the general populace. Educational training is increasingly important for human resource development, the formation of human character suited to life within an expanded economy, improvement of the nation's life, and popularization of democracy. For these reasons, we must implement educational training of youths from 15 to 18 years old, a world-wide task.

As of 1960 the rate of enrollment in high school is 59.8%. It is estimated that this rate will rise in correlation with the rise of per capita income to 72% in the target year of this plan. It is necessary to establish more high schools, especially technical schools, since the number of students desiring to enter high school will increase during the period 1963–65.

By the target year of this plan, 24.4% of the population over 25 years old will have completed secondary education, doubling the 12.6% level of 1955, and the educational standards of the nation will have risen one step higher.

40
Request for Measures for the Establishment and Promotion of the Advance of Technical Education (*Gijutsu Kyoiku e no Kakkiteki Shinko Saku no kakuritsu Shinten ni kansuru Yobo*)

Federation of Economic Organizations and
Japanese Federation of Employers' Associations

August 25, 1961

Source: Sengo Nihon Kyoiku Shiryo Shusei, vol. 7 (Tokyo: Sanichi Shobo, 1983), pp. 117–118. Translated by James Vardaman.

In accordance with current rapid economic growth and technological innovation, the industry of our nation requires a large number of engineers. However, the number of graduates in the sciences and engineering has not kept up with this need.

This lack is liable to be increasingly felt as the economic structure continues to expand and as production structure and industrial technology advance. Furthermore, as we take into account the demands for technological support from developing nations, a deficiency of engineers will become a grave matter and one which may prove to be a bottleneck in future economic growth. In order to improve this situation—to raise the technological standards of our nation, to increase future international competitiveness, and to maintain long-term economic prosperity—it is extremely important for us to make rapid strides, both quantitative and qualitative, in our nation's technical education, which now falls several steps behind that of the West.

Although promotion of technology has been a major policy of the government for several years, implementation of this policy has been ineffective and it has not met the needs of the nation's constantly growing economy.

Confronted with this, we have seriously examined the possible solutions and come to the following conclusions: First, it is vital that the government take initiatives to establish and implement basic policies for the positive advancement of technical education. Given the urgency of the situation, it is also vital that the government establish emergency measures to remedy the current scarcity of engineers and call upon the cooperation of private industry.

We hope the reformed cabinet will take as its central concern the issue of strengthening technical education policy and we expect that the cabinet will eagerly support the following as urgent and significant national policies.

1. Government plans for the expansion of technical education, particularly the proposal to increase over a seven-year period the number of university students in the faculties of science and engineering to 16,000 above the current figure, requires a fundamental reexamination because these plans do not adequately address the current requirements of industry. In order to bring this about as rapidly as possible, we call for concrete plans that involve the national, public and private universities and which can be implemented more rapidly.

2. We call for major increases in the national budget and subsidies for expansion and modernization of technical educational facilities in schools. The government should take action to expand technical education in national and public schools at national or public expense. The government should also foster secondary measures such as increasing various subsidies, expanding the range of subsidies, raising national budget financing to financial institutions and exempting related donations from taxes.

3. It is urgent that the government establish measures concerning the expansion of technical education, including the hiring of teaching staff, increasing research funds and wages, and planning for promoting industry-academic cooperation. We especially request that the government consider drastic, exceptional measures concerning securing teachers and increasing wages.

4. The government should consider sufficient financial measures and other

positive national aid policies for sound growth and enrichment of technical high schools and the technical colleges which have recently been established. Furthermore, as a transitional measure, technical colleges should be carefully and effectively integrated with the currently existing educational system.

In this crisis, we in industry express our willingness to cooperate with these policies when they are established and promoted by the government.

41
Prime Minister Ikeda's Campaign Speech for the Upper House of the Diet
(*"Hitozukuri" Enzetsu)*

May 25, 1962

Source: Sengo Nihon Kyoiku Shiryo Shusei, vol. 7 (Tokyo: Sanichi Shobo, 1983), pp. 62–63. Translation by James Vardaman (abridged).

. . . Upon what grounds are we to hope for the development of a nation? Surely they are the grounds of the dissemination of education. And surely it is education and the development of technology which will bring about world peace and the greater happiness of all humankind. Perhaps our greatest aim as human beings is to free ourselves from the limitations of nature. To wit, the road to improving the culture of humankind is through surmounting the restrictions of nature by means of machines and technological progress. The progress of science and technology over the recent centuries has brought about the evolution of our way of life. Already the recent developments in man-made satellites have pushed the boundaries of progress beyond the limits of this earth into the development of space, and we have entered an age when human civilization can be constructed beyond this planet.

I believe that education is not merely the singular path toward the development of one nation, but also the foundation stone upon which is built world peace and the happiness of all humankind. Ladies and gentlemen, our precursors perceived this and, from the beginning of the Meiji period, they made special efforts on behalf of our nation's education. Ought we not to recall that what brought forth the progress of our nation today, despite the fact that defeat in war caused us to lose territory and left us surrounded by destruction, is the education which our forerunners bequeathed to us? This is not only true of Japan. It is worth noting that great emphasis was put on the dissemination of education in Great Britain in the nineteenth and twentieth centuries, and more recently in America and the Soviet Union. But we are fortunate that in these terms Japan may be called first among the nations. Japan today faces difficulties stemming from the rapid increase in the number of high schools. But in terms of the percentage of graduates of compulsory education who go on to high school, our nation is first or second in the world. In terms of the percentage of those who go on to college, Japan is second only to the United States, and ahead of England, Germany, France, and Italy. Japan's education has progressed this far, but these are only statistics. In terms of the quality of that education, although I would like to boast, I fear, unfortunately, that I cannot. Therefore, it is toward the issue of quality in education, from compulsory education through university, that we must henceforth direct our endeavors. I shall not mention the Japan Teachers' Union, but in compulsory education and in university education ought we not to take heed when education is used as an instrument of revolution?

Ill-informed as I am, even I have seen how education is being used as a means of revolution. I am painfully aware that we, together with the people of this nation, must conceive sufficient measures to deal with this. Who among us can assert that there is no need to worry when rights are insisted upon and duty is forgotten, when self-interest is mistaken for freedom, when respect for the individual and the world are lost, when love for one's home and one's homeland are lost, and when one loses sight of one's own homeland? The ancient sages said that it is not the enemy without that destroys the nation, but the weakening of moral principles within. The moral strength of our citizens is the best means of resuscitating our nation and realizing a truly democratic country. With this in mind, I am considering the expansion and strengthening of government policies concerning compulsory education, and as one effort in the direction of strengthening the ties between our nation and the youth and children who constitute the nation's foundation, I am considering a system of free distribution of textbooks. Moreover, I need not point out that if we are to build the nation of Japan, we must build human beings (*nigen o tsukuru*). Japan is restricted in territory and limited in resources, but the Japanese people themselves have an excellent constitution. Through education, the Japanese people can continue to cultivate this superb character and contribute not only to their own country but also show their fiber to the world through their efforts toward the peace of our nation and that of the world.

Since the formation of my cabinet, I have taken substantial budgetary measures to provide for the promotion of compulsory education and the development of scientific technology. In addition to furthering these measures, I am making efforts toward the improvement of the quality of our teachers, from professors in the universities to teachers within compulsory education, who are concerned with the fundamentals of the formation of human beings *(hito zukuri)*. Furthermore, I have instructed the Minister of Education that the current system of management of the universities is in need of reexamination— of course, academic freedom will be maintained. This is the general overview of my convictions concerning the problems which we are now facing in education.

Allow me to reiterate: In order to build a superior nation, a nation that will be trusted throughout the world, it is necessary for all of the Japanese people to love their homeland and their nation's culture and history, to attain sound judgment and superior technique, and to cultivate a character that will be respected by people throughout the world. That is precisely what new nation-building *(kuni zukuri)* entails. And I believe it is the exclusive means of contributing to world peace. . . .

42
Contributions of Education to Economic Growth

November 5, 1962

Source: "Japan's Growth and Education: Educational Development in Relation to Socio-Economic Growth" (1962 White Paper on Education) (Tokyo: Ministry of Education, 1962), pp. 7–9.

It is not necessary here to review the important role of education in achieving the social and cultural development of a country. Recently however, special attention has been directed to the relationship between educational and economic developments.

Many newly independent countries striving for rapid development in Asia and Africa are becoming deeply convinced that expanding and raising the level of education is the prerequisite for socioeconomic development.

Meanwhile, in the industrially developed countries, such human factors as scientific creativeness, technological talents, laborers' skill and the abilities to use completely all available resources have been recognized as affecting economic development, physical capital, and the labor force. The development of these factors, which might be identified as "human resources," will depend largely on the quantitative and qualitative development of education. For future economic growth to occur it is necessary to increase investment in the development of all available national resources. Education directed to the development of "human resources" should be considered as one of the most important forms of investment.

Under these circumstances, education should be looked upon not as a mere item of consumption but as an investment in economic growth. Education is an indispensable factor in the full utilization of the fruits of this period of rapid acceleration of technological innovation. In this context, regarding education as an investment should be more emphasized.

In this chapter, the relationship between education as an investment and economic growth will be observed from this point of view.

1. Role of Education in Economic Development in Japan

The contributions of education in achieving the modernization of our country since the Meiji Restoration (1868) might be evaluated from various points of view. Recently the interests of countries abroad have centered on the role of education in achieving the economic development of Japan.

The first point that was considered was the economic reconstruction after World War II and the prosperity that followed in Japan. The remarkable recovery from the economic losses suffered from the war and the following spectacular economic growth in this country as well as in West Germany are deemed miracles in the current world. It is said that this economic development has depended mainly on such human factors as knowledge and talents which had been accumulated since pre-war periods. Such accumulated knowledge and talents are no doubt the very results of education in the past.

The second point to be mentioned is the fact that Japan is included among such countries as Canada, West Germany, Israel, the USSR and the USA, which have achieved exceedingly rapid economic growth in this century.

Political, social, and cultural factors undoubtedly contributed to the economic growth of those countries, but the effects of these factors varied among countries in both kind and weight. The countries mentioned above as having achieved rapid economic growth, however, have one factor in common: namely, the important role of their educational institutions. Furthermore, it should be noted that the educational systems of such countries were intentionally modernized and strongly oriented toward technological progress and economic development. Japanese modern education also had been developed in this direction.

The third point in comparing the role of education in achieving economic development in these countries and in Japan is the introduction and diffusion of a modern educational system during the so-called "take-off" period to overcome disadvantages.

Japan now [1962] is approaching the economic level of developed Western countries, in advance of other Asian and African countries. This is despite Japan's relatively late start in modernization of society and industry, her overcrowded population, and her very scarce natural resources. Like Japan in Asia, Denmark in Europe is mentioned as a country which overcame such disadvantages of underdeveloped status, overcrowded population and scarcity of natural resources. A common basis for the economic development of Denmark and Japan has been the introduction of a modern educational system, especially the spread of general elementary education to farm families who constituted the major part of the labor force in the beginning of modernization. Thus, the role of modern education in achieving economic development in Japan may be said to have been very important.

Education in the early Meiji Era, mentioned above as the third point, supported the foundation on which the modern Japanese economic system was created rather than contributing directly to economic growth. In other words, the diffusion of elementary education raised the quality of the people's skills, modernized their thought, and made it possible for them to participate successfully in modern economic activities.

The second point mentioned above shows that Japanese education had successfully met the needs of industries that had developed on the bases founded earlier.

The first point stated above indicates that the unexpectedly rapid revival from the socioeconomic collapse following World War II, and the following prosperity in Japan resulted largely from the accumulated efforts of pre-war education.

Thus far, the high evaluation of the role of education in achieving economic development in this country should be attributed to the effort of the people who restricted consumption and invested the money thus saved in education. That the rate of educational expenditures to national income in Japan was among the highest in the world substantiates this statement.

43
Problems and Strategies in Manpower Development during Economic Growth: Report of the Economic Investigation Council *(Keizai Hatten ni okeru Jinteki Noryoku Kaihatsu no Kadai to Taisaku)*

Economic Investigation Council

January 14, 1963

Source: Keizai Shingikai (Economic Investigation Council) (Tokyo, 1963). Translation by James Vardaman (excerpts).

Chapter I: The Necessity of Manpower Policy

Significance of Manpower Policy

This report is concerned with the basic direction of our nation's future manpower development. First, we shall briefly deal with the scope and vision of human resource development in order to understand its characteristics. We have regularly associated manpower with economic growth. Needless to say, the issues that we must address are not only concerned with economic factors, but the economic underpinnings of our lives play a crucial role in improving the quality of our lives. Through productive activity we human beings realize these improvements. We should not ignore the role of the human being as a consumer in the economy, and when we consider man as the key to economic development we must focus on issues regarding the work force. In dealing with the development of human resources and the economy, we must be concerned with ways to cultivate skilled workers and ways to use those workers effectively. However, we must recognize a certain limitation, namely that manpower policies address only one element of man's economic life, and therefore such policies are only one way to enrich one's life. The rationale for cultivating and utilizing human resources in the work force must be considered as part of a larger organic whole whose goal is the improvement of human life and so the rationale must be adjusted to mesh with other policies.

The manpower policies which we have taken up herein place less emphasis on our nation's history and on comparison with foreign nations and more emphasis on the enrichment of the lives of our people.

We have focused on manpower as labor and have considered that its relationship with economic growth has always been necessary for the improvement of the national standard of living. In short, the goal of a manpower policy is to develop economic conditions for the enrichment of life and to develop manpower as an element in promoting economic growth. We believe that in such policies lies hope for the improvement of our lives and for the growth of respect for other human beings. Therefore, equal educational opportunities and the right to choose a profession by one's free will are the basic premises of this policy. . . .

The Background of Manpower Policy

Perception of Manpower Policies

Our present society, economic system, and practices, and the rationale foundations upon which they rest change as the society and the economy grow and change. Some elements which may have been practical in former times have been transformed in response to the new era. But adjustment to rapid change is usually delayed. In many cases these rationales may have a negative effect and may actually work against a smooth transition to a new situation. In such instances we need to be willing to reform the obsolete systems, practices, and ideas and endeavor to promote a successful transformation.

As we have just pointed out, the Japanese economy is now in a period of revolutionary change. Economic development, especially technological innovation, will have a profound impact on the reformation not only of the economic structure itself, but of our society and culture. If we ignore the situation we currently face it will generate serious confusion, and we will not be able to attain the economic growth that we had expected. If we recognize that human beings bear the burden of technological innovation, we realize that development of human resources is extremely important. How are we to deal with the issue of manpower development in this era of technological innovation?

Economic Development and Human Resource Utilization

As we have seen, high economic growth, centering largely on technological innovation, is expected in Japan. Thus it is imperative that we foster the development of human beings who can serve this purpose and that we utilize these people effectively. The present system of educational training, however, does not aim at developing the type of human talent that is equipped for such economic progress. Current forms of management and labor-management relations in the business world where such resources are most widely used are still in the early stages of technological innovation themselves. The gap between the education system and the demands of society has grown larger than we expected. Therefore it is necessary to review the content and the system of education for manpower development along with economic progress and to review the various factors involved in management and labor-management relations, in order to attain effective resource utilization.

Considering the issue of human resource cultivation in Japan from this standpoint, our prime concern is to improve the overall skills of the people in general. Doing this involves the major task of establishing vocational training in schools and in society as a whole and tying this together with the eventual goal of completing secondary education. It is essential to develop skilled workers, such as technicians and specialists, who will directly support and promote economic development, and therefore develop people with greater skills ("high talent").

In utilizing human resources it is also essential to modernize management of systems and labor management, and—of even greater importance—to rationalize the wage system. We must especially take into account the specialists, the middle and senior management groups, and female workers because they will continue to be pivotal in the future. It is also necessary to cultivate and utilize human resources from an international viewpoint, in line with respective international exchange activities. . . .

Chapter III: The Basic Direction of Manpower Development

Reformation of School Education

Enrichment of Science and Technology in Higher Education

First, it is essential to expand the scale of facilities of science which will be the base of scientific and technological advancement and to improve the teaching of subjects such as mathematics, physics and chemistry. Second, it is necessary to establish new departments in conjunction with basic education that take a moderate course between the current science and technology departments in order to train creative technicians who can develop new techniques and contribute to the advancement of technology by keeping abreast of technological innovation. . . . Third, we need to provide practical education for technology graduates who are to become industrial workers and to emphasize practical exercises for that purpose. Western Europe and the Soviet Union have adopted practical exercises on a long-term basis. An ideal engineer should be able to balance theoretical knowledge with the ability to use that knowledge in practical situations. Fourth, in the faculty of agriculture it is necessary to implement a more basic scientific perspective in promoting technological innovation in agriculture. . . . Fifth, we recommend the expansion of new advanced professional schools that would help meet the need for engineers. Sixth, it is especially necessary to enrich education related to scientific management technology in response to increased automation of business. And finally, it is necessary to improve the content of education and the scholarship system in graduate schools in order to foster the growth of creative scientists and technicians.

Improvement of Secondary Education

It is necessary to reform full-time upper-secondary schools to address both the demands of industry and the increase in the number of students who are going to high school. Within the basic curriculum we encourage the introduction of vocational subjects, especially practical subjects, which are simple, basic, and suitable to a broad range of students. Within the vocational curriculum we recommend the enrichment of technical high schools and basic subjects such as machinery, electronics and chemistry. We also recommend that teaching methods in certain subjects be reconsidered, including the introduction of an on-the-job training system. It is necessary to improve the content of subjects taught in agricultural high schools in order to provide appropriate knowledge for managers who will in the future administer large-scale mechanized operations. It is necessary to bolster . . . sections such as stock breeding, fruit culture, gardening, and machine and agricultural management, as well as to train people who will work in farm product processing, agricultural engineering, and related industries.

In part-time high school education . . . , we hope that employers, especially employers in medium and small enterprises, will be understanding and cooperative. We recommend the following ideas in the system of secondary education for those who have been unable to attend high schools in their present form. Currently schools require students to attend school during the daytime several times each week and divide education into a general course and a vocational course. Various forms of education should be developed according to the principle that a "subject" is taught in a classroom, but "practical training" is done in a real situation. The general course is open to all students, while vocational educational training varies according to occupations. We submit the following as a plan for secondary education. We recommend that some students be allowed to enter special vocational training institutes and farms that satisfy requirements for staff and educational content.

3. *Improvement in Education by Implementing
Meritocracy* (noryokushugi)

In order to implement a meritocratic system throughout education we encourage careful analysis and observation of the ability and guidance or those responsible for academic career development. Junior and senior high school is an important time for determining one's future occupation. We recommend the following be implemented for career guidance: employing a full-time counselor in junior and senior high schools; installing one expert in each school district to supervise the counselors in each school, and establishing a special organization to investigate and study issues of school guidance and to collect and distribute information. It is also necessary to improve the functions of vocational guidance. . . . Further, the standardized system of automatically promoting pupils to higher grades should be reformed into a more flexible system that takes into account individual abilities. It is worth examining the possibility of allowing pupils with sufficient ability to skip to higher grades, for example from the first year to the third year of high school. . . . This would also prevent a student with insufficient ability from moving to the next higher grade or school. The entrance examination, the only existing method of evaluating a person's ability and one which has made significant contributions, should nevertheless be reformed into a more rational system. This means it is necessary to administer a nationwide qualifying entrance examination aimed at allowing entrance to schools of higher levels based upon objective criteria. Only candidates who succeed in this exam should be allowed to take regular entrance examinations given by each university. If enforcement of the formerly stated policy is combined with rectification of the social custom of emphasizing a person's academic career, it would be possible to reduce the burden of examinees and revise the entrance examination system. This type of examination should be administered on numerous occasions each year to prevent the effect of accidental factors. An additional method would be to have an outside organization prepare the examinations on the bases of objective standards. . . .

The elimination of redundant elements of education is needed in order to develop students' talents efficiently. Although such endeavors have been made through the revision of the course of study, we hope that it will be further improved. We also recommend the establishment of combined junior and senior high schools, where students of special abilities may study. As to the matter of handicapped children, we encourage special education so that they can develop their potential and attain skills appropriate to their abilities. Manpower development goes well beyond school education. We need to provide re-education, adopting various kinds of human resources. Each individual and each enterprise would be greatly changed with such an effort. Many varieties of social education and systematic re-education will be necessary in the age of technological innovation. We should search for solutions to these problems by enhancing the cooperation of industry and education. Moreover, adult education for the middle-aged is necessary to enable them to cope with the changes in contemporary society and to keep up with their professions. . . .

44
Japan Teachers' Union 1966 Convention Goals

May 1, 1966

Source: Nikkyōso (Japan Teachers' Union), *Dai Sanjūunikai Teiki Taikai Gian* (Proposals of the Thirty-second National Convention) (Tokyo, May 1966), p. 1. Translated by James Vardaman.

1. Intensify the joint struggles of all public servants for the early attainment of a large salary increase.

2. Oppose dismissals of teachers, increase the number of teachers over and above the limit set by the government, and increase the education budget for the improvement of education and our working conditions.

3. Intensify our struggles for teachers' rights and recapture our fundamental labor rights.

4. Oppose education controlled by the central government, promote the independent research and study of education, and abolish the achievement tests and the Nōken Test. Promote the People's Movement for a New Education in order to provide secondary education for all.

5. Oppose the "invasion" of Vietnam, destroy the United States–Japan Security Treaty, prohibit the nuclear rearmament of Japan, return Okinawa from American control, and intensify the People's Movement for Peace.

6. Establish our labor union at each workshop (school), intensify the unity and solidarity of our 600,000 members, and expand our organization.

45
The Image of the Ideal Japanese
(Kitai Sareru Ningenzo)

December 15, 1966

Source: Ministry of Education, Central Council for Education, "Report: Concerning the Expansion and Consolidation of Upper Secondary Education" (Tokyo, 1966). Translated by James Vardaman.

Part I—Problems Facing the Japanese Today

1. Characteristics of Modern Civilization

This is the age of science and technology. However, industrialization has had a dehumanizing effect upon man. The extraordinary progress of natural science, industry and technology has shown the danger that man may be controlled by machines. Thus man is in danger of being mechanized for the sake of technological advancements.

The economic prosperity which Japan has been enjoying has produced hedonistic tendencies and a spiritual vacuum. If this continues, the long-range prospects of sustained prosperity are threatened. The continued industrialization of Japan must cultivate man's creativeness. In this modern age, the "humanity" of man must be elevated. Otherwise man will merely be a means of production in an industrial society.

2. Contemporary International Situation

The experience of defeat in World War II has brought about a serious transformation in the way the Japanese people think about their country and society. Our people are laboring under the delusion that everything in Hawaii's past is wrong, with the result that they ignore Japanese history and the national ethos. To be sure, there are negative aspects about Japan's past, but there are also so many positive characteristics that must be understood in developing a new image of a Japanese man.

Today Japan finds itself in the middle of the conflict between East and West, North and South. Japan must, therefore, be conscious of this position and must be acceptable to the world at large. However, this does not mean that we are to forget that we are Japanese. We can be effective citizens of the world with a clear awareness of our international responsibilities when we are truly Japanese. We must be strong-minded and resolute, both morally and spiritually, to maintain the independence of our nation.

3. Japan Today

Democracy in Japan is still in an immature state of development. There is much confusion about the understanding of democracy, which has not yet taken root in the Japanese mind. Opinions are divided between those who interpret democracy from the standpoint of independent individuality and those who interpret it as a class struggle. If the latter position prevails, the essence of democracy will be destroyed. After the war, the Japanese people lost their traditional virtues of national solidarity and national consciousness. In addition, a firm sense of individual dignity has not been achieved. While continuing the development of individuality, it is also our task to assume a common responsibility for our country.

Part II—The Ideal Japanese

1. The Ideal Japanese as an Individual

  A. To Be Free. Man has human dignity which is the foundation for human rights. The fundamental element of that dignity is freedom. But responsibility accompanies freedom. The postwar tendency to stress freedom and rights while ignoring responsibilities and duties is a misinterpretation of freedom. To be free means to accept responsibilities.

  B. To Develop Individuality. Man is unique because of his individuality. Men are equal in dignity but different in individuality. By developing one's talents, one can fulfill one's individual mission.

  C. To Respect Oneself. Man loves himself instinctively. But it is important for man to love himself correctly, which means to cultivate one's ability and respect for life. Then will the purpose of life be appreciated. Mere pursuit of pleasure deteriorates man, so one must know what is more important in life than mere pleasure. Through this, one can come to realize oneself.

  D. To Be Strong-Minded. A reliable and trustworthy man is a strong-minded and courageous man who does not follow others blindly. He is also a person who can share happiness and sadness with others.

  E. To Be Reverent. As a basis for the above, it is important to have reverence for the origin of life. At the source of our being are our parents, our nation, and mankind. Love for mankind, human dignity and true happiness grow out of this feeling of reverence for life's origin.

2. The Ideal Japanese as a Family Man

  A. The Home as a Place of Love. Love is inherent in man, but it must be purified and disciplined by morals in the home. Chastity, filial duty, and love between brothers and sisters are the moral traits to be cultivated.

  B. The Home as a Place of Rest. The home will provide a haven of rest amidst our busy society. It is a place where man can find himself within our mass society and mass civilization.

  C. The Home as a Place of Education. The atmosphere of the home influences children and helps them grow up. Parents, in turn, train themselves through the education of their children. Children must listen to their parents. We must, however, never forget the dignity of parents as well as parental love for children.

3. The Japanese as a Member of Society

A. Respect for Work. Society is the source of production which provides greater happiness for its members. For that purpose we must love our work and devote ourselves to it. Through work we can live a good life and help others also to live a better life.

B. Contribute to the Social Welfare. The development of science has given us many blessings as well as many troubles. It has indeed helped us to solve many of man's problems. However with the development of industry, the growth of cities, traffic congestion, air pollution, etc., man is threatening his existence with the deterioration of his environment. Our modern society has become so interrelated that the individual's welfare cannot be separated from the general welfare. Hence it is essential that a spirit of social service be promoted based on a sense of social solidarity.

C. Creativity. In this age of popularization of culture, society tends to be pleasure-seeking and wasteful. We must develop a productive and creative society emphasizing our traditional virtues of work and economy. A constructive and creative man loves his work and devotes himself to it, be it on the farm, in the factory, or in the school.

D. Respect the Social Norm. The most conspicuous deficiency of Japanese society is social confusion. Japanese are not sensitive enough to social justice. It is most important to observe the laws which guarantee our freedom.

4. The Ideal Japanese as a Citizen

A. Proper Patriotism. It is through the state that we find the way to enjoy our happiness and contribute to human happiness throughout the world. To love our nation properly means to try to enhance the value of it. The man who is indifferent to his own nation is the enemy of his own country.

B. Respect for Symbols. We have loved and respected the Emperor. This was not separated from loving Japan and respecting its mission."The Emperor is the symbol of Japan and the unity of the people. This position is based on the will of the people wherein lies the sovereignty." We must give deep thought to the fact that loving and respecting the Emperor is synonymous with loving and respecting the Empire.

C. Development of Japanese Character. Those nations that contributed most to the world have all had their distinctive characteristics. And so it was during and after the Meiji period when the unique characteristics of the leaders and people of those days made the modernization of Japan possible. We can be distinctively Japanese today by looking back upon our own history and traditions.

46
Course of Study for Junior High Schools: Moral Education

1969

Source: Ministry of Education, *Lower Secondary School Course of Studies* (Tokyo: Ministry of Education, 1969), pp. 145–48.

I. To make an effort to respect human life, maintain security, and lead a life of moderation and harmony.

    1. To respect the lives of others and to secure the sound growth and development of both mind and body.

    2. We should try to lead a steady life with self-control, and not give way to impulse.

II. To understand the basic habits of daily life and to regulate them.

    3. Try to form such habits as keeping things in order and try to deal with everything systematically.

    4. Try to understand the meaning of courtesy so as to be able to use appropriate language and to behave appropriately according to the time and place.

III. Try to cultivate a positive attitude toward work and the habit of carrying through a task to completion.

    5. Do not hesitate to make a decision, but carry out courageously those acts you believe to be right.

    6. Carry out your duties and responsibilities with confidence and persistence, overcoming all obstacles.

IV. Always try to think independently, decide things for yourself, and accept the responsibility for what you do.

    7. Try to have pride as a man, and develop your self-control.

    8. Do sincerely whatever you choose to do, and accept the consequences willingly.

V. Try to respect others' opinions on the basis of understanding and confidence, and try to learn from them.

9. Try to respect everybody's personality and tolerate others' different opinions and actions.

10. Try to listen to others' opinions with modesty and a desire for self-improvement, and not be complacent.

VI. Try to know the value of work and seek a fulfilling life that may lead to real happiness.

11. After accomplishing what you must do, you will know the job of work. In doing so you will come to understand the basic concept of a profession.

12. Determine for yourself a way of life which will satisfy you from the bottom of your heart, not acting only from immediate desires and present pleasures.

VII. Try to build a positive and sincere attitude toward life not allowing yourself to be directed by others, but to love truth and realize your own ideals.

13. Try to judge things objectively and rationally and to search continually for truth.

14. Do not compromise too easily and do not indulge in unnecessary daydreaming, but try steadily to realize your ideals.

VIII. Be humane and try to cultivate a rich mind which responds to what is beautiful and noble.

15. Recognizing that man has both frail and weak aspects as well as strong and noble aspects, try to develop an attitude of loving human beings.

16. Love nature, aspire to beauty and try to develop your mind so as to feel that creative force which is greater than man.

IX. Try to establish a good human relationship with friends, male or female, understanding, respecting, and encouraging each other.

17. Try to establish a constant relationship with friends, loving and respecting them and helping them develop.

18. Boys and girls should come to understand each other's characteristics, through pure-minded association.

X. Try to understand the significance and aims of the groups to which you belong and try to enrich community life.

19. Build a wholesome family life through affection, consideration, and respect for each family member, realizing your role as a family member.

20. Try to value the unity of groups; do your share willingly to contribute to the betterment of the community.

XI. Try to understand the spirit of law and the meaning of order; so that you can learn to discipline yourself.

21. Honor the rules of groups, cooperate with and evaluate each other so that you can improve the order and discipline of the group.

22. Value the attitude of respect for law; try to carry out your responsibilities to the letter as well as to assert your rights.

23. Make a clear distinction between public and private affairs, and try to develop the morality necessary as a member of a democratic society.

24. Love justice and conquer selfishness and narrow cliquishness; try to work together to bring about an ideal society which has no discrimination.

XII. Love your country as a Japanese and try to aim to be a man who can contribute to the welfare of his fellow men, as well as to contribute to the development of our country.

25. Deepen your understanding and affection toward our land and culture and try to be useful in transmitting and creating still more excellent traditions.

26. Be always aware of the international point of view and try to be a man who can contribute to world peace and the happiness of all mankind.

47
A Proposal Concerning the Fundamental Issues of Education *(Kyoiku no Kihon Mondai ni Taisuru Teigen)*

Japan Federation of Employers' Association

September 1969

Source: Nikkeiren (Japan Federation of Employers' Association), (Tokyo, 1969)

There is serious debate today concerning the forms which education ought to take in the school, at home and in society at large.

In our separate report, "Opinions of Industry Concerning the Fundamental

Issues of Education," we have discussed the issues and we now make the following proposals to solve the urgent problems we face.

We call on the government and other related organizations to give full consideration to the purport of industry's views and call on them to deal firmly with the fundamental problems.

1. Learning a lesson from the 6–3–3–4 educational system's failure to adapt to diversification in education, we call for drastic reforms, especially in secondary and higher education.

Furthermore, we urge that consideration be given to making the age for entering school one year earlier.

2. The system for training primary and secondary school teachers and instilling them with a great sense of their mission in society should be firmly established.

3. An impartial third-party system should be established to examine qualifications of university faculty and staff.

4. A qualification authorization system should be established to provide a unified standard for the recognition of university students' graduation and credentials.

Furthermore, through the creation of this type of qualification system, equal educational opportunities should be devised for those who do not go on to university.

5. The mass media, including television and radio, should be actively utilized on behalf of school education and social education.

6. In home education and primary education, great social emphasis should be attached to discipline (politeness, gratitude, sense of public duty, kindness) appropriate to the new social circumstances.

7. Government and local public organizations should secure locations for the improvement of physical fitness of children, students and young adults and expand the facilities therein.

48
Problems Concerning Students

1964

Source: Higher Education in Postwar Japan: The Ministry of Education's 1964 White Paper, ed. and trans. John E. Blewett (Tokyo: Sophia University Press, 1965), pp. 93–114.

Section 1: University Entrance Examination

1. Entrance Examination under the Old System

1) University Applicants in Prewar Days

The former school system was a multi-track one, each track having its own steps of advancement. For example, in order to enter a university one went first to a middle school (or an elementary course of a higher school), then through the advanced course of a higher school, or the university preparatory school. Those who wished to attend technical colleges had to be graduates of middle or girls' high schools. Higher vocational schools required diplomas from either a middle school or an upper-type vocational school.

The above, however, were general rules, and, as ordained by the Minister of Education, those who proved to have attainments equal to or higher than the graduates of accredited schools could also, theoretically, enter institutions of higher learning. It was, in actuality, simplest to go through a middle school. As Table 48.1 shows, most of the students in the advanced courses of higher schools and university preparatory schools as well as in normal schools and higher vocational schools were graduates from middle schools. That is to say, the possibility of attending a university was more or less determined by whether one entered a middle school or not. And most of the middle school students were from well-to-do families. Thus, the number of entrants into middle schools in 1935 and 1940 respectively, 80,641 and 110,486, was very much smaller than the number of those now entering high schools.

Table 48.2 shows that the competition to enter high schools was considerably keener than that for university preparatory schools or technical colleges. This was due to the fact that higher schools were the direct routes to the imperial universities. Entrance to universities was easy since the annual registration quota of the national higher schools, which constituted the large majority of all higher schools, corresponded roughly with the freshman entrance quota of the national universities while graduates of university preparatory schools were admitted to the university departments as a matter of natural process. As indicated in the same table, entrance into technical colleges and higher vocational schools was comparatively difficult.

2) The Amelioration of Entrance Examination Methods

The severe competition to enter higher schools resulted in a tendency to put excessive emphasis on the purely academic side of education, and middle school students were bedeviled by preparations for entrance examinations. Several attempts were made to rectify the situation.

Table 48.1

Type of Previous Education of Entrants to Higher Schools and Technical Colleges in 1935 (unit: %)

Kind of school		School of graduation	Middle school	Girls' high school	Candidates for technical schools	Other	Total
Higher	Total	100.0	—	—	—	100.0
	National	100.0	—	—	—	100.0
	Public	100.0	—	—	—	100.0
	Private	100.0	—	—	—	100.0
University Preparatory	Total	84.8	—	13.6	1.6	100.0
	National	93.5	—	3.6	1.9	100.0
	Public	99.1	—	0	0.9	100.0
	Private	84.1	—	14.4	1.5	100.0
Technical	Total	55.2	14.8	25.2	4.8	100.0
	National	88.3	3.6	4.2	3.9	100.0
	Public	25.9	59.5	3.3	11.3	100.0
	Private	55.0	13.5	26.9	4.6	100.0
Vocational	Total	81.2	0.3	17.1	1.4	100.0
	National	82.3	—	15.8	1.9	100.0
	Public	64.5	—	35.5	—	100.0
	Private	80.4	1.2	18.2	0.2	100.0

Notes:
1. "Candidates for technical schools" means those who were approved for technical or vocational education as equal to or above middle school graduates.
2. Special sections of national universities are not included.
3. Middle school graduates include those who finished four years of middle school or the normal courses of higher school.
4. Girls' high school graduates include those who finished four years of the same.

Table 48.2

Rates of Competition for Entrance into High Schools and Universities in 1935, 1940 (unit: 1)

Type of university		High schools	Universities	Technical colleges	Vocational schools
1935	Total	6.7	1.4	2.0	6.0
	National	7.3	1.7	2.9	6.8
	Public	4.2	1.2	2.7	6.8
	Private	1.8	1.1	1.9	3.2
1940	Total	6.3	1.6	2.6	4.4
	National	6.5	1.5	2.1	3.9
	Public	5.0	1.3	3.5	7.1
	Private	4.6	1.6	2.6	4.6

Note: Special sections of national universities are excluded.

Table 48.3

Educational Background of Entrants into Old-System Universities (1935) (unit: %)

Type of university	Schools of graduation	Higher schools	University preparatory schools	Technical colleges	Other	Total
Total		36.2	44.8	15.2	3.8	100.0
National	Total	81.7	7.6	6.5	4.2	100.0
	Imperial	86.6	5.5	3.5	4.4	100.0
	Government	59.6	17.0	19.7	3.7	100.0
Public		—	83.5	16.5	—	100.0
Private		3.4	72.3	20.0	4.3	100.0

Notes:
1. Hiroshima and Tokyo Universities of Literature and Science are not included in government universities.
2. Technical schools include vocational schools.

The revision of entrance examination methods made in 1927 by higher schools and higher vocational schools was one such attempt. According to this revision the applicant's grades in his former schools were to have value equal to the results of the entrance examination. The subjects of the examination were restricted to three or less for the advanced courses of higher schools, and four or less for the higher vocational schools. Character judgment based on an oral test was allowed, and the selection of applicants was to rest on these three factors plus a physical examination. The universities gave selected examinations only when the number of applicants exceeded the freshman entrance quota. The subjects of the examination in this case were selected from the courses taught in the higher schools.

According to the University Law, those who had completed a university preparatory school or the advanced course of a higher school, or those who had ability equal to such students or above were qualified to enter a university. Thus a graduate of a normal school or a higher vocational school could apply for a university, but in reality, except for universities which had special affiliations with these schools, it was difficult for an outsider to be admitted. This is brought out in Table 48.3.

After the war, it was decided that the selection of entrants for higher schools and technical colleges should be based on an overall judgment of four factors: written test, oral test, a report from the principal of the applicant's former school, and a physical examination. The questions asked in the written test given in 1946 covered the entire middle school curriculum, and were not limited to specified subjects. This was in consideration of the confused state of affairs in education during that period. The content of this particular examination was inadvertently very similar to that of the later scholastic aptitude test. In 1947 the written examination was subdivided into intelligence and achievement tests. The intelligence test for national universities was formulated by the Question Planning Committee of the Education Ministry, and after 1948 was given apart from entrance examinations under the name of scholastic aptitude test.

2. Entrance Examinations to New-System Universities

In 1949 the new-system universities were formally inaugurated, with the graduates from the new-system high schools as their first-year students. The selection of entrants was based on the results of the written examination (scholastic aptitude test and achievement test), a report from the principal of the applicant's former school, and a physical examination. The achievement test was, naturally, formulated in accordance with the educational method of the new-system high schools, but since not a few of the applicants were graduates from old-system schools efforts were made to formulate questions applicable to both systems.

The subjects of the examination were: Japanese, social studies, mathematics, science, and foreign languages. These were given as fundamental subjects, although at times some subject was excluded. The students were allowed some choice in the questions they wished to answer. Further, in consideration of the possibility that the university staff that formulated questions might not have sufficient understanding of the educational content and the objectives of the new-system high schools, pamphlets on the method of question formulation, with sample questions, entitled "Explanation of the Method of Selective Examination," were distributed to the universities.

3. Scholastic Aptitude Test

The intelligence test which was given as a part of the written examination in 1947 was separated from the entrance examination in the following year and came under the jurisdiction of the Scholastic Aptitude Test Control Committee, and was given throughout the country simultaneously. It was decided that all applicants for entrance to national, public, or private universities of both old and new systems, higher schools, and technical colleges must take the national scholastic aptitude test or one given by an individual university. Although an applicant had a choice between the two, those who wished to enter national universities were required to take the national aptitude test, and even the private universities gradually began to depend on it for such reasons as the difficulty of making up examination questions for their own institution only.

The aim of this aptitude test was to forestall such undesirable phenomena as excessive study and competition arising from too much emphasis on the purely scholastic side of the examinations, and to select students fitted in all respects to acquire higher education. Consequently this test was designed to examine, with comparatively simple materials, the applicant's intellectual power of application, and so, theoretically, did not need special preparation on the part of the examinee. The test was divided into parts on humanities and sciences. Average scores, learned by national sampling, were published, and by comparing one's own test result with this average, one could know one's relative ability and aptitude and could receive suitable guidance.

The aptitude test was given once a year and both its method of administration and content were gradually improved. However, neither the universities which should have used it in their selection of entrants, nor the high schools which should have used it for guidance of students took advantage of it. It was discontinued in 1955, as criticism of the increasingly keen competition for university entrance became audible.

Criticism was raised, above all, by the parents of those who failed in the aptitude test, which constituted the first step of the entrance examination, and who therefore lost the opportunity to take the scholastic achievement test. Their point of contention was that even though the aptitude test was to determine the inherent abilities of a student, the way in which it was administered seemed to deny the efforts made by an individual.

The second criticism was raised by the high schools which contended that the preparation for the aptitude test was an added burden on the students who had to study for the scholastic achievement test, and consequently caused disturbance in the normal course of education. Later, a follow-up study was made by the National Research Institute for Education, comparing the results of the aptitude and scholastic achievement test with the college grades, in order to determine the validity of the aptitude test. According to this study these facts were discovered: (1) compared with the scholastic achievement test, the aptitude test had a closer relationship with the specialized studies of the universities than with the courses in general education; (2) when the applicants fresh from high schools were compared with the *rōnin* [high school graduates who have taken and failed the entrance exam at least once], the achievement test results of the latter were better, but no marked difference was noticeable in their aptitude test results; (3) of the students who received the same marks in the scholastic achievement and the aptitude test, the new-system high school graduates scored better grades in the universities. These findings testified to the importance of the aptitude test, as a supplement to the scholastic achievement test, in determining the abilities of the students.

4. The Present Condition of University Entrance Examinations

The new school system took a single-line form of progression, which meant that an increase in the number of those desirous of acquiring higher education resulted directly in the increase of university entrance applications. In other words, more enrollments at new-system middle and high schools means more applications for university entrance. The universities have enlarged their quota of registrations, but some differences depending on the original form of these universities—whether they evolved from old-system universities, higher schools, technical colleges, normal schools, etc.—could not be avoided. This in turn resulted in a concentration of applicants at universities of famed and established traditions. This concentration has also been abetted by the fact that society, what with the actual difference in the abilities of graduates, tends to favor those from known universities.

The percentage of new high school graduates who applied for university entrance and the number of freshman enrollees between 1958 and 1963 shown in Table 48.4 indicates that every year 90 percent of the new graduates of high schools could be admitted to a university—if there were no *rōnin* and if students were not too particular about what university they would enter. In actuality, however, students tend to prefer known universities; also, many take examinations at two or more schools for safety's sake, a practice which makes the number of applications far larger than the real number of applicants. Both factors help to intensify the competition in entrance examinations.

The concentration of applicants at certain universities can be given as the reason for the existence of *rōnin*, who may be divided into three categories: (1) Those who failed to pass a university entrance examination the preceding year; (2) Those who after entering universities of their second choice are trying to apply for the universities which they originally wanted to attend; (3) Those who did not, initially, expect to enter universities but, from change of circumstances, decided to go on to higher education.

Thus the actual situation of *rōnin* is too complicated to be pinned down with complete exactness.

Figures 48.1 and 48.2 on page 179 show what percentage of entrants into four-year universities were new high school graduates and what percentage were *rōnin*, as well as the relation between number of applicants and number of entrants. The percentage of university entrants represented by new high school graduates went down from 1955 to 1957, then gradually turned upward. Even before 1954 the percentage of *rōnin* was quite high, due to the fact that there was an accumulation of *rōnin* who were graduates of the old-system higher schools. Year after year this accumulation has gone on so that the large number of *rōnin* is one reason for the intense competition for university entrance.

5. Improvement of Entrance Examinations

Efforts to improve the method of entrance examinations so that they will become a dependable means of judging the applicants' abilities have been going on year after year. As for the achievement test, it has been stated earlier that at the

Table 48.4

Graduates from New-System High Schools; University Applicants and Entrants (1958–63) (unit: person)

	High school graduates (A)	Applicants (*Rōnin* excluded) B		B/A		Entrants (C)		C/A		C/B	
		Universities (B_1)	Junior colleges (B_2)	B_1/A %	B_2/A %	Universities (C_1)	Junior colleges (C_2)	C_1/A %	C_2/A %	C_1/B_1 %	C_2/B_2 %
1958	776,753	161,785	34,983	20.8	4.5	146,377	34,888	18.8	4.5	90.5	99.7
1959	854,377	177,260	39,874	20.7	4.7	155,686	37,889	18.2	4.4	87.8	95.0
1960	933,738	197,847	44,506	21.3	4.8	166,761	42,318	17.9	4.5	84.3	95.1
1961	956,342	203,852	49,365	21.3	5.2	179,622	47,278	18.8	4.9	88.1	95.8
1962	1,016,181	225,643	57,835	22.2	5.7	201,125	55,613	19.8	5.5	89.1	96.2
1963	987,426	231,457	63,027	23.4	6.4	215,884	61,417	21.9	6.2	93.3	97.6

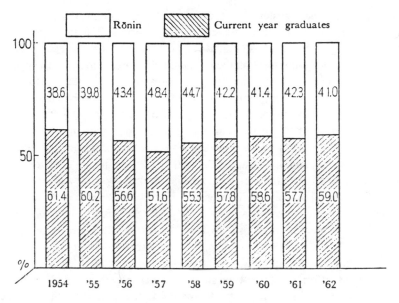

Figure 48.1. **Ratio of Current Year High School Graduates and** *Rōnin* **among University Entrants (1954–62)**

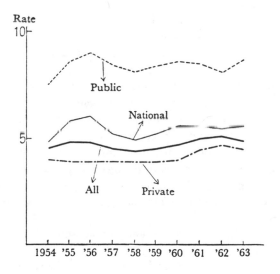

Figure 48.2. **Rate of Competition for University Entrance (1954–63)**

beginning of the new system the Education Ministry published principles for formulating questions together with sample items. From 1953 on, a special committee within the Ministry has studied the achievement tests of each preceding year, and published pamphlets on their findings. In these pamphlets the Committee explains how to make up questions by showing samples taken from every subject and points out their merits and defects. They are distributed annually to all the universities and to the boards of education of all the prefectures, for the purpose of bridging the gap between high school education and the university entrance examination, of preventing any undesirable influence the latter may have on the former, and of upgrading the quality of examination questions.

In a comprehensive study of the entrance examination system, the Central Council for Education made the following points in its 1962 report: (1) In reality, the selection of university entrants is made upon the basis of only one written examination given simultaneously to large numbers. (2) There is not enough direction and guidance in high schools, and cooperation is lacking on the part of the universities which could, but do not, help to lessen the fierce competition by such means as offering information about entrance possibilities. (3) Communication among universities and between them and the high schools is deficient. (4) Students can take entrance examinations as many times as they wish.

The writers of the report stated that they judged that, in order to solve these problems and to establish a totally objective and reliable method of examination, a juridical foundation composed of those affiliated with high schools, universities and the Minister of Education should be established. Upon this suggestion, the Research Institute was established on January 16, 1963, by the cooperative effort of high schools, universities and the administrative authorities. This institute concerns itself chiefly with high school students and studies the method of weighing objectively their knowledge and abilities. It also gives a common achievement and ability examination and tries to help improve university entrance examinations and methods of guidance of students.

In November 1963 the first achievement and ability examination was given to 360,000 volunteers. The institute, in cooperation with the universities, plans to conduct a follow-up study on the results of this test, comparing them with the results of the university entrance examinations and grades after entrance. It is hoped that this examination, after three years of experiment and research, will become a useful aid to the betterment of university entrance examinations.

Section 2: Economic Life of Students and Scholarships

If a person possesses the ability to profit from higher education but is prevented from doing so for financial reasons, it is a loss not only for himself but also for society and his country. It is for this reason that our Constitution and the Fundamental Law of Education state that national and local public organizations should make efforts to equalize educational opportunities and to encourage those who are talented but poor. This idea, though in a different form, already appeared in 1870, and the Educational Code of 1872 also advocates scholarships for poor and talented students as well as provisions under certain circumstances for remission and forgiveness of debts incurred by such students. At present the Japan Scholarship Society, established in 1944, is our chief national foundation granting scholarships to indigent students.

At the end of the war, students who came back from the front or the factories faced poverty, progressive inflation, and deep social unrest. The financial resources of their parents were sorely depleted and most of the students were obliged to support themselves. As a consequence many had to withdraw from school or give up hopes of entering institutions of higher learning. The financial situation of students during this period can be learned from Figure 48.3 on page 182. In the light of the difficulty they faced, it was urgently desired that some measure of protection and encouragement be provided for them, since it was on their shoulders that the reconstruction and the future of Japan depended. Consequently there was a marked increase in the scholarship grants. In 1948, 40,000 students received some scholarship assistance, an increase of four times over 1946. During the 1946–1948 period the amount of assistance given monthly was increased on five occasions. Subsequently, with the stabilization of society and the economic growth, our national endeavor at encouraging students and raising their academic level through financial assistance grew rapidly in scope and content.

1. Student Life

Before discussing the conditions for scholarship assistance, let us consider the actual situation of student life at present. As a basic rule the school fees and the living expenses of a student are borne by his family. Figure 48.4 (page 183) presents a breakdown of the families of university students according to their annual income, while Table 48.5 on page 182 shows the average yearly expenses of a university student.

If we take, for example, the students of national universities and study the expenses borne by their families as shown in Figure 48.5 (page 184), we find that whereas families in higher income brackets can send their children to universities with comparative ease, those in middle or lower income groups must shoulder a comparatively heavy financial burden and may well run into difficulties. So, a considerable number of students have to supplement their income by taking on part-time jobs, as indicated in Figure 48.6 (page 184). This situation is somewhat taken for granted. However, in view of the physical and the mental burden such extra-curricular work imposes on students, the question should not be lightly dismissed. All things considered, we must admit that it is still difficult for a great many families in our country to send their children to institutions of higher learning. On the other hand, to let the complete financial burden fall on the students themselves can cause a great future problem.

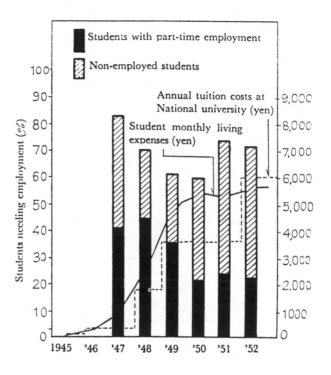

Figure 48.3. Finance of Students in Postwar Years (1945–52)

Table 48.5

Average Living Cost of Regular University Students (1961) (unit: yen)

Type of university		Living quarters		
		Own homes	Dormitories	Private lodgings
National	School expenses	36,246	27,668	28,812
	Living costs	35,774	71,687	99,759
	Total	72,020	99,355	128,571
Private	School expenses	65,515	57,931	60,193
	Living costs	50,267	96,426	123,388
	Total	115,782	154,357	183,581

Notes:
1. Students' living costs include school and living expenses.
2. Junior colleges are excluded.

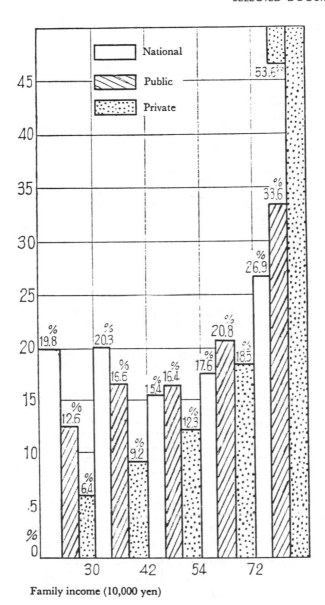

Family income (10,000 yen)

Note: 1 Family income in 1961 for 100 percent each of students in national, public and
          private universities.
       2 Based on the 1961 report issued by the Statistics Bureau, Prime Minister's Office,
          concerning income of city workers, divided into 5 categories.

Figure 48.4 **Students According to Type of University and Family Income (1961)**

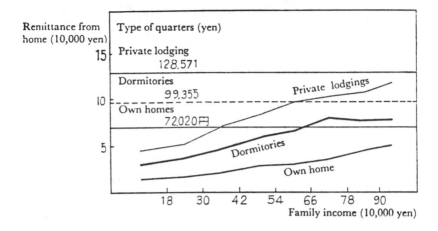

Figure 48.5. **National University Students (Daytime) According to Family Finance, Individual Living Quarters, and Remittance from Home (1961)**

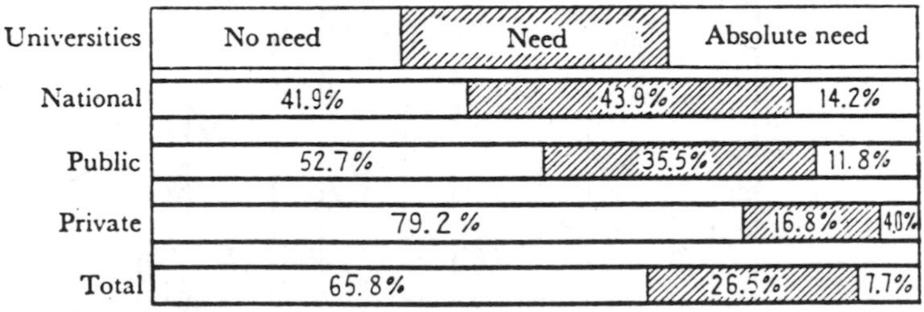

Universities	No need	Need	Absolute need
National	41.9%	43.9%	14.2%
Public	52.7%	35.5%	11.8%
Private	79.2 %	16.8%	4.0%
Total	65.8%	26.5%	7.7%

Figure 48.6. **Part-time Work According to Student Need for It (1961)**

If the present situation continues, equality of educational opportunity will become an empty letter to people in lower income groups, and the loss in potential human resources can hardly be calculated. For this reason the extension and improvement of the scholarship system is not a matter which concerns only education but is an indispensable condition for the future development of our country.

2. Present State of the Scholarship System

We will now look more closely at the operations of the Japan Scholarship Society, the most important organization of its kind in our country. The society at present grants scholarships to students who go on to institutions above the middle school level. Recipients are expected to repay the total amount within twenty years after graduation. There are two kinds of scholarship: general and special.

Table 48.6

Scholarships According to Types, Amounts, and Recipients (1963)

Types	Monthly amount (yen)	Number of actual recipients
General		
High schools	1,500	68,879
Higher technical schools	1,500	724
	2,500	110,090
Universities	3,000	
Graduate Schools		
M.A.	10,000	6,490
Ph.D.	15,000	
Special		
High schools	3,000	
	3,000*	38,000
Higher technical schools	4,500**	
Universities	5,000*	27,000
	8,000**	

Notes:
*Indicates students living at home.
**Indicates students living away from home.
1. Scholarships for medical interns and for students in special art courses and correspondence courses are excluded.
2. Scholarship for prospective vocational arts teachers are included in those for university students.

The former are given to highly qualified students who cannot afford to continue studying for financial reasons, the latter to exceptionally talented students who are financially unable to enter higher schools. The kinds of scholarship, monthly sums payable, and number of recipients scheduled for 1964 are shown in Table 48.6.

Following are some special characteristics of the system. (1) Special scholarships are given to students of the third year of middle or high school, including graduates of one year who pass a national examination, to help them after they have entered school. The amount granted is larger than that of a general scholarship but after graduation the recipient has only to repay a sum equivalent to the latter. (2) Scholarships for graduate students are meant to encourage them to become scholars who will contribute to the future development of the arts and sciences. In consideration of the fact that graduate students receive little parental support, their scholarships are appreciably more generous than are those for undergraduates. (3) Recipients of either undergraduate or graduate scholarships who after graduation accept appointments at schools or other specified educational and research institutions may have their total indebtedness forgiven depending on the number of years of employment.

Funds for the Japan Scholarship Society are derived from national subsidies

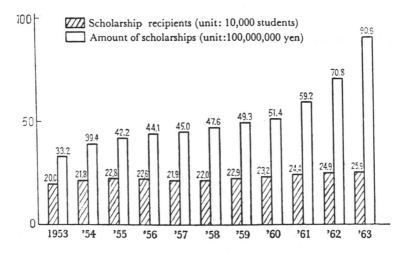

Figure 48.7. **Annual Number of Recipients and Total Appropriation for Scholarships (1953–63)**

and the repayments of formerly granted scholarships. Reflecting a national demand, the total appropriation for scholarships more than doubled between 1953 and 1963, as shown in Figure 48.7. Of the 820,000 students enrolled in 1962 at national, public and private undergraduate universities, graduate schools, and junior colleges, 140,000 received some assistance from the Japan Scholarship Society, one out of every six. Funds for special and graduate scholarships have been augmented during recent years. Special scholarships were first granted in 1958 to first year high school students. As shown in Figure 48.8, by 1963 there were 65,000 recipients, and grants totaled 3.58 billion yen. Recipients of graduate school scholarships numbered 6,500 in 1963 and a total of 1.04 billion yen was expended [Figure 48.9 on page 188]. Unfortunately, of the total of 9.33 billion yen which should have been returned by the end of 1962, 41 percent was still due. All efforts have been [made] to expedite the repayment and with considerable success, but it is fundamentally a question for the conscience of the recipients.

In concluding this section on scholarships, we can say that the scale of assistance has gradually become greater, and the living standard of our nation has also risen, but that, nonetheless, much remains to be done.

Section 3: Student Welfare, Guidance of Self-Governing Activities, and Employment

Student welfare and guidance, a relatively new sphere of activity characterizing postwar university education, includes such activities and institutions as the following: personal contact with professors, directors, guarantors or guidance per-

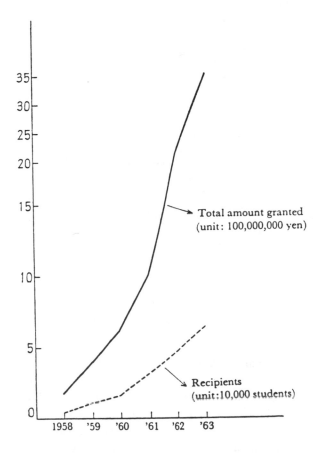

Figure 48.8. **Special Scholarship According to Number of Recipients and Amount Granted (1958–63)**

sonnel; promotion of sports; school loans; student cafeterias, stores, and dispensaries.

During the years immediately after the termination of the war, welfare activities were mainly centered on alleviating the financial plight of students. In 1947 a Student Welfare Committee was established in the Ministry of Education, in order to study the means of materially helping students. On another level, research in establishing a welfare and guidance program which, free from the former type of control, would help realize the aim of new-system universities, was carried on by the cooperative effort of the Ministry of Education and the universities. Research on a type of program to be based upon the Fundamental Law of Education and the School Education Law materialized in March 1949 in a report entitled *Activities of Student Personnel Sections in the Universities,* submitted by the Committee on Improvement of Student Life.

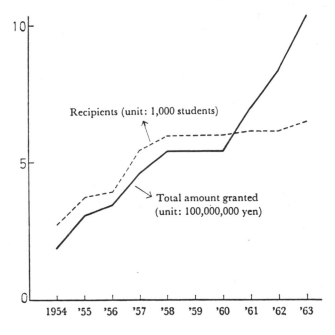

Figure 48.9. **Scholarships for Graduate Students (1954–63)**

In these circumstances the Enforcement Regulations for the National School Establishment Law which were promulgated in June 1949 (Ministry of Education Ordinance No. 213, 1949), clearly indicated that a department of student welfare and guidance should be provided in every national university. In 1951, a clause calling for "a special organ for the betterment of student life to be established in a university," was added to the University Standards published by the University Accreditation Association. In October 1956 it was decided by the Ministry of Education in the Standards for University Chartering that a system which provides for full-time welfare directors must be organized.

In January 1963 the Central Council for Education submitted a report on fundamental matters concerning the meaning of welfare and guidance in the universities, direction and management of students' self-governing activities, the system and administration of welfare guidance; further, it clarified the role of welfare and guidance in university education.

Because of the fact that memories of the meaning of "student guidance" in prewar years lingered and the fact that, since the beginning of the new system, the research activities of professors have been valued more highly than their zeal in teaching and the fact that social upheavals reflected so directly on student activities that counteractive measures to radicalism had to take precedence over

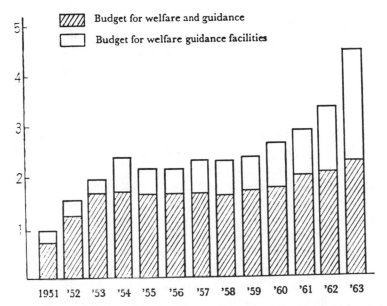

Note : 1 " Welfare and guidance budget " means fees for medical staff, dormitories, student
guidance, extra-curricular education, health maintenance, vocational guidance.
2 "Budget for welfare and guidance facilities " means construction or maintenance
fees for athletic fields, dormitories and pools.

Figure 48.10. **Expenditure for Welfare and Guidance at National Universities**
(1951–63)

welfare and guidance, the true meaning of the latter has not always been understood by people in general. According to the Council's report, the prime significance of welfare and guidance is that it plays a unique function in the formation
of character, a function which cannot be fulfilled by academic education. Welfare and guidance services should, therefore, help to make the academic side of
education more effective.

Welfare and guidance activities, if spelled out in greater detail, comprise at
least the following:

a) counseling by specialists to help students solve their problems;

b) extra-curricular educational activities carried on in student residences and
halls, gymnasiums, and the like;

c) guidance in students' voluntary activities such as those carried on in self-
governing associations, cultural and sports clubs;

d) orientation and leadership training;

e) health services, financial aid, and activities to improve the physical environment of students.

Figure 48.10 shows the costs for such activities at national universities from
1951 to 1963. A look at the condition of welfare and guidance facilities in these

universities will give us a more concrete understanding of this matter. Student residences in new-system universities are mostly a legacy from old-system higher schools and colleges, army barracks, or dormitories for factory workers. They were converted to student residences in order to meet the postwar housing shortage, and as such, looked more like welfare institutions for the indigent than educational facilities. The situation remains somewhat the same at the present. The condition of the buildings is, as shown in Table 48.7, far below what is desirable. Most are wooden structures, with nearly 40 percent of the total being converted from army barracks and factory workers' dormitories. Over 30 percent of the buildings are 30 years old or over.

The budget of national universities allocated for the improvement of these facilities is shown in Table 48.8 on page 192, and, as can be seen, the marked and rapid progress of the past few years is clear.

In July 1962 the Student Welfare and Research Committee in a report on the management and administration of student residences and the ends to be attained through their improvement urgently demanded that the current situation be rectified, so as to make the residences integral and effective parts of university education. This report led to research on the part of the universities as to the true position of student residences in the overall educational program, their management and administration, and the types of educational guidance to be used in them. Much is hoped for from these endeavors.

Student halls, imitations of the unions of American and European universities, have developed remarkably in recent years as centers for extra-curricular activities. Closer association with teachers; increased sociability and improved etiquette; needed relaxation and enjoyment—these are some of the reasons for such halls. With the foundation of Clark Hall at Hokkaido University in 1959, the establishment of student halls has gone on apace so that in 1963 there were 19 in national universities. With this kind of improvement going on, the most urgent task now concerns the organization and betterment of centers for health services and counseling.

As stated above, much importance is placed on extra-curricular education in the universities, one form of which is the self-governing activity of the students. This is recognized by the universities as a reliable extra-curricular means of education to foster a spirit of independence among students, to develop their social consciousness, and to assist them in their efforts at mutual improvement. In reality, however, owing to some misdirected movements of the students, the self-governing activities have not infrequently been confused in the popular mind with political or other social movements. Even students and university authorities and professors have not been immune from this misunderstanding.

An outstanding characteristic of postwar student activity is that, against the background of the self-governing associations at each university, a minority of student activists has mobilized the student body at large to participate in special political movements in order to realize the wishes of its own groups. That is,

Table 48.7

Dormitory Buildings According to Original Purpose and Age (1961)

	Original purpose of dormitories (%)							Buildings according to years of existence (%)						
	Total	Dormi-tories	Army bar-racks	School build-ings	Factory dormi-tories	House	Other	Total	0–10	11–15	16–20	21–30	31–40	41 and above
Men														
Total	100	63	10	4	8	6	9	100.0	22.6	6.4	17.3	22.2	18.9	12.6
National	100	61	12	5	8	4	10	100.0	16.3	6.9	17.0	23.2	21.5	15.1
Public	100	66	—	17	17	—	—	100.0	17.6	19.7	61.1	1.6	—	—
Private	100	65	8	1	7	12	7	100.0	58.9	2.0	13.1	18.8	6.6	0.6
Women														
Total	100	62	8	5	3	14	8	100.0	37.2	8.2	7.7	12.9	11.3	22.7
National	100	59	14	5	1	9	12	100.0	26.1	9.9	8.1	5.0	6.4	44.5
Public	100	50	—	—	—	25	25	100.0	23.5	42.6	—	—	33.9	—
Private	100	65	4	4	4	17	6	100.0	49.6	4.6	7.8	21.9	15.2	0.9
Total	100	62	10	4	6	9	9	100.0	26.0	6.8	15.1	20.1	17.1	14.9

Table 48.8

Improvement of Dormitories (1951–63)

Year	Area improved (tsubo)	Amount spent (1,000 yen)	Index
1951	2,076	40,965	100
1952	3,217	91,360	155
1953	3,002	72,258	145
1954	443	17,273	214
1955	1,263	44,678	61
1956	1,062	45,281	51
1957	3,171	86,743	153
1958	1,983	79,663	96
1959	1,325	67,715	64
1960	1,505	83,090	72
1961	4,961	348,869	239
1962	8,070	621,129	389
1963	8,951	780,791	431
Total	41,029	2,379,815	—

Note: Both new construction and repairs of old buildings are included.

Table 48.9

Student Associations in National Universities According to Type and Number (1963)

Type	Self-governing associations	Student amity associations	Student councils	Other	Total	Number of universities	
University-wide	8	3	6	—	17	—	17
Faculty-wide	170	32	26	11	239	15	55
	178	35	32	11	256	15	72
Total (%)	(69.5)	(13.7)	(12.5)	(4.3)	(100.0)		

efforts at self-assistance, necessitated by the disintegration of the traditional order and the financial chaos of postwar Japan and fed by the struggles in 1948 against raises of tuition, increasingly took on a political coloring until they issued forth in the organization of Zengakuren. Taking these facts into consideration, the Central Council for Education report of 1963 stresses, first, the necessity of clearly differentiating between students' self-governing activity and their political and other social movements which have no relation with university education proper, and emphasizes that only so can one comprehend fully the meaning and the significance of student self-government.

There are two typical forms of self-governing activity: (1) that of associations which include all students; (2) that of individual and voluntary clubs, study circles, or groups organized for sports or cultural pursuits. All national universities have student self-governing associations, as indicated in Table 48.9. Although much effort has been expended to guide them correctly, what with the previously mentioned circumstances and the indifference of many students, they have not achieved the educational results expected of them at the beginning. Participation in sports clubs and cultural circles in national universities is as shown in Table 48.10. The number of students belonging to such groups is roughly 140,000 (the total enrollment in national universities is 200,000), and their activities are becoming more and more lively.

After the unrest of the immediate postwar years, as social life and the economy became stabilized, directly political movements also subsided. There are many reasons for this turn of events, one being that the constituent political factions split into sub-factions and fought among themselves. This division and in-fighting continues with increasing intensity. On the other hand, the political movements of active minorities grew in violence, and not a few of them resulted in direct infringement of the law. In Table 48.11 on page 195, the number of political and social assemblies of students in Tokyo from 1960 to 1962 is shown. To help guide the self-governing activities of students in the right direction is an important task not only for student personnel workers but for the universities as a whole; it is also the responsibility of the students themselves. The healthy growth of self-government depends in the last analysis on the realization of the students themselves and active guidance on the part of the universities, and as such remains one of the most important tasks of university education.

If we turn to a consideration of the employment situation of the students, we can begin with the truism that it naturally reflects the conditions of the industrial world. As 1952 and 1953 were years of economic adjustment and also a time when a large number of graduates from both old- and new-system universities were coming into the labor market, the government, apprehensive of imminent employment difficulties, established a planning center on student employment and asked the help of the industrial world in order to forestall possible social unrest. Recent economic growth has resulted in an ever increasing need for new labor so that the university graduates of today, especially those from science and engineering departments, are in great demand. Even with the 100 percent increase in the number of graduates between 1946 and 1962 [see Figure 48.11 on page 195], it is still not sufficient to meet the demand in full. The present high rate of employment is shown in Figure 48.12 (page 196).

Formerly, over half of each year's graduates were employed by large corporations, but recently medium and small enterprises have begun to demand university graduates, and they are offering salaries not too far below those of the giant firms. Hence, more students are being absorbed by medium and small business and the employment condition has markedly improved. However, there are still some companies which discriminate against women or night-school graduates, and improvement along this line in the future is to be desired.

Because of the comparative shortage of university graduates, competition on

Table 48.10

Number of Students Circles and Clubs in National Universities (1963)

	Cultural circles			Athletic clubs			Other			Total			Average
	University-wide	Faculty-wide	Subtotal	University-wide	Faculty-wide	Subtotal	University-wide	Faculty-wide	Subtotal	University-sity-wide	Faculty-wide	Subtotal	
Number	1,268	1,354	2,622	1,079	1,035	2,114	11	2	18	2,358	2,396	4,754	per university 68.9
Member	39,650	35,603	75,253	45,088	23,068	68,156	673	422	1,095	85,411	59,093	144,504	per circle 30.4

Notes:

1. 220 organizations with unspecified membership are not included.
2. Cultural circles include academic (language study, humanities, and social sciences, science) artistic (music, fine arts, theatre, arts, literature), social hobby groupings. Athletic clubs include baseball, tennis, field and track, mountain climbing, volleyball, basketball, judo etc.

the part of companies to secure and employ them starts earlier every year. This sort of thing disturbs the last year of university education and is detrimental to the attainment of its true objective. So every year the university authorities meet and through the Ministry of Education implore the companies to cooperate. Their efforts, however, have not proven very successful. As shown in Figure 48.13, untimely offering of jobs and selection of employees before September have been increasing steadily, until in recent years over half of the seniors have acquired employment by the middle of their last year.

Table 48.11

Sociopolitical Gatherings of Students within Tokyo Area during 1960–62

	Number of gatherings	Gatherings at which students were arrested	Number of participants	Number of arrestees
1960	46	16	242,000	289
1961	56	27	35,000	86
1962	51	18	30,000	132

(unit: 10,000)

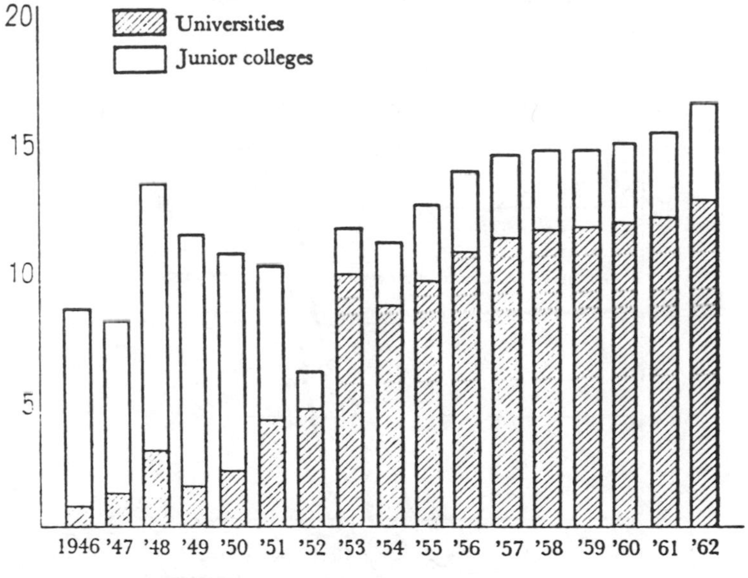

Note: "Universities" includes old-system universities; "Junior colleges" includes old-system colleges, preparatory schools, higher schools, technical schools and teacher training schools.

Figure 48.11. **Number of Graduates from Postwar Universities and Junior Colleges (1946–62)**

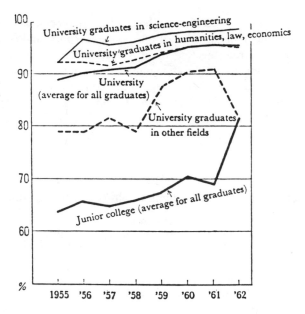

Figure 48.12. **Employment of University and Junior College Graduates (1955–62)**

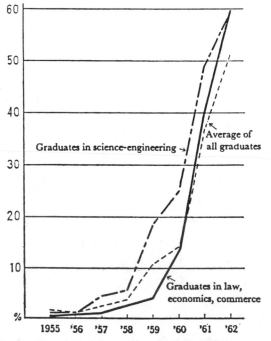

Figure 48.13. **Graduates Who Secured Employment before September (1955–62)**

49
Reviews of National Policies for Education: Japan

January 11, 1970

Source: Organization for Economic Cooperation and Development Report on Japanese Education (Paris, 1971) (excerpts).

A viewpoint widely accepted among Japanese intellectual and political leaders that amounts almost to an official position is that "the mystery of Japan's extraordinary growth" lies in its social investment in education. Furthermore, no country has been more certain in its support of the proposition that such educational investment must rest on a strong base of primary and secondary education. Primary education was virtually universal by the turn of the century, providing a base for a steady increase toward universal secondary education. With the post–World War II reforms, compulsory education was extended up through ninth grade, and today the upper secondary schools enroll more than 80 percent of the age group. Furthermore, Japanese schools are generally recognized as among the most effective in the world. Although completely modern in their conception, their excellence is perhaps rooted in the long tradition of concern for education in Japan. Schools were developed throughout the feudal domains during the 300 years before the first modern Code of Education creating an integrated system was issued in 1872. By that date there were already about 17,000 different schools in Japan and, it is estimated, male literacy was already 40 to 50 percent, female, perhaps 15 percent.

Yet the fact that Japan's educational policy today stands at a critical juncture is widely recognized and proclaimed by Japanese authorities. Thus, the Central Council for Education has said that in keeping with other aspects of Japanese economy and society, "The educational system has expanded . . . its quantitative increase bringing with it numerous qualitative problems." Judging from the current proposals made by the Central Council, the content of these qualitative problems is urgent and profound.

The Central Council proposals call for a sweeping reordering of the schools based on the rapid changes that have taken place in Japanese society. Schools that have performed so well in training people for particular roles in the earlier growth of industrial society must instead prepare them for changing roles in a fluid technological and "information" society.

The schools have essentially selected out the students in a series of entrance exams from one school level to another, preparing and channeling them toward particular levels in the social-economy. Instead they now would be asked to concentrate on the human development aspect of education because the pupils must emerge as individuals capable of self-selection and of continuous personal growth as they move along with a dynamic society.

Thus the Central Council calls for major reforms in preschool education and in the primary and secondary schools would:

1. Prepare the individual for life-long development. Education would be adapted to the stages of human development and to human variations in this development during the preschool and school years. Revised curricula and new pedagogical technique, the restructuring of the schools—beginning with the new kindergartens through to the 12th grade—and the amelioration of the entrance examinations, would all be geared to this objective.

2. Extend and guarantee equality of educational opportunity in line with the public demand. This would involve not only the elimination of the steep competition in entrance exams but, to make this less necessary, the wide diffusion of high quality schooling which could be diversified (secondary schools) to fit students' actual needs; also it would involve the reform of technical schools and the support of private schools to raise their standards and reduce the burden of these schools on the fee-paying parents.

3. Prepare the teaching staff to play their role as the major agents for educational change. Teacher training linked with research would be upgraded in new, high-level institutions while at the same time teaching would be opened to more people; training would emphasize new levels of sophistication in the fields of human physical and mental growth as well as a longer period of practical apprenticeship in the schools; accordingly, to recruit and retain teachers, their salary and status would have to be appreciably revised.

Throughout all of these Central Council proposals also runs the concern that education lay a foundation in the youth for an integrated national society based on the distinctive qualities of Japanese traditions and culture.

In the face of the broad scope of this plan of reform, the Examiners' remarks here can only seem somewhat fragmentary. However, it may be significant that we believe that our remarks are in general supportive of the directions outlined above.

Early Childhood Education

There is a deep national concern for the welfare of children in Japan. This concern has extended to a general feeling that preschool education must receive much more study and support. An anxious desire to compensate for less healthy urban environments and an increasing recognition of the developmental signifi- cance of the early years of life have given rise to proposals to extend education downward from the usual school age of six to the age of five, four or even to earlier years to age zero—and to pre-birth training of parents, and particularly mothers, for the tasks of parenthood.

In practice there are three immediate proposals:

i) *To provide more public support for nursery schools* for children between the ages of three months and five years.

ii) *To provide public kindergarten education for all,* though in the first in- stance for five-year-olds.

iii) *To lower the compulsory school age to five years. . . .*

Conclusions

Discussions around these topics in Japan seem to lead to a consideration of the following conclusions:

i.) There should be a broad and increasing public support for the whole range of preschooling in response to the obvious need and demand. Compulsory school attendance from age five may be the most convenient framework in which to develop and support national standards for kindergarten education, and to inte- grate this first year into the subsequent school program. For nursery schooling (three months to four years) the goal could be to make this available to all, though not compulsory.

ii.) Experimental action research programs, particularly stressing evalua- tion of the long-term results, could be organized to investigate and develop various forms and styles of nursery schooling, sorting these out with respect to a number of key factors such as age and other child characteristics, paren- tal circumstances and participation, teacher characteristics, etc. Such investi- gation should provide the basis for policy in organizing and constantly improving this level of education.

Parallel experimental programs could be conducted for the development and evaluation of kindergarten level education. Also to these programs could be attached fundamental research into the basic factors of early child development as they are related to and affect the efficiency of subsequent learning processes during later school years.

iii.) Teacher training for nursery schooling and for kindergarten need not be considered in terms of more years of university training. Rather, the training needs for such teachers should be deduced from their functions as they are prescribed in developing preschool programs. Teachers should be selected in terms of personality characteristics as much as for their academic qualifications.

iv.) An investigation could be made of the various semi-institutionalized forms of private nursery schools and kindergartens in order to assess how far public control would be beneficial to their standards of operation.

v.) Systematic provision of courses in child care and development could be offered to parents. The suggestion from prominent private sources in Japan to mount a national campaign dealing with the developmental needs of children from early infancy might also be considered for public support.

In all, these suggestions look toward a new and more systematic basis for preschool education, toward involving parents more closely in the initial educational experiences of their children and toward mitigating handicaps generated in unfavorable home environments.

Diversity and Uniformity

Primary Schools

The primary schools in Japan are still organized on the basis of a traditional graded system in which all children proceed at the same time, grade-by-grade, through a uniform curriculum. The Council has proposed to emphasize the development of children's basic abilities at this grade level but also to explore how to do this in a " 'non-graded' system, under which individualized guidance is offered to pupils according to the degree of their progress," and a decision to move forward on this combined basis would be very promising. There have been regular and notable revisions of curriculum contents—particularly for mathematics—but such a newly informed approach involving the codification of contents as well as more advanced forms of organizing the learning process in the classroom might lead to new avenues to meet outstanding problems in primary education.

For example, a major problem called to the Examiners' attention with respect to the primary schools was the problem of developing effective mastery of the Japanese language. By standards of other OECD countries Japanese presents extraordinary learning difficulties, the curriculum requiring, for example, the mastery of 881 separate and unique written characters during the first six grades. About 400 additional characters are required in grades seven to nine, which complete the basic vocabulary for reading a Japanese newspaper. It is not surprising, in the light of this burden, that although an important proportion of school time is spent in learning to read and write, the last national survey of language achievement registered only 67.2 percent general mastery of Japanese at the sixth grade level and 45.6 percent at the ninth grade. These results, however, seem not out of line with those of other countries with respect to the learning of the vernacular, and this problem of increasing the efficiency in this field is an international one.

Concern with this problem seemed to leave little room for the possible consideration of reforms or innovations to bring foreign language teaching into the primary schools. The growing importance of Japan's position in international economic and political affairs seems to the Examiners to suggest a striking need to explore in this direction in search of an effective foreign language program. Reorganization of the school environment to encourage individualization in the learning process may produce ways to bring foreign languages in a natural manner to the earlier school age groups on a practical and economical basis.

Secondary Schools

Secondary education inevitably poses a great dilemma for all societies: how to achieve, on the one hand, the adaptation of curricula to the *differing needs* of children of differing aptitudes and abilities, and how, on the other hand, *to keep children together* for as long as possible in common and cooperative activity with peers of widely differing abilities and career prospects. One has to avoid rating any of the children as inferior at any time since such a rating seriously hinders their intellectual and moral development and since the discriminatory segregation which usually follows leads to an increasing social distance in adult life between the "high" and the "low."

Japan represents a careful effort to extend the *lower secondary school* nondiscriminatory schooling through to the age of fifteen. The absence of streaming, the refusal to create special classes except for the specially handicapped and the devices for mobilizing the brighter students to help the less bright struck us as among the most attractively human features of the lower secondary schools. Much of the last year of lower secondary school is, however, focused on the entrance examinations to high schools. In many prefectures, mock tests are held every month designed to place every child in his exact place in the ability range so that he can apply for the right high school. It is surprising if the less bright children do not suffer—particularly the 20 percent who do not proceed to upper secondary school—and we were struck by the general absence of discussion of this problem. It is difficult to know whether the determination of teachers to ensure that their pupils do not suffer is such that no problem exists, or whether this is indeed an area in which more research might be desirable.

If research were considered within this school level, we would suggest that it focus not only on the existing system and practice but also on active experiments involving whole schools and new methods of teaching. It might specifically consider the extent to which pupils might be allowed more scope in the design and choice of their own curriculum, and the extent to which such activities could facilitate the adjustment of curricula to the needs of pupils of varying abilities and dispositions, and at different stages of their development.

By contrast, *upper secondary education* is highly differentiated in two senses. There exists, first, a diversification between general academic high schools and vocational high schools and, second, a differentiation between academic high schools in terms of ability as measured in entrance exams. From this diversification three major problems arise:

Differentiation between the Academic High Schools

The *first* problem is the *differentiation of the academic high schools* which is carried out to a high degree in some prefectures. According to the Ministry's survey, in 1969, in 26 prefectures, some groups of children competed for entrance to seven or more schools, graded according to prestige and entrance standard. The depressing character of the school to which the bottom seventh of the achievement range was consigned is not hard to imagine. The Tokyo reforms, which limited the achievement grading to a four- or five-step division seems generally held to be an advance. In order to minimize social differentiation, however, it might be better to differentiate classes and courses *within* more heterogeneous comprehensive schools, rather than to differentiate by ability *between* schools. This would require a wider span of facilities and teachers within the school but would also make the school a less artificial introduction to society as a whole. The same end could be partially achieved by greater common activity involving sports and other extra-curricular activities between neighboring schools.

In general, what is gained in efficiency by an early separation of pupils in terms of their future career goals and their ability to assimilate knowledge is lost in terms of a rigid social class structure and in terms of an increased social distance between the high and low in society. We feel that schools should cater to different *levels* of ability, and/or different standards of facility and teaching. Each type of school should accommodate children of different abilities and should have teachers of similar qualification and the same standards of physical plant.

The *private upper-secondary schools,* it should be noted at this point, which enroll one-third of the students at this level, are, with a few outstanding exceptions, much under-financed and at the bottom of the quality—and prestige— pyramid. Thus a restructuring which would be operative for this important segment of the secondary schools, would have to include new legal and administrative mechanisms and substantial new financial resources.

*Differentiation between General Academic High Schools
and Vocational High Schools*

The *second* problem concerns *vocational education*. In Japan the ideal of diversification by aptitude has (as will always happen in *any* society where a lathe-mechanic is paid less than a university teacher) become confused in the public mind with differentiation by ability, and as a consequence, the vocational schools—with some exceptions—have become low prestige schools which can recruit only children of lower ability who have little chance of entering the "best" academic schools. The reason most frequently given for this was that the vocational schools cannot, given their curriculum, prepare children adequately for the conventional entrance examinations for conventional universities.

Moral Education

A widespread concern for what is variously called "moral education," "spiritual education," or "human enrichment" is found among all groups concerned with education in Japan. Dissatisfaction is voiced by many over the failure of elementary and secondary schools to afford adequate education of this type. Different groups, however, clearly have different conceptions of what the content of such "moral education" or "human enrichment" should be. For some it implies discipline, a respect for national values and for heroes of the past; for others it signifies the development in individuals of strength of mind and of a critical independence of national symbols; yet others see it as conformity to an antiestablishment critique of national heroes and values, and for a further group it has the traditional, liberal arts connotation of enriching oneself by becoming a skilled consumer (and even an amateur producer) of aesthetic values.

There seemed to be agreement that the schools should reflect the demand for moral education in their curricula; it is not something to be left to the pupils or students to be pursued in their spare time. In a country so clearly divided on political matters as is Japan, however, the use of the educational system for the teaching of one ideology or one specific set of political attitudes would seem to be out of the question. Nor, it appears, would a search for some kind of common national ideology to guide education lead to any fruitful results. This, however, need not imply that the educational system will have to avoid any attempts at moral education or even, at political education.

The Ministry of Education however, has great formal control over the contents of Japanese education—perhaps in this respect one of the most centralized in the world. It has:

i) The power to determine the courses of study in each subject, a power which is exercised in the form of such detailed prescriptions that the teacher's freedom to vary the curriculum is restricted.

ii) Licensing power over all textbooks to be used.

This power has inherent in it the danger of possible uniformity in the political values offered in connection with such subjects as history. Also, centralization and required uniformity largely prevent the wide variety and experimentation in content and teaching methods so greatly needed to improve education if it is to meet the needs of modern society. Thus what commences as an effort to control the value content of education also has serious negative effects on the purely educational side.

Conclusion

No one will deny that technically Japan's primary and secondary schooling is excellent. The international recognition given to Japan as the leading country in the teaching of mathematics at this level is only one testimony to the high levels achieved.

Hence it is on a high plateau of accomplishment that a restructured school system and new directions in curriculum and teaching procedures can be developed to implement the reforms proposed by the Central Council. These kinds of reform measures, even if begun immediately, must be seen in their long-term perspective. A strategy for their implementation will undoubtedly involve the participation of the teachers and the community, the organization of action-research and experimental projects, a coordinated effort in revitalizing teacher training programs, and the support of new laws, regulations and budget. The Examiners are interested in the perspective plans and the possible timetable of all this.

Meanwhile, the Examiners feel that possibly there is a readiness for some practical measures aimed at the development of the students' personalities through a more flexible and less pressured scheme of education, with more free time, more curricular freedom, more diversity in extracurricular activities, and more cooperation among pupils. The time may have come to devote more attention to such matters as *cooperation,* in addition to discipline and competition, and *creativity,* in addition to receptivity and imitation.

Some of this can probably best be obtained by leaving much of the organization of extracurricular activities to the pupils themselves. Pupils might also be allowed to develop responsible, individual decision-making, by having some hours every week with a choice of learning activities at similar levels of difficulty and play-appeal. They might also be consulted in such matters as choice of textbooks and the design of timetables.

The Objectives of University Reform

It is clear that this present, inflexible and hierarchical university structure cannot meet the generally accepted educational objectives of the highly technological society now in existence in Japan. Students' futures are still largely determined according to the type of university to which they obtain entrance, and little allowance is made for the further development of their abilities beyond that designated by their university "label." We were told by some that this situation is changing, but very little evidence was offered of the nature of this change, either in the substance of university education or in the perceptions of prospective employers or of students.

The objectives which seem to underlie many of the reform proposals currently under discussion in Japan emphasize further the inadequacy of this structure. Extracting some of the most common proposals it is evident that the Japanese are seeking a system of higher education which will:

1. Meet the needs of society for tertiary level training of a directly utilitarian, vocational kind;

2. Assist in the discovery and further development of knowledge;

3. As living levels rise, releasing and raising levels of aspiration, meet the rising demand for university education—a demand which cannot be denied in a democratic society;

4. Encompass simultaneously, as in primary and secondary education, the objectives of *diversity* and *uniformity* in human development, allowing a maximum development of different talents with a minimal creation of social distinctions between different types of skills and occupations;

5. Provide independent and autonomous "critical" centers for society;

6. Ensure the university's effective response to and participation in society and in its social, cultural and economic processes.

University Reform

In conjunction with improvements in primary and secondary education, the above objectives for university level education might be reached by a number of courses. However, the Report of the Central Council for Education, drawing material from its deliberations and hearings during the past year, indicates how these would involve a general transformation of the university along the lines of:

1. Expansion, particularly the multiplication of centers of higher quality.
2. Diversification.
3. Structural innovation and reorganization.
4. Administrative autonomy.

... *Restructuring Higher Education for Diversity*

In response to the need for greater flexibility in higher education, the Central Council, in its "Master Plan for Higher Education," has suggested the establishment of five categories of higher education with the maximum possible amount of movement of students and staff between the different establishments.

i) Of the five types proposed by the Central Council, the *"Junior College"* appears to meet a special and clear need in Japanese society, particularly for women. However, the Examiners would stress that the character of these institutions could be geared to the particular need to provide programs for some people, and not programs of inferior quality. Defined in this way the offerings of such institutions could be diversified, away from being "colleges for brides," and educational "blind alleys" which stop most of their students from moving on to further education later in their careers.

ii) The *"Technical Colleges"* also appear to meet a clear and specific need in Japanese society, but the same provisions that are suggested above for students of Junior Colleges should also apply to those of other institutions, so that properly qualified and motivated students do not find the Technical Colleges "dead ends."

iii) The *"Universities"* are to redirect their energies into more socially relevant activities and, to this end, three types of curricula are suggested by the Central Council, all to be completed in a period not exceeding four years and, preferably, within three. "Type A" curriculum will provide, for those going into a wide range of occupations, a general and broad base of knowledge; "Type B" will offer a systematic, academic training for those who intend, after graduation, to go into specific professions in which academic skills are demanded; "Type C" will train "specialized personnel like teachers, sailors, artists and athletes." Most importantly, within these curricula, the previous distinction between general and specialized education will be abolished. Students will be more readily able to study the mixture of subjects in which they are interested and, if necessary, move from one type of curriculum to another.

In order to produce the above type of curricula, however, with a sufficient range of content and adequate tuition, it seems clear that many of the present, sharp divisions between faculties, institutes and schools will need to be broken down. There seems to be a widespread consensus in Japan that these divisions are detrimental to the intellectual atmosphere of the universities and inefficient also from the point of view of the optimal organization of research and teaching.

University Entrance Procedures

The Effect of University Entrance Examinations

In the entire educational debate in Japan, there seems to be no point on which there is greater agreement than that the present university entrance procedures are unsatisfactory. In fact, the condemnation of the system of university entrance examinations is so universal that it may be worth mentioning some of the contributions that have been made by the system so that its shortcomings as well as alternative procedures can be explored in fuller perspective. Many of these positive and negative arguments also apply to the entrance examinations to schools of lower levels, including kindergartens, and examinations for jobs.

What can be remembered is that the entrance examinations are open to all and hence are an instrument for equalizing opportunity regardless of social origin. The grading of the papers also to a large extent eliminates subjective evaluation and is not subject to outside pressures, making in general for a "fair" system. The only deviations from this fairness are the privileges of pupils from the "attached" schools at some private universities, and the system at some others of adjusting the entrance examination pass mark to the size of parents' "voluntary donations" to university funds. The system stimulates diligence, concentration, self-control and competitiveness. Moreover, through this system, Japan has achieved a reasonably effective leadership and an adequate supply of specialized skills for a number of decades.

As this system currently operates in Japan however, it cannot be supported on any such grounds. As the primary system of social selection, or the chosen method of "social birth," it exerts an enormous social pressure on Japanese youth and their families and has seriously distorting effects on the students, on the schools they attend before university, on the universities themselves and on society at large.

However, reform of this entrance examination system will represent the relief of a symptom of a far larger malaise. As long as the universities continue to be a narrow topped hierarchy, intense competitiveness will remain a feature of the system. Any new procedures should be viewed as part of a strategy to break through the present rigidity of educational and occupational stratification in Japan and the destructive strains imposed on thousands of young Japanese, and it is within this context that the Examiners place this discussion.

The Effect on Students

Students, it is said, become more interested in examination techniques than in real learning and maturation. Parents make strategic plans for launching their children on "escalators" leading to the most prestigious career lines by moving into districts with high schools enjoying a reputation as recruitment grounds for elite universities, and they try to get their children into primary schools leading to such secondary schools and into kindergartens leading to such primary schools, some of them attached to universities. There are proverbial stories in Japan of the educational mothers, the *kyoiju mama,* who even register under false addresses in order to launch their children into the Bancho primary school leading to Hibiya High School or the private Azabu middle school. The pressure on the individual student becomes so great that it probably is even reflected in the suicide curve, which has a life-cycle maximum for both sexes at the age of university examinations and an annual maximum for boys in the month the results of the examinations are known. Of course, at that age, and particularly during spring, there may also be *predisposing* factors such as loneliness, but failure at university entrance examinations would certainly be among the *precipitating* factors. Several years of the student's life become so dominated by preparation for the examinations that all kinds of extra-curricular activities and broader educational objectives are slighted.

The Distortion of Education at the Primary and Secondary School Levels

The distortion effect on the secondary schools and down to the primary schools is very frequently pointed out. As has been mentioned, the whole school system, particularly at the higher secondary school level, runs the danger of being turned into a cram system for the entrance examinations and distracted from its true educational objectives. Curricula are shaped to meet the examination requirements rather than the needs of students in terms of their current levels of maturation and their future educational and career needs.

The Distortion of University Education

The *distortion effect on the university* is also severe. Since the entrance examination is used by society as the primary certificate of scholastic ability, rather than achievements while in university, there is less incentive for students to work seriously at university studies. While this situation has the beneficial effect of granting leisure to some and time for broadening extracurricular activities to others, it does diminish the total significance of the university experience.

The Effect of the Entrance Examinations on Society

The most important distorting effect of the entrance examinations may in fact be *on society itself,* although the entrance examination in this case is, as already stressed, both a cause and an effect of certain social pressures. In the popular mind, universities are ranked in a strict hierarchy of prestige, secondary schools are ranked in terms of the number of students they can place in prestigious institutions, and graduates are judged by many employers and others in terms of the university, and faculty of a university, into which they win admission through the examination system, rather than in terms of what they know and are able to do. Thus there is a general belief that a student's performance in one crucial examination at about the age of 18 is likely to determine the rest of his life. In other words: the university entrance examination is the primary sorting device for careers in Japanese society. The result is not an *aristocracy* of birth, but a sort of *degree-ocracy*. The system is egalitarian and flexible as compared to a hereditary class system, but rigid and arbitrary as compared to systems in which individual performance over a much wider span of time helps sort people into appropriate careers and offers an opportunity for the motivated individual to catch up educationally and even change occupational status as he develops his capacities. This pattern will not change greatly as long as the "lifetime employment pattern" lasts. But simply within the educational sphere one can do something to modify it by changing the criteria by which individuals are rated by prospective employers.

Reforming Entrance Procedures

This problem of selection, given this imbalance of supply and demand, is truly formidable. We list below some of the measures for improving student selection which might help the educational authorities to distribute the "better" students a little more rationally among the "better" universities in a manner which generates less tension.

The Use of High School Reports

The most commonly suggested alternative is to *use high school reports*—grades plus teachers' personal evaluations—either as the sole selection criterion, or as the most heavily weighted component. The major *advantages* are that this:

i) reduces the unfairness of the "single-throw" entrance examination system;

ii) minimizes distortion of the high school curriculum which comes at present from students giving disproportionate attention to math, English and Japanese language, the most common entrance examination subjects;

iii) through the reports of teachers, doctors and other responsible persons could help to identify disadvantaged students whose promise might not be adequately revealed by school records or tests, and;

iv) could allow for the system to be flexibly adapted to admit students of promise from vocational high schools and other persons who may not have completed a high school course but would qualify from other experiences.

The experiences that could merit consideration might include individual study of an unusual kind or any achievement which could be taken as evidence of intellectual ability, maturity and seriousness of intent.

On the other hand, heavy reliance on high school reports has *disadvantages* in that:

i) it might accentuate the role-learning element in selection which some of the better entrance tests are moving away from;

ii) the disparity in quality and grading standards between 4,900 different high schools would be beyond the capacity of the most able admissions officer to assess adequately so it could never work "fairly";

iii) like the present system, it also forces students into certain universities even against their own will.

Nevertheless, we believe that there are some advantages in diversifying the selection procedures by using high school report cards—especially if they are used in combination with either or both of the other two methods listed below.

National Achievement Tests

The first is a *national achievement test.* These have hitherto met with opposition as they were regarded by teachers as attempts at the enforcement of national uniformity. To hold the key to university entrance is to hold power and prestige, and this problem seems also to be an important element in the conflict. These charges would be met if (a) the test were set by joint university–high school bodies in cooperation with the Ministry of Education; (b) there was not a single test but three or four set by different bodies. This would ensure a certain amount of diversity and experimentation in the curriculum, while liaison between the test boards and interchange of examiners could maintain comparability of standards. The tests would have the further advantage of serving as a leaving certificate for children who do not proceed to university, and a qualification for university but not through the conventional route through the academic high school.

Scholastic Aptitude Tests

The *second* alternative technique which arouses almost universal opposition is the *scholastic aptitude test.* There is no reason to suppose that the same objection would be aroused if (a) it were very thoroughly prepared, (b) there was no question of its use being required before its value was proven, and (c) the test allowed for varying interpretations of what is an "apt" university student.

It is worth noting in passing that we were struck by the contrast between the poor opinion generally held of the expertise commanded by the former Educational Test Research Institute and the high opinion held of the professional competence of those engaged in the private sector industry that offers preparation for entrance examinations, supplies mock examinations and so on. The fact that this industry would be threatened by a reform of entrance examinations does, of course, present a very real obstacle to such reforms. Might it not be possible to harness the expertise which is available by bringing it into the public sector in a national testing service based on cooperation between high schools and universities as Subcommittee XXVI suggests? It might even be possible to absorb some of the existing private enterprises into a new public corporation as ongoing entities.

An Alternative

The use of a mixture of the above measures in a university entrance procedure would almost certainly be a significant improvement over the present system. It would better predict success in university studies. It would also diffuse the psychological strain imposed on the child though without lessening it in total. It would not, however, take the pressure off the high schools. The concentration of anxiety on university selection depends on (a) the lifetime employment system which gives enormous importance to the *first* job one gets (since it is likely to be also one's last) and hence to the educational qualifications with which one gets it, and (b) the very steep prestige gradient by which Japanese universities are differentiated. These are the two factors which differentiate Japan from the other industrial countries and which make what is a somewhat worrying problem in other countries an acutely perplexing problem in Japan.

50
Social Education in a Rapidly Changing Society (Kyugeki na Shakai Kozo no Henka ni Taio Suru Shakai Kyoiku no Arikata ni tsuite)

Social Education Council

April 30, 1971

Source: Social Education Council, "Kyugeki na shakai kozo no henka ni taio suru" (Social Education in a Rapidly Changing Society), in Kanda Osamu and Yamazumi Masami, eds., *Shiryo Nihon no Kyoiku* (Tokyo: Gakuyo Shobon, 1978), pp. 45–48. Translated by James Vardaman.

Part I: The Change of Social Conditions and Social Education

Society today is undergoing immense changes and among the many issues facing people are some that must be dealt with in education. Therefore, we shall first analyze the rapid changes within society and seek an overview of how they affect social education.

1. Education and Changes in Social Conditions

The following changes have taken place within society and brought about many educational problems.

(1) Demographic Changes

Changes in the population structure by age groupings have been remarkable, and as a result of declining fertility rates and the increase in average life expectancy, our nation's population has begun to age rapidly. Together with the increase of young people pursuing higher education, this has produced a shortage of young workers. This in turn has increased the demand for development of human resources, improvement in quality of the population, and fuller application of middle-aged labor and latent labor. Because more women are working, there is a problem of the decrease of education within the home. There is also a problem of young people leaving their jobs and making quick job changes. The aging of the population also results in concern for the use of increased leisure time and for the meaningful use of one's post-retirement years. In future years, how people use their leisure time will become increasingly important in determining how full a life they are able to live. Education bears a major responsibility in solving these problems.

(2) Change in Home Life

Not only is there a decrease in the number of children per family, but a notable increase in the percentage of nuclear families. Moreover, accompanying the change in the industrial structure, the household has become the unit of consumption as parents and grown children come to live separately, children no longer are able to see their parents at work, and children and parents rarely work together. These tendencies, together with the expansion of durable consumer goods and the decrease in time required for domestic chores, have produced the phenomena of "My Home-ism," the increase of working wives, "education mothers," the generation gap, the declining role of the household as socializing agent, the encouragement of consumer desires, and educational problems. Furthermore, television and radio have made major intrusions into home life and have considerable influence on family life and the consciousness of young people. A major concern for education now is how to relate to these changes and how to employ them in an effective manner.

(3) Urbanization

Urbanization has become a significant phenomenon as industry and population gravitate toward urban areas, causing problems such as the so-called loss of nature, traffic congestion, and pollution. Urbanization of lifestyle and individual consciousness have spread throughout the land, and solving the problems mentioned has become extremely important. With the development of megalopolises and the extension of required commutes, the need for development of extensive social education has increased. . . . Newcomers to the cities, especially young people, sometimes find it difficult to adapt to their new environment, becoming lonely or falling prey to the temptations of the city. It has traditionally been a problem for farm-born youth to make their way in the big cities, but now we are also faced with the opposite problem of city-born youths who have little affinity for nature and little consciousness of a native place. . . . As a result of urbanization, young people are increasingly leaving the countryside and the populations in the provinces are declining, so it is becoming more and more urgent to increase educational opportunities in these outlying areas.

(4) Raising Levels of Education Received

There has been a major increase in the average number of years of education received and the level of that education. With the increase in education levels and the increase among that portion of the population that has a desire for learning and the concomitant ability to learn, it is only natural that the level of educational content has risen. On the other hand, school education sometimes becomes too much of a burden for some students and they are unable to adjust to school life. Social education should cooperate closely with school education, and at the same time that it seeks to attain higher levels of content and quality it should take into full account the educational difficulties of those who are left behind as a result of this trend toward higher levels.

(5) Industrialization and the Information Age

Innovation within technology has increased rapidly, and this has resulted in a significant alteration of the employment structure, with a decline in the number of people involved in primary industries and an increase within the secondary and tertiary industries as enormous organizations evolve. With industrial progress has come a serious alienation in which the worker feels like a cog in a machine, like a slave to the equipment, and like one of "the lonely crowd." On the other hand, the "information society" resulting from the advance of media has overpowered the individual with excessive information and in constantly changing fashion. Both individuals and the society as a whole are left with a great confusion, even opposition, of values.

(6) Internationalization

Industrial progress has brought about a rise in the economic strength of our nation. The rise in our international position and the increase in our international responsibilities, coupled with epoch-making advances in transportation and communication, have made every field, from politics to economics to culture, more international. The life of the Japanese people has exceeded the bounds of our nation and come into both direct and indirect relationship with other nations around the world. Therefore, education must be considered from a broad international perspective and must take into consideration international exchange, influence, and cooperation.

Part II: Lifelong Education and Social Education

1. Societal Change and Social Education

In order to deal with constant change and develop to the maximum the individual's character and ability, it is necessary for people to be constantly learning, making use of every opportunity. Especially in terms of the increase in life expectancy rates and the increase in leisure hours, it is necessary to offer as many educational opportunities as possible throughout life. In addition, as society changes, the number of people who are unable to adapt to that change increases, resulting in certain tensions within society, and the educational needs of the people advance and diversify. To deal effectively with these changes, we must view education from the perspective of an entire lifetime.

The necessity for lifelong education is apparent; even a person with a reasonably high level of education must still continue to learn as knowledge and technology continue to grow. However, lifelong education not only demands that one continue learning, it also requires the organic unification of home education, school education, and social education. There is a tendency to neglect the close cooperation required among these three aspects of education. There are gaps between them, and there are also areas of overlap. We must reexamine education in its entirety from the perspective of lifelong education.

2. Lifelong Education and Social Education

In lifelong education it is necessary to deal with diverse educational subjects over a lifetime. School education is limited in time and is therefore insufficient. Flexible education, which replies to the changing and diverse demands of the individual and the locale, becomes more important. In lifelong education, the role of social education is paramount. Social education should adjust as society changes, but also actively cultivate humanity and help to guide members of society. . . .

3. The Meaning of Social Education

Social education is often imagined as the actions of groups (such as youth or women's organizations), as facilities (such as public halls and libraries), and as schools and lectures. And it is true that the impression we get from this term is of a passive form of education such as a lecture and of serious contents. . . . Although these traditional aspects of social education will continue in the future, this narrow view of social education cannot fully meet our expectations of education within this rapidly changing society. We must extend our conception of social education to cover a wider variety of opportunities and places within the people's lives.

Social education should encompass everyone from children to senior citizens, levels from basic to advanced, means from individual learning such as reading a book by oneself to group activities such as discussion and group sports, and content from intellectual to cultural to physical. . . . However, no matter how broad we draw the boundaries of social education, not every form of learning will be included. . . . There is an intrinsic mutual relationship between the desire for education or educational activity and activity to raise them by means of education.

51
Basic Ministry of Education Guidelines for the Reform of Education *(Kongo ni okeru Gakko Kyoiku no Sogoteki na Kakuju Seibi no tame no Kihonteki Shisaku ni tsuite)*

Central Council for Education

June 11, 1971

Source: Central Council for Education, *Basic Guidelines for the Reform of Education for the Development of an Integrated Educational System for Contemporary Society: Report of the Central Council for Education* (Tokyo: Ministry of Education, 1971), pp. 3–23 (abridged).

Part I. Basic Guidelines for the Reform of School Education

Chapter 1. The Role of School Education in the Future Society

I. Basic Problems of Human Development in the Future Society

Education is for human development, that is the development of character and various human aptitudes and abilities in integrated personalities. Because of the rapid changes in contemporary society, individuals find increasing difficulty in developing personalities suited to their environments. Schools thus take on growing importance as agents for helping individuals adjust to their environment and to develop integrated personalities. As we consider the ideal schools for the future, we are forced to study the process of human development and the problems that changing environments pose for this process.

1. *The Diversity of Environments.* Man has grown and developed over the course of history by adapting to the environments in which he has lived and by transforming these environments to realize his needs. The process of human development is complicated and subtle. In order to understand the problems involved we need to take account of the following essential imperatives:

(a) As men living in the natural world, if we are to maintain and develop our lives in a sound manner, we should adapt ourselves to the rules of nature and come to understand the relationship between man and nature. In this way we can create a rich life which is harmonious with nature.

(b) As men leading a social life, we should establish a variety of human relations and actively participate in social activities. Through these we acquire the consciousness of social solidarity, responsible attitudes and behavioral abilities which enable us to realize not only our own goals, but also to aid others in their efforts.

(c) As active men who seek a meaningful life, we should understand and where necessary criticize the values we have inherited. With this understanding we can prepare with strength, creativity, and purposefulness for the future.

These imperatives are organically interrelated. In human development, it is necessary to aim at the balanced development of individual personalities imbued with love and respect for nature and life which can cope with these imperatives.

Differences between the sexes is another aspect that needs to be considered in our thinking on human development. It is a matter of course that men and women are equal as human beings. It is an important future task to enable every individual—regardless of their sex—to realize their unique potential while allowing each sex to make its natural contribution to their maintenance and development of mankind and culture.

2. *The Challenge of Changing Social Environments.* Considering that human development is taking place in the setting of our rapidly changing society, what problems are created that we must pay special attention to?

(a) Scientific and technological progress and a high rate of economic growth create a gap between nature and man, and thus destroy the foundations of our lives. With the improvement of economic conditions and the increase of free time, individuals enjoy the opportunity to live more active and enriched lives. At the same time, there is a growing need for individuals to master the rapidly expanding knowledge and technology, and to use it for the sake of individual and social progress.

(b) Due to urbanization and the growth in population, increasing numbers of our society find that they are required to live and work in densely populated environments isolated from nature. Maintaining our physical and spiritual health in the dynamic urban setting is often a problem. The urbanized way of life also poses the challenge of maintaining social solidarity and standards of public morality. People need the strength of character to avoid loss in today's society of mass organizations.

(c) Changes which have occurred in the structure of the family and kinship relations are exerting a considerable impact upon the setting for the human development of infants and youth. How modern families can make a better contribution to the development of basic character and human feelings in their children becomes a problem of great urgency.

(d) The prolongation of our life span along with the growing need for man-power has increased the possibility that aged persons can lead healthy and en-riched lives. It is necessary to take measures which will allow old people to take advantage of this opportunity.

(e) Because of higher levels of education and the desire this creates for social participation, because of the increasing need for manpower, and because of increasing spare time in homes, women in increasing numbers are seeking op-portunities for various activities outside their homes.

(f) Due to expanding international exchange and the development of mass media, events which are going on all over the world in different cultures are giving new stimulus to our daily lives. The international stimulus contributes instability to our value systems. Furthermore, many of our people have confused attitudes toward the nation because of our defeat in the war. In consequence, there is much ambiguity in our society concerning the basis of nationhood, and much conflict with respect to the meaning of democracy. This turbulent setting is unprecedented in the history of our society, and yet it is within this setting that we must succeed in the difficult task of human development.

The present state of society is not fixed in nature. It should be the purpose of all our national policies to improve social conditions.

Through social policy we can improve the external conditions. But there will not be real improvement unless we develop individuals who have personalities suited to the changes. Individuals without the appropriate personalities will feel a sense of alienation even when social conditions conform to the highest concepts of social welfare. Without adaptive changes in the process of human develop-ment, it is possible that as social conditions improve members of the future society will come to lose their sense of purpose and will seek satisfaction in immediate pleasures. Today, the tendency of escapism, and the inclination to violence and sex which can be seen among some young persons underline the importance of adaptation in the process of human development, if we are truly to improve our future society.

Chapter 2. Basic Guideline for the Reform of Elementary and Secondary Education

I. Central Problems in Elementary and Secondary Education

As was indicated in the discussion of the basic problem of human development, it is necessary in today's society for every individual to develop the strength of personality to live an independent self-controlled existence. This strength does not come simply from learning various knowledge and skills. Rather it comes as the individual's personality develops to the point where it has the capacity to integrate these various abilities and talents in a meaningful whole. The objective of education for the development of personality should be to help people acquire the abilities for building a satisfactory and spontaneous life, for adapting to social realities, and for the creative solution of difficulties. The Japanese people, showing tolerance for the values of others, should realize their national identity, and on the basis of the rules of democratic society and their national tradition should contribute to the peace of the world and the welfare of mankind through the development of a distinct but universal culture.

Thanks to the postwar educational reforms, nine years of compulsory education have become established, equality of educational opportunity has been promoted, and the educational level of the people has been significantly improved. There is no doubt that these reforms together with the educational heritage have been the basis for the school system's considerable contribution to Japan's socio-economic development. But today the school system is faced with the problem of how to cope with the qualitative changes that have occurred as a result of quantitative expansion. Also there are many problems in the school system which stem from the hasty reforms introduced in the unsettled situation of the postwar occupation. On the basis of our evaluation of school education's past accomplishments and the need for it to accomplish new tasks, we conclude that the main objectives in the reform of elementary and secondary education can be summarized as follows:

1. As elementary and secondary education provide the basis on which individuals develop throughout their lives, importance should be attached to pupils developing their personalities to the full and acquiring an understanding of their nature. To do this, school education must be improved so that teaching takes account of each individual's development, using methods which flexibly take account of both the normal stages of human growth and the special characteristics of individual students.

2. It is the government's responsibility to maintain and improve the standard

contents and level of public education, to guarantee equality of opportunity in education, and to work toward the diffusion and development of the kind of school education the public demands. In order to fulfill this responsibility, the government must take proper actions based on a long-term view of educational development, enlisting the understanding and support of the people.

3. Especially in elementary and secondary education it is the educator who determines the substance of education, but it is increasingly difficult to attract good teachers for these levels. As much will be expected from school education in the future, it is necessary to take comprehensive steps to improve the conditions for training and rewarding school teachers so that highly-qualified people will join the teaching profession and will conduct their education with confidence and pride.

II. Basic Guidelines for the Reform of Elementary and Secondary Education

1. Developing a School System Adapted to the Different Stages of Human Growth. In order to study measures for resolving the problems in the current school system and to implement gradual educational reform, experimental pilot projects must be carried out with the following aims:

(a) Experiment with ways to improve the effectiveness of primary education by establishing institutions which provide continuous education for youths from the ages of four or five through what is now the lower years of elementary school.

(b) Establish an institution which provides a consistent program of secondary education as an experiment to find a solution to the problems caused by the current division of secondary education into upper and lower schools, and introduce educational guidance as well as diversified courses so that students can plan their courses according to their abilities and interests.

(c) In addition to the two experiments above, other experiments such as linking the upper grades of elementary school with the lower grades of lower secondary school and the upper grades of lower secondary schools with upper secondary schools should be attempted.

(d) Extend the idea of the educational program offered at present in the technical colleges, i.e., a consistent set of courses covering both secondary education and the first stage of higher education, to other subject areas and educational establishments.

2. Reforming the Curricula in Accordance with the Characteristics of Each School Level.

(a) Promotion of consistency in the curricula offered from the elementary school to the upper secondary school, careful selection of curricula contents, and further examination of the subjects taught, especially so as to improve basic education in the elementary school.

Especially in the lower secondary school, it is necessary to discover ways for teachers to observe students and, based on careful consideration of each student's individual characteristics, to provide students with the guidance they need to select their future courses. While students at this stage will receive some common courses, this is the point where their educational careers will begin to differentiate.

(b) Diversification of the curricula of the upper secondary schools to enable students to choose courses suited to their particular abilities and interests. In this context, while the courses are diversified, it should be made easier for individual students to transfer from one major to another as their abilities develop and their interests change. The system should also be structured so that students may advance to schools of a higher grade from various courses.

3. Improvements of the Students' Guidance in Selection of Courses. The difficult but important task of education is to guide students to select suitable courses at each level of education. While hoping that individual students will develop new potentialities, it is necessary to recognize their demonstrated abilities as objectively as possible. To do this effectively, however, schools require the understanding and cooperation of individual families and society in general.

4. Improving Educational Techniques in Order to Develop the Students' Individual Abilities and Interests. The success of education depends not on what is superficially studied but on what is actually learned. In this learning process, teaching skills and techniques are as important as the content and level of education offered.

It is very important, therefore, to make the best use of teaching techniques which can be adapted to individual abilities and interests at each school level in order to ensure the attainment of educational objectives. To this end the following measures should be given particular attention:

(a) In order to provide effective education which will both conform to educational objectives and prove suitable for individual pupils' characteristics, measures for more flexible class management such as "instruction by grouping" shall be considered.

(b) So that students can pursue their studies in a rational manner and in a fashion suited to their individual characteristics, measures which increase opportunities for individual study should be considered.

(c) Measures to develop a flexible system with simultaneous guidance given to students of different grades should be considered as this may be more effective than giving guidance to students of one grade at a time.

(d) Measures to allow exceptional students to skip some grades in high school and enter higher educational institutions at a comparatively early age should be considered.

5. *Maintaining and Improving the Standard of Public Education and Equality of Educational Opportunity.* The government should reform the administrative and financial arrangements which regulate education in order to ensure equality of educational opportunity with attention, in particular, to the following:

(a) Maintaining curriculum criteria and other educational standards at an adequate level and improving them by means of continuous reexamination in the light of changes in society's needs.

(b) Ensuring the public nature of private schools so that they play an important role in public education, improving their educational conditions, and relieving students in these schools of their extra financial burdens.

(c) In keeping with the diversification of employment opportunities, more flexible means of education should be provided for young people already at work.

6. *The Positive Expansion and Development of Kindergarten Education.* In view of the importance of education for small children and the popular demand for kindergarten education, the government should actively promote the following measures for the improvement of kindergarten education:

(a) Declare that all five-year-old children who so wish may be enrolled in kindergartens, and make it the obligation of municipal authorities to establish sufficient numbers of kindergartens to achieve this objective. Financial aid from the national and prefectural governments will be necessary for this.

(b) Together with the measures explained in (a), coordinate the geographical distribution of kindergartens so that both public and private kindergartens can adequately play their respective roles and at the same time take necessary financial matters in order to enrich the quality of the education and decrease the expense of enrolling kindergartens.

(c) Improve kindergarten curricula on the basis of research on pre-primary education.

(d) Change over from individually-operated kindergartens to incorporated kindergartens in as short a period as possible.

7. *Positive Expansion and Improvement of Special Education.* It is an important responsibility of the government to guarantee equality of educational opportunity to all the people according to their ability. There are people who are mentally and physically handicapped and not suited to study in ordinary schools or to be taught with the teaching methods of ordinary school education. To provide the opportunity of special education for these people the government should take administrative and financial steps as soon as possible to implement the measures described below:

(a) Hold the cities, towns, or villages responsible for establishing a sufficient number of special classes to accommodate all the mentally retarded children so that they can receive compulsory education.

(b) Diversify the forms of education so as to meet the various needs of the physically and mentally handicapped children. This would include sending teachers to those children unable to attend school because of medical treatment or other reasons.

(c) The government should take a more active role in improving the facilities for special education by means of establishing institutes for children with dual handicaps of a serious kind, etc.

(d) Improve the treatment of the physically and mentally handicapped children through earlier discovery and training of them, improvement of the facilities for their education after compulsory education, and through promotion of closer cooperation between the diverse authorities responsible for the mentally and physically handicapped.

8. Improvement of the Structure of Management within Schools and the Administrative Structure of Education. In order to establish a structure within each school which can perform integrated activities in pursuit of the objectives of public education and that can hold itself responsible to the public, appropriate measures for reforms could be considered with emphasis on the following:

(a) Establishing an administrative organization within schools in which the responsibility for various school activities is properly divided, thus ensuring a lively and well-organized school program under the guidance and responsibility of the school principal.

(b) Unifying the system of local educational administration so it coordinates public and private schools.

(c) Devising means for hearing the criticisms and wishes of the people concerning education so they can be incorporated in educational policy and administration.

9. The Training and Recruitment of Teachers and Improvement of Their Status. As the role of teachers is going to be increasingly important in the future, the following measures should be comprehensively enforced to secure the best possible teachers for the educational system and to improve the quality of their work as well as their social and economic status.

(a) In principle, the teachers of elementary education and a certain percent of teachers in secondary education should be trained in institutions of higher education with special curricula for that purpose, hereafter called "teachers' colleges." On the other hand, distinguished teachers should be secured by means of inducing into the teaching profession the graduates of ordinary universities with high qualifications. In doing so measures should be taken to balance the demand and supply of teachers of the different areas throughout the country.

(b) In addition to improving the teachers' colleges as explained above, the government should take appropriate steps to train teachers and to expand the financial aid system for students in order to secure necessary teachers for compulsory schools.

(c) It may be necessary to consider a system in which prospective teachers are put on trial for about one year in an actual teaching situation and employed on a full-time basis only if their performance proves satisfactory. This will improve the training program and the new teachers will develop more self-confidence and a higher level of teaching ability under these conditions.

(d) A system of licensing talented individuals who, although they may not have proper teaching certificates, are sufficiently erudite and experienced must be extended in order to invite them to teach in schools.

(e) Means must be found to establish institutions of higher education designed for advanced educational research and teacher training, and a system should be started which gives teachers graduating from these institutions a special status and salary in accordance with that status.

(f) A teachers' pay improvement must be made to keep the teachers' salaries at a level high enough to attract distinguished persons into the teaching profession, and at the same time to create a salary scale which will provide teachers with suitable increases in salaries as their abilities become more specialized and their administrative responsibilities are increased.

In addition, since the people put a high value on education and expect much from the teachers, it is desirable that teachers form their own professional organizations and make efforts to improve their skills through mutual exchanges of experiences. In this way the teachers may earn the respect and trust of society and public recognition that the teaching profession is a specialty based on highly developed skills and a firm professional ethic. If the teachers will make efforts to improve their quality continuously by means of such training, their constructive opinions will be socially accepted and they will meet the people's expectations of them.

10. The Promotion of Research on Educational Reform. In view of the present, rapid pace of change and the pressing need to improve the quality of education, a center must be set up to promote and integrate research which pertains to educational reform, as well as to carry out a special program of research and development on education.

52
Basic Guidelines for the Reform of Higher Education

1971

Source: *Basic Guidelines for the Reform of Education: Report of the Central Council for Education* (Tokyo: Ministry of Education, 1972), pp. 24–43 (abridged).

I. Central Problems in the Reform of Higher Education

1. The Demand for the Expansion of Higher Education and the Growth of Scientific Research

Institutions of higher education should be developed for the future that are able to provide education to meet the diversified educational needs of a great number of people as well as to raise the standards of scientific research, and train teachers and research workers who can transmit and develop this research.

2. The Demand for Specialization and for Integration of the Content of Higher Education

Tomorrow's system of higher education must be designed, in close connection with secondary education, to help people develop professional skills useful in their future careers. At the same time it should encourage people to acquire the abilities and cultural background that they will need to handle the increasingly difficult problems of our developing society.

3. Special Features of Teaching and Research Activities and the Necessity of Their Efficient Administration

Institutions of higher education must guarantee freedom and respect for those who perform their teaching and research activities. At the same time, given the increasing size and complexities of universities, due in part to the growing specialization of disciplines, more emphasis should be placed on integrating the university as a whole by rationalizing its organization and by making its administration more efficient.

4. The Necessity of Guaranteeing the Autonomy of Universities, and at the Same Time, of Curbing Their Exclusiveness

Institutions of higher education should be guaranteed autonomy in their teaching and research activities. However, when too much emphasis is placed on autonomy these institutions become exclusive and so far removed from realities that they cannot fulfill their social responsibilities. In the future, organizational devices must be developed which keep the universities "open" and prevent their teaching and research activities from becoming outdated.

5. The Necessity of Respecting the Spontaneity of Institutions of Higher Education and, at the Same Time, of Providing Assistance on the Basis of a Coordinated National Plan

In reforming institutions of higher education it is necessary to restructure their organization in such a way as to respect and encourage their spontaneous creativity and, at the same time, to coordinate their activities and assist them from the perspective of a national plan.

II. Basic Guidelines for the Reform of Higher Education

1. The Diversification of Higher Education

In order to diversify Japanese higher education in the future, institutions must be categorized according to the students' qualifications and the number of years required for the completion of an average course of studies. At the same time it is desirable to provide different types of curricula in accordance with the aims and nature of the education. It is also necessary to establish a system where students can easily transfer from one category of institution or one type of curriculum to another. . . .

2. Directions of Curriculum Reform

Curriculum in [universities and junior colleges] should be developed along lines allowing for the provision of comprehensive or more specialized forms of education. The goals of general education pursued by existing universities can be more effectively attained if the following improvements are made:

(1) General education has, in the past, sought to give students overall knowledge of various disciplines, an understanding of scientific method, a grasp of problems in the context of the development of culture and a correct understanding of humanity and value. All these aims should be included in the revised programs of study and pursued integrally.

(2) Whatever fundamentals are required in specialized education should be integrated into the specialized education programs of the respective institutions.

(3) Foreign language training should aim at giving students a knowledge of foreign languages and the ability to use these languages for communicating with

people of other societies. Language training centers may be set up on campuses to provide this training, and it is desirable to develop tests of language ability. (The education of those majoring in foreign languages will be considered on a different basis).

(4) Health and physical education should be improved by giving adequate guidance in extracurricular athletic activities and by supervising the health of all students more thoroughly.

3. The Direction of Improving Teaching Methods

It is desirable to effect an improvement in the teaching methods used in institutions of higher education in accordance with their teaching patterns, i.e.:

(1) In the teaching of systematic theories, the quality and efficiency of lectures can be raised by utilizing broadcasting, VTR (video-tape recorders), and other technological devices.

(2) Seminars, experiments and practice sessions in small groups should be used more so that students acquire a clearer understanding of material presented in lectures and obtain the ability to apply what they have learned.

(3) As regards student athletics and student activities on the campus, specialists should be appointed who can give guidance and assistance thus enabling students to enjoy student life thoroughly.

4. The Necessity of Making Higher Education Open to the General Public and of Establishing a System of Certification

For the purpose of making it possible for all the people living in our future rapidly changing society to receive education at any time and whenever necessary, higher education should be made available not only to students in specific age groups or with particular educational qualifications but also the public at large. This means that it should be made easier for all institutions of higher education to accept those requiring reeducation and also that educational opportunities should be expanded by using methods other than those of the traditional credit system of school education. It should be made possible for those acquiring a certain number of approved credits from various categories of institutions to be granted a higher education degree.

5. The Organizational Separation of Teaching and Research

In order to achieve a balance between the teaching and research activities of the faculty in institutions of higher education, the structure of the teaching body should be reformed into one carrying out education for students. At the same time, all teachers should be provided with an environment conducive to research, in accordance with the aims and characteristics of their institutions. For this purpose, in the case of [graduate schools and research centers] it is desirable to separate the teaching and research organizations and to develop each of them in a rational fashion. It is necessary to clarify the teaching and research responsibilities of scholars, and thus to eliminate the conflicts between teaching and research organizations which might arise from their distinctive aims and objectives.

6. Institutions . . . (Provisionally To Be Called "Research Centers")

The "research center" is a teaching and administrative organization giving research training to those who want to engage in advanced academic research leading to a doctor's degree. As a rule, it will have a faculty with some full-time teachers of its own. Therefore, if these research centers are to be established in affiliation with other institutions, [graduate schools] or research institutes where an appropriate research and training organization already exists should be chosen. Of those admitted to engage in research, those chosen as assistants for the teaching and research activities of the Center or in other institutions should be given appropriate renumeration.

7. The Size of Institutions of Higher Education and Rationalization of Administrative and Managerial Organizations

Institutions of higher education should avoid becoming too large simply in order to meet managerial needs or to become financially self-sufficient. They should be of such a size to optimize their coherent functioning as educational institutions. For the benefit of research, exchanges between institutions of higher education and research institutes should be encouraged by developing close relationships and cooperation between them.

8. Improving the Employment of Teachers

Institutions of higher education should secure an adequate number of qualified academic staff for achieving their purposes. At the same time, institutions of higher education should improve their administration regarding teaching staff. They should prevent that stagnation in teaching and research which results from insularity; they should make use of the opinions of experts from outside the institution in the selection and evaluation of the performance of their teaching staff: they should limit the time that one teacher can remain in a specific position; they should also limit the numbers of teachers on their staff who have been trained in any one university.

At the same time, teachers' salaries and other conditions of employment must be extensively improved in order for institutions of higher education to attract highly qualified staff and to make it easier for personnel to move between higher educational institutions as well as from other organizations into higher education. Improved salary schedules should be developed so that they become a means for encouraging teachers to exert greater efforts in their work.

9. The Direction To Be Taken for the Reform of Establishment Procedures for National and Public Universities

Among institutions of higher education, national and public universities are considered to have the character of governmental agencies but at the same time it is thought that special consideration should be given to them owing to their unique characteristics. They, therefore, are in a position where conflicts easily develop with the governmental authorities in terms of administrative affairs. Furthermore, because of the way in which these institutions are organized, their internal governing bodies tend to be conservative in making decisions and to lack a sense of autonomy and responsibility. Therefore the following two types of reforms are proposed . . . :

(1) The present form of establishment for governmental universities should be abandoned and these universities should be incorporated in a new form that increases the autonomy they have over internal management while preserving their public character and their claim to public funds.

(2) The universities should improve their administration, establish responsible management, and clarify the relationships they maintain with those bodies that provide subsidies for their operations.

10. Improving Governmental Financing of Higher Education, the System of the Costs Being Borne by the Beneficiaries and the Scholarships System

To develop higher education further . . . it would be desirable for the government to give qualified private institutions of higher education a subsidy amounting to a certain proportion of their expenditure reasonably estimated and fixed in terms of the institutions' objectives and the nature of their activities. The government should provide these subsidies in a manner consistent with its long-range education plan, and the institution should be permitted to use the subsidies flexibly and effectively. The provision of financial resources for national and public institutions of higher education should also be considered in terms of an educational plan. In the case of national and public institutions, the educational expense, including tuition fees borne by the beneficiaries should be made more suitable.

The aim of these policies would be to reduce differences in the finances available to different institutions because of their form of establishment and the types of courses they specialize in.

When the government's measures for dealing with the above problems are discussed, a thorough examination should also be made of the national scholarship system, with the intention of increasing equality of educational opportunity and of encouraging talented individuals to enter these areas where they are most needed.

11. A National Plan for Coordination of Higher Education

National financial aid will be indispensable for the future operations of institutions of higher education. In order to utilize its resources to the full, the government should develop a long-range plan for higher education as a whole which recognizes that different types of higher education occur in different categories of institutions, and hence proportions the enrollments according to institutional category and specialized field and ensures a fair regional distribution of institutions. It is, therefore, necessary to make such a plan now from the standpoint of the nation as a whole, to establish a new public framework responsible for its realization, and to reform and enrich higher education.

12. Improving the Students' Environment

In order to make higher education fruitful in the best sense of the word, in addition to all the above-mentioned reforms, an enriched student life should be promoted in institutions of higher education by improvements in extracurricular activities and other aspects of student life. For the development of the character of students, the "dormitory" has been found to be very important, and it is important for institutions of higher education to improve their dormitories. Since both now and at a latter stage some institutions may not be able to provide "dormitories," some other ways should be found to offer the educational advantages of "group life" that the dormitories provide. In addition, some other methods must be found by which students may be given the chance to have more interpersonal communication both among themselves and with other members of society. All students should be provided adequate food and accommodations. If institutions of higher education cannot accomplish this alone, then the government must consider some appropriate measures.

13. Improving the Selection Procedure for Students

Because the student selection system has an undesirable effect on the whole system of education in Japan we must try to improve it. The aim should be that in the selection of students for higher education, the records of those who, at the secondary level, studied the planned curriculum conscientiously should be fairly evaluated, and that qualified students should be able to gain admission to higher educational institutions suited to their individual abilities without special preparation for entrance examinations. The improvement of the selection procedure must be based on the following principles:

(1) School records showing what students have accomplished in senior high school should be used as one criterion in selection.

(2) A common aptitude test should be developed and utilized as a means to compensate for differences in the standards of evaluation of different senior high schools.

(3) When a university wants, it may initiate a test to examine certain abilities needed for a specific field, require essays, and conduct personal interviews. Then the results of all these should be used in making a comprehensive judgment.

53
The Formation of Human Character in the New Industrial Society—The Ideal Form of Education from a Long-Term Perspective (*Atarashii Sangyo Shakai ni okeru Ningen Keisei—Chokiteki Kanten kara Mita Kyoiku no Arikata*)

Japan Economic Investigative Council

March 15, 1972

Source: Nihon Keizai Chosa Kyogikai (Japan Economic Investigative Council) (Tokyo, 1972). Translated by James Vardaman.

Basic Premises

Following World War II, our nation has achieved a high-growth economy by aiming at heavy chemical industrialization, and this has been backed by remarkable progress in education both preceding and following the war. Our nation is now moving out of this stage into a more advanced state of "post-industrialization." At this stage, while establishing material prosperity, air and water pollution have spread and traffic accidents have occurred frequently. Likewise, as urbanization has progressed the sense of community has collapsed. In the world of education we have witnessed several problems such as student rioting and juvenile delinquency coupled with other problems. The system of values which seems to have been established during industrialization is shaking, and questions are being raised concerning the existing order both within and without.

At this historical turning point, we must recognize that it is extremely important to devise new measures for dealing with education. As the ideal means of forming the human character of our nation, we particularly call attention to the importance of "life-long education" and call for means to implement it as soon as possible.

Proposals

1. The Role of Home, School, and Social Education

The new educational view known as life-long learning presses for revolutionary change in the commonly accepted notions of education we have heretofore embraced. It requires particularly serious reflection on the disproportionate emphasis on school education in our nation and a greater emphasis on education in the home, the fundamental locus of character formation.

The standpoint of life-long education reminds us once again that school education, following education in the home, is the second fundamental locus of learning and that the university is no longer, as it once was, the culmination of education. This is not to deny the significance of school education. On the contrary, it has become necessary to clarify the role of school education at each level of the formation of human character.

In addition to the importance of home education and school education, the third component of social education, which should continue throughout one's life, has taken on increasing significance. In the reform of our nation's education, we should commence with an accurate recognition of the particular roles that each of these three components is responsible for and of how these three functions complement one another. Taking into due consideration the fundamental view that learning is a life-long process, we must thoroughly support all types of social education, including education within enterprises.

2. Abolition of Standardized Education and International Comparisons

In order to deal with a new society in which various types of human qualities are cultivated, not only domestically but in a larger international realm, we ought to abolish standardized school education. We ought to actively promote various opportunities for learning, including facilities outside of the traditional school system. From this point of view, it is of paramount importance to drastically reform the entrance examination system.

It is also desirable that each citizen will deepen his or her understanding of international society in order to cope with the progress of multifarious, multilateral international exchange. In particular, language education should be improved.

3. Improvement of the Working Conditions and the Quality of Teaching Staff

Accompanying increasing requirements for the development of education to deal with the new industrialized society is the demand for the improvement of the quality of teachers. Although this ultimately depends on a teacher's own self-awareness and efforts, it is first necessary to greatly improve the treatment of teachers, reform teacher training, and radically revise the teacher appointment system.

4. Respect for the Formation of Character and the Breaking Down of Excessive Attention to Academic Careers in Business

Once the workplace is recognized as a place for character formation as part of life-long learning, we ought to expect that the "humanization of organizations" will aim at establishing individuality, developing individuality, and raising morality. Moreover, business must take the initiative in abolishing the detestable practice of placing excessive significance upon academic career. Furthermore, the so-called practice of "buying rice before it is reaped"—recruiting new employees before they graduate from school—has harmful effects and should be abolished at once. For this purpose, it is first of all desired that leading business enterprises will work in cooperation in implementing this policy.

5. Promotion of Equitable Industry–University Cooperation at Home and Abroad

We should promptly rectify the sometimes "cozy relationship" between funding and research—wherein a particular corporation maintains a restrictive relationship with a particular university professor—and maintain conditions for research under industry–academia cooperation based on mutual trust.

In the future, the sphere of demands for joint research in such fields as environmental control will enlarge throughout the world. Therefore, it is desirable that we actively promote not only domestic industry–university cooperation but also a broad international exchange.

6. Modernization of Educational Facilities and Development of Local Communities

It is necessary immediately to enlarge and provide educational facilities, which are the basic physical conditions for accomplishing complete education. Specifically, we should raise educational efficiency by promoting the introduction of new equipment for dealing with information.

It is also desirable to provide open educational facilities for the local regions to serve as the focus of the community in promoting the strengthening of local development. Taking the educational environment into account is extremely significant for the development of local regions and economic growth.

7. Complete Reform of Educational Administration and Increased Expenditures for Education

In order to establish a unified educational policy and efficiently implement it with the consensus of our nation's citizens, we must completely reform educational administration in general, including, of course, the framework of the Ministry of Education.

There are many problems, which involve not only the Ministry of Education but also other ministries and agencies, in providing abundant opportunities for learning both at home and abroad through the cooperation of home, local community, school, and business. We propose the establishment of new cabinet-level National Educational Council (*kokumin bunkyo kaigi*) to advise the Prime Minister regarding basic educational policies and the establishment of a strong secretariat for its activities.

It is necessary to drastically increase budget allocations for the various educational requirements.

It would be extremely meaningful if our nation, which has raised its international economic standing, were to declare at home and abroad in UNESCO's "International Education Year" (1970) and in commemoration of the centennial of the founding of our nation's educational system, that its fundamental policies are based on education.

54
How Japanese Education Ought to Be *(Nihon no Kyoiku wa dou Arubeki ka)*

The Japan Teachers' Union Committee to Consider the
Educational System

June 14, 1972

Source: Japan Teachers' Union, *How Education in Japan Ought to Be: The Idea and
Problem of Reformation* (Tokyo: Japan Teachers' Union, 1972). Translated by James
Vardaman (abridged).

... (2) The Aims of Education: Our View of the Image of the Japanese

When one person educates another, he hopes and anticipates that the one who
receives the education from him will become as he imagines. Those connected
with educational matters have to be able to firmly restrain themselves so as not
to hinder, with narrow-mindedness, self-righteousness, or force, the development
of the unlimited possibilities of the children and the youth so as to allow the
independent development of a free personality for a bright future.

However, assuming that one maintains this self-restraint and maintains the
fundamentals of respect for humanity and the foundations of education, it should
be admissible for one to possess an earnest wish or expectation for the student to
be as one imagines. For, actually, a powerful education filled with passion is not
possible where there is no such wish or expectation.

The Imperial Rescript on Education (Kyoiku Chokugo) [1890], as a statement
of the ideal of what a Japanese should become, held sway over teachers and
young people for a long time. Following World War II, there was a stubborn
movement to preserve *The Imperial Rescript on Education,* and another, more
obscure movement to establish something to replace it. In 1951, Education Minister Teiyu Amano made public a tentative statement of the idea under the name
of *The Practical Enactment of a Citizenry* (Kokumin Jissen Yoryo); in 1966,
fifteen years later, the Central Council for Education included "The Image of an
Ideal Japanese" as part of its report "Concerning the Expansion and Consolidation of Upper Secondary Education."

It centered, as did Amano's trial statement, on the image of a Japanese who
was expected to have "respect and affection for the Emperor," and it promoted
the ideal of a person filled with patriotism and admiring Japan as a great country.

In this latter statement, we cannot find a positive attempt to accomplish the principles of the sovereignty of the people, respect for human rights, or the love of peace which the Constitution promotes. It was a rather strange mixture, opportunistically forged from the old value system and the values of industrial society and forced upon the people. On the whole it was lacking self-restraint and modesty.

We should be very careful and object to any attempt to revise the vision of man presented in the Constitution, or The Fundamental Law of Education, and to force upon the people a distorted ideal of man which in the future can cause Japan to repeat an earlier mistake.

What ideal shall we emulate? Basically, an ideal should be chosen and built up by the individuals themselves in the process of thinking over what life is and imagining their own futures. A man ought to draw his own individual image. While admitting that this is best, we still have our own vision of the future. What kind of person do we want to cultivate?

1. A person like that described in the Constitution and the Fundamental Law of Education.
2. A person who respects others—a person who does not allow discrimination.
3. A person who loves justice.
4. A person who loves truth.
5. A person with a rich sensitivity and vitality.
6. A person who seeks international solidarity.

D. From "Oil Shock" to Economic Giant, 1973–1990

55
Features of Education in Japan: Background

1975

Source: Japan Teachers' Union, *How to Reform Japan's Education: A Report of the JTU Council on Educational Reform* (Tokyo, July 1975), pp. 24–30; 48–50 (abridged).

... B. Ability-First Principle

1. Ability-First Policy

The term "ability-first principle" came to existence for the first time in 1963 in a report of the Economic Commission, an advisory organ to the Cabinet, on "Problems and Measures to Develop Abilities of Men in Economic Development."

An educational policy based on ability-first principle was stressed as early as in 1951 in a report of the Ordinance Revision Commission. Later, the idea was emphasized in an "Views Concerning Technological Education to Meet with the Need of the New Age" issued by Nikkeiren (Japan Federation of Employers' Associations) in 1956, a typical national economic organization of Japan, and also in the "Views for the Promotion of Scientific, Technical Education" issued by the same Commission in 1957.

The report of the Economic Commission in 1963 was issued to formulate a policy based on the opinions of the above-mentioned Commission in 1951 and 1956. In June 1963, 6 months after the issuance of the report, the Education Minister requested the Central Council for Education to study "Extension and Fulfillment of Upper Secondary Education." In answer to the request, the Council started its activities by studying the report of the Economic Commission.

Thus, the Council placed emphasis upon the importance of "diversification of upper secondary education" in its report of October 1966. Diversification of school subjects based on ability-first principle has become the main line of educational reforms since then.

Ability-first principle and diversification of subjects based on it were introduced to meet with the requirements of enterprises, which consider men as a labor force rather than human beings, by developing youngsters, after selection, into efficient, advantageous manpower.

2. "Diversification" of Upper Secondary Education
(Senior High Schools)

Educational policy based on ability-first principle was initiated from the reorganization of upper secondary school education at senior high schools, in conformity with the report of the Central Council for Education of 1966 on "Extension and Fulfillment of Upper Secondary Education." The Government had already introduced a course system into junior high schools through the revision of Course of Study in 1958. Through the revision of courses of study at senior high schools in 1960, normal courses had already been divided into two courses of A and B, while introducing a course system in the name of "types." This has enabled the authorities to select students according to "abilities, aptitude, and types of academic course chosen in universities." [The] 1966 report by the Central Council for Education was to systematize a course system, as a system of "diversification," under which all students are involved.

In the 1960s, the rate of students who advanced to schools of higher grades was much higher than in the 1950s. This was a reflection of the growth of people's demands and movement for secondary education in complete form. And yet, "diversification of course" in senior high schools was a distorted measure, based on ability-first principle, to cope with the upsurge of demands for higher education for all children who so desire.

With this report of the Central Council for Education as a basis, the Council on Scientific and Industrial Education reported in favor of diversifying vocational education in 1967; and from 1968 to 1970, courses of study in primary schools, junior high and senior high schools were revised to justify discrimination in education contents as well as stages of development, in the name of diversification. In junior high schools, a technical course was established for boys while a homemaking course was established for girls; and in senior high schools a physical education course for boys and a homemaking course for girls.

In addition to these changes, a plan to "assort" courses has been put into practices, by inaugurating Technical Colleges, Temporary Training Schools for Teachers, etc.

The idea disclosed by the Central Council for Education in 1971 in a form of Report to the Cabinet was nothing but a program to promote this policy of diversification in entire spheres of education ranging from infants up to university students. Thus, a single-track university system in higher education, which characterized postwar educational reform, has been lost.

3. Education to Intensify Discrimination and Rivalry

Parallel with the reorganization of the schooling system on the basis of ability-first principle, a formula to rank, select and classify children in accordance with the already-established concept of "abilities" has been more and more deeply infiltrated into education contents, as seen in the statewide execution of the national scholastic achievement test.

Emphasis was placed upon the importance of teachers' guidance to help children to enter into senior high schools, under the pretext of eliminating harmful effects of competitions at the time of entrance examinations. Such emphasis, however, has proved to be meaningless because it is no longer possible for teachers to meet with the demands or desires of students or their parents today. What they can do is to distribute students, in accordance to their schooling records, by means of yes-or-no tests, to schools that seem to be adequate to schooling records of students concerned.

Further, "consolidated observation and guidance" at junior high schools was emphasized, but this, too, has resulted in selecting students on the basis of their schooling records, instead of conducting scientific approaches to correctly grasp aptitude as well as abilities of students concerned. This together with the policy of enlarging school districts and broadening school ranking, has contributed only to turning junior high schools into places to prepare for entrance examinations.

To cope with these fresh contradictions, education authorities attached importance to reports of students' schooling records by principals, and called for "thorough education based on Course of Study." "Improvement" of an entrance examination system (for senior high schools) through the attachment of importance to students' schooling record reports was nothing but the imposition of intensified studies upon students and teachers as well (in strict accordance with the Course of Study), according to the correlative evaluation system, which is not only an uneducational, but also an irrational and an unhumanistic method.

Under these circumstances, more importance is attached upon entrance examinations for boys, and guidance for girls has been belittled or neglected under the excuse that girls have special womanly traits rather than necessity to work hard for entrance examinations.

C. Narrow Nationalism in Education

Education policy for the past decade has come to take a nationalistic taint, together with the emphasis upon the ability-first principle, and promoted particularly through (1) the reactionalization of and State's control over education contents, (2) intensification of managerial control over teachers and (3) centralization of education administration aimed at strengthened State control.

This trend has become more and more apparent since the 1950s, and has been the core of education policy under the new Japan–U.S. Security Treaty from the 1960s toward the 1970s.

1. Tendency for Nationalism and Intensification of Control

Moves for nationalization and intensified State control of education contents first appeared in the Government's policy on textbooks. As early as in 1951, immediately after the system to enforce the use of State textbooks at schools was abolished, the Ordinance Revision Commission recommended the drafting of standard textbooks by the Education Ministry. With a leaflet entitled "Deplorable Problems Concerning Textbooks" published by the Democratic Party in 1955 as an impetus, "Bill on Textbooks" was presented to the Diet in 1956. Textbook examiners were appointed to carry out authorization of textbooks. Many textbooks suffered deletions and modifications of descriptions due to intensive examinations, and many were made disqualified. Many writers refused writing. Descriptions concerning the National Constitution or the Pacific War were made subject of such forceful deletions or modifications, while any deviations from the contents of the Course of Guidance were not allowed even in connection with mathematics or science. Their object was to intensify bureaucratic control over textbooks.

Further, revision of the curriculum of primary schools and junior high schools took place in 1958. "Ethics" was introduced into curriculum and the Course of Study formulated by the Education Ministry came to have a legal binding power. The revision was said to meet with a rapidly changing period as symbolized by technological progress, and elevate Japan's position in the world. Importance was attached to moral education, attainment of fundamental scholastic abilities, and improving the quality of scientific and technological education. Features of such revisions were, however, to beautify the aggressive war in the past, accentuate the position of the Emperor, glorify the policy of the Government, give weight to people's duties rather than their rights, and regard countries of Asia and Africa as underdeveloped countries. In a word, the revision of the curriculum was attempted to reactionarize education contents to comply with the new Japan–U.S. Security Treaty setup.

Secondly, the revision was aimed at confining teachers' educational activities within the framework of Education Ministry's Course of Study, restraining free and creative teaching activities.

Parallel with the revision of the curriculum, as mentioned above, "institution classes" were organized for teachers and a "Scholastic Achievement Test" was conducted on a national basis for pupils of junior high schools. Whatever the reasons might have been given by the authorities, the aims of the two attempts were to impose on teachers and children a type of education complying with the new Course of Study as a link in the chain of a policy to develop talent.

With the passage of the Law on Free Distribution of School Textbooks in 1963, measures for authorizing textbooks were made extremely severe, and the number of authorized textbooks was reduced greatly. For instance, textbooks on social study for junior high schools decreased from 30 different types before 1963 to only 8 types in 1969, 71% of which were monopolistically published by 3 big textbooks producing companies, while the prefectures that adopted concentratively only one type of authorized textbooks numbered 7, and those that adopted two different types number 16. This provided local government administrators, including those of towns, cities, etc., the right to select textbooks, and teachers who were teaching children lost means of choosing textbooks most suited for children concerned.

2. Centralization of Education Administration

The second important point in carrying out control and regimentation of education was to centralize educational administration. In 1951, the Ordinance Revision Commission denied a public election system of the Education Board and proposed an appointment system, parallel with a step to strengthen the Education Minister's authority, for instance the Minister's interference with the activities of the Board of Education. At the same time, the Commission proposed the establishment of a unified, highest deliberative organ to control all matters connected with educational administration.

In 1956, the Government rammed through the Diet, by mobilizing the police, a bill concerning the organization and operation of local educational administration, and introduced an appointment system to education boards. The Law stipulates the Education Minister's right to ask for legal measures toward education boards, as well as a system to appoint a Superintendent of Educational Affairs by approval.

Establishment of the Law contributed to strengthening bureaucratic control over education vertically from the Education Ministry—Prefectural Education Board—Regional Educational Board—Principal—classroom teachers, on the one hand, and provided supervisor teachers with the right to supervise educational activities, to enact and carry out managerial regulations, to establish a system for notification and approval of teaching materials, as well as to conduct efficiency evaluation system upon teachers, etc. Thus, the Education Ministry attempted to establish a firm control over day-to-day educational activities.

The Educational Reform Council that played an important role in the postwar education reform proposed in autumn 1951 the establishment of a Central Education Council based on an indirect election system for the purpose of "realizing democratic education in complete form." In disregard of the Reform Council's proposal, the Ministry of Education set up a Central Council for Education based on an appointment system in June 1951, and started deliberations of the report of the Ordinance Revision Commission from January 1953.

One year after its inauguration, in January 1954, the Central Council for Education submitted a report concerning the maintenance of political neutrality in the field of education, on the basis of which two laws concerning education were formulated in order to intensify control over education on the pretext of prohibiting political activities of teachers and maintaining educational activities. The enforcement of these laws made democratic ideas and systems which were obtained as the result of the postwar educational reform completely null and void.

Structure and functioning of educational administration were further consolidated in the 1960s. Instances of such were . . . payment of Superintendent Allowance for principals and head teachers and the increase of its amount, forceful execution of a teachers' efficiency rating system, scholastic achievement tests conducted at the national level by the Education Ministry, and at prefectural levels by prefectural and regional Boards of Education, a drastic increase in the number of supervisor teachers, increase of their supervisory visits to schools, etc. At the same time, on the grounds of normalizing education, maneuvers for splits, transfers, and thought control over members of the Teachers' Union were practiced in some prefectures. These measures were taken not only in connection with administrative spheres, but also in relation to activities within and without the field of education as revealed in the revision of the Social Education law in 1959.

Measures taken by the central and local governments to attain their ends were clearly proved by the measures taken by the Government at the time of "reversion" in Okinawa in May 1972. The Central Government made ineffective various laws and systems, including a democratic Education Board system which the people of Okinawa Prefecture had established on the basis of the so-called *democratic law,* and forcefully applied laws and regulations of mainland Japan in order to carry out uniform administration with the latter.

3. Policy to Govern Teachers

Supervisory and managerial structure was reinforced at schools. Parallel with the organization of a Planning Committee or Steering Committee, an Administration Chief, Curriculum Chief, Grade Chief, etc., have newly been appointed to supervise ordinary classroom teachers. The task was to compel teachers to be faithful executors of education controlled by the State, by setting up a centralized managerial structure with a small proportion of teachers acting as managerial staff. The system to control classroom teachers ranges from the principal down to classroom teachers by the medium of head teachers, School Affairs Chief, Administration Chief, and Chiefs of various sections. This structure was further reinforced through the legislation of head teachers' positions, the execution of a system to dispatch Social Education Chiefs to schools, and the enforcement of the 5-stage Wage Law. Thus, educational practices of teachers are under constant watch and control by upper-rank teachers. Under these circumstances, there appeared those who viewed "staff meetings" useless. While on the other hand, a two-head teacher system was adopted at some schools with lady teachers as a second, or subhead teacher, further intensifying discrimination against lady teachers. . . .

Reinforcement of control has greatly hindered the progress of free and creative educational activities and studies by teachers, on the one hand, and imprinted officialism in the minds of some teachers, emasculating their spirits and creating a dark atmosphere at their places of work, on the other. The feeling of freedom and liveliness prevalent in schools in the immediate postwar period have [*sic*] been lost, schools have been turned into government offices, and teaching into a mere business. Teaching is performed in a crude and lifeless atmosphere giving an unfavorable impression to children. . . .

4. Measures to Cope with Problems of Youth and Attempt to Obtain "National Consensus"

Under "the high economic growth policy" derived from the so-called "double the income program" in the 1960s, special importance was attached to the questions of young people, "in order to create men who will be the core of a nation" under their conception. While placing emphasis upon public peace, labor, culture as central themes of internal politics, the Government intended to bring up youth [as] "Japanese" by reinforcing its measures for character building, imprinting patriotism and necessary knowledge and technologies.

[The] 1963 report of the Central Council for Education was made a basis for such practices by the Government. They put into practice measures "to cultivate wholesome youth" by strengthening measures to cope with juvenile delinquency. In 1966, the Central Council for Education brought forward the so-called "Image of Men Expected by the Nation" in reply to the inquiry of the Government, in which the Council recommended "all youngsters ranging from 15 to 18 years of age to be cared for in some types of educational institutes." The idea of the Central Council was to control the thinking of young people and formulate "national concurrence" to nationalistic direction.

With sharp increase of "juvenile delinquencies" in those days as a momentous change, they intended to tighten measures for young people. They helped prefectural governments to build and reinforce regional youth organizations, enforce acts or regulations to protect and upbring youth, establish home education courses, etc.

Greater importance was attached to these measures particularly since 1965, when the Japan–South Korea Treaty was concluded. The Special Bureau on Youth was set up in the Prime Minister's Office, and a People's Congress for the Cultivation of Youth was inaugurated to carry out movement for such objectives. Similar organizations were established also at the prefectural level. These organizations have carried out activities to organize youth from a moral point of view under the slogans of wholesome group activities, wholesome homes, purification of social environment, etc.

The "Economic, Social Development Plan" disclosed in 1967 gave prominence to "home education" and "measures for the youth." In the same year, the Social Education Council stressed the urgency of "planting in the minds of young people the feeling of oneness to mass, love for their homes, native country and the State" in its report to the Government entitled "Guidance to be given to Youth Organizations." To comply with the proposal, activities to organize sport organizations, etc. for youngsters have been accelerated.

Further in 1971, the Social Education Council reported the result of its studies on "How Social Education Should Be to Cope with Radical Changes in Social Structure." Here, too, the aims of these proposals were to enforce thought control, particularly toward youngsters. Having accepted these proposals, a number of Youngsters' houses, Outdoor Activity Centers, etc., have been built by central and local governments, under a similar guiding principle as described above. . . .

I. How to Reform Content of Education

A. Basic Principles

Our task here is to search for the methods, system, and formation of the content of education that may help children and youth to develop fully their personal possibilities—physically, mentally, morally, and aesthetically—in every opportunity inside school and out.

First of all, we will present the essential principles for the organization of the content of education.

1. Completing basic knowledge and self-formation of a world view. Children will grow to pursue their own work and way of living in the future. It is essential for children to have an enriched life now in order to acquire fundamental abilities for their varied activities in the future. School owes children the acquisition of basic scholastic ability as its primary responsibility. In this view, we must select and create such content of school education that can cultivate basic scholastic ability, creative intellectuality, and self-formation of a view of the world and life. At the same time, in teaching this content, we must endeavor to foster children's self-awareness of popular sovereignty as well as necessary political sense, and critical and active manners.

2. Well-selected, systematic, and coherent content of education. The content of education is to be carefully selected to meet every stage of children's growth and to achieve required results effectively within a certain period of time. For this purpose, the content of education should be continually enriched by all the cultural spheres of art and science in order to meet the needs of the time, and should not be isolated from the fruits or heritage of art and science. As a matter of course, the content of education should not segregate the achievements of art and science, but adopt them systematically and coherently to meet the demands of children and youth in their every stage of development. In order to fulfill this aim, it is necessary to make the best use of historical and current research achievements in educational science on the premise of academic freedom in research.

3. Organizing multifarious activities of children and youth. It is not school education alone that can contribute to the development of children's physical, emotional, and mental ability. If we neglect children's life outside school, we can achieve little success in school reform. Therefore, in order to enrich and encourage children's life, it is necessary that the content of education adequately include collective autonomous activity, exploring and problem-solving activity, creative and vital activity using body and mind, actual life experience, linguistic activity, and play inside school and outside. These activities and experiences are to be more leveled off in the advanced stage of youth. In this way, we will help children and youth in school and in other educational institutions to establish gradually their own view of the world and of life, and to be people who think creatively [and] possess vitality and sense for constructing a new society and life in the future.

4. Respecting spontaneous activity of children and youth in educational methods. In educational practice, it is important to create and spread scientific methods, teaching techniques, and learning processes and forms for securing children's full growth while respecting many teachers' free and creative activities and making the best use of achievement in educational science. At the same time, we must carefully find the way to integrate the two activities: the one is to teach children art and science, and the other is to have them learn spontaneously in their actual situations.

5. Spontaneous curriculum-making and democratization of its procedure. In order to meet the task of what to teach children and youth, it is necessary to have school curriculum spontaneously organized by all school staff, and its formulation drastically democratized. In this respect, the existing system of various councils and committees for special investigation must be abolished, because their role has been mainly to subordinate educational content and methods to the needs of economics or to utilize them for political control. We must newly establish in each local governing body a democratic council for examining the content of education, which should be composed of specialists in the cultural spheres of art and science, researchers and practitioners in educational activity, and those who can widely represent the people's demands. In addition, it is necessary to establish a central organization of adjustment and association for the activities of these local councils. . . .

56
Japan's Private Universities

1987

Source: Japan's Private Colleges and Universities: Yesterday, Today, and Tomorrow (Tokyo: The Japan Association of Private Colleges and Universities, 1987), pp. 54–70.

The distinguishing characteristic of private colleges and universities is that they adopt an original and independent approach to education, based on the principles of free thinking and self-accountability, that allows their graduates to respond flexibly to the demands of society. Throughout their history private universities have been keenly influenced by the ideals of their founders, and this founding spirit at each school has been continually reexamined and reinterpreted in light of the changing times.

In material terms—school grounds, athletic fields, and student facilities—the private universities have gradually been able to provide themselves with the proper educational environment and to cultivate close working relations with local communities to create schools with distinctive campus atmospheres. On an abstract level, to be discussed later, they have made diligent efforts to reassess the contents of what they teach, searching for an educational program best suited to the times. In short, private universities are striving on both the material and abstract levels to develop and maintain a school spirit based on respect for individuality and to offer an education that intimately reflects that spirit.

Private universities often are accused of taking an assembly line approach to teaching—mass-production education. Some universities have opted for mass education for management reasons and to absorb all those seeking a college degree, but some schools—women's colleges and medical and dental schools, for example—also offer small classes. Because class size is usually geared to the educational objectives of each school, universities should not be accused indiscriminately of mass-production education. Even schools that have developed into centers of mass education offer small seminars, field trips, and other intensive teaching programs to instill in their students a sense of belonging and the motivation to learn. Moreover, the number of teaching hours for private university faculty members is greater than for their national university counterparts. In these and other areas, private schools are working hard to prevent mass education from diluting the quality of the education they offer.

Building Character Through a Liberal Education

In the prewar period, universities emphasized the training of specialists who would become society's elite. After World War II, the philosophy of universities under the new system changed to stress the training of well-educated generalists through specialist programs. As the universities became centers of mass education, they grew increasingly aware of their role in the formation of character. The goals of private colleges and universities and the ideals on which they were founded have always been to educate the next generation. But unlike the national universities, which focus primarily on research, the private schools do not believe their mission is merely to provide a knowledge-intensive education through specialized studies. They have constantly maintained that a liberal education is of paramount importance in building character.

In recent years, fewer and fewer students are reading books. This trend is not confined to the private universities. But private schools are making concerted efforts to tailor programs in reading and other skills specifically to help students overcome these shortcomings. Their promptness in initiating these programs again shows their predisposition to appreciate the strategic importance of a liberal education in their students' lives.

Innovations in Course Offerings and Academic Structure

The private universities have displayed originality in creating faculties and professional schools, departments, courses of study, majors programs, and curricula that have allowed them to respond flexibly to the needs of their students and of society. As a result, they have also played a pioneering role in teaching and research. No national university, for example, has ever had a single inclusive school of social welfare. Schools of this kind are numerous, however, at private universities, notably at Christian and Buddhist colleges and others with religious affiliations because of religion's inherent concern with social problems. Private schools have also taken the initiative in creating schools or departments of business administration, international and human relations, and dentistry (Table 56.1).

These pioneering efforts have also given rise to new approaches to education that effectively call into play the principles of free thinking and self-accountability on which the private schools justly pride themselves. The years since the Meiji Period have seen the development of women's education, especially at the Christian colleges (Table 56.2, page 249); correspondence courses to satisfy the learning desires of those unable to enroll in ordinary college classes (Table 56.3, page 250); and night-school classes for those already in the work force (Table 56.4, page 250).

More recent examples reflecting Japan's increasing participation in the world community include the admission of foreign students and returning Japanese students who have been educated abroad (Table 56.5, page 251), as well as affiliations and exchanges with foreign universities. Waseda University has been a pioneer in international exchange. Its international division, established in 1962, by fiscal 1978 had admitted 1,173 students from 62 U.S. colleges and universities. In the Kyoto-Osaka area, Kwansei Gakuin, Kansai, Doshisha, and Ritsumeikn universities were among the first to experiment with inter-university exchange programs, recognizing credits earned in one another's graduate and undergraduate courses (Table 56.6, page 251). Showa University has a Research Institute for Biomedicine in St. Petersburg, Florida, with ties to the University of South Florida, that serves as a training center for young researchers and as the site of student exchanges.

Ever since the Meiji government first hired foreign specialists, non-Japanese teachers have made outstanding contributions to Japanese education. Foreign teachers have also played an important role at private universities. Some schools were even founded by non-Japanese, and many private schools, though not all, see nothing unusual about having foreign professors or presidents (Table 56.7, page 251). In marked contrast, the national universities have only recently decided to appoint foreigners as regular full-time faculty members.

Other pioneering efforts are being made in the area of continuing education. To expand their ties with the alumni who play important roles in college affairs, for example, many private universities are extending continuing education opportunities to them. A great many universities publish alumni bulletins to further these efforts.

Changing conditions—increasing costs and teaching loads and diminishing enrollments—are forcing a reevaluation of night schools and correspondence courses for working people. Despite these difficulties, the private universities have found ways to cope with social change and fulfill their responsibilities as educational institutions. Sports and other extracurricular activities will continue their important role in developing students' characters and skills. Because these activities also enhance a school's prestige, they are warmly supported and granted a positive place in private school education.

Table 56.1

Departments Unique to Private Universities

Department	Entering enrollment capacity	Department	Entering enrollment capacity
Literary Arts	600	Industrial Engineering	1,400
Theology	165	Veterinary Science and Animal Husbandry	470
Buddhist Studies	390	Agriculture and Veterinary Science	1,380
Linguistic and Cultural Studies	200	Dairy Farming	380
Social Science	600	Oceanography	760
International Relations	200	Health Education	100
Industrial Sociology	700	Environmental Health Studies	100
Political Science and Economics	1,300	Nutrition	430
Politics and Economics	3,190	Performing Arts	2,240
International Politics and Economics	150	Plastic Arts	594
Management and Information Studies	400	Home Economics	
Information Science	100	Acupuncture and Moxibustion	220
Hygiene	500	Total (25 departments)	100
			16,669

Source: Ministry of Education, *An Overview of Universities Nationwide*, 1983.
Note: As of May 1, 1983. Departments and enrollment capacities include day and night courses.

Table 56.2

Number of Female Students and Women's Colleges (Fiscal 1983)

	Number of colleges and universities		Number of students			Women's colleges and female students as percentages of the total		
	Women's colleges	Total	Male	Female	Total	Number of colleges	Number of students	% of total
National	2	95	342,107 (289,971)	93,405 (84,787)	435,512 (374,758)	2.1%	21.4% (22.6)	22.5% (21.3)
Local-Public	8	34	36,305 (31,484)	17,212 (16,145)	53,517 (47,629)	23.5	32.2 (33.9)	4.1 (4.1)
Private	76	328	1,040,751 (1,011,293)	304,713 (295,952)	1,345,464 (1,307,245)	23.2	22.6 (22.6)	73.4 (74.6)
Total	86	457	1,419,163 (1,332,748)	415,330 (396,884)	1,834,493 (1,729,632)	18.8%	22.6% (22.9)	100.0% (100.0)

Source: Ministry of Education, *Report on Basic School Statistics,* 1983.

Notes:

1. "Number of students" includes undergraduates, graduate students, special students, auditors, and research students. Figures in parentheses refer to undergraduate students only.

2. "Women's colleges" under the category of "Number of colleges and universities" refers to undergraduate enrollment only. In addition to the numbers cited above, 2 national universities and 1 private university had no undergraduate students.

Table 56.3

Private University Correspondence Courses

Fiscal year	Number of universities	Entering enrollment capacity	Number of students admitted	Number of students enrolled	Number of graduates
1950	6	34,500	15,254	12,227	—
1955	7	35,500	10,838	43,819	1,727
1960	8	37,500	12,620	46,655	1,858
1965	9	38,500	19,320	59,905	1,926
1970	11	44,200	20,692	77,391	2,158
1975	11	44,200	28,308	88,594	1,955
1980	12	49,600	26,162	91,612	2,087
1983	12	53,300	23,308	72,662	3,096
Total to 1983	—	—	—	—	64,927

Source: From a survey by the Association of Correspondence Schools at Private Colleges and Universities.

Notes:

1. Because statistics are not available for some schools prior to 1955, these schools have been omitted here.

2. "Entering enrollment capacity" and the "Number of students" in all three categories refer only to students in the regular course of study.

Table 56.4

Universities Offering Night-School Classes (Fiscal 1983)

Establishing body	Number of universities	Entering enrollment capacity	Number of students admitted	Number of students enrolled	Number of graduates
National	13	1,940	1,903	8,951	1,320
Local-Public	5	704	639	3,430	507
Private	48	20,570	26,346	104,882	18,657
Total	66	23,214	28,888	117,263	20,484

Source: Ministry of Education, *Report on Basic School Statistics,* 1983.

Note: "Number of students" in all three categories refers to undergraduates.

Table 56.5

Admissions of Japanese Students Returning from Abroad (Fiscal 1983)

	Total number of universities	Number of participating universities	Number of participating faculties	Number of applicants	Number of students admitted			
					1983	1982	1981	1980
National	95	13	23	151	51	27	23	11
Local-Public	34	3	4	8	2	3	2	4
Private	328	59	150	1,238	388	221	277	183
Total	457	75	177	1,397	441	251	302	198

Source: Ministry of Education, *Survey of the College Admissions Screening Process,* 1983.

Table 56.6

The Undergraduate Credit Transfer System (Fiscal 1982)

	Total number of universities	Number of participating universities			Number of students using the system		
		Domestic	Foreign	Total	Domestic	Foreign	Total
National	95	19	47	51	225	157	382
Local-Public	34	—	1	1	—	2	2
Private	326	6	40	43	111	646	757
Total	455	25	88	95	336	805	1,141

Source: Ministry of Education, *Data on Universities,* No. 90, 1984.
Note: The number of universities that accept credits from foreign universities: national 88, local-public 2, and private 170.

Table 56.7

Number of Full-Time Foreign Faculty Members

	Public universities		Private universities	Total
Fiscal year	National	Local		
1979	227	22	691	940
1980	294	22	811	1,127
1981	301	27	852	1,180
1982	334	24	897	1,255
1983	326	32	927	1,285

Source: Ministry of Education, *Report on Basic School Statistics* (relevant annual editions).

Table 56.8

Full-Time Staff at Association Member Affiliated Schools

	Number of schools	Full-time teachers	Full-time non-teaching staff
Junior colleges	45	1,411	1,022
Special schools	26	236	118
Miscellaneous schools	4	13	9
High schools	92	4,630	1,313
Middle schools	47	1,148	265
Elementary schools	12	257	87
Kindergartens	41	299	71
Total	267	7,994	2,885

Source: From a survey by the Japan Association of Private Colleges and Universities.
Notes:
1. As of May 1, 1983. Based on statistics provided by the 84 association member schools.
2. Teachers cross-appointed to both middle and high schools are counted under high schools.

The Role of Affiliated Schools

One approach to providing an education that stresses character formation has been to establish close relationships with affiliated elementary or secondary schools; this approach has been adopted by many private schools. In fact, many private colleges began as elementary or secondary schools and only later developed into institutes of higher learning. Some lay great importance on offering an integrated education from kindergarten through college (Table 56.8), despite the inherent difficulties in this approach. Because their founding ideals thrive best under these conditions, schools such as Keio and Doshisha that have made continuous use of this approach can distance their students from the harsh entrance examination system and produce graduates that have distinctive personalities.

Not all affiliated schools have been successful. In the past, preferential treatment given by colleges to applicants from affiliated high schools has been criticized as a ploy to secure large enrollments, one that allows the admission of students with low scholastic abilities. In recent years, though, as university entrance exams have become more difficult, the academic standards of affiliated schools have steadily risen. They may even have overemphasized their college preparatory role because more and more students are applying to colleges outside the system. A worse result is that the evils of Japan's "entrance-exam hell" now affect younger and younger students, not only those going on to colleges, but even those entering high schools and middle schools.

Nevertheless, in these times of overheated competition to get into the right college, affiliated schools have helped private universities preserve their founding ideals and distinctive school spirits. They also suggest a direction in which the private universities of the future might move. If the many professional training schools, business schools, and other adult education facilities at the private colleges and universities are also considered, the system of affiliated educational institutions is seen to offer a diversified approach well suited to the age of lifelong education we are entering.

One reason private universities have been able to maintain a relatively free educational environment is that, except at certain faculties of medicine, the teaching staff is not organized into a system of professorial chairs, as is the case at the national universities. Because the private schools are not tied to this rigid system, faculty members can move freely into new fields of research, then put this research to immediate use in the classroom. Moreover, the way is open for talented young teachers to advance to professorships regardless of the numbers involved. However, this freedom to appoint and assign faculty members can lead to an arbitrary personnel policy and occasionally can also adversely affect education.

Innovative Admission Policies

The diverse approaches to education at private universities are apparent from the time they begin to screen candidates for admission. Though all private schools prefer to admit students with high scholastic achievements, some, reflecting the ideas of their founders, may also wish to select students with distinctive personalities and high potential. Many universities base admission decisions on entrance examinations in only three subject areas, unlike national universities which test in more areas. This approach makes allowance for those students who, while not outstanding in every subject area, have excelled in particular fields of interest. High schools have complained, however, that students planning to enter private universities are less diligent with examination subjects on which they will not be tested in the entrance exams. Nevertheless, private schools strive to provide a diverse range of elective examination subjects to satisfy individual aptitudes and needs.

Private universities have also broken new ground in implementing and expanding an entrance system based on high school recommendations. Instead of staking everything on the entrance examinations, this practice, which has spread throughout the entire college entrance system, allows students to be admitted on the recommendation of their high school principals and on the basis of their achievements during the previous three years. Most private institutions with affiliated high schools have always relied on recommendations, so this is a well established practice with a long history.

Applicants are usually admitted by recommendations on the condition they do not apply to any other college. This procedure is gradually gaining approval (see

Table 56.9

Admissions to Association Member Institutions from Affiliated Schools

			Students admitted			
Fiscal year	Applicants	Students admitted on the basis of entrance examinations	Students recommended by affiliated high schools	Students recommended by other high schools	Others	Total
1979	1,530,402	122,758	15,339	11,803	827	150,727
1980	1,454,710	124,497	15,631	12,712	666	153,506
1981	1,416,730	122,877	15,900	13,807	1,218	153,802
1982	1,403,466	120,205	15,404	15,522	1,899	153,030
1983	1,444,610	120,762	15,849	17,563	2,404	156,578

Source: From a survey by the Japan Association of Private Colleges and Universities.
Note: "Others" includes foreign students in Japan, graduates from foreign high schools, returnees, and students admitted in accordance with the regulations for foreign students and by certificate examination.

Table 56.9) because students who apply in this way are more strongly motivated to enter a specific university than those who take the entrance exams as a safety measure should they fail to be accepted by a national university or the school of their first choice. The recommendation system also has the advantage of giving students a sense of belonging at their universities from the moment of early admission; in this way, it can help improve educational effectiveness.

As the number of years of formal schooling steadily rises for Japanese society as a whole, more students are changing majors or adding new ones. Schools are experimenting with policies that can respond to diversifying student needs. Special admissions policies are also being adopted to allow mature students to enter regular university courses (Table 56.10). The faculty of law at Rikkyo University, for example, has developed a radical admissions policy that has won high praise for its pioneering role in this area. The introduction of older students into a student body made up entirely of the same age group has created some problems, but this policy has also provided a new incentive for learning for students entering from high schools that prepared them only to pass college entrance exams. It points the way to the open university of the future.

The candidate-screening process is an essential first step in any college's plans for development. Most private universities are making almost desperate efforts to be innovative in this area. The trend today is not to rely on the single criterion of scholastic achievement tests that reflect only a student's skill at exam taking. Interviews, short essays or questionnaires, and participation in student

Table 56.10

Admissions of Mature Students (Fiscal 1983)

	Total number of universities	Number of participating universities	Number of participating faculties	Number of applicants	Number of students admitted			
					1983	1982	1981	1980
National	95	45	104	1,176	369	367	266	253
Local-								
Public	34	9	12	204	69	55	30	38
Private	328	104	145	6,834	3,595	4,329	3,653	2,964
Total	457	158	261	8,214	4,033	4,751	3,949	3,255

Source: Ministry of Education, *Survey of the College Admissions Screening Process,* 1983.

Note: "Mature students" refers to those who have worked for a while after high school graduation, to housewives, and others, but not to so-called *rōnin*.

government or athletic and cultural activities during high school are used to select ambitious students who on admission will strive to develop themselves through their studies. There can be no doubt that the success of these efforts has contributed greatly to the recent rise in stature of the private colleges and universities.

Specialized Studies

One problem frequently singled out in the postwar system of education arises from efforts to acquire a broad knowledge through a dual system of study in general and specialized subject areas. General education courses especially, it is said, often merely repeat what was taught in high schools; teachers fail to gear their lectures to their students' level, and as a result the students often lose the desire to study once they enter college. To overcome these problems, schools are experimenting with ways of motivating their students to learn.

Most private schools, for example, have no special liberal arts department consisting exclusively of teachers responsible for general education courses. Instead, a faculty member is assigned to a specialized department, and teaching is tailored to its needs. Freshmen attend lectures in specialized subjects to develop a desire to learn and the sense of belonging to a department. As upperclassmen, they are made to take general education courses as a way of arousing their interests and providing a broader view of scholarship (Table 56.11, page 257). Sometimes seminars are integrated into general education courses: small classes and more specialized areas of study are used to maintain student enthusiasm for learning despite the mass-education systems they may encounter after admission (Table 56.12, page 258).

All universities have made efforts of this kind, especially in general education, but the private universities with their keen appreciation of the vital importance of education must intensify their interest in teaching methods for both general education and specialist programs. The need for both theoretical and practical studies of university teaching methods is being addressed in many ways. Kwansei Gakuin University, for example, after being rocked by campus unrest, established the Institute for Integrated Educational Research and Development to improve the quality of private-university teaching and to develop teaching methods suited to the times. Many faculties of medicine are also tackling the issue of educational reform: Juntendo University, for one, has set up a medical education research center and now holds workshops every summer for faculty members.

Today, private universities may be derided as leisure lands, and at one level these charges cannot be denied. What is important is that the private schools are creating educational systems truly characterized by originality and independent thought to stop this trend. Thus, despite the many problems they face, we can entrust Japan's private colleges and universities with our hopes for a brighter future.

Students who spend four years in a lively campus environment increasingly value the ties within the university community, among faculty and students, parents and alumni, because these are the ties that help create a distinctive school spirit. As one expression of this sense of community, many private universities have formed parent associations and other support groups. These groups hold meetings to report on the school's educational system and its founding ideas and on current programs and extracurricular activities being offered. In this way, they convey a sense of the school's distinctive spirit and heighten the feeling of belonging to the university community through question-and-answer and other exchanges between the school and its students' families. This community spirit has drawbacks too. It can create a mentality of dependence within the educational system that has frequently led to problems. Nevertheless, a university community has a human mix of strengths and weaknesses, and whether these are good or bad, liked or disliked, each school has come, over the years since its founding, to possess its own unique features and characteristics.

Table 56.11

Specialized Courses within General Education (Fiscal 1983)

	Total number of universities	Schools providing general education in 3rd and 4th years	Schools providing specialized courses in 1st and 2nd years				Total
			Schools where specialized courses are compulsory in 1st year	Schools where specialized courses are compulsory from 2nd year on	Schools where specialized courses are elective	Total	
National	95	70 (48)	71 (31)	53 (16)	46 (17)	87 (51)	90 (62)
Local-Public	34	22 (20)	23 (14)	12 (3)	14 (11)	29 (24)	29 (26)
Private	328	257 (234)	279 (208)	103 (53)	123 (92)	318 (270)	322 (295)
Total	457	349 (302)	373 (253)	168 (72)	183 (120)	434 (345)	441 (383)

Source: Ministry of Education, *Data on Universities*, No. 90, 1984.
Note: The figures in parentheses show the number of schools making use of specialized courses in all faculties.

Table 56.12

Innovative Approaches to Smaller Classes (Fiscal 1982)

	Total number of universities	Small foreign languages classes	Small beginning foreign languages classes	Small supervised lab or field work groups	All students participate in small seminars	Small supervised graduation thesis work groups (including research and writing)	Other innovative approaches	Total
National	95 (353)	24 (39)	6 (10)	60 (132)	43 (86)	66 (172)	25 (82)	83 (239)
Local-Public	34 (79)	7 (18)	1 (2)	10 (12)	13 (28)	19 (45)	5 (5)	26 (62)
Private	326 (712)	117 (201)	43 (56)	126 (165)	143 (291)	231 (389)	73 (129)	287 (542)
Total	455 (1,144)	148 (258)	50 (68)	196 (309)	199 (405)	316 (606)	103 (216)	396 (843)

Source: Ministry of Education, Data on Universities, No. 90, 1984.
Note: The figures in parentheses refer to faculties.

57
Ministry of Education Directive Concerning the Prevention of Delinquency of Pupils *(Jido Seito no Hiko no Boshi ni tsuite [Tsutatsu])*

Ministry of Education

November 25, 1980

Source: Ministry of Education, *Sengo Nihon Kyoiku Shiryo Shusei,* 12 (Tokyo: Sanichi Shobo, 1983), pp. 393–394. Translated by James Vardaman.

To: Chiefs of Education, Boards of Education,
Governors of Municipalities and Prefectures,
Presidents of National Universities with affiliated primary and secondary schools

Recently the rise in delinquency of pupils has continued unabated, and it is most regrettable that there have been incidents where this has led to social problems. According to the report of the National Police Agency, this trend is characterized by an increase of delinquency in younger age groups, an increase in incidents involving youths in motorcycle gangs, and an increase in cases of school violence involving junior high school students.

In this regard your special guidance has been requested formerly in the "Directive Concerning Prevention of Problem Behavior of Pupils," issued March 7, 1978. Once again, we ask you to give consideration to the following concerns, make them thoroughly understood throughout the organizations under your supervision, and provide further guidance in the prevention of delinquency of pupils.

1. Please give careful consideration to the appropriate carrying out of school educational activities in order that children do not turn to problem behavior as a result of maladjustment to school education.

(1) Carefully select the materials for teaching students, strive for the improvement of teaching methods, and be certain that students can fully understand the materials, so that they will become enthusiastically involved out of interest and liking. Moreover, devise its extension by various opportunities in school educational activity and by conducting guidance in accordance with the individuality and ability of each pupil.
(2) While cleaving to an organized system of course guidance, attach importance to consultation about plans so that pupils may firmly choose a course for themselves with a clear awareness of purpose vis-à-vis the future.

2. It is important to deepen understanding of students and for all teachers to join together in dealing with pupil guidance.

(1) Teachers should endeavor to develop close relations with pupils, develop a deep understanding of each and every pupil, and make efforts to cultivate desirable relations with them.

(2) While all teachers should obtain a deeper realization of the importance of pupil guidance, since there cannot be an appropriate means of dealing with the problematic behavior of pupils when teachers carry out divergent means of pupil guidance, all teachers should arrange a system of cooperation among themselves and actively work as one in the guidance of students.

If there appears anything out of the ordinary in the behavior or attitude of students, teachers should maintain close communications between the students of that grade, homeroom teachers, the supervisor of that grade, and the guidance supervisor, in order to carry out appropriate measures to solve the problem as early as possible.

(3) Schools should clarify their policies in regard to pupil guidance and endeavor to make those policies clear to the pupils themselves. Even trivial instances of violence should not be overlooked, but should be dealt with in a firm manner.

3. It is necessary that schools cooperate fully with homes and local community organizations.

(1) Schools should maintain even closer communications than ordinary with the homes of pupils and take advantage of every opportunity to build an understanding of the schools' policies concerning guidance. Schools and homes should exchange information concerning students' everyday behavior and cooperate in the nurturing of pupils.

(2) Schools should endeavor to maintain close relations with neighboring schools and local community organizations and groups, exchange information concerning trends of and strategies for dealing with delinquency, and come to grips with problem behavior of pupils. And, when necessary, schools should join together with and cooperate with these organizations in the prevention of pupil delinquency.

58
Concerning the [Ministry of Education] Survey of Actual Conditions of Moral Education in Public Elementary and Junior High Schools (*Koritsu Sho-Chugakko ni okeru Dotoku Kyoiku no Jisshi Jokyo no Chosa ni tsuite*)

August 5, 1983

Source: Mombu Jiho, no. 1274–1279 (July–December 1983), pp. 72–74. Translated by James Vardaman.

[In May the Ministry of Education carried out a survey of the actual conditions of moral education in all of the nation's public elementary and junior high schools. Under the name of the bureau chief of primary and secondary education, notification concerning the results was sent to the chairpersons of the boards of education of the respective prefectures, regions, and municipalities. . . .]

Bunshosho 213
5 August 1983

To: Chairperson of the Respective Boards of Education
From: Takaishi Kunio, Bureau Chief of Primary and Secondary Education

"Concerning the Survey of Actual Conditions of Moral Education in Public Elementary and Junior High Schools" (Notification)

As indicated in the title above, the survey referred to in Bunshosho 213, dated 5 August 1983, has been carried out and you are herein advised of the results. The attached is the summary of those results.

It is hardly worthy of mention that moral education plays an extremely important role in the character formation of children in school education. Especially in recent years there has been an upward trend in the number of occurrences of problem behavior of school pupils, and there is strong demand for the complete implementation of moral education.

In light of the significance of moral education, as a result of this survey, it appears necessary to establish the following improvements. Please give this due consideration and give guidance to the elementary and junior high schools under your supervision.

(1) There are some schools which have not drawn up an overall plan for moral education or an annual plan for guidance of the "moral education" class periods. They should do so promptly.

(2) There are schools in which the class time allotted for "moral education" is substantially below the standard number of hours. Care should be taken to guarantee the appropriate number of hours.

(3) The guidance materials for "moral education" periods are insufficient for systematic application; therefore, it is necessary to carefully prepare and enrich these materials and make efforts toward their effective, systematic application.

(4) Common consensus concerning "moral education" among all teachers is lacking. You should therefore employ occasions such as in-service training to deepen the mutual understanding among the teachers within the schools. Such occasions for study and training are currently insufficient and so, in order to improve the ability of teachers to provide guidance, such opportunities for training should be increased.

(5) At present, the cooperation between the school, home, and local community is not all that it might be. Therefore, the entire school should actively come to grips with this problem.

(6) A small number of schools has yet to place a time period clearly labeled "moral education" in the weekly time schedule. This should be rectified.

[Hereafter follows a summary of the report. This is one excerpt.]

IV. Guidance Concerning Basic Habits of Daily Life

(2) The five top-ranking topics of moral education which schools hoped to emphasize in the 1983 school year, in accordance with the course of study for respective schools, are as follows. Elementary schools: unreasonableness and persistence (14.8%); politeness and promptness (13.5%); trust and friendship (9.7%); independence and self-reliance (9.4%); respect for life, health, safety (8.5%). Junior high schools: basic habits of daily life (28.3%); improving group life (10.4%); strong will and persistence (.8%); and love for fellow man (9.3%).

59
Moral Education

1983

Source: Ministry of Education, *Course of Study for Elementary Schools in Japan* (Tokyo, 1983), pp. 111–117.

I. Overall Objectives

The objectives of Moral Education are based on the basic spirit of education stated in the Fundamental Law of Education and the School Education Law. Moral Education, in other words, is aimed at realizing a spirit of respect for human dignity in the actual life of family, school, and community, endeavoring to create a culture that is rich in individuality and to develop a democratic society and state, training Japanese to be capable of contributing to a peaceful international society, and cultivating their morality as the foundation thereof.

In the class of Moral Education, based on the above objectives, instruction should be given so as to develop pupils' ability to practice morality by maintaining close relations with moral education conducted in the class of each Subject and in Special Activities, and supplementing, intensifying, and integrating this moral education through systematic and developmental instruction, by enhancing pupils' ability to make moral judgment, by enriching their moral sentiments, and by seeking improvements in their moral attitudes and the willingness for practice.

II. Contents

1. To hold life in high regard, to promote good health, and to maintain safety. As for the major teaching contents, it is desirable that, in the lower grades, one should learn to take care of one's health and to protect oneself from risks; and, in the middle grades, to make efforts to maintain health and safety for oneself and others; and, in the higher grades, to hold in high regard the lives of oneself and others.

2. To observe good manners, and to live in an orderly manner. As for the major teaching contents, it is desirable that, in the lower grades, one should learn to greet others in daily life, to be tidy, and to be punctual; and, in the middle grades, to observe good manners and make effective use of time, according to the situation; and, in the higher grades, to recognize the importance of observing good manners and to live in an orderly manner.

3. To keep oneself neat and tidy, and to make good use of goods and money. As for the major teaching contents, it is desirable that, in the lower grades, one should learn to keep oneself neat and tidy, to distinguish one's belonging from others, and to use things carefully; and, in the middle and higher grades, to make efforts to put things in order efficiently and to make surroundings clean and neat, to recognize the value of goods and money, and to make appropriate use of them.

4. To act according to their own beliefs, and not to be moved unreasonably by others' opinions. As for the major teaching contents, it is desirable that, in the lower grades, one should learn to conduct one's own matters by oneself and to express oneself clearly; and, in the middle grades, to think carefully and to act according to one's own beliefs; and, in the higher grades, not to be moved unreasonably by the opinions and actions of others.

5. To respect another's freedom as well as one's own, and to be responsible for one's own acts. As for the major teaching contents, it is desirable that, in the lower grades, one should learn to act with a feeling of ease, and, in the middle grades, to take responsibility for one's own acts, and, in the higher grades, to consider the relationship between freedom and responsibility.

6. To act always cheerfully and sincerely. As for the major teaching contents, it is desirable that, in the lower grades, one should learn to be cheerful and spirited, not to tell lies or deceive others, and, in the middle and higher grades, to act always sincerely and lead a cheerful life.

7. To love justice and hate injustice, and to act righteously with courage. As for the major teaching contents, it is desirable that, in the lower grades, one should learn to love justice in one's own frame of mind; and, in the middle grades, to distinguish between justice and injustice, and to overcome temptation; and, in the upper grades, to carry out correct actions positively and with courage.

8. To endure hardships and persist to the end for the accomplishment of one's right aims. As for the major teaching contents, it is desirable that, in the lower grades, one should learn to bear hardship, and, in the middle grades, to persist to the end with patience, and, in the upper grades, to be steadfast and accomplish goals undaunted by obstacles or failures.

9. To reflect upon oneself by listening attentively to the advice of others, and to act with prudence and live an orderly life. As for the major teaching contents, it is desirable that, in the lower grades, one should learn to listen to the opinions of others, admit frankly one's own mistakes or faults, and to behave unselfishly; and, in the middle grades, to live a life of moderation; and, in the upper grades, to reflect always on one's words and behavior, to act with prudence and to live an orderly life.

10. To love nature, and to have affection toward animals and plants with a tender heart. As for the major teaching contents, it is desirable that, in the lower grades, one should learn to become intimate with nature and love and care for animals and plants with a tender heart, and, in the upper grades, to protect nature with love and care.

11. To esteem beautiful and noble things, and to have a pure mind. As for the major teaching contents, it is desirable that, in the lower grades, one should learn to take care of beautiful and noble things, and, in the higher grades, to respect noble things and have a pure mind.

12. To know one's own characteristics, and to develop one's strong points. As for the major teaching contents, it is desirable that, in the lower grades, one should learn to notice one's own characteristics, and, in the higher grades, to know one's strong points and to develop them.

13. To be always filled with aspiration, to aim toward higher goals, and to strive for their realization. As for the major teaching contents, it is desirable that, in the lower grades, one should learn to do things with zeal and to feel the joy of accomplishing things; and, in the middle grades, to set goals for oneself and strive toward their realization, and, in the higher grades, to strive toward higher goals and proceed with hope.

14. To think about things in a rational way, and always to have an attitude of inquiry. As for the major teaching contents, it is desirable that, in the lower grades, one should learn to think fully before one does anything; and in the middle grades, to make efforts to have always an attitude of inquiry; and, in the higher grades, to value truth and to behave critically and with judgment and determination, always being broad-minded.

15. To apply one's original ideas, and to cultivate actively new fields. As for the major teaching contents, it is desirable that, in the lower grades, one should learn to work by applying one's original ideas, and to carry out positively what one thinks is right; and, in the middle grades, to conceive of new ideas and methods; and, in the higher grades, to cultivate actively new fields.

16. To be kind to everybody, and to care for the weak and the unfortunate. As for the major teaching contents, it is desirable that, in the lower grades, one should learn to be kind to friends and younger people; and, in the middle grades, to comfort and encourage willingly the weak and unfortunate; and, in the higher grades, to consider the positions of other people by putting oneself in their place, and to have warm relationships with everybody.

17. To respect those who devote themselves to others, and to appreciate their work. As for the major teaching contents, it is desirable that, in the lower grades, one should learn to appreciate those who take care of others; and, in the middle grades, to respect and appreciate those who devote themselves to public welfare; and, in the higher grades, to admire the great achievements of one's predecessors.

18. To trust in and to be helpful to one another. As for the major teaching contents, it is desirable that, in the lower grades, one should learn to be friendly and help [others] and give encouragement to others; and, in the middle grades, to give friendly advice; and, in the higher grades, to trust in friends and not to betray them.

19. To be fair and impartial to everybody without prejudice. As for the major teaching contents, it is desirable that, in the lower grades, one should learn not to be occupied with one's personal likes and dislikes, and, in the middle and higher grades, to be fair and impartial to everybody without prejudice.

20. To understand others' feelings and positions, and to forgive others' faults generously. As for the major teaching contents, it is desirable that, in the lower grades, one should learn to forgive others' faults; and, in the middle grades, to understand others' positions and forgive others' faults; and, in the higher grades, to respect generously the opinions and positions of others which differ from one's own.

21. To understand the rules and the significance of making rules by oneself, and to follow them willingly. As for the major teaching contents, it is desirable that, in the lower grades, one should learn to obey rules and regulations, and, in the middle and higher grades, to understand fully the significance of rules and regulations and obey them willingly, and to make good rules on one's own and make improvements to them according to circumstances.

22. To assert one's rights properly, and to perform one's duties faithfully. As for the major teaching contents, it is desirable that, in the lower grades, one should learn to perform one's duties faithfully, and, in the higher grades, to assert one's rights properly, and to understand the relationship between rights and duties.

23. To appreciate the value of work, and to cooperate actively in the service of others. As for the major teaching contents, it is desirable that, in the lower grades, one should learn to strive to work; and, in the middle grades, to work together in the service of others; and, in the higher grades, to understand the significance and value of work and to work willingly in the service of others.

24. To take care of public property, and to protect public morality with a full awareness of being a member of society. As for the major teaching contents, it is desirable that, in the lower grades, one should learn to take care of public property and not to cause trouble to others, and, in the higher grades, to protect public morality and to serve the public willingly.

25. To love and respect all members of one's family, and to strive to have a good home. As for the major teaching contents, it is desirable that, in the lower grades, one should learn to have gratitude and affection toward one's parents; and, in the middle grades, to perform one's role in the family as a member of one's family; and, in the higher grades, to understand the positions of the respective members of one's family and to make efforts to have a good home.

26. To love and respect people at school, and to strive to establish good school traditions. As for the major teaching contents, it is desirable that, in the lower grades, one should learn to have gratitude and affection toward people at school; and, in the middle grades, to have affection toward school and to strive to make school a pleasant place; and, in the higher grades, to realize one's responsibility as a member of the school and to strive for the establishment of good school traditions.

27. *To love the nation with pride as a Japanese, and to contribute to the development of the nation.* As for the major teaching contents, it is desirable that, in the lower grades, one should learn to cultivate one's feelings toward the nation as a citizen; and, in the middle grades, to learn to love one's home town and to protect the land, culture, and traditions of the motherland; and, in the higher grades, to be aware of one's responsibility as a Japanese and to strive for the development of the nation.

28. *To have proper understanding of the love toward the people of the entire world, and to become an individual who can contribute to the welfare of mankind.* As for the major teaching contents, it is desirable that, in the lower grades, one should learn to cultivate feelings of friendship toward foreign peoples and to cooperate with kind hearts toward them, and, in the higher grades, to respect the lives and cultures of foreign peoples, and to cooperate with them in contributing to the peace of the world and to the welfare of mankind.

III. Preparation of the Teaching Program and Points for Special Consideration in Teaching

1. In preparing the teaching program, considerations should be given to taking up and emphasizing the particularly important contents on the basis of the correlation between Moral Education conducted in the class of each subject and in special activities, and to linking the several contents to one another for teaching.

2. The matters mentioned in [section] II indicate the major desirable contents according to the stages of the grades. In preparing the teaching program, careful consideration should be given to these matters.

3. The teaching program should be prepared specifically according to the realities of the region and pupils, and should be treated with flexibility and not be viewed as fixed.

4. In instructing pupils, consideration should be given to deepening mutual understanding among the school, the families and the community so that the effectiveness of teaching may be further enhanced.

5. It is important to be aware of the level of the pupils' morality at all times. However, it is not proper to apply the same rating method that is used for each subject with respect to the evaluation in the class of Moral Education.

60

Prime Minister Yasuhiro Nakasone's Formal Request on Education Reform at the First General Meeting of the Provisional Council on Educational Reform and His Address

September 5, 1984

Source: *Discussions on Education Reform in Japan* (Tokyo: Foreign Press Center, 1985), pp. 13–14 (excerpts).

At the first general meeting of the Provisional Council on Educational Reform on September 5, 1984, Prime Minister Yasuhiro Nakasone asked the Council to deliberate a set of urgent questions according to Article 2, Clause 1 of the Law for the Establishment of the Provisional Council on Educational Reform, together with his reasons for making the request.

Request: Concerning basic measures for achieving necessary reform in various areas for the realization of education that will match social changes and cultural development in Japan.

Reasons: Education in Japan has advanced rapidly since the end of World War II. But the drastic social changes and the increased number of students receiving higher education have had great impact upon education, giving rise to many problems.

At the same time, we need an educational system that matches society's further changes and cultural developments that include changes in the industrial structure, the advance of an "information society," greater expectations for lifelong education, and trends to internationalization in various fields.

For our country to build up a creative and vigorous society into the twenty-first century, we must appraise various problems that exist in the present education system and work toward the realization of an education system that can keep abreast of progress around us. It is therefore a pressing task to carry out necessary reform in pertinent areas, in conformity with the spirit of the Fundamental Law of Education, and establish a basic policy of reform.

The following is excerpted from Prime Minister Yasuhiro Nakasone's address at the first general meeting of the Provisional Council on Educational Reform:

"The circumstances that surround us today, both at home and abroad, are changing rapidly. I firmly believe that Japan is now at a point where a new future must be sought through the implementation of various necessary reform measures in the political, economic, social, educational, cultural and other areas. As for education, reform must be pursued from a long-range perspective and as a responsibility of the entire government. For this reason, we have brought into effect this new Law for the Establishment of the Provisional Council on Educational Reform, and created this council whose members are respected and learned citizens representing various sectors of society.

"The success and prosperity which Japan now enjoys were made possible by the people who grew up under our country's fine education system. There is no doubt that our educational standard is highly rated in the international community. However, we are no longer without problems, as indicated by the increasing incidence of classroom violence and juvenile delinquency in recent years, the social climate that overemphasizes educational background, the standardized nature of the Japanese education system, and the need for further internationalization. I believe that new situations requiring reform have arisen along with the passage of time over our 40-year postwar history.

"Moreover, in the case of our country in particular, the recent rapid changes in the industrial structure and the advance of "information oriented society and an aging society" not only affect the school education system but also give rise to a more pressing demand for a wider range of opportunities for lifelong education. Also, as internationalization advances in various fields, the internationalization of education becomes a vital issue. These social changes and cultural developments call for an educational system that can truly match the trends of the times.

"For our country to build up a creative and vigorous society into the twenty-first century, we simply cannot avoid addressing the problems that exist. We must keep up with new developments to effect educational reform.

"My inquiry today is based on this standpoint. But educational reform must also aim at fostering our country's own traditional culture and encouraging young people to be aware of their Japanese identity in contributing to the international community. We must help them learn social codes of conduct that are universal to mankind, pursue high ideals and maintain good health, and develop their personality and creativity.

"I ask you to consider the purpose of this council and thoroughly discuss education and its related issues from a broad and long-range viewpoint."

61
Study of Educational Reform and Improvement of Entrance Examination System: Prime Minister Yasuhiro Nakasone's "Seven-Point Proposal" on Educational Reform

December 10, 1983

Source: Discussions on Educational Reform in Japan (Tokyo: Foreign Press Center, 1985), pp. 13–14.

Prime Minister Yasuhiro Nakasone revealed a "seven-point proposal" on educational reform at a press conference held on December 10, 1983, in Kagoshima City while stumping for the December 18, 1983, general election. The proposal summed up Nakasone's views on educational reform, which he stressed during election campaign.

The seven points are:

(1) to consider changing the present so-called "6–3–3" school education system,

(2) to revise the upper secondary school entrance examination system and discontinue reliance on test results as the main yardstick of students' academic success,

(3) to revise the university entrance examination system,

(4) to promote extracurricular activities, such as community service activities,

(5) to reinforce moral education,

(6) to encourage a more cosmopolitan outlook, and

(7) to improve the quality of teaching staff by revising training and hiring programs.

In announcing his seven-point proposal at the press conference, the Prime Minister explained that he was firmly committed to implementing his brand of educational reform if he could win popular support for it. When asked how he intended to handle the financial aspect of the educational reform issue, he said that he would tackle the issue step by step, starting with the measures that were the least difficult to implement. He also noted that since the issue had to be approached over the medium to long term, he would make necessary financial readjustments along the way.

The following is the full text of the seven-point proposal.

(1) To start considering changing the present so-called 6–3–3–4 school education system: the quality of education under this system must be scrutinized and the system reviewed for radical reorganization.

(2) To revise the present upper secondary school entrance examination system and discontinue reliance on test results as the main yardstick by which to determine students' future academic course: the entrance examination system must be made more flexible and thoroughgoing measures taken to discourage school authorities from trying to determine students' scholastic aptitude by the grades they make on commercially prepared tests.

(3) To revise the university entrance examination system, including the joint first stage achievement test (*kyotsu ichiji*) and promote upgrading of the quality of higher education: the system must be revised to enable students to advance to higher education in keeping with individual ability, aptitude, and area of interest. Qualitative improvement of higher education, by giving more flexibility to the programs offered, is also called for.

(4) To promote extracurricular activities, such as community service activities and group training programs, and recognize such activities as a legitimate part of school education to encourage students' personality development: various kinds of work experience, including community service activities, as well as group trips and training sessions at facilities for youths, must be given more emphasis as part of school education. Students' performance in these activities should be appraised appropriately.

(5) To reinforce sensitivity training and moral education to encourage well-rounded personality development: the home, school, and community must work together closely in making this possible. Various youth groups, women's groups, PTA (Parent–Teacher Association), and sports and cultural associations should organize pertinent activities in each community to teach children discipline and assist them in their character formation as well as provide them with opportunities for sensitivity training, moral education, and physical education.

(6) To encourage students to become internationally minded people capable of functioning in the international community, their education should be aimed more at nurturing cosmopolitan views and upgrading foreign language ability, as well as making Japanese universities more compatible with foreign institutions of higher learning: Japanese universities should be internationalized to accept more non-Japanese students and should offer programs on international understanding and better English language programs to nurture citizens worthy of the trust and respect of the international community.

(7) To improve the quality of teaching staff by implementing better training programs and more realistic hiring systems, as well as by accepting mature and highly respected members of society as teachers: there is room for improvement in the current staff education system, hiring practices, and training programs. More teaching positions should be made available to mature and highly regarded members of society.

62
Progress Report by "Quality of Education" Panel of the Central Education Council

November 15, 1983

Source: Discussions on Educational Reform in Japan (Tokyo: Foreign Press Center, 1985), pp. 15–19.

On November 15, 1983, a panel on the quality of education submitted a progress report to the 13th Central Education Council (chairman: Takamura Shohei) at the Council's final general meeting.

Recommending a sweeping change in the quality of the nation's elementary and secondary education, the panel mapped out a basic concept of and the issues involved in the next wave of education reform which is to be the last of such reforms in the twentieth century.

A more diversified and flexible school education was stressed as a means for nurturing "the ability to teach oneself" which, the panel said, would prepare the younger generation for the anticipated period of drastic changes in society preceding the arrival of the twenty-first century.

Specifically, the panel stressed a flexible school education system resulting from a consistent education system that makes for smooth transition from the kindergarten level to elementary school level and from the lower secondary to upper secondary level.

The panel also recommended that repeated studies be made to find the most desirable method of making the school education system more flexible.

Emphasis on "Ability to Teach Self"

Preface

The Progress Report consists of five chapters. The first chapter gives an overview. In the second chapter, which is entitled "Changing Times and School Education," the report predicts new changes as society moves deeper into an "age of internationalization," "age of advanced information" and an "aging society," and stresses the ability to cope with such changes.

In discussing the present state of school education, the report cites three major problems and offers solutions. These problems are: (1) undesirable conduct of students, (2) excessive competition in school entrance examinations, and (3) standardized school education.

As a related issue, the report also stressed the role of the home and community in educating the young.

The report further recommended that special attention be given to (1) nurturing "the ability to teach oneself," (2) the basics of learning, (3) individuality and creativity, and (4) respect for culture and tradition. These four points were mentioned in view of social changes and the level of personal development achieved by children.

The report repeatedly stressed the need to give more diversity and flexibility to school education to let children develop their ability, personality and interests.

Chapter Three, entitled "Fundamental Issues Concerning the Quality of Elementary and Secondary Education," deals with the issue of compulsory education.

The report recommended a departure from the traditional standardized concept of compulsory education to one that can more flexibly accommodate [the] individual student's ability, aptitude and interests, especially on the lower secondary school level where education tends to become specialized.

The report also pointed out that lower secondary schools of today try to overload their students with knowledge of a fairly high level, in the belief that compulsory education must be complete in itself. However, this thinking is no longer practical today when the great majority of lower secondary school graduates go on to higher education and there are greater opportunities for lifelong education.

The report then discussed the meaning and role of elementary and secondary education as follows:

• Elementary education: This is for encouraging children to take interest in learning. Aside from reading, writing and arithmetic, children should also be taught basic good manners, discipline and common sense. Their mental and emotional development should also be accompanied by healthy physical development.

• Secondary education: While students at this level should be awakened to their responsibilities to society or the nation, attention should also be given to their ability and aptitude as individuals who are on the way to becoming young adults. Traditionally, the nation's education system tended to ignore this aspect because lower secondary school education is regarded as part of compulsory education. In the future, however, every attempt should be made to recognize each student's individuality and independence as a person under a more flexible and diversified education system.

The last part of this chapter dealt with the question of continuity from one level of education to the next. Noting that 93 percent of five-year-old children today attend kindergarten or day care centers and 94 percent of lower secondary school graduates advance to upper secondary schools, the report stressed better continuity from one level of school education to the next, especially from kindergarten to elementary school and from lower secondary school to upper secondary school.

• Kindergarten–elementary school: Although older kindergarten children and younger elementary school children have a great deal in common in terms of mental and emotional development, a clear gap exists between kindergarten and elementary school in the organization of curriculum and method of teaching. The report recommended that this gap be eliminated to assure better continuity.

• Lower secondary–upper secondary: The quality of lower secondary school education should be reviewed, and some of the subjects presently taught in lower secondary schools should be considered for inclusion in the upper secondary curriculum if need be. The report also mentioned the improvement of the secondary school entrance examination system as a vitally important issue.

Reorganization of Elementary School Curriculum

Chapter Four, entitled "Curricula for Elementary and Secondary Schools," discusses the quality of education and the method of teaching from the kindergarten level through upper secondary school level, and makes specific recommendations for reform.

1) Kindergarten education: A review of the 1964 guidelines on kindergarten is called for, in view of recent changes in social environment and the need to clarify the kindergarten's role in relation to elementary education and education in the home.

2) Elementary school curriculum: The school curriculum for younger elementary school children should differ from that for older children. Consequently, the present curriculum requires reorganization, whereby Japanese and arithmetic lessons should be given more emphasis. Further studies are needed to determine the most desirable curriculum for younger elementary school children.

3) Elementary education guidelines: While encouraging participation in various community activities and programs in addition to routine classroom drills for thorough mastery of the basics of learning, opportunities for extra coaching should also be given to slow learners. In the future, various new teaching methods should be introduced, including private coaching and group instructions, to create more diversified standards by which to assess students' academic performance.

4) Lower secondary school curriculum: This should be reorganized on the understanding that lower secondary school education is merely the first stage of secondary education. The quality of education calls for improvement, and consideration should be made to lengthen school hours and increase the number of optional subjects. Consideration should be given to interrelation among curricula, moral education and extracurricular activities.

5) Secondary education guidelines: Diversified methods of teaching should

be introduced, including opportunities for extra coaching for slow learners. In implementing such diversified and flexible teaching arrangements to accommodate the needs of individual students, thorough studies should be made to determine what subjects to include, how they are to be taught and when to start. Also, the present standard of grading the student's academic performance should be made more flexible.

6) Upper secondary school curriculum: The expansion of lower secondary school optional subjects would call for a greater diversification of upper secondary school education, which should be achieved by allowing numerous subjects to be included among upper secondary optional subjects. Special attention should be given to revising the subjects for social studies. Furthermore, in connection with raising the academic standard of upper secondary school education, one important issue that requires to be addressed is that of smooth transition from the upper secondary level of education to higher education.

7) Guidance on way of living in adolescence: Secondary school students are at a stage in life when moral education and guidance on life in general are of vital importance.

8) Vocational education: A more systematic approach is called for in preparing lower and upper secondary school students for professional life. In view of the recent progress in electronics technology and service industry, a review of the present vocational school system would also be in order.

9) Credits and years of school attendance: Studies should be made to introduce the benefits of the credit earning system to upper secondary education. Also to be recommended is the implementation of a credit exchange system for upper secondary schools, as well as a system for evaluating the academic performance of students who were transferred from vocational schools or overseas schools.

10) Improvement of the secondary school entrance examination system: While this task is to be carried out on the initiative of prefectural authorities in keeping with their respective local situations, the main emphasis should be on making the system as flexible as possible. In addition to revising the entrance examination system, a broader screening system should be adopted for the selection of applicants. Lower secondary schools should not be turned into cram schools to prepare students for upper secondary school entrance examinations, and for that, it would be necessary to look into the possibility of accepting more upper secondary school candidates on recommendation from their lower secondary schools as well as of admitting them on a trial basis.

In the fifth and last chapter, entitled "Problems in the Elementary and Secondary Education System," the report discusses the school education system which is now under growing public pressure to change.

The report pointed out that the school education system is not merely a hierarchy of schools for different levels of education, but a comprehensive system combining various systems and practices that support public education.

The report stressed efforts to give maximum flexibility to the present school education system through the establishment of new types of upper secondary schools, the improvement of the upper secondary school entrance examination system, and the creation of secondary schools that combine the lower and upper levels.

The report recommended that an appropriate new school education system be considered if the present system is found to be incapable of being made more flexible.

The report concluded that "thorough studies are called for in the future in addressing various problems concerning the creation of a more flexible and desirable school education system."

63
Yomiuri Shimbun Opinion Survey on Education

March 1984

Source: Discussions on Educational Reform in Japan (Tokyo: Foreign Press Center, 1985), pp. 25–29.

In a *Yomiuri Shimbun* opinion poll conducted on 525 prominent members of society in March 1984, 70 percent of the respondents said that compulsory education in this country was being distorted by an overemphasis on the school entrance examination system, and 60 percent lamented the absence of moral education in the classroom. These figures revealed the respondents' deep-seated dissatisfaction with the present school education system in Japan.

The pollees were selected from about 13,500 names registered in the 1984 edition of the Yomiuri Annual Who's Who, which lists society's prominent members classified by the seven fields of:

1. politics, administration, law and labor;
2. economy and business;
3. humanities;
4. natural sciences;
5. literary art;
6. fine arts, music, drama, and sports;
7. local communities.

The 525 names, consisting of 75 from each of the seven fields, were selected by the random sampling method.

Compulsory Education

The pollees were first asked to compare the schooling they received as students with what today's elementary and lower secondary school students are getting, and to judge whether the present public education system was better or worse than in their times. Those who responded "worse" slightly outnumbered those who saw the present situation in a more positive light.

Thirty-four percent of the respondents said that the present situation was "relatively worse" or "worse," outnumbering those who did not think so.

In a nationwide opinion survey conducted by the Yomiuri Shimbun in late February 1984, 50 percent of the respondents said that the present situation was worse than in their own times, and 57 percent said they were "relatively dissatisfied" or "dissatisfied" with the present school education system.

Asked what they thought were some of the problems besetting the nation's compulsory education, seven out of ten pollees said "overemphasis on the school entrance examination system," while 60 percent pointed out "the absence of moral education." More than 40 percent lamented the poor quality of teachers and their inability to deal with dropouts.

Of those who cited the negative effects of the excessive emphasis on the school entrance examination system, about 70 percent were people who were involved with education in one form or another. This category made up 60 percent of all the pollees.

As for moral education, 85 percent of educational and business leaders lamented its absence, although the corresponding figure was 31 percent among those in the field of humanities.

On the other hand, a high positive rating of over 80 percent was made on the availability of "better school facilities than before." Those who gave this positive evaluation included those who were generally critical of the present education system.

In this survey, the respondents were also invited to write down their comments. Excerpts:

—"Teachers don't care enough about their pupils and are doing quite poorly in helping them develop personality."

—"The Education Ministry and Japan Teachers' Union *(Nikkyoso)* are too bureaucratic."

—"It is hard to understand why lower secondary school English classes have to be reduced to give mere 'relaxed hours' *(yutori-no-jikan)*."

—"Physical education is being underestimated."

There were also some positive comments, among which was that "state-designated school textbooks have been abolished and all school textbooks are now distributed free of charge."

In summary, the prevalent view among the pollees was that while schools of today are better than in the past in terms of facilities and other material aspects, there was much room for improvement in the quality of education and teachers in general.

Teachers

Severe judgment was passed on the quality of teachers. Only three percent of the pollees said that today's teachers were better than in the past, in contrast to 46 percent who thought to the contrary.

The survey asked the respondents to define the characteristics of today's teachers in relation to five factors which included personal appeal, ability to teach and compassion toward their pupils.

Sixty-two percent said that today's teachers were lacking in principle, and 54 percent judged them to be wanting in personal appeal, indicating that there was considerable dissatisfaction with the quality of teachers as persons.

In another nationwide Yomiuri Shimbun opinion poll conducted in 1982 on the subject of the quality of school teachers, only five percent of the pollees said that they could rely on "the majority of teachers," and 18 percent said that "relatively many" could be relied upon. On the other hand, 23 percent and 36 percent, respectively, replied that the number of teachers they could trust were "few" and "relatively few." Thus, both the 1982 and 1984 surveys revealed similar results.

In the 1984 survey, the respondents from the economic and business circles were the severest critics of teachers of today. Those who said they could trust only "few" and "relatively few" teachers accounted for 63 percent, which figure was considerably higher than in the 1982 nationwide survey.

Opinion was split on how to increase the number of teachers who could be relied upon. Those who said "select the right people regardless of age and career background" and "give them continuous training after they have been employed" came to over 50 percent each, while 40 percent recommended "better conditions of employment."

In this connection, some expressed sympathy with the plight of teachers of today who, they noted, were overburdened with miscellaneous tasks.

School Entrance Examination System

The so-called deviation value *(hensachi)* is the yardstick by which students are advised to choose which lower or upper secondary school to go to. Many of the pollees, of all ages and fields, responded that this system was creating problems.

While 24 percent endorsed the "deviation value" as a "necessary yardstick," 62 percent rejected it, and 70 percent said that the present system whereby students are given guidance "ignores the student's aspirations and personality."

But on the question of how to improve the present upper secondary school entrance examination system, diverse views were expressed. Fifty-five percent recommended that "the students' character and such nonacademic activities as student government, club and volunteer activities be given more consideration," 36 percent recommended "less emphasis on the results of scholastic achievement tests," and 31 percent called for "more interviews with applicants."

The majority of the respondents gave a negative evaluation to the joint first stage achievement test system for public universities.

Only four percent insisted on keeping the system, whereas 45 percent and 38 percent, respectively, called for "changes" and "abolition." The proportion of those who demanded the system's abolition came to 44 percent among those from the education and related fields.

Causes of Juvenile Delinquency

Juvenile delinquency has become a problem not only in lower secondary schools but also in elementary schools. The survey asked the respondents to select as many reasons as they saw for this problem.

"Overprotective parents who can't discipline their children properly" and "prevalence of materialistic thinking in society" rated more than 60 percent each, followed by "absence of moral education" (50 percent) and "overevaluation of children's academic performance on the part of parents" (46 percent). Those who blamed the problem on teachers and the school education system were unexpectedly few.

The proportion of those who held "overprotective parents who can't discipline their children properly" in grave responsibility amounted to close to 80 percent among the respondents who were critical of today's compulsory education system.

The corresponding figures were 75 percent among those in the fields of fine arts, music, drama and sports, and local community leaders, and 58 percent among literary artists and writers.

The survey further asked the pollees to pick one out of "home," "school" or "society" as the main reason for juvenile delinquency. Fifty-four percent chose "home," 24 percent "society," and 10 percent "school."

A considerable number of people responded, however, that the three were closely interrelated and therefore it was not realistic to single out just one.

In the 1982 nationwide survey, 42 percent cited "absence of discipline in the home" as the cause of classroom violence, and 28 percent gave "deterioration of the social environment" as the reason.

Education Reform

Varied views were given on educational reform, and the only recommendation that was supported by over 50 percent of the pollees was that the quality of teachers be improved. The recommendations that received 40 percent support were "reinforcement of moral education," "modification of the university entrance examination system," and "modification of the 6–3–3–4 school system." These were followed by "modification of the upper secondary school entrance examination system," "improvement of the quality of education," and "reduction of class size," in that order. Only about one percent of the pollees encouraged "jumping classes" and "greater variety of optional courses."

Broken down by field, high proportions of local community leaders (72 percent), economic and business leaders (66 percent) and those in the political, administrative, legal and labor circles (64 percent) questioned the quality of teachers.

As for the issue of moral education, nearly 70 percent of local community leaders and economic and business leaders considered this to be an important issue, while only 20 percent of those in the humanities field and 36 percent of literary artists and writers shared that view.

As for the modification of the "6–3–3–4" system, 58 percent of economic and business leaders supported this, whereas the support rate was lower among all others. With those in the education and related circles, for instance, the support rate was 38 percent and ranked below "improvement of the quality of teachers" and "modification of the university entrance examination system."

64
Seven Recommendations to Revitalize School Education

The Kyoto Group for Study of Global Issues
Chairman: Matsushita Konosuke

March 13, 1984

Source: The Kyoto Group for Study of Global Issues, *Discussions on Educational Reform in Japan* (Tokyo: Foreign Press Center, 1985), pp. 31–34.

While the following recommendations were made with due appraisal of the successes which this country has so far had with education, they also aim to promote educational reform as far as possible within reasonable means. These recommendations apply to the nation's elementary and secondary education only.

Principle of Fair Competition

The sort of education that can match the needs of the twenty-first century must be ruled by the principle of fair competition in all areas. A diversified and technologically sophisticated society requires many different types of talented citizens. For that, the school must be a place where students are motivated to learn. An environment must be created which encourages free competition not only among students but also among teachers to become better educators.

Where there is no fair competition, there can be no progress. Under apathetic teachers who have no interest in self-improvement through fair competition, it would be impossible to expect the sort of education that will help each student fulfill his personal potential.

Ideally, education should be free and independent of constraints and interference from public authorities as much as possible. In particular, we would like to see as much decontrol as possible—if not any outright abolition of various restrictions—in the education system. We strongly believe that today's standardized school system and the use of standardized teaching materials will create a monolithic value system. In such an environment, children's spontaneous motivations and aspirations can be easily stymied. They may well become disillusioned with school, and some may choose to drop out of school. Seen in this light, we recommend that a new free and flexible school education system be worked out—one that does not necessarily follow the conventional 6–3–3 formula.

A More Flexible System

It would also be worth considering a system whereby students without high school diploma can still hope to acquire qualifications for higher education or employment. It would be necessary to make the education system more flexible in such a way that once children have been taught the basics of education in elementary school, they will have as much freedom as possible in deciding what they want of the next step of education. For some, it may be to pursue special areas of study, and for others, it may be to seek new areas where they can be more comfortable. The ultimate ideal would be to give ample leeway to those who are eager to study. Some may wish to study on their own or at private academies before they enter university. Some may wish to go back to school after some years of job experience. There should be a wide choice of ways in which people can study.

We also recommend that school authorities practice greater flexibility in their selection of students. The present student admission system serves only to make "standardized" people out of youngsters, not individuals with distinct personalities —the types who can truly adjust to the anticipated social changes into the next century. We call for efforts to diversify the standards of student selection.

As for the establishment of new schools, we believe that a gradual shift should be made from the present reliance on public schools to private schools, and free competition should be encouraged among these schools for the betterment of the quality of education.

We ought to remind ourselves that, during the period of drastic transition brought about by the Meiji Restoration, many private academies sprang up to generate a new wave of education for the next generation. The spirit of renovation came from within every individual who sensed the dawning of a new era. Today, we are undergoing a period of renovation that compares with the Meiji Restoration. Now is precisely the time to openly welcome the creation of many types of new private schools so that children may have a wide choice of schools where learning can be truly enjoyable and rewarding.

Moral Education

Each of these new schools should have a clearly defined set of principles of education of its own, and be expected to follow through these principles. In this connection, teaching social norms would be a very important consideration.

While some people may say that this is forcing moral education on children, we believe that certain rules are vital to society's sound functioning and progress and it would be in the interests of children to be taught these rules clearly, if they are to live happily in the next century. Needless to say, the teaching of social norms must not be limited to the classroom. The home, community and place of work should all be responsible, especially the home. Education, after all, starts in the home where children's characters are formed. Still, the school is also partially responsible for children's character formation. The home and school must join hands in educating the young.

Seven Recommendations to Revitalize School Education

1. Diversification of school education through relaxation of rules on establishment of new schools. We recommend that the current rules on the establishment of new schools be relaxed, so that anyone who is truly interested in education should be permitted to open a school. This would increase the variety of schools. We believe that the different potential of each individual school child can be best developed only when there are schools with distinctive characteristics run by dedicated educators with a firm and sound philosophy of education.

2. Relaxation of the school zone system. The present school zone system should be vastly relaxed to enable children to attend schools of their choice. The school zone system was created to ensure egalitarian education, and it has certainly served a useful purpose to this day. However, now that equal educational opportunities exist virtually for all, we think it is high time that a new system that gives students a greater freedom of choice be considered.

3. Employment of dedicated teachers. We recommend that the present teaching license system be revised to allow unlicensed people to teach full-time or part-time, provided they have the ability, aptitude and genuine interest in education. We also recommend that more opportunities for training be made available to teachers. It may also be worth considering the introduction of limited periods of service and a system of reappointment of teachers according to circumstances.

4. Greater flexibility in the years, contents and methods of education. The abilities of individual children cannot be fully fathomed by any single yardstick. To ensure that each child receives education that matches his abilities, the present demarcation of school years by age should be made less rigid. Early developers should be allowed to jump classes, while slower learners might need to repeat, even during the compulsory education. As for children who reveal special talents in certain areas, they may benefit greatly from being allowed to attend more advanced classes in these particular fields.

The contents and methods of education should also be decided freely by school operators, be they the national or local government, private bodies or individuals, and not be required to follow any fixed formula. However, where such basics of education as reading, writing and arithmetic are concerned, we recommend that a standard academic aptitude system be adopted for each age group to make sure that no child is left behind the minimum level of education required of every citizen.

5. Review of the present school system. While the present 6–3–3 system has its merits and therefore should not be rejected outright, we strongly believe that this system should not be regarded as the one and only "right" system. We see nothing wrong with schools that follow, for example, a 6–4, or 6–6, or even 5–4 system. The choice should be left to each school. Furthermore, any student who has passed the aforementioned standard academic aptitude test should have the freedom not to attend school, if he so wishes.

6. Abolition of the "deviation value" (hensachi) system. We oppose the present practice under which students are instructed to choose schools based on their "deviation value." The choice of schools should be left to each student, and the school authorities should try to guide the student along a course that is considered most suitable for him. And each school should have the liberty to set its own student admission standards in accordance with the sort of education offered. In other words, each school should have its own school entrance examination system. Some schools may decide to accept students on the basis of comprehensive standards of evaluation, including records on such extracurricular activities as cultural, artistic, athletic and community service activities.

7. *Enforcement of moral education.* There are certain social norms which all human beings are expected to conform to such as:

a) taking responsibility for one's words and actions,
b) kindness and consideration for others, and
c) respect for law, social rules and justice.

All these are indispensable to society's sound progress.

But no one can be forced into observing social norms by intimidation or sheer exercise of power. Children must be helped to understand why the norms are necessary through real-life experiences. Needless to say, this is the responsibility of the home and society at large. Still, we believe that schools should also be expected to remain positively committed to this.

65
A Proposition from Businessmen for Educational Reform: In Pursuit of Creativity, Diversity, and Internationality

Education Council, Japan Committee for Economic
Development (*Keizai Doyukai*)

July 1984

Source: Education Council, Japan Committee for Economic Development, *Discussions on Educational Reform in Japan* (Tokyo: Foreign Press Center, 1985), pp. 35–42.

An Introductory Remark

It is the common hope of businessmen to expand their corporate activities and strengthen their system in line with progress being realized by the Japanese economy. However, it is extremely difficult to forecast the environment in the forthcoming century, and the determination of strategies for survival is a major task for a great number of enterprises.

In such an environment, "acquisition and fostering of human resources" are considered to be more significant than any other aspects of society. Listing the qualifications expected of young people would accompany certain risks, but in abstract terminology, they can be classified into the three categories of "creativity," "diversity," and "internationality."

Creativity should be ranked as the most desirable qualification, although it is difficult to determine who has creative potential. The development of diversity, an antonym of uniformity, is hoped for in many areas in society. A combination of human resources each having a variety of unique characteristics is the source of strength for an enterprise, assuring flexibility in dealing with an uncertain future.

In the area of internationality, we must remind ourselves of the increasing expectations people in other nations have of the role to be played by the Japanese. Although Japanese products are diffused throughout the world and Japanese factories are increasingly being set up in foreign countries, Japan's closed system can still be strongly seen in various fields of society such as education, and meeting the needs of internationalization has long been delayed.

The following items clarify the opinions of this committee on the tasks and plans which various groups in society must deal with in order to realize creativity, diversity, and internationality.

First, we start by discussing how enterprises, government agencies and other bodies should deal with new employees, then consider the individualization of universities, improvement of college entrance examinations and lower and upper secondary school system reforms. Then, we shall make reference to internationality and how to cope with the era of high technology.

1. Revision of Personnel Evaluation Standards in Business Enterprises and Government Agencies

Standards of personnel evaluation vary depending on the characteristics of each institution, and such evaluations are subject to change together with the changes of the times. However, standards set without a principle and concentration on passive activities may invite a loss of energy not only in the organization but in the entire society.

Business enterprises must place importance on the fact that their philosophy and methods in employee relations policy (especially in recruiting) have great impact on the educational field. Businesses must accumulate their individual ideas.

In the same manner, national qualifying examinations (government employees, teachers, judicial officers, diplomats, doctors, etc.), which have considerable influence on society, must be reviewed in terms of their own philosophy and method.

The following points are mainly focused on companies. Items (1) through (4) relate to employee relations in general, and items (5) and thereafter relate to the recruitment process of employees.

(1) Carry out a policy for employees which respects the individuality of employees.

(2) Respect specialists and try to utilize their skills.

(3) Have a positive policy for employees that will foster the potential capabilities of women.

(4) Give consideration to those who wish to engage in meaningful volunteer activities such as Japan Overseas Cooperation Volunteers so that those activities would not be disadvantageous regarding remuneration, promotion, and so on.

(5) Provide employment opportunities throughout the year to prevent excessive homogeneity.

(6) Give opportunities to applicants who have graduated from college 2–3 years previously.

(7) Positively accept those who have experienced foreign education due to their fathers' overseas assignments or those who graduated from foreign universities, regardless of age or period of employment. The above would strengthen a company's ability to internationalize and, at the same time, internally resolve a part of worker problems, which accompany overseas assignments.

(8) Encourage recruiting from as many schools as possible. When there are plural applicants who appear to be equal in ability, the company should try to select the person who has the smallest number of fellow alumni or alumnae members within the company.

(9) Upon selection, place importance on the characteristics of the applicants such as "way of life," "way of thinking," and "critical mind."

(10) It is desirable to examine not only academic capabilities but also the personal traits necessary for the relevant subject of the national qualifying examinations.

2. Individualization of Universities

During the past several decades, the wave of uniformity and self-effacement surged upon various fields in society. This trend seems to be common throughout the world and observed in the formative period of industrial societies. In our country, this trend was obvious to the extreme because of a more rapid industrialization process than that of western nations, as well as the national character of the Japanese, who tend to lean toward uniformity.

During this period, the evaluation of universities has tended to be uniform; therefore, people have become conscious of the rank order of universities. In order to emerge from such a past and meet the diversified needs of the Japanese people in future society, each university must develop a basic philosophy and a unique atmosphere rooted in the characteristics of the community, without following blindly the poor examples set by others.

(1) A university that has a certain degree of history and record should develop a unique curriculum and when conducting education, it should positively adopt methods (such as case study, or a combination of video lectures and group discussions) not necessarily limited to a traditional lecture-oriented education. It is desirable for the Ministry of Education to make positive evaluations of these efforts.

(2) Try for individualized admission screening method to select students who fit the atmosphere of the university.

(3) It is desirable that upon selection, many universities evaluate the records of volunteer activities or work study, or capabilities and records in sports, or art.

(4) From the standpoint of promoting the individuality of private universities, conduct a fundamental review of the payment standard of national subsidy support to private universities and begin to introduce amendments.

3. Improvement of the Joint First Stage Achievement Test

We have come to a time of making a fundamental revision of the joint first stage achievement test for 5 subjects in 7 areas. Giving examinations on two basic subjects, Japanese language and mathematics, would seem to be a natural selection for the second stage achievement test: however, there is a concern that the existing method in which other subjects largely depend on a single measure is creating an undesirable influence on elementary, lower and upper secondary school education. It is desired that the respective universities and departments consider the implementation of a unique examination method for subjects other than Japanese and mathematics.

(1) Limit the subjects of the joint first stage achievement test to two subjects, Japanese and mathematics, and carry this program out 3 to 4 times per years.

(2) When the above item is realized, it is desirable that many private universities utilize it.

(3) For foreign language, it is desirable to adopt formats such as those in the English Proficiency Examination or TOEFL (Test of English as a Foreign Language) in which the four skills of "reading," "writing," "hearing," and "speaking" can be comprehensively examined. The first stage test, which does not examine "hearing" and "speaking," should be eliminated since it has an undesirable impact on lower and upper secondary school English education. However, it may remain if the TOEFL or EPE-style method is adopted to a large degree bearing some risk and higher costs.

(4) Social science subjects shall be eliminated from the joint first stage test since the current system demands mere memorization of facts. The knowledge on these subjects would be better evaluated in the second stage test. However,

the social sciences are no less important, and the second stage test needs to confirm how much efforts the student should put into social studies by examining study reports from lower and upper secondary school records. Also, it is desirable that the second stage test should help discover the students' ability and the potential for social sciences by introducing screening methods such as essay, interview, and other written tests incorporating special ideas.

(5) For the same reason, it is desirable to delete the natural sciences from the first stage test and conduct the screening in the second stage test. Considerations equivalent to those given to social science must be given to the natural sciences because of its importance. This is especially true when we consider the fact that the graduates of the social sciences or the humanities lack interest in the scientific fields in comparison to western nations.

4. Revision of the 6–3–3 System

If a choice is to be made between the 6–3–3 system and 6–6 system without any preconditions, the selection would be the 6–6 system without any examinations, in which students can devote themselves to study without anxiety.

However, it is extremely difficult to modify the existing 6–3–3 system to 6–6 in a single step. Also a negative impact of lack of variety could be anticipated in a different sense. Much less it is unrealistic to call for the actualization of new concepts such as 5–4–4 and the like. At this point, realistic steps aimed at the diversity of the school system are desired.

(1) Allow the existence of the 6–6 system along with 6–3–3 by partially amending the School Education Law.

(2) It is desirable that enthusiastic private schools advance into the 6–6 year system when the above-mentioned amendment of the law is realized.

(3) Different regions may have different opinions, so it is desirable that in the case of public schools, about 20% of the schools shift to the 6–6 year system, and develop in line with the 6–3–3 system.

(4) Consideration should even be given to financial benefits as in the existing system, for the first 3 years of the second 6 years (period of compulsory education) when the 6–6 system is realized.

(5) There is an increase in students who pass the college entrance qualifying examination through private institutions other than regular high schools. The existence of such students bypassing the conventional route and private institutions should be positively evaluated.

(6) We would like to propose moving a step forward and abolishing qualifying proficiency examinations for entry into schools of higher learning, and leave acceptance or refusal of entry to the discretion of the accepting schools. This will vitalize education with the systems of "6–3–0–4" or "6–3–3–0–2" and social mobility shall be promoted. Also, the activities in items (5) and (6) will be a

stimulant to the "stagnation" of current education, and, at the same time, become a trigger for increasing educational institutions not depending on national fund subsidies for support.

5. *Advancement to Internationalization*

There is no guarantee that man's mind will be further directed toward the outside with the progress of economic internationalization. In our country, the closed door trend deeply remains not only toward foreign nations but in many fields domestically. A policy to overcome such a trend must be positively followed.

(1) Education to foster tolerance toward people who are different and interest in them should be conducted at home, in preschool and at elementary schools.

(2) Affection for and mastery of one's own culture is essential to understanding foreign cultures as well as to establishing one's own identity. Contents of study and its method in Japanese language and history at elementary, lower, and upper secondary school levels must be significantly improved.

(3) In English language study at lower and upper secondary school levels, serious considerations must be given to the four skills of "reading," "writing," "hearing," and "speaking" as clearly stated in the course of study. In the present-day education, attention to the three areas other than "reading" is lacking in general.

(4) An attempt should be made to change the beginning of the academic year from April to September. This would facilitate the exchange of teachers and students with the majority of foreign countries which begin the academic year in September, and would also allow the mutual exchange between summer programs.

For the business circles, such a shift is expected to cause inconveniences in the first year since the entry of college graduates would be shifted from April to September, but there would be no loss and much to gain in the long run.

(5) Capabilities in languages other than English, German, or French should be given more consideration. For instance such linguistic capability should be counted as advantage at college entrance examinations. Even if colleges do not provide special language courses, it is desired that efforts made outside of school be evaluated and credits be given.

(6) Business enterprises and government bodies should note the trend of a decline in the aspiration of youth to learn a special language, and make efforts to provide various measures including some incentive measures.

(7) More and more foreign students are wishing to learn specific technologies or skills in Japan during a short stay. It is desirable to add curricula in English for the convenience of these foreign students.

(8) Acceptance of foreign teachers in schools and employment of foreigners as regular employees in companies should be positively promoted over a broad area.

6. Strengthening Education in Science and Technology

It is commonly said that the industrial strength of our nation is supported by the excellent technologies involving "application" and "development," but much is dependent on other developed nations in the "basics" field. In the future, however, the research on basics should be pursued to enhance Japan's contribution to the world.

The field of "basics" especially requires creativity; therefore, this must be seriously challenged in order to eliminate the common view that Japanese abilities are limited. To achieve this objective, education, which aims at tapping the creative ability of individuals at various levels of school education, must be promoted.

(1) When allocating the budget, the government shall place importance on science and technology (especially on the basic science) and conduct assessments from a long-term perspective.

(2) Companies with sound financial status should positively expand and strengthen the activities in basic research.

(3) In accordance with (2) above, colleges should try to expand their science departments.

(4) Cooperation between the industry and the academic circles is desired in the upstream, namely in the basic study, rather than in the downstream, where the product reaches the consumer market.

(5) Establish new educational institutions whose purpose is to foster creativity in science and technology in the early period.

Select 2 or 3 schools from among the national universities having science departments, and directly link 3-year subsidiary schools (similar to upper secondary schools attached to colleges). This would provide opportunities to begin early studies in an exclusive field as well as to take more upper-level classes appropriate to the skill level.

General study courses, important for broad character formation for science students, should be organized so that classes can be taken at appropriate times during a 7-year period.

7. Education for the Information Society

As a result of the widespread use of computers, changes in education are now called for.

Ideas must be introduced to the new methods in curriculum programing, the operation of classes and self-study involving the positive use of computers. At what level of the current compulsory education system should a child start learning computer is a recent topic of discussion.

If it starts too early, there is a danger of lacking a basic understanding in figures or letters, and, if too late, it becomes difficult to acquire skills as in the case of musical instruments and sports.

When a comparison is made between Japan and the United States for lower secondary education, computer utilization is seen more in the U.S., and it appears necessary that Japan catch up.

In the area of educating computer software system engineers, if the current trend continues, the current shortage is not expected to be filled even when we enter the next century. The growth of manpower in the field of software as well as hardware is the primary task for the future.

(1) A meeting should be held to seek advice from various groups in Japan in the educational and business circles regarding at what level of the current compulsory education to introduce computer usage. It would take time to reach conclusion, but immediate guidance is called for.

(2) A comprehensive plan must be prepared for educating software engineers and programmers. The needs must be met especially at commercial and industrial upper secondary schools, and if such upper secondary schools and special training schools are combined, the effect of education would further be improved.

(3) There is a need to conduct training programs for teachers so that they also possess the knowledge and skills relating to computers. The preparation of a fundamental system is called for.

(4) Development of educational materials, which combine audio-visual materials and computers, is an immediate task. In the U.S., attractive programs, which include the [insertion] of games into case studies are [common]. Japan is largely lagging in this field.

66
Japan Teachers' Union's Views on the Bill to Establish the Provisional Council on Educational Reform

March 27, 1984

Source: Discussions on Educational Reform in Japan (Tokyo: Foreign Press Center, 1985), p. 43.

Following the approval by the Cabinet on March 27 of the bill for the creation of the Provisional Council on Educational Reform, Japan Teachers' Union *(Nikkyoso)* released on the same day the following statement.

The Bill for the Creation of the Provisional Council on Education Reform Threatens to Violate the Neutrality of Education

1) The bill stipulates that this provisional council is to be an advisory panel to the prime minister in conformity with Article 8 of the National Government Organization Act, and that the council's chairman is to be appointed by the prime minister. As such, the bill creates a potential threat of control and interference in education by the party in power for the sake of implementing the party's education policy. We cannot support such a council which is as undemocratic as the Extraordinary Administrative Reform Council.

2) We hold the government in deep mistrust for adopting, also on the same day, the bill for the amendment of the Teachers' License Act which will have the effect of undermining the principle of liberal training of teachers. We question this move by the government, made without public consensus, and at the very time when a comprehensive educational reform is being sought by the public at large.

We are also concerned that the council is expected to follow the recommendations made by the Central Education Council, the Extraordinary Administrative Reform Council and the Round-Table Conference on Education, all of which are critical of and opposed to the principles of post–World War II education. Lastly, we cannot accept this bill which absolves the ruling Liberal Democratic Party of its failure to assume responsibility for educational administration.

3) For the time being, we intend to reinforce popular movement for the attainment of such pressing goals as the early introduction of smaller classes of no more than 40, the increase in the number of teachers, the elimination of mammoth-sized schools, the creation of new upper secondary schools, and the substantial increase in aid to private schools and universities.

67
The Japan Socialist Party's Counter-Proposal to the Establishment of the Provisional Council on Educational Reform

March 21, 1984

Source: Discussions on Educational Reform in Japan (Tokyo: Foreign Press Center, 1985), pp. 45–47.

At a special committee meeting on educational reform held on March 21, the Japan Socialist Party drew up a counter-proposal to Prime Minister Yasuhiro Nakasone's plans for the creation of the Provisional Council on Educational Reform.

The following is an outline of the JSP proposal.

The deterioration of education, which is apparent from the recent phenomenal rise in the incidence of juvenile delinquency and violence at schools as well as in the number of children who refuse to go to school, is a matter of grave concern requiring immediate attention.

The present education system overemphasizes the so-called deviation value *(hensachi),* and this is only one of the reasons why the vast majority of people in Japan find the present system extremely unsatisfactory. The need to reform education is felt by all.

The deterioration of education today is certainly not without cause. We have a situation in which children and adolescents are not given due recognition for their capacities and talents as individuals. Each youngster's worth as a human being is gauged by his academic performance. This fans fierce rivalry and competition with his peers, with the result that nobody can really enjoy learning.

Educational reform is said to be worth 100 years of planning and efforts by the state. Considering the great importance of the matter, our party calls for the establishment of an organ that will deal with this matter in a truly thoroughgoing and democratic manner. We believe that such an organ should be entrusted with the task of drawing up reform measures by popular consensus.

Political Neutrality of the Organ

1. The Prime Minister's Provisional Council on Educational Reform Violates the Neutrality of Education

(1) The risk of having an advisory panel to the Prime Minister. After World War II, the only time that an advisory panel to the Prime Minister handled the

issue of education was from 1946 through 1949. This panel was called the Committee for Education Renovation. This happened at a time which can hardly be called "normal"; the country had just been defeated in a major war.

Education is one area which should be free of political interference. But an advisory panel to the Prime Minister is bound to be subject to direct political interference. We see a grave threat to the political neutrality of education, which is guaranteed under Article 10 of the Fundamental Law of Education.

(2) Hypocrisy of "Nakasone Educational Reform." Prime Minister Yasuhiro Nakasone, who openly calls himself a constitutional revisionist, once said that "educational reform must follow administrative reform . . . (by carrying out educational reform) we may be able to settle some pending problems concerning the Constitution."

For him, educational reform is part of his overall revisionist concept directed at "reviewing postwar politics totally."

From what he has said, it is clear that the goal of his idea of educational reform differs, right from the start, from the sort of reform sought by the parents of today's schoolchildren and the public at large. We must say that Nakasone's idea of educational reform is politically inspired, and we regard political motivations as being highly dangerous.

2. Establishment of a Consultative Organ to Replace the Central Education Council (Chukyoshin)

We recommend that a consultative organ be created in the Ministry of Education, instead of the proposed advisory panel to the Prime Minister that violates the neutrality of education. In creating such a consultative organ, which should be called the "Education Council," we recommend that the present Central Education Council (Chukyoshin) be dissolved. We call for the dissolution of Chukyoshin because it has often served merely to fulfill the Education Ministry's self-serving interests by having members who were chosen quite arbitrarily. We see Chukyoshin as an organ that does not serve the interests of the public.

We recommend that the new Education Council consist of supraparty members who, representing various fields and walks of society, are genuinely committed to education. The appointment of members should be approved by the Diet.

The number of members should be limited to around 20, and their term of office should be two years in principle, although they may be reelected for a second term. The new Education Council should adopt only unanimous decisions as a rule. We recommend this in order to make sure that the decisions reflect the public consensus on educational reform measures. We also recommend that each session of the Council be conducted in public, and that the Minister of Education limit his prerogative to the presentation of guidelines on matters to be deliberated by the Council. The Minister of Education should not interfere with the Council in such matters as the choice of specific topics of discussion, the manner in which the discussions are conducted, and the conclusions reached by the Council.

68
Introductory Note on the National Council on Educational Reform

no date, probably 1984

Source: Reports on Educational Reforms (Tokyo: National Council on Educational Reform, n.d., probably 1984), pp. iii–vii.

1. Background

The educational system in Japan has undergone several important reforms. One of the most important two reforms took place immediately after the creation of a modern national state under the Meiji Restoration, when the Government Order of Education was promulgated in 1872. The Order and accompanying statutes laid the foundations of Japan's modern national system of education.

The other major reform took place immediately after World War II with the enactment of the Fundamental Law of Education, which defined the aim of education and set forth the basic principles for education in the new democracy.[1] Under this law and the related School Education Law, compulsory schooling was extended from six to nine years and a new "6–3–3–4 system" was introduced, comprising six years of elementary school, three years of lower secondary school, three years of upper secondary school and four years of university. This new system, based on the principle of full equality of educational opportunity, is now widely recognized as having greatly contributed to the present prosperity of the nation. It improved educational standards for the people, provided for character formation for the young, and produced a highly qualified work force.

Dramatic advances in science and technology, as well as rapid economic growth since World War II, have brought about changes in the nation's industrial structure, a redistribution of the labor force, and other major social changes, such as urbanization and computerization. The education sector has also witnessed remarkable quantitative development. The proportion of children going on to upper secondary schools, for example, has grown from about 40% in the early postwar period to more than 90% today.

These rapid changes in the social environment and this quantitative expansion have had great impact upon education in this country. A number of problems have arisen, such as a lack of discipline among school children and intense competition for entrance to universities. Many people have pointed out that the present-day method and content of school instruction fail, in large part, to respond to the diversity of ability and aptitude of students.

At the same time, with the improved standard of living and the growing proportion of older citizens in Japanese society, there are increasing demands by the public for more opportunities for education throughout life.

These social problems and the growing demand for a system of lifelong education have led to a call, once again, for comprehensive reform of the educational system.

2. The Characteristics of the National Council on Educational Reform

It became a matter of urgency for the government to examine its policies and practices related to education and to produce necessary reforms, so as to respond to the above-mentioned demands of the people, to make education relevant to changing social circumstances and the cultural development of the nation and to expand opportunities for lifelong education. Accordingly, in August 1984 the government established the National Council on Educational Reform as an advisory body to the Prime Minister. The Council was created under the "Law for the Establishment of a National Council on Educational Reform." It was charged with dealing with educational reform from a long-term perspective, with the support of all relevant government authorities.

The Council was organized as follows:

(1) The Purpose of the Council. The purpose of the Council was to propose relevant reforms of various government policies and practices related to education to enable the educational system to respond to recent social changes and cultural developments, and thereby to achieve the aim of education as defined in the Fundamental Law of Education of 1947.

(2) Subjects to be considered by the Council. The Council was to conduct a comprehensive study of various government policies in education and related areas. On the basis of this study, the Council was to consider and propose strategies for necessary reforms.

(3) The composition of the Council. The Council was composed of 25 members, citizens of exemplary character and respected judgment, who were appointed by the Prime Minister with the consent of the House of Representatives and the House of Councillors. In addition, 20 specialist members were also appointed.

(4) The term of activity of the Council. The Council was to work for three years from August 1984.

3. The Reports of the Council

In August 1987, the Council finished its work after presenting its final report to the Prime Minister. During its term of activity for three years, the Council held 668 meetings including 90 plenary meetings. It also organized 14 public hearings in different regions. During the same period, the Council sent 7 missions to 13 countries in Asia, Europe, and North America to study the educational structures and practices in these countries. Each mission spent several days in one to four countries, visiting respective educational authorities and institutions.

In accordance with its own policy that it should publish a series of reports successively, the Council published four successive reports during the three years.

The first report: June 26, 1985
The second report: April 23, 1986
The third report: April 1, 1987
The fourth and final report: August 7, 1987

Note

1. Article I. Aim of Education: "Education shall aim at the full development of personality, striving for the rearing of people, sound in mind and body, who shall love truth and justice, esteem individual value, respect labor and have a deep sense of responsibility, and be imbued with an independent spirit, as builders of a peaceful state and society." (Fundamental Law of Education of 1947)

69
Summary of First Report on Education Reform

June 26, 1985

Source: First Report on Educational Reform (Tokyo: Provisional Council on Educational Reform, June 26, 1985), pp. 1–9.

Introduction

With a long-term perspective as a basic prerequisite, the Council has been examining various problems so as to cope with both the present condition of education and the national demands for education. The Council hereby presents its first report in accordance with its own policy that it should publish a series of reports successively.

Part I. Basic Direction of the Educational Reform

Section 1. Present Condition of Education

(1) Japan's education has become a driving force for the economic and social development of the nation. Our educational system has marked relatively high standards, particularly with regard to elementary and secondary education, as compared with educational standards in many other countries. In this respect, it has obtained a high international reputation.

(2) On the other hand, our educational system involves a lot of problems. For example, it has not adequately responded to the need for internationalization. And a number of ill effects have been exposed due to the uniformity and rigidity of the structure and operation of the educational system. The competition in entrance examination and various manifestations of the state of confusion in education such as school bullying and juvenile delinquency have grown very serious. They are deep-rooted and interwoven with the present conditions of the family, the school, and the community.

(Some examples of major causes and explanations for these phenomena are presented in the report.)

(3) The development of modern science and technology has brought about many problems such as the spread of materialistic ideas, the absence of feeling, less contact with nature, and a lack of due regard for the dignity of life.

(4) Since the establishment of a modern national state in the Meiji era, one of the national goals of Japan was to catch up with the industrialized nations in Europe and North America. The educational system has placed emphasis on the efficiency of importing and rapidly disseminating the science and technology and statutory institutions originated in some advanced countries. As a result, uniform content and methods of teaching were adopted. In recent years education in Japan has not successfully kept abreast with the changing times and the growing demands of society.

Section 2. Significance of the Educational Reform

(1) The "first education reform," which took place in the Meiji era, was intended to contribute to the development of the national state and modern industry. The "second educational reform" immediately after World War II identified such principles as the full development of personality, due regard for the dignity of the individual and equal opportunity as basic guiding principles. But it

followed the line of the prewar education policy since the Meiji era, which aimed at making education instrumental in helping the nation modernize and catch up with advanced countries.

(2) Japan's present educational system, which was formulated through the first and second educational reforms, has brought about a number of problems outlined in Section 1. It has tended to cause a lot of problems such as the denial by some people of the values and advantages of our traditional cultural assets and the down-playing of moral education. All the advantages and disadvantages of both the prewar and the postwar educational systems are in urgent need of review in order to inherit and develop the advantages and overcome the disadvantages and limitations.

(3) Today on the eve of the twenty-first century, we are facing the age of transition—transition to an internationalized society, transition to an information-centered civilization, and transition to an "80-year-career" life-style. The further advance of science and technology in the twenty-first century will require the reexamination of our way of living and the recovery of human dignity. Education must respond to these requirements of the new age.

(4) It is the earnest hope of the public that our educational system restore vitality and creativity, as well as enriched humanity, and that our schools revive their primary function. We must review thoroughly the whole educational system and carry out needed reforms boldly and carefully from a renewed point of view.

Section 3. Functions of the Council

(1) Regarding the state of confusion in education, the solution to which the public is keenly calling for, the Council should not only suggest emergency measures. What is more important is to make basic and comprehensive suggestions for solutions.

(2) The Council should suggest the future direction of education with a view to helping to create a society with creativity and vitality relevant to the twenty-first century.

(3) The Council should point out the importance of certain eternal values such as respect for freedom, discipline, consideration for others, enriched aesthetic sentiments, and the reverence for nature.

(4) The Council should grasp the distinctive individuality of Japanese culture and society, and suggest what the educational system should do in order to develop the consciousness of children as being Japanese citizens.

(5) The Council should review the educational structures and policies administered by the Ministry of Education, Science and Culture and other Ministries and Agencies, as well as those which are the responsibilities of local governments, and suggest basic strategies for introducing reforms into these structures and policies.

Section 4. Basic Concepts for Reform

The coming educational reform will be undertaken in accordance with the spirit of the Fundamental Law of Education. The Council hopes to realize an educational system which will pay due regard to the dignity of individuality and which will aim to create a culture rich in individuality. The Council also aims at helping to develop Japanese citizens who are competent to inherit the traditional Japanese culture and who are competent to make a relevant contribution to the international community while maintaining the consciousness of being a Japanese. To achieve this aim, the Council has identified eight "basic concepts for reform" as listed below. The first basic concept, that is, the "Principle of putting emphasis on individuality" is the fundamental principle which is implicated in all the other concepts.

In promoting educational reform, the improvement of the quality of education and research should always be attempted. Further, appropriate financial measures should be taken in the context of the whole national government finance.

1. Principle of putting emphasis on individuality
2. Putting emphasis on fundamentals
3. Cultivation of creativity, thinking ability and power of expression
4. Expansion of opportunities for choices
5. Humanization of the educational environment
6. Transition of a lifelong learning system
7. Coping with internationalization
8. Coping with the information age.

Part II. Major Issues to Be Considered by the Council

The Council has been deliberating on educational reform to cope with social change and cultural development in the nation. The reform also aims at helping to solve various problems referred to as the state of confusion in education. In this deliberation the Council has identified the major issues to be considered as listed below. These issues are to be considered by the Council during the course of its deliberation for three years on the basis of the "Basic Concepts for Reform" mentioned above.

(1) *Basic requirements for an education relevant to the twenty-first century.* (Aims of education; analysis of the past and present of education, and future prospects for education.)

(2) *Organization and systematization of lifelong learning and the correction of the adverse effects of undue emphasis on the educational background of individuals.* (Correction of the adverse effects of undue emphasis on the educational background of individuals; development of a lifelong learning system;

vitalization of formal education, and vitalization of educational functions of family and community.)

(3) *Enhancement of higher education and individualization of higher education institutions.* (Diversification and individualization of higher education institutions; scientific research and graduate schools; and the organization and management of institutions of higher education.)

(4) *Enrichment and diversification of elementary and secondary education.* (Basic direction of the substance of education; structure of the school system; moral education; health education; education of the handicapped; and class size and other educational conditions.)

(5) *Improvement of the quality of teachers.*

(6) *Coping with internationalization.*

(7) *Coping with the information age.*

(8) *Review of educational administration and finance.* (Distribution of functions between governments and nongovernmental bodies; responsibilities of the national and local governments and the distribution of functions between different levels of government; school administration and management; and educational costs and financing of education.)

Part III. Immediate Specific Proposals for Educational Reform

The Council has reached particular conclusions with respect to a certain number of issues among those outlined in Part II, and has worked out the specific proposals noted below as a breakthrough for the reforms relating to the issues that the Council should deal with in the future.

(1) The Council has dealt with the issue of rectifying the adverse effects of undue emphasis on the educational background of individuals, recognizing that this undue emphasis constitutes one of the background factors affecting the excessive competition in entrance examination and the so-called state of confusion in education.

(2) The Council has dealt with how to reform the procedures for selecting university entrants. This was an attempt to cope with the trends in which distinctive characteristics of individual universities have been reduced and educational programs at upper secondary and other schools have been hampered due to the ranking of universities according to the level of academic achievement of incoming students, as well as due to the classification of students according to the "deviation value" of their test scores.

(3). Many of the present educational problems clearly concern the secondary education level in particular. With the increasing percentage of children going on to upper secondary education, students enrolled in institutions on the upper secondary level have been more diversified in terms of their purpose of enrollment in these institutions and in terms of their motivation, aptitudes and other factors.

In view of this situation, it is necessary to provide diverse opportunities for learning, each offering diverse routes leading to higher education and other post-secondary education and training, and thus to give young people possibilities and challenges, as well as positive prospects for the future. From this point of view the Council has decided to submit some proposals on structural reform contributing to the diversification of opportunities and to the increase in the routes leading to post-secondary education.

Section 1. To Correct the Adverse Effects of Undue Emphasis on the Educational Background of Individuals

It can be considered that the adverse effects of our undue emphasis on the educational background of individuals may be solved through creating a lifelong learning society based on a long-term perspective, since this undue emphasis on educational background is deeply rooted not only in today's educational and learning system but also in the social customs of this country and the way of behavior of the Japanese people. In addition, comprehensive corrective measures have to be developed in two other dimensions: education in schools and universities, and the practice of hiring employees at industrial firms and government offices.

In particular, it is desirable that educational institutions on the one hand and industrial firms and government offices on the other should establish a good liaison and cooperation with each other, without blaming each other, and should endeavor to help correct any evil effects. For this purpose, while there is undoubtedly a need to reform the education in schools and universities, the Council appeals to industrial enterprises and government offices for further positive efforts in improving their hiring practices and personnel management, with a view to ensuring an assessment of the diverse abilities of employees and with a view to vitalizing the activities of each organization.

Section 2. To Correct Excessive Competition in Entrance Examinations

(1) Reform of the Procedures for Selecting University Entrants

In order to help remedy the evil effects of the competition for university admissions, which are characterized by an excessive emphasis on "deviation values" of the applicants' scores on achievement tests, the Council requests that every university attempt to reform the content and methods of its entrance examinations to ensure an independent and distinctive selection process.

The Council proposes that the existing "Joint First-Stage University Entrance Examination" now required for all applicants to national and local universities be replaced by a new "Common Test" for voluntary use by any university, national, local or private. With a view to ensuring the effective introduction of the common test, the legal status and functions of the National Center for University Entrance Examination should be examined and a relevant reform should be introduced, so that the common test may be utilized by all universities on an equal footing and so that upper secondary school representatives may participate in planning the test.

At the same time, efforts should be made to introduce such measures as: strengthening admission services at each university; improving educational guidance at secondary schools; providing students with an opportunity to apply to two or more national universities in a particular year; and making special arrangement for applicants, including those who are graduates of vocational courses of upper secondary schools.

(2) Diversification of Opportunities and Increase in Educational Routes

1. Liberalizing and Giving More Flexibility to the Qualifications for University Entrance. Based on the basic perception that the opportunity for higher education should be as diverse and broad as possible, the government should consider, as soon as possible, concrete measures for granting university entrance qualifications to students who have completed an upper secondary course lasting three years or more at special training schools, as well as to other competent people.

2. Six-year Secondary Schools. Local governments, nonprofit corporations entitled to set up institutions of formal education, and other appropriate bodies should be allowed to set up six-year secondary schools at their discretion. A six-year secondary school should be a new type of school designed to contribute to the continuous and progressive development of the personality of students by combining the existing lower secondary and upper secondary education, and thus providing a consistent education suitable for adolescents.

3. "Credit-System" Upper Secondary Schools. With a view to enabling students to have easier access to an upper secondary school education in accordance with their aspirations, schooling career, and living circumstances, a new type of upper secondary school ("credit-system" upper secondary school) should be established that will recognize the acquisition of credits for each subject, as well as grant qualification for graduation from an upper secondary school course on the basis of the total number of credits each student acquires in various subjects.

70
Reforms to Invigorate Education and Inspire Public Confidence

April 23, 1986

Source: Summary of Second Report on Educational Reform (Tokyo: National Council on Educational Reform, 1986), pp. 12–26.

Chapter 1. Transition to a Lifelong Learning System

Section 1. *More Provision of Learning Opportunities throughout Life*

To ensure the transition to a system for lifelong learning and respond to the needs of people at different stages of life, we must develop and improve the whole range of educational systems and opportunities now widely available as formal education, nonformal education or education in the home. To this end, various learning opportunities appropriate to different stages of life should be provided.

a. The educational function of the home should be restored: it should be the starting point of a lifetime of learning. Importance should be attached to the community's providing education for young people. In addition, attention should be paid to the provision of more learning opportunities for women and older people, as well as developing vocational skills of individuals, to help us cope with such changes as the aging of the population and the greater maturity of society.

b. Institutions of formal education have an important role to play in the process of lifelong learning. From this point of view, consideration should be given, at the elementary and secondary levels, to enabling children fully to acquire basic skills and knowledge, as well as to having them develop a capacity for independent learning. Adapting education to the developmental stage of children should be considered. In addition, vocational education in schools should be promoted.

Further, at the higher education level, attention should be given to helping students fully acquire specific skills and knowledge in specialized fields, as well as to helping them develop, in particular, broad powers of thinking. Efforts should be made to invigorate the educational function of institutions of higher learning.

c. To cope with the changes in society and in the national economy, universities, upper secondary schools and other educational institutions should be developed so that adults have the opportunity to learn. To this end, special consideration should be given to securing more flexibility in the system of learning, with a view to making the entrance requirements for these institutions more liberal and flexible. In addition, attention should be paid to ensuring that what is learned can be put to use in the vocations and daily life of adults.

Section 2. Cooperation among Family, School and Community for Lifelong Learning

The roles and responsibilities of the home, school, community and other bodies concerned with education need to be made clearer as regards the whole system of lifelong learning. In addition, it is necessary that all these parties cooperate closely with each other.

a. The limits of the role of schools should be clarified, and the educational potential of home and community should be recovered and utilized.

b. The possibility of shifting from a six-day to a five-day school week should be considered.

c. The functions and facilities of educational institutions should be opened further to people in the community. Attention should be given to educational services provided by universities and other institutions for the community. Community centers to train and do research to promote industry in the community should be considered.

d. The administration of education for adults and out-of-school youths, as well as laws and regulations relating to this area of education, should be thoroughly reviewed from the standpoint of ensuring the transition to a lifelong learning system and in light of the necessity for making the administration adaptable to the changing circumstances in the new age.

Further, the development of the individual's vocational capabilities should be promoted in diverse ways, in effective cooperation with formal education programs in universities and other institutions.

e. In order to provide people with the motivation and willingness to learn, we should consider appropriate measures for encouraging them to participate in learning activities, such as arrangements for recognizing certain university credits for extension courses.

f. The vitality of nongovernmental bodies should be utilized to promote programs for lifelong learning. At the same time, proper coordination and collaboration should be secured among different government programs for lifelong learning so that these programs may be efficiently carried out.

Chapter 2. Recovery of the Educational Power of the Home

Section 1. Significance of Education at Home

Behind the various manifestations of the current "state of desolation" in education, such as group bullying, school violence and juvenile delinquency, lies the serious fact not only that schools face a number of problems but that the home is not sufficiently achieving its educational potential.

If the waste and ruin of the minds of children today is to be overcome, it is essential that parents develop a basic relationship of mutual trust with their children in early childhood and that, on the basis of this relationship, their discipline is timely and proper to help their children develop self-control, consideration for those around them and other necessary virtues. This is a crucial responsibility of parents.

In the past, Japanese people have tended to think of education as consisting merely of formal schooling. It is most important for all parents to reflect on this and to become conscious of their own role and responsibility.

In addition, it is necessary that schools rectify the closed attitude they take in attempting to solve bullying or other problems by themselves and endeavor to maintain closer relations with children's families. In this connection, it is important that, instead of simply trying to compensate for the declining educational role of families, schools endeavor to involve families in the problem, taking the specific circumstances of each family into account.

Government authorities must therefore formulate and implement relevant measures to restore the educational role of the home.

Section 2. *Invigoration of Education at Home*

Unified efforts by three parties are necessary for the rearing and education of children: the home, the school and the community. The family should be aware of its role and responsibilities in education, while efforts should be made to help the home recover its educational power by building a sound foundation for family life and adopting other relevant measures.

a. We should enrich learning which will prove useful for parenthood. With this in view, the contents of courses on homemaking and other relevant school courses should be reviewed.

b. Efforts should be made to provide more counseling services for young people. In order to build a sound basis for family life, infant-care leave for women should be more widely available, and women's discussion groups should be encouraged at kindergartens or other facilities concerned with children's education and health. Assistance should be given to certain families to help restore their educational power.

c. In order to cultivate in children such sentiments as reverence for life and nature, and in order to help them develop sound minds and bodies, we should give them more opportunities to experience and study nature directly. In addition, urban children should have an opportunity to live in rural areas, and rural children in urban areas. Further, the educational power of the community should be utilized and vitalized.

d. Family, school, and community should cooperate with one another, while each should fulfill its own function. These three parts of society should make unified efforts to create a better environment for bringing up and educating children. From this standpoint, activities of Parent–Teacher Associations should be revitalized, community members should be encouraged to participate in school activities, and the existing school lunch programs should be reviewed.

Chapter 3. Reform of Elementary and Secondary Education

Section 1. Enrichment of Moral Education

The home is the first and fundamental site of the character formation of children. As children grow up, their life experience expands from home to school and from school to community. Thus it is necessary that schools make efforts to enrich moral education through all educational activities, in cooperation with the family and the community.

a. Emphasis should be attached to teaching basic manners and customs, in elementary education, as well as developing both self-restraint and willingness to follow social norms in daily life. In secondary education, emphasis should be placed on developing in students a good attitude toward life, as well as on enabling students to deepen their insight into themselves.

b. Children should be encouraged to participate, as appropriate to their developmental stage, in empirical learning activities in the natural environment, as well as in communal living, volunteer activities and social service activities.

c. Regarding moral instruction as a concrete part of the elementary and lower secondary school curriculum, its contents should be reviewed and efforts should be made to concentrate it into certain essential matters. Further, in order to help children develop the ability to put moral principles into practice, moral instruction should be carried out in closer relation to "Special Activities" and other school activities.

d. To contribute to the enrichment of moral education at school, the use of appropriate supplementary teaching materials should be encouraged.

e. In improving teacher training, both initial and in-service, attention should be paid to improving teachers' capabilities concerning moral education.

Section 2. Improvement of Contents of Instruction

(1) Basic Direction for the Improvement of Contents of Instruction

In elementary and secondary education, children should fully acquire the basic and essential knowledge and skills necessary to cultivate sound character formation for life. In our changing and developing society, children should also be assisted in developing the ability for self-education, which comprises the will, attitude, and ability to learn voluntarily and independently. In addition, attention should be paid to diversifying of the content and methods of instruction, as well as to making school activities open to the public as far as possible.

a. Instruction should be concentrated on the essentials at all levels—elementary, lower secondary, and upper secondary. The amount and level of difficulty of what is taught should be reviewed to ascertain whether it is appropriate for children at respective school levels. Based on this review, more effort should be made to select essential subjects.

In this effort, emphasis should be placed on the following: developing creativity, the ability to think clearly, judgment and the power of expression; giving children a deeper understanding of the tradition and culture of Japan and developing their awareness of themselves as Japanese citizens; improving their physical fitness and upgrading health sciences education; and fostering children's ability to act independently, a skill necessary in our changing society which is growing more international and where information technology is spreading.

At the elementary school level, in particular, stress should be placed on enabling children to master the basic skills of reading, writing, and arithmetic and to develop good social attitudes and aesthetic sensibilities.

b. At the elementary school level, efforts should be made to diversify the contents of what is taught, putting value on the development of distinctive personalities. To this end, the kinds of required and elective subjects, as well as the nature and content of both general and vocational education, should be reexamined.

Career guidance services should be improved so that students may consider their own future careers and achieve self-realization.

c. Teaching methods should be diversified and evaluation practices improved so that students receive instruction appropriate to their individual characteristics and thereby develop sound and balanced personalities.

d. In order to make school activities more open to the public, students should be provided with an opportunity to participate in community activities and volunteer services. Upper secondary schools should expand collaborative programs for vocational education with industrial firms, special training schools or other establishments. Upper secondary schools should also provide people in the community with more opportunities to learn at these schools.

(2) The Structure and Content of School Subjects
and Other School Activities

The structure and content of school subjects and other school activities should be reviewed in light of the basic direction described above (1). It is also necessary to take into account the developmental stage of children, the continuity of education, and systematization of the content of instruction.

a. Some integration of existing subjects should be implemented for the lower grades of elementary school.

b. The structure and content of courses in social studies at secondary schools should be examined. The contents of homemaking courses, as well as the nature of this subject (e.g., what part should be required for all students) also should be reviewed.

c. To enhance health education, the nature and content of courses in moral instruction, special activities, and health and physical education and other related subjects should be examined.

(3) Improvement of Practical Application of Statutory and Other Systems Affecting the Content of Instruction

It is necessary that laws and regulations affecting the content of what is taught at school be made as flexible as possible, so that schools may organize appropriate curricula compatible with changes and developments in society, the actual circumstances of each school and community, and the developmental stages as well as diverse personalities of students. This way a sound continuity in the content of instruction may be secured between the different school levels.

a. Regarding the courses of study for elementary, lower secondary, and upper secondary schools as prescribed by the national government, the provisions therein should be made broader, so that individual schools may employ diverse creative devices in organizing their own curricula. Depending on the nature of the respective subjects, attention should be given both to defining more clearly the basic and essential subject matter and to enriching the description of what comprises each subject. With regard to the organization of the curriculum at individual schools, consideration should be given to providing schools with more choices, as well as to allowing some of them to adopt exceptional practices.

b. In connection with the nature of course contents, consideration should be given to the possibility of defining the duration of an upper secondary school course more flexibly—specifically in terms of "three years or more." In addition, the advantages of the credit system should be utilized.

c. Efforts should be made to ensure better continuity and cooperation between the different school levels. In the selection of university entrants, favorable consideration should be given to graduates from vocational courses at upper secondary schools.

Section 3. *Improvement of the Quality of Teachers*

(1) Improvement of Teacher Training and Certification System

In order to attract as many competent teacher candidates as possible, the present system of teacher training, which is now open to university students, should be maintained. However, the existing structure of teacher training courses, as well as the existing method using working people as teachers, should immediately be revised, as these methods have many problems and difficulties.

a. The content of professional training courses and other subjects offered as part of teacher education should be reviewed with a view to making teachers better able to cope with the recent changes in the mental and physical condition of school children, as well as with the changing curricula of elementary and secondary schools.

b. Regarding practice teaching by prospective teachers, the duration, content, and other aspects of this should be reviewed, and the introduction of in-service training programs for beginning teachers considered. Further, the appropriate allocation of time for classroom observation, classroom participation, practice teaching and other activities should be examined for each school level to which prospective teachers will be assigned.

c. Whenever necessary, universities should be allowed to provide special one-year or half-year teacher training courses for university students and adult citizens who have not earned credits in the required professional teacher training subjects but who wish to obtain a teaching certificate.

d. More flexibility should be introduced into the teacher certification system, with a view to enabling it to cope with the diversification of upper secondary school education, to attracting competent people to teaching positions in vocational and other practical subjects, and to strengthening foreign language teaching.

e. In order to attract more adult citizens working in other sectors to the teaching profession and thus to revitalize formal education, a special system of teacher certification (to be authorized by each prefectural board of education) should be introduced. Further, provisions for exceptions should be included in the teacher certification system so that certain subject areas may be taught by part-time lecturers with no teaching certificate.

(2) Improvements in the Procedures for Appointing New Teachers

It is crucial to attract to the teaching profession an adequate number of competent people. It is necessary to improve the procedures for appointing new teachers.

a. The methods for selecting new teachers should be diversified to allow an overall assessment of the abilities and aptitudes of applicants on the basis of a variety of factors.

b. The time schedule for recruiting new teachers should be advanced so as to follow the practices of other professions.

(3) Creation of In-Service Training Programs for Beginning Teachers

It is important to provide novice teachers with in-service training at the beginning of their teaching careers and thus help them make a successful start in their educational service. To help teachers in public schools develop the skills required for their profession as well as a firm sense of mission and broad grasp of knowledge, we should immediately consider concrete measures to introduce in-service training programs for beginning teachers based on the following:

a. Immediately after hiring, all beginning teachers should be required to undergo one year of training under the guidance of supervising teachers. The training should concern both actual teaching and other duties of teachers.

In administering training for beginning teachers, each school should establish a systematic mechanism whereby the supervising teachers and all other teachers at the school will cooperate in the training of beginning teachers under the leadership of the principal.

b. Specially appointed supervising teachers should be assigned to schools where beginning teachers have been placed. Further, every prefectural government should develop an appropriate structure for administering in-service training programs, including the appointment of supervisors in charge of these programs.

c. With the introduction of the above in-service training programs, the conditional period of initial appointment for beginning teachers should be extended from six months to one year.

(4) Systematization of In-Service Training of Teachers

The great expectation of the public toward schools and instructors demands that teachers constantly train and enlighten themselves, ever aware of the importance of their professional responsibilities.

a. The division of responsibilities among the national, prefectural, and municipal governments for the in-service training of teachers should be made clear, and an overall system of training should be planned in which training programs at the different levels are incorporated into a whole. This would ensure the systematic and well-planned administration of in-service training programs, beginning with the school-based training provided in close connection with teachers' daily educational work at school.

b. In-service training programs at regular intervals throughout teachers' professional careers should be planned. These periodic programs will allow teachers to reflect on their own teaching experiences, acquire new professional knowledge, revitalize themselves and further improve their own capacity for classroom and other activities.

c. In order to encourage teachers to participate in training for self-enlightenment, government authorities should endeavor to strengthen financial assistance to voluntary organizations with programs for in-service teacher training. The government should also expand programs for awarding honors to teachers for outstanding accomplishments.

Section 4. Improvement of Environmental Factors Affecting Children

It is necessary to consider ways of providing children an environment that will help them develop healthy hearts and minds. Various environmental factors affecting education should be improved to humanize the educational surroundings so that children may receive education appropriate to their differing personalities.

a. In order to provide children an education appropriate to their differing personalities, we should strive to eliminate excessively large schools and plan proper measures to secure an optimum size for every school.

b. Regarding class organization and staffing of schools, the national government's current plan for improving staffing, including its plan for reducing the maximum class size to 40 for elementary and lower secondary schools, should be fully implemented. Once success in the current national plan has been achieved, elementary and lower secondary school staffing should be further improved, taking into account both future demographic trends in school population and relevant statistical data, such as pupil–teacher ratios, from the advanced countries of Europe and North America. Some provision for flexibility should be incorporated into the national standard regulations for class organization.

c. Improvements should be planned for physical facilities and equipment in schools, including outdoor spaces, with a view to cultivating in children a balanced personality, as well as making them adaptable to a variety of teaching methods.

d. The improvement of class organization and staffing of upper secondary schools should be planned so that these schools can organize and implement diverse curricula.

Section 5. Dealing with School Bullying

School bullying today is a very worrisome problem. Most importantly, educators and other concerned people should recognize this problem as their own problem and do their best in dealing with it. While we should also work for both improvement in various factors affecting education and humanization of the educational environment, the problem of bullying must primarily be solved by implementing overall reforms involving the home, school, and community. Some immediate measures, however, should be taken in parallel to these long-term solutions.

a. Pupil guidance programs at school, particularly counseling services, should be strengthened.

In addition, the function of the Health Room at school should be enhanced, and a cooperative relationship, including the smooth exchange of information, between nurse teachers and classroom teachers should be strengthened.

b. Schools with especially difficult guidance problems should be given priority, as far as possible, in the placement of competent teachers and the employment of other relevant remedies. Likewise, priority should be given to these schools in enacting government programs to make school size optimum (including eliminating excessively large schools) and in providing better physical facilities, including improvements in outdoor environment.

c. Each municipal board of education should improve its function of educational counseling for students, parents, and community members. Each prefectural or municipal board of education should improve the structure of its secretariat so as to respond quickly with guidance and advice, especially to schools with difficult problems.

d. When, despite their best efforts, schools find it difficult to solve specific problems by themselves, they should seek cooperation from relevant community organs concerned with education, child welfare, police matters or the like.

Further, schools should make clear who is responsible for educational activities or for school management. When necessary, they should also take disciplinary measures, such as suspending problem students, and they should follow strict policies in the personnel management of teachers. Through these means, schools should endeavor to conduct proper educational activities and school management.

e. Government ministries and agencies and other organs concerned should implement further measures as needed to solve school bullying problems. These various parts of government should also strive to cooperate with each other in the exchange of information and in other ways. The Ministry of Education, Science and Culture and other organs concerned should endeavor to determine the actual extent and gravity of the [highly publicized] school bullying problem, as well as the background and causes of this phenomenon. They should make active efforts to publish relevant information on the findings of their study of the problem, as well as on the measures they take to help solve it.

71
Reform of Elementary and Secondary Education

April 1, 1987

Source: Third Report on Educational Reform (Tokyo: National Council on Educational Reform, 1987), pp. 32–44.

Elementary and secondary education provides young people a foundation for lifelong learning. It plays an important role in fostering in young people the basic qualities required for their character formation, in having them acquire basic and fundamental knowledge and skills needed for cultivating a rich personality and a positive social attitude, and in developing their genuine academic abilities, strong bodies and generous minds. In its second report, the Council identified the following "goals of education for the twenty-first century": (1) the nurture of open and generous hearts and minds, strong bodies, and richly creative spirits; (2) the development of free and self-determining spirits and public-minded character; and (3) the cultivation of Japanese competent to live as members of the world community. It must be stated that whether these goals can be realized or not depends basically on elementary and secondary education in the future. For this reason, reforming elementary and secondary education is an important task for the current education reform.

From this point of view, the Council, in its first report, made proposals for six-year secondary schools and "credit-system" upper secondary schools, and, in its second report, made recommendations with regard to: the basic direction for the improvement of teaching content; moral education; health education; improvement of class organization and other educational conditions; and the improvement of the quality of teachers.

After submitting the second report, the Council deliberated the remaining issues: school textbooks; upper secondary education; preschool education; education of the handicapped; making schools open to the public and securing a sound base of school administration and management; school attendance districts; and dealing with private education industries including *juku* (i.e., a variety of private profit making nonformal educational institutions). The consistent basic theme behind the deliberations on these issues was the qualitative improvement and diversification of elementary and secondary education. The Council has been carrying out its deliberations, paying special consideration to the basic concepts for the coming educational reform which the Council itself defined— namely, greater respect for individuality, emphasis on fundamentals, humanization of the educational environment, and the expansion of opportunities for choices. With regard to the textbook system, the Council paid special attention to improving the quality of textbooks and to increasing the public's confidence in both the textbook system and the content of textbooks. In respect to upper secondary education, the Council gave careful consideration to providing diverse educational opportunities on the basis of the most flexible ideas available, as well as to expanding opportunities for choices. Regarding school administration and management, the Council took the idea of "making schools more open."

Section 1. Reform of Textbook Systems

Elementary and secondary education plays a very important role in developing a foundation for character formation throughout one's life, as well as in fostering people who will shape our future nation and society. In this elementary and secondary education, school textbooks, as well as teachers' capabilities for teaching, have played a basic and key part in school programs.

Today's textbooks, however, involve a number of problems. For example, they are hampering distinctive teaching because their contents are uniform and all-inclusive. While they present common contents in an orderly and concise form, emphasis is placed on transmitting knowledge, and little attention is paid to developing in students thinking power or creativity, or to enhancing the willingness to learn. Textbooks have not always succeeded in presenting neutral and impartial knowledge. Further, in the context of the anticipated internationalization and of the predominance of information technology in the future, there is a growing need for more distinctive and more diverse textbooks. The existing textbook authorization system is not adequately open, and the screening is apt to enter into too much detail.

Therefore, it is an important task for us today to review overall and reform both the existing textbook systems and the contents of textbooks, from the perspective of the future and with a view to ensuring the improvement of the quality of textbooks so that textbooks may help students develop thinking ability and creativity and may also help teachers enrich their classroom instruction by increasing students' willingness to learn.

The ways and means to be adopted in this reform must be based on the principles specified in the second report, namely, (1) that bold and careful deregulation be implemented, (2) that the principles of freedom, self-determination and self-responsibility in education be firmly established, and (3) that diverse opportunities for choices be expanded. They must be put into practice, taking account of the real conditions surrounding textbooks.

From this point of view, in studying this issue, the Council has paid full consideration not merely to the statutory systems related to textbooks, including the authorization of textbooks, but also to various aspects including the improvement of textbook writing and editing; enhancement of research and evaluation on textbooks; the use of diverse supplemental materials, as well as effective use of textbooks; the improvement of teachers' capacity for instruction; and the relationship between textbooks and such factors as the school curriculum and the improvement of entrance examination systems.

(1) Basic Direction for Reforms

In order to realize a better elementary and secondary education system for the twenty-first century, keeping abreast with social change and cultural development in Japan, it is very important to reform the whole systems related to textbooks, which represent major teaching materials for different subjects and which systematically arrange relevant information in accordance with the structure of the curriculum.

a. In the context of information technology's growing impacts on education, as well as the growing diversification of teaching materials anticipated in the future, the content of textbooks and methods of using them should be reviewed, with a view to helping promote diverse approaches in teaching and learning in which due regard is paid to the individuality of students. In this review, textbooks should be studied as *learning* materials used by students, rather than as *teaching* materials used by teachers in their instruction.

b. Reforms of textbook systems must be carried out in light of the historical background and present problems of textbook systems, the changes in environmental factors around education resulting from the betterment of educational and cultural standards in Japan and from the maturing of our society, and the impact of the further spread of information technology and further internationalization on textbooks and teaching materials. In these reforms, emphasis should be given especially to the following aspects: (1) improving the quality of textbooks and encouraging creative innovations in their contents; (2) publishing diverse and distinctive textbooks; (3) fostering students' creativity, thinking ability and the power of expression; (4) making teaching relevant both to students' real needs and to their stages of development, selecting the appropriate priority content of teaching, and maintaining the optimum level of teaching; and (5) ensuring public confidence in education, securing the neutrality and equity of education, and safeguarding equal opportunity for education.

(2) Improvement of Textbook Writing and Editing and the Establishment of Appropriate Structures for Research and Development on Textbooks

Under the present legal framework, textbook writing and editing are primarily undertaken by private textbook publishers. The quality of textbooks depends to a great extent on the creative efforts by private publishers. In order to make the most of the spirit of the present system, it is necessary for each publisher to improve the quality of textbook writing and editing, and to establish responsible structures for writing and editing.

a. It is desirable that textbook research in the private sector be expanded and that textbook publishers strive to secure excellent authors and editors of textbooks.

Further, with respect to indicating authors or editors in a textbook, the textbook publisher should make clear who is responsible for the writing and editing of the textbook. To this end, the publisher should, for example, show in each textbook the name of the person who has the main responsibility for editing the textbook.

b. Research centers which are run by either a private body or the government or sponsored jointly by private and government bodies and which extensively conduct research, development and evaluation on school curriculum, textbooks, methods of instruction, teaching materials and other matters should be expanded and improved. These centers should also counsel textbook publishers on textbook writing and editing.

1. Textbook publishers are apt to be excessively dependent upon textbook authorization authorities. While the existing textbook authorization system should be amended, textbook publishers must be expected to overcome their own passive attitude and make positive and independent efforts to become more creative in producing better textbooks. To this end, publishers should be urged to improve drastically their own capability for writing and editing textbooks, to make clear where the practical responsibility for writing and editing textbooks lies, and to acquire self-determining and self-helping attitudes in producing textbooks.

2. In order to support the self-helping efforts of textbook publishers, research and development on textbooks and other teaching materials must be promoted as a basic requirement.

Research on the desirable contents of textbooks and comparative studies on textbooks and other teaching materials in other countries are needed. In addition, the impact of social trends—further spread of information technology, more internationalization and more maturing of our society—on textbooks should be studied, taking account of broader issues of the school curriculum and teaching methods. These studies and research are integral to developing excellent textbooks and teaching materials. Establishing and strengthening such research and development are of great importance.

3. To contribute to better international understanding through textbooks, more encouragement should be given to such international efforts as information exchange on textbook research, and international joint research related to comparative studies on textbooks by educators and researchers in and out of Japan.

(3) New System for Textbook Authorization

The existing textbook authorization system needs to be reformed to ensure that appropriate content of teaching, publication of diverse and distinctive textbooks, and public confidence both in textbook systems and in the content of textbooks may be enhanced.

a. Textbook publishers should be encouraged to make creative and innovative efforts in preparing textbooks, and textbook authorization should emphasize judging each proposed textbook's qualification as a school textbook.

b. Judgment on whether each proposed textbook is qualified or not should be made in general and broad terms. To help explore creative and innovative efforts by textbook authors and editors, the existing national standard regulations for textbook authorization should be reviewed and simplified and so that they concentrate on essential provisions.

In reviewing the existing guidelines, the present provisions on "basic general requirements" and "specific requirements" should be restructured and amended to emphasize the accuracy and qualitative level of textbook content, as well as neutrality and equity.

In some subjects, textbook publishers should be allowed to prepare a volume of textbooks for two or more grades, not merely for a single grade. They also should be allowed to prepare a separate volume for a particular area of a certain subject.

With regard to the existing main and supplementary standard regulations on textbook authorization, all detailed technical provisions for preparing textbooks, including those on editing techniques and designs, should be abolished or simplified. It is desirable that, for example, a "Guide for the Preparation of Textbooks" be prepared by the above-mentioned research center or by joint work of governmental and nongovernmental bodies, so that the guidebook instead of the above provisions is made available to textbook publishers as a reference for writing and editing textbooks.

c. With a view to ensuring a fair and appropriate authorization of textbooks, existing procedures for screening textbooks should be reviewed, and the process simplified. The present screening of textbooks in three stages—examining the first draft text, examining the second draft text, and examining the printed final draft text—should be replaced by screening in a single stage.

d. With a view to carrying out textbook screening in a general and broad perspective, the present system and composition of the Council on Textbook Authorization and textbook examination officers should be reviewed. With regard to the selection of members of the Council on Textbook Authorization, consideration needs to be paid to securing an appropriate composition of the Council.

e. The decision of the Minister of Education, Science and Culture on approving or disapproving specific textbooks should be based on the recommendation of the Council.

On the basis of the recommendation of the Council, the Minister should be allowed to direct a textbook publisher to amend the content of a proposed textbook before he approves the textbook.

f. The reasons for the Ministry's judgment on specific textbooks, as well as an outline of the process of examining the textbooks, should be made public in an appropriate way.

g. The interval of textbook authorization should be longer than under the present practice (three years), taking account of the level of school, kind of subject and other matters.

h. With regard to upper secondary school textbooks, the present provisions in the national regulations for textbook authorization related to these textbooks need to be reviewed to make screening procedures for these textbooks simpler than those for elementary or lower secondary school textbooks. Further, consideration needs to be given to abolishing the screening of textbooks for certain subjects for upper secondary schools, taking account of such factors as the methods of classroom instruction in these schools, the maintenance of the quality of upper secondary school textbooks, implications for university entrance examinations, and various circumstances around upper secondary textbooks.

The present system of the Ministry's approval of the price of an upper secondary school textbook should be reviewed with a view to mitigating government control on this matter.

1. Under the present system the screening of textbooks enters into too much detail. The system needs to be reformed to encourage textbook authors and editors to make self-helping efforts and to be more creative in preparing textbooks.

The textbook authorization system has a positive function of contributing to the development of better textbooks, as well as a function of eliminating inappropriate textbooks. In the future, emphasis should be placed on judging if each proposed textbook is qualified to be a school textbook, and the present national regulations and procedures for textbook authorization, as well as the system and composition of the Council on Textbook Authorization and textbook examination officers, should be reviewed.

2. The existing national standard regulations for textbook authorization comprise two kinds of requirements: "basic general requirements" that all textbooks have to meet in common and "specific requirements" that all textbooks for each subject have to meet. In reviewing the existing standards, these requirements need to be restructured and amended, and provisions in the national standard regulations concerning editing techniques and designs be abolished or simplified.

3. The present process for textbook screening comprises three stages: the examination of the first draft text submitted for the first time to the Ministry; the examination of the second draft text which has incorporated some revisions in accordance with the opinions of textbook examination officers on the first draft; and the examination of the final draft text for the purpose of confirming that the text is appropriate for use in schools. This three-stage process should be simplified, and replaced by a single-stage process.

4. The present system of textbook screening is not open. In order to help improve the quality of textbooks and to help enhance the public's confidence in textbooks, it is necessary to publish, in an appropriate way, an outline of how each proposed textbook was examined.

5. At present, textbooks are subject to the Ministry's authorization once every three years. This interval should be lengthened so that textbook publishers

may devote more energy and time to the work of writing and editing textbooks, thus improving the quality of textbooks.

(4) Adoption and Supply of Textbooks

a. Local boards of education should strive to further improve the mechanism and procedures for adopting textbooks and ways of publishing the reasons for adopting particular textbooks. In this effort they should take into consideration such objectives as ensuring the adoption of suitable textbooks, promoting research on textbooks, and ensuring fair competition among publishers.

Local boards of education should further strive to reflect better the opinions of schools, teachers, and parents in their policies and practices.

b. With a view to increasing the interest of the public in textbooks, ordinary book stores should be encouraged to sell textbooks, and such facilities as public libraries and citizens' public halls should be encouraged to keep and display textbooks.

c. It is advisable that the existing structure for the supply of textbooks be more open.

1. The adoption of textbooks to be used in municipal compulsory schools is the responsibility of the local board of education. For the purpose of adopting textbooks, each prefectural board of education designates a number of textbook adoption areas. Some of them coincide with a single municipality or *gun* (county), while the others comprise two or more municipalities or *gun*. A single textbook for each subject is adopted jointly by the municipal boards of education within the adoption area.

In jointly adopting textbooks, the boards of education usually set up a textbook adoption council that appoints a group of teachers or other experts who are commissioned to make relevant studies on textbooks.

In order to make such a process of textbook adoption more effective, it is necessary to improve the mechanism and procedures for textbook adoption and the ways of publishing the reasons for adopting particular textbooks.

2. Under the present system, textbook publishers assume responsibility for supplying individual schools with textbooks. In practice, textbooks are supplied to individual schools through designated wholesale and retail bookstores under the responsibility of each publisher. It is desirable that this structure for textbook supply should be more open.

(5) Free Distribution of Textbooks

With regard to the present system of free distribution of compulsory school textbooks, some believe that this system should be maintained to encourage the ideal of free compulsory education.

On the other hand, various other systems have been suggested, making parents pay for school textbooks; distributing textbooks among children on a loan basis; limiting free distribution to certain textbooks only; and distributing certain textbooks on a loan basis. Behind these opinions are consideration for parents' financial ability to pay for textbooks and for economic efficiency in education, as well as educational considerations about the impact of the system on people's attitude toward textbooks and on methods of instruction, and for the improvement of the quality of textbooks.

This issue should be further studied in light of future social and economic changes, the change in people's opinions on education and on textbooks, and future trends in the whole elementary and secondary education system, including textbooks. For the time being, the free distribution of textbooks for compulsory education should be continued.

(6) Long-Term Issues for Textbook Reform

As regards textbook systems, there is the opinion that efforts should be made to realize free publication and free adoption of textbooks in the long run, while there is also the opinion that we should be cautious about the abolition of textbook authorization and the shift to the free publication of textbooks. The question of what policies should be implemented for textbook systems in the future is very closely related to such diverse factors as the capacity of private publishers to write and edit textbooks, people's views on textbooks, the real situation in entrance examinations, and the improvement in the quality of teachers. It also has much to do with what view should be held on the role of the national government in education. With a view to developing better textbooks, it is necessary for us to cope flexibly with the above changes. In addition, it is crucial that relevant research and studies on textbook systems should continue in the future.

72
Reforms for Coping with the Changes of the Times

April 1, 1987

Source: Third Report on Educational Reform (Tokyo: National Council on Educational Reform, 1986), pp. 127–139.

Section 1. Coping with the Change to a More International Society

In No. 3 and No. 4 of the "Outline of the Progress of Deliberations" (published in January 1986 and in January 1987, respectively) and in the Second Report (published in April 1980), the Council has already referred to the significance of the "internationalization" with which Japan is now faced. It does not seem to the Council that internationalization should be perceived as an invariable concept. As a matter of fact, the substance of internationalization changes with the times. The measures taken in the given conditions of today to cope with internationalization may become out-of-date tomorrow. Internationalization ought to be regarded as a process of people's efforts whereby they accumulate daily practices to achieve the objectives of this concept, while constantly reflecting on the essence of the concept.

If we adopt this point of view, it is quite natural that there is no quick-acting medicine on which the educational system in Japan can depend to cope with internationalization. Although promising buds of internationalization have been witnessed everywhere, and a variety of pilot experiences have been accumulated, a new stock of knowledge and wisdom must be accumulated after repeated trial and error and after groping our way and changing ourselves. What is required in Japan today is the internationalization of "people" subsequent to the internationalization of "goods," "money," and "information." This process requires a change in our consciousness and a reaffirmation of humanity. Therefore, a firm attitude toward groping our way without being afraid of failure can be regarded as most important.

Along with the internationalization of Japanese society, there are a wide range of issues to be dealt with in education. While careful consideration has to be paid to respective issues, we must always remember the necessity of reviewing fundamental problems involved in education in Japan. What appears most crucial is that, through the process of internationalization, the Japanese education system should create and acquire the capacity to evolve both itself and mechanisms needed to cope flexibly with the constantly changing demand of the times.

While internationalization efforts in the education sector are aimed at promoting the evolution of Japanese society into a more international one, the fact remains that without changes in society the education sector would be unable to push forward its internationalization. Now the Japanese economy is going to be more open and the international exchange of persons is going to be increasing. In this context, while dealing properly with immigration control and other government services, more emphasis should be given to positive policies and measures that would allow foreign nationals to be active in various sectors of Japanese society. In addition, sufficient favorable attention should be given to foreign nationals with the right of permanent residence in Japan. In brief, it should be remembered that the attitude of the whole Japanese society is being challenged in the context of internationalization.

(1) Internationalization Efforts by the Education Sector on Its Own Initiative—Innovations Recommended

In order to make our educational programs cope with internationalization, it is most important that various experiments based on a firm conviction be made at different levels and fields of education.

a. It is desirable that schools research and develop content and methods of educational programs to cope with internationalization and that communities carry out extensive activities for international exchange. In brief, a variety of creative devices should be attempted.

b. In order to help make these creative devices possible and to encourage them, national and local government authorities need to take the lead in working out various innovations without adhering to precedents. Resource center services for education for international understanding should be enhanced. The exchange and dissemination of information on concrete attempts for internationalization in different fields should be encouraged.

c. The national government should prepare a "White Paper on International-ization in Education" presenting a synthesis of concrete attempts for internationalization in education and indicating the direction of government policies.

(a) It is important that schools should attempt various creative devices to help promote internationalization by carrying out various activities for research and development related to the content and methods of relevant educational programs. What is important in these efforts is to ensure that the opinions of those parents and teachers who have lived abroad be fully reflected and utilized in these attempts.

In a world where nations are more interdependent, the activities of nongovernment organizations play an important part in international exchanges. It is expected that plural and multilayered exchanges under various projects including sister-city arrangements will be further promoted on a voluntary basis.

(b) With a view to stimulating fresh plans and creative devices, the national and local government authorities are requested to take the lead in working out various innovations, without adhering to precedents, in implementing a selective allocation of budgetary funds and in mitigating government control over detailed matters. It is also necessary, for example, that resource center services for education for international understanding be enhanced with a view to helping disseminate the results of studies, as well as newly developed teaching materials, on education for international understanding. Administrative support should be provided to shape networks of schools, private organizations and other related agencies for the exchange of information concerning various attempts for internationalization in education, with a view to making such exchange of information more active.

(c) The national government should prepare a "White Paper on Internationalization in Education" presenting a nationwide synthesis of concrete attempts for internationalization and indicating the direction of government policies in this aspect. It is expected that the preparation of such a white paper would facilitate a wide dissemination and utilization of relevant information and would help create an education system equipped with the capacity to change itself to cope with the changes of the times.

(2) Some Specific Proposals

1. The Interest in, and Tolerance of, Foreigners and Other People Somewhat Different from Ourselves

—Schools open to the international community

Every school in Japan should aim to become an open school where foreign children, as well as those Japanese children who have returned from a long stay abroad, can easily enter at any stage and study together with other Japanese children and where full advantage is taken of their experience overseas. To this end, the following policies need to be actively adopted:

a. Each school accommodating foreign children and those Japanese children who have returned from a long stay abroad should have a specialist teacher who plays a key role in counseling services for these children and their parents, and in Japanese language instruction for these children. In addition, teachers with some experience abroad should be actively utilized, and the invitation of foreign teachers should be promoted.

b. New elementary or secondary schools (i.e., new international schools) for foreign children and Japanese children who have returned from overseas study, together with other Japanese children, should be established in order to promote the research, development and dissemination of new educational programs and methods relevant to the age of internationalization.

c. Competent authorities should take appropriate measures whereby attendance by a Japanese upper-secondary school student at a secondary school in a foreign country may be recognized as the equivalent to attendance at an upper secondary school in Japan.

(a) One of the most important tasks for Japanese society is that people have an interest in, understand, and accept foreigners and other people somewhat different from themselves and increase mutual contacts with them. Every school in Japan should aim to become an open entity where foreign children, as well as those Japanese children who have returned from a long stay abroad (including children of repatriates), are readily accepted and given the opportunity to study together with other Japanese children. It is necessary that an environment leading to mutual enlightenment between foreign and Japanese children be created by taking advantage of the overseas experiences of these children in Japanese schools and in the Japanese education system and by providing Japanese children with the opportunity to understand other cultures. Further, as pointed out in the Second Report, the opening of Japanese schools overseas to non-Japanese should be promoted as far as possible.

(b) As part of measures for enabling Japanese schools to become open schools as mentioned above, each school accommodating foreign children and Japanese children who have returned from a long stay abroad should have a specialist teacher who plays a key role in counseling services for these children and their parents, as well as in Japanese language instruction for these children. In addition, relevant measures should be taken to make systematic use of those teachers who have served Japanese schools overseas. For example, these teachers may be appointed to the position of specialist teacher mentioned above. Improvements should be made in the selection, training and economic status of teachers sent to Japanese schools overseas, as well as in the methods for teachers' study abroad.

Further, positive efforts should be made to invite more foreign teachers to lower and upper secondary schools in Japan, and they should be more effectively utilized not only for foreign language instruction but for other educational activities and international exchange activities at the community level.

(c) So far, schools in Japan have not had much experience in accepting the above children, especially foreign children. Accordingly, research and development should be carried out on appropriate educational programs and methods of instruction for these children. The new international schools mentioned above should be granted the status of the elementary, lower secondary or upper secondary schools as provided for in Article 1 of the School Education Law. They should serve as demonstration schools to carry out research and development on educational programs and methods, and materials of instruction for foreign children and those children who have returned from a long stay abroad. They should also disseminate the results of such research and development. These international schools should seek Japanese teachers who can communicate with foreigners in a foreign language, and should actively utilize the service of foreign teachers.

(d) In order to give Japanese upper-secondary school students more opportunities for study abroad, and to ensure that students who have returned from study abroad be smoothly accepted in upper secondary schools in Japan, relevant measures should be taken whereby a student is allowed to study abroad without losing the status of student at his or her school or even without taking a long leave of absence, and whereby attendance at a foreign secondary school may be recognized as equivalent to attendance at an upper secondary school in Japan.

(e) With regard to the existing international schools in Japan, which have been increasing along with the progress of internationalization, various arrangements should be made for giving those who have completed a particular course in these schools the qualification for advancing to Japanese educational institutions of a senior level, so that they may be smoothly admitted to these institutions.

2. Assistance to Other Countries with the Development of Human Resources

—Arrangements for students from overseas

a. There is an urgent need to improve and enhance the whole structure for accepting students from overseas. In particular, it is necessary to attach more importance to such warm-hearted arrangements as the provision of more opportunities for foreign students to have heart-to-heart contacts with Japanese people and the strengthening of follow-up service for those who have returned home after completing their study in Japan.

b. With a view to further promoting educational exchanges, consideration should be given to providing foreign students with more opportunities for short-term study in Japanese institutions of higher education.

(a) In its first report, the Council proposed a number of policies for a dramatic increase in the number of foreign students to be admitted to Japanese institutions of higher education. A statistic of student exchange indicates that the majority of Japanese students studying abroad are in Europe and North America, while the majority of foreign students studying in Japan come from Asian countries. Japanese students should become aware that countries other than European or North American countries have many things in which Japanese people should be interested. It is desirable that Japanese students' destinations for their study abroad be more diversified.

(b) During recent years foreign students studying in Japan have been rapidly increasing. Various efforts for developing appropriate structures for accepting foreign students have been made on the community level jointly by governmental and nongovernmental organizations. Various forms of assistance have been increasingly given foreign students by many volunteers. In the future, in addition to the improvement of institutional structure, physical facilities, and other environmental factors for foreign students, more thoughtful arrangements will be needed which may include: providing a variety of information for students in foreign countries who wish to study in Japan; warm-hearted arrangements for foreign students concerning their accommodations, including opportunities for home-stay experience; follow-up services for former foreign students who have returned home, including reinviting them to Japan and sending them Japanese scientific publications.

(c) It is necessary that consideration be given to providing foreign students more opportunities for short-term study in Japanese institutions of higher education, including study in an attractive summer school.

3. Language Education Useful for Communication

—English and Japanese as international languages

a. In teaching of foreign languages, especially English, emphasis needs to be placed on the mastery of an international language (lingua franca) as a tool for international communication. From this point of view, a basic review should be made of the content and methods of English language instruction throughout lower and upper secondary schools and institutions of higher education.

b. With regard to Japanese language instruction for foreigners, there is urgent need to carry out scientific research on the Japanese language as a lingua franca and to develop appropriate teaching methods and materials. The training of Japanese language teachers should be accelerated, and efforts should be made to ensure that the Japanese language be more widely learned and used in foreign countries.

(a) As pointed out in the Second Report, English language instruction in Japan today is very inefficient. It is necessary to make a basic review of the teaching content and methods of this subject.

In English language education in the future, emphasis should be placed on mastery of the English language as an international language as a tool for international communication. The content and methods of the teaching of this language should be reviewed to help simplify the content and to develop students' skill in active communication with foreigners.

In the light of this requirement and of the spirit of the recommendations made in the Council's second report, and in order to strengthen collaboration among different school levels, comprehensive studies should be made of the content and methods of English language instruction throughout lower and upper secondary schools and institutions of higher education, by providing representatives from different school levels opportunities for joint discussions.

(b) The teaching of English as a national language, not only as an international language, should not be neglected. Further, the importance of learning foreign languages other than English must be emphasized. It is necessary that university students should be able to choose a second foreign language not only from among French, German, and Spanish but also from the languages of Asian nations neighboring Japan. For this purpose, mutual recognition of credits earned in other universities should be promoted. In addition, consideration should be given to introducing some qualifying examination to be administered by an external organ to award certain university credits to students for their learning in special training schools or other institutions or in summer schools. With regard to foreign languages other than English, French or German, even dictionaries basic to learning these languages have not adequately been compiled so far.

Government actions or others' endeavors to improve this situation are needed.

Further, keeping in mind the need of children who have returned home from a long stay abroad, a wide range of foreign languages should be offered as selective subjects in upper secondary schools, and attention should be paid to help increase the kinds of foreign languages given in university entrance examinations.

(c) Demands of foreigners for Japanese language instruction have been increasing quantitatively, and the content demands themselves have been diversified. It is a pressing task to take active measures to respond to these demands. It is necessary to delineate the difference between teaching Japanese for foreigners who wish to learn this language to communicate (in other words, as an international language) and the learning of Japanese as part of studies of Japanese classics. Scientific research on the Japanese language is required, as is the development of appropriate teaching methods and materials. In particular, it is necessary to establish undergraduate and graduate courses for teaching Japanese as a foreign language. It is also necessary to ensure that the Japanese language be more widely learned and used in foreign countries, for example, by sending Japanese teachers of the Japanese language, as well as teaching materials and aids, to foreign universities who request them, under exchange programs between Japanese and foreign universities.

Meanwhile, with regard to teaching the Japanese language as the national language for Japanese, the acquisition of the skill of reading, writing, and speaking accurate and beautiful Japanese is indispensable for inheriting and developing Japanese classics and culture. From this point of view, the importance of rigorous teaching of the national language for Japanese must be emphasized.

4. Establishing the Identity as a Japanese and Regarding Oneself as a Relative Being

—A task for lifelong learning

a. Japanese people are requested to have the identity of being a Japanese and, at the same time, to have the attitude and ability to regard themselves as relative beings. More specifically, they are required to have a profound knowledge about Japanese culture, to regard Japanese values as relative ones, and to enrich and enlighten themselves spiritually.

b. In addition, Japanese people have to acquire sociability as a basis of human relations. For instance, while they are staying in a foreign country Japanese people must acquire such basic manners as are accepted in common in the international community, including paying due regard to the national flag and national anthem of each country. They should also become modest enough to respect native culture and customs of the country where they are staying. Due attention should be paid to these factors in the discipline of children within the family and in Japanese schools.

(a) Japanese people must objectively perceive the position of Japan in the international community. To cope with this position, they must have pride in Japan's culture—in other words, what has made Japan what it is today—and in the implications of this culture for all mankind. It is important for Japanese people to have both sufficient thinking power and ability of expression to explain this Japanese culture to foreigners, drawing on their logic and their mentality.

In addition, Japanese people need to learn specifically that there are a great variety of different life-styles, customs and value systems in the world, and to acquire the attitude and ability to look at Japan's image in a relative manner, from a global and objective perspective. Further, based on the perception that Japan cannot survive in isolation from Asia, they must without fail strive to learn the real state of affairs in these neighboring Asian countries. The knowledge required for citizens living in such an international community needs to be incorporated into the teaching of Japanese and world history and geography, in which the perspective of comparative cultures should be emphasized.

(b) Japanese people living in the international community must acquire the sociability which is a requirement for human relations in Japan and in the international community and the basic manners which are accepted in common.

For example, all parents and all teachers living abroad should make every possible effort to acquire valuable life experience by adapting themselves to native society and teach their children the modest attitude of respecting the differing native culture and customs.

(c) All these requirements are applicable not only to school children but also to adult citizens in general. To meet these requirements is an important task for lifelong learning. It should be noted that increasing efforts in this area is in itself the internationalization of education, which will lead to the internationalization of Japanese society as a whole.

73
Higher Education Reform Proposals

August 1987

Source: Fourth and Final Report on Educational Reform (Tokyo: National Council on Educational Reform, 1987), pp. 37–46 (excerpts).

**Section 2. Diversification and Reform
of Institutions of Higher Education**

As we move toward the twenty-first century, our institutions of higher education
should, in accordance with diverse demands of the public, contribute both to the
development of qualified human resources and to the advancement of creative
scientific research. They should also play an important role in providing people
with opportunities for lifelong learning. To this end, the individualization, diversification, and enhancement of these institutions should be promoted. They
should be more opened to, and more cooperative with, society. Further scientific
research should be promoted. In order to provide basic conditions facilitating
these measures, the autonomy and self-control of individual institutions should
be secured with regard to their organization and management, the quality of
teaching and other staff should be improved, and a sound economic foundation
should be developed for these institutions.

*1. Individualization and Enhancement of
Institutions of Higher Education*

(1) Enrichment and Individualization of Institutions of Higher Education

In order to enhance the educational activities of our universities and to help each
institution to organize its own distinctive educational programs, the structure and
content of both general and specialized educational programs should be examined. Universities should be allowed to develop distinctive structures for education and research, free from traditional frameworks. In addition, the existing
credit system should be re-examined, and more flexibility should be introduced
in regulations on semesters, terms or academic years, so that the advantages of
the credit system may be fully utilized. Further, the possibility for students to
transfer between different universities or between different faculties within a
university should be increased. In order to effect the above reforms, such national regulations as the Standards for the Establishment of Universities should
be thoroughly reviewed. Efforts should be made to broaden and simplify the
provisions in these regulations.

*(2) Diversification of Higher Education Institutions
and Mutual Cooperation among Them*

Institutions of higher education should be encouraged to develop in diverse
ways, and mutual cooperation and exchange should be promoted among institutions. With these as aims, the government should study the following measures:
diversifying the departments and curricula in junior colleges and giving more

flexibility to the content of education in these colleges; expanding the categories of courses in colleges of technology so that they may offer courses other than the existing engineering or mercantile marine courses; changing the general name of this category of institution (presently *Koto senmon gakko*).

All possibilities should be reviewed in formulating future plans for the University of the Air. Utilization of correspondence courses of the higher education level needs to be examined, based on a new mode of thought and in the context of the development of new media for providing information.

In light of the goal of creating a lifelong learning system, competent authorities should consider the introduction of a "credit accumulation system" by which completion of a university degree program may be recognized on the basis of the total credits earned, including those obtained in other educational institutions.

(3) Drastic Improvement and Reform of Graduate Schools

A drastic improvement and reform of graduate schools is our urgent task. The roles of master's and doctor's programs should be classified, and the possibility of defining the standard length of a master's or doctor's program as one year, depending on the field of study should be studied. The introduction of a system under which excellent students may be allowed to enter graduate schools after they have completed the third year of an undergraduate course should be considered. Regarding the structure of graduate schools, diverse patterns, including "independent graduate departments" (i.e., graduate degree programs which have no corresponding programs at the undergraduate level in the same university) should be encouraged. Further, graduate schools should strengthen their own staff, facilities and equipment. The whole existing system of academic degrees should be re-examined.

(4) Evaluation of Universities and the Opening of University Information to the Public

Universities are requested to become more conscious of their social obligations and responsibilities and to verify and evaluate constantly their own educational and research activities, as well as the extent of their contribution to society, in light of the basic philosophy of the university. They are also requested to make information on their own educational, research and other activities widely available to the public, both inside and outside Japan.

2. Liberalizing and Giving More Flexibility to the Qualifications for University Entrance

Based on the basic perception that the opportunity for higher education should be as diverse and broad as possible, the government should consider as soon as possible concrete measures for granting university entrance qualifications to students who have completed an upper secondary course lasting three years or more at special training schools, as well as to other competent people.

Further, regarding university entrance qualifications, studies should be made of liberalizing and giving more flexibility to these qualifications.

3. Positive Promotion of Scientific Research

(1) Promotion of Basic Research in Universities

In order to promote basic sciences so as to bring them to a level worthy of international recognition, the following measures should be taken: the creation in universities of flexible research structure; a review and improvement of the organization and activities of research institutes affiliated with universities, inter-university research institutes and the like; the expansion of post-doctoral fellowship programs for developing competent young researchers; a major review and strengthening of the present institutional structure for supporting research activities at universities; and an increase in government funds for scientific research. Special consideration should be given to the encouragement and enhancement of the humanities and social sciences.

(2) Strengthening of Cooperation between Universities and Society

In order to strengthen cooperation between universities and society, use of part-time lecturers and visiting professors should be considered, while relevant measures should be taken to enable university teachers to cooperate with research activities of governmental and nongovernmental bodies. In addition, the following measures should be taken: giving more flexibility to master's programs in graduate schools; opening research findings to the public, as well as strengthening scientific information systems; further expanding joint research programs among industry, government and universities; and ensuring the successful introduction and effective use of nongovernment funds for public universities, including the introduction of endowed Chairs.

(3) Promotion of International Exchange for Scientific Research

The university is by nature an international institution. Scientific research is basically an activity jointly undertaken by all mankind. If Japan is to be trusted and respected in the international community and is to make a relevant contribution to the cause of world peace and progress, then the nation must strengthen its activities for international exchange in science and culture. To this end, the following measures should be taken on the basis of the improvement of higher education from an international point of view.

To promote international exchange for scientific research, the following measures should be taken: actively expanding international exchange of researchers, especially young researchers; promoting exchange programs based on agreements between Japanese universities and universities overseas; and encouraging Japanese universities to participate in collaborating on joint, international scientific research. To deal with the above activities, efforts should be made at universities and other institutions to strengthen the internal mechanisms for the administration of international scientific exchange programs.

4. Establishment of a National Council on Universities and Colleges

A National Council on Universities and Colleges should be set up as a standing committee responsible for deliberating on basic issues of higher education in Japan and for providing necessary advice and assistance to universities and colleges. The Council should be authorized to make recommendations to the Minister of Education, Science and Culture.

5. Financing of Higher Education

If the quality of higher education is to be improved, it is essential for government authorities to strive to increase public spending on higher education, while reviewing the state of affairs in higher education. In addition, it is also necessary to facilitate the introduction of diverse funds for institutions of higher education from various sources and thus to reinforce the autonomous financial basis for these institutions.

a. In further increasing public expenditures for higher education, competent authorities should emphasize such tasks as: the promotion of basic and creative scientific research; the promotion of various activities related to the internationalization of universities; and the improvement and activation of graduate schools. With regard to the promotion of and financial support for private educational institutions, the government should greatly expand subsidies to private educational institutions for their distinctive educational and research projects, while basically maintaining and improving the system of subsidizing current expenditures of these institutions.

b. There should be closer cooperation between the community and institutions of higher education. In particular, universities or other institutions in a locality and the local government should together take relevant measures to facilitate a cooperative financial relationship based on the initiative of both sides.

c. Conditions favorable for accepting donations should be provided for institutions of higher education, so that they may receive more donations.

d. More flexibility should be given to the budgeting and accounting systems and practices in national universities, and individual national universities should be encouraged to set up their own funds and affiliated foundations, so that they may have more financial autonomy and be provided full scope for their initiatives in financial management. Further, consideration should be given to opening the properties of national universities to the community for its use, as well as to more efficiently utilizing the site of a national university by, for example, putting it under management by a trust company.

e. In light of the future development of higher education, programs for financial aid to students should be improved, and the expansion of these programs should be considered.

The Organization and Management of Universities

(1) Securing the Autonomy and Self-Control of Individual Universities

The creation of an appropriate structure for ensuring the autonomous organization and management in each university is indispensable. With regard to national universities, an appropriate structure for ensuring autonomous and responsible administration and management should be created. In addition, proper leadership by the president, faculty deans and other university officers should be developed. With regard to private universities, the president, the administrative bodies assisting him in the academic management of the university, and the faculty meetings should make clear their own responsibilities. Based on cooperation between the academic side and the board of trustees, the private university as a whole should carry out its social responsibilities. With regard to local public universities, they are expected to make their educational and research activities open to the community, and to develop fresh ideas with a view to contributing to the development of the community.

(2) Teachers and Administrative and Clerical Staff

a. In order to recruit teaching staff from a wider source, relevant measures should be implemented to give more flexibility to qualifications for university teachers so that universities may appoint teachers from among citizens who have worked in other sectors, as well as foreign nationals.

b. The possibility should be explored of introducing a definite term of office for university teachers, with the aim of eliminating the closedness of teacher appointments, and of facilitating the mobility of teachers. Consideration should be given to the salaries, research environment, and other conditions of teachers with a limited term of office.

c. Active measures should be taken concerning the training of researchers and the fostering of prospective researchers. In this connection, consideration should be given to the content of work, salaries, official title, and other factors of research fellows.

d. It is advisable that universities positively engage themselves in evaluating teachers' accomplishments in education and research, and that university teachers devote themselves to self-improvement efforts.

e. In order to help activate the educational and research programs of a university, its structure for business administration should be reorganized and the functions of that structure should be improved. In addition, improving the quality of the administrative and clerical staff should be attempted by enriching the systematic and professional in-service training of these staff members.

(3) "Open" Universities

Universities should assume the responsibility for opening themselves wide to society, responding to the demands of society, and thus making public contributions. Each university should set up and utilize an advisory board in which outside people participate. Universities should become more active in offering extension courses, lectures for citizens, and other activities for community service, in making their facilities available to citizens for their use, and in admitting working adults as students. They should develop and improve relevant mechanisms to cope with the increase in information systems.

7. Types of Establishment of Universities

It is desirable that the type of establishment of national and local public universities be thoroughly examined to help create the ideal pattern of control of a university and the mechanism by which the national government should participate in the administration of universities. The Council requests the national government authorities and university people deal actively with this particular subject.

74
Implementation of Educational Reform

August 1987

Source: Fourth and Final Report on Educational Reform (Tokyo: National Council on Educational Reform, 1987), pp. 94–98.

Whether the current educational reform will be successfully brought about or not is a very important issue affecting the future of our country. What is most important is that the Council's recommendations for educational reform should be immediately implemented. In addition, because of its nature, educational reform must be continuously carried out for a long time. For this reason, the period of more than ten years remaining in the century is extremely important, if the present educational reform is to be carried out fruitfully. The destiny of Japan in the twenty-first century will be greatly affected by whether this educational reform is successfully brought about or not.

If the current reform is to be carried out continuously in the future, the following measures and attitudes will be necessary.

(1) After receiving the reports presented by the Council, the government has determined to pay the greatest regard to the recommendations made therein, and has been making relevant efforts for educational efforts, developing various mechanisms for carrying out reforms as the responsibility of the entire government. These efforts, however, have only just begun. Accordingly, in order to ensure the implementation of educational reform in the future, the government should take all possible measures with the best possible mechanisms.

(2) In view of the role and responsibility to be assumed by the Ministry of Education, Science and Culture in the entire government's efforts for educational reform, the Ministry should develop a powerful mechanism and actively carry out relevant measures to implement educational reform in accordance with the recommendations made by the Council.

(3) In addition, the local government, which is directly responsible for educational administration in a particular locality, has an important role to play in carrying out educational reform steadily and successfully. In the coming years, based on this perception, the local government—the local board of education, in particular—will have to make positive efforts toward educational reform on its own judgment and responsibility.

(4) Further, in order to make educational reform truly effective, the government will need to take appropriate financial measures for bringing about educational reform, with regard to such aspects as: the improvement of basic research; the qualitative improvement of higher education; the promotion of international exchange in education, science and culture; the improvement of children's mental and physical health; and the improvement of the quality of teachers. In taking these measures, the government should always cope with social and economic changes expected to take place in and out of Japan.

(5) During the past three years, the Council has successively presented a number of recommendations with the aim of ensuring an educational reform based on a broad national consensus. The issues in educational reform are not limited to those pointed out by the Council. Besides, there are some issues on which the Council has worked out no definite conclusion, either because of

immature circumstances or because of further comprehensive studies remaining to be made, or for some other reasons. In the years ahead, it would be necessary for the government to make further review of the structure of the formal education system, the content of formal education, and other aspects related to education, including those which have not been pointed out in the Council's report, and to make further efforts toward relevant reforms in an active and flexible manner, while coping with the changes in our society and the progress of the times.

In Conclusion

The Council has finished its mission with this report. The recommendations which the Council has made regarding a wide range of aspects represent only the first stage of the present educational reform, which will be carried out for a long time. Needless to say, the government should take all possible measures by the best possible means to ensure the implementation of educational reform for the twenty-first century. However, it is time for all the people to begin concerted efforts toward educational reform.

Any reforms cannot be implemented without people's eagerness or boldness to overcome barriers to them. Above all, an educational reform affects not only administrative systems or their management. It is a long-range program which should be carried out with the firm will of the people and their untiring cooperation.

During the three years since its inauguration, the Council has carried on an active dialogue with the public with a view to meeting its great expectations for educational reform. The dialogue was held by organizing 14 public hearings in different regions throughout the country and by publishing four interim reports of the progress of its deliberations. Thus the Council has made all possible efforts to bring about an educational reform based on a broad national consensus.

The deliberations by the Council provided an opportunity for an unprecedented national debate on educational reform—a great symposium on education. The Council considers that this in itself is of great significance in promoting educational reform. The Council believes that a great many opinions expressed by many people in different sectors, as well as the statements presented in the progress reports, will be fully utilized in the implementation of educational reform in the coming years.

For any nation and for any society, the basic mission of education lies in conveying the cultural assets created and developed by ancestors to the next generation, and also in bringing up young people who will carry the future of the nation on their shoulders. It will be our national task to meet the challenges of the future and to constantly carry out educational reform. Without this endeavor, it would be impossible for us to develop our society into a creative and energetic one.

The Council sincerely hopes that, with the present educational reform as a clue, every teacher, every parent, every student and everyone else will tackle educational reform with enthusiasm for the sake of our children and grandchildren, who will become responsible citizens of Japan and the world in the twenty-first century.

INDEX

A

Abe Yoshishige, address by, 82–85
Ability-first principle, 236–37, 238
"Ability to teach oneself," emphasis on, 272, 307
Academic freedom, 22, 90, 97, 132–33
  Communist Party membership and, 119–20
  struggle to restore, 67
Academic year, changes in, 289
Achievement tests
  improvement of joint, 287–88
  Japanese scores on international, 13
  national scholastic, 210, 239–40, 254
Activities of Student Personnel Sections in the Universities, 187
Ad Hoc Reform Council, 3, 24
"Administration of the Educational System of Japan," 6, 62–64, 72
Admission policies
  university, 253–55
  See also Entrance examinations
Adult education, 89, 99, 305
"Advanced nation disease," 28
Affiliated schools, role of, 16, 252–53
Aging phenomenon, Japanese population, 26, 212, 217
Allen, H. W., 69
All Trade Unions of Japan, 114
Amano Ikuo, 26–27
Amano Teiyu, 11, 234
American Association of University Professors, 119
Anderson, Ronald S., 77, 112, 118
Asahi Shimbun (publication), 21, 66
Azabu middle school, 207

B

Baby boom, effects of, 14, 15
Bancho primary school, 207
"Bill for Emergency Measures of University Administration," 23
"Bill on Textbooks," 239
Birthrate, 14, 17, 25–26, 129, 212

Blind, education for the, 101, 103, 104, 107, 140
Board of Education
  organization, 117–18
  powers and duties, 118
Board of Education Law (1948), 9, 11, 129–30
  text, 117–18
Bullying, 28–29, 298, 305
  dealing with, 312–13
  See also Violence
Bureau of Educational Reform, 40, 44
Bureau of Social Education, 40, 43
Businesses. *See* Industry

C

Campus unrest. *See* Student movement
Canada, 157
Catholic University of Chile, 66
Censorship
  by Occupation forces, 7
  Japanese constitutional prohibition, 97
  of textbooks, 52, 59
Central Council for Education, 8, 24, 180, 192, 234, 236, 237, 240–41, 242, 292
  reform proposals, 197–98, 200, 204, 205–6, 215–23
  replacement of, 294
  reports, 136–39, 164–67, 272–76
Centralization of education, 12–13, 40, 240–41; *See also* Decentralization of ecuation
Certification
  high-school equivalency, 143
  law, 130–31
  need to establish system of, 226
  teacher, 69, 88, 130–31, 309–10
Charter Oath, 75–76
Childbirth, teachers' miscarriage/stillbirth rate, 129
Children
  home life of, 124, 125–26
  See also Juvenile delinquency; Students
China, 84

Edward R. Beauchamp is Professor of Historical and Comparative Educational Studies at the University of Hawaii at Manoa. A specialist on Northeast Asia, Beauchamp's recent publications include *Japan: A Source Book* (with Richard Rubinger, 1989), *Windows on Japanese Education* (1990), *Schoolmaster to an Empire* (1991), and others. He is currently completing a documentary study of education during the Occupation of Japan, and another of education and reform in east-central Europe. Beauchamp received his Ph.D. from the University of Washington and has been a Fulbright Professor at Keio University and International Christian University (both in Tokyo) and at Eotvos Lorand University in Budapest. He has served as visiting professor at Dankook University (Seoul), Naruto University of Education, Indiana University, and the University of Washington.

James M. Vardaman, Jr., is Professor of English at Surugadai University, near Tokyo. After receiving a master's degree in Asian Studies at the University of Hawaii at Manoa (1976), he began his teaching career in Japan, where he has lived for almost two decades. He is the co-editor of *The World of Natsume Soseki* and has translated literature by Mori Ogai and other Japanese writers. At present he is translating one volume on Japanese literary theory and another of interpretation of the Lotus Sutra.